THE ESSENTIALGARDENBOOK

conran
OCTOPUS

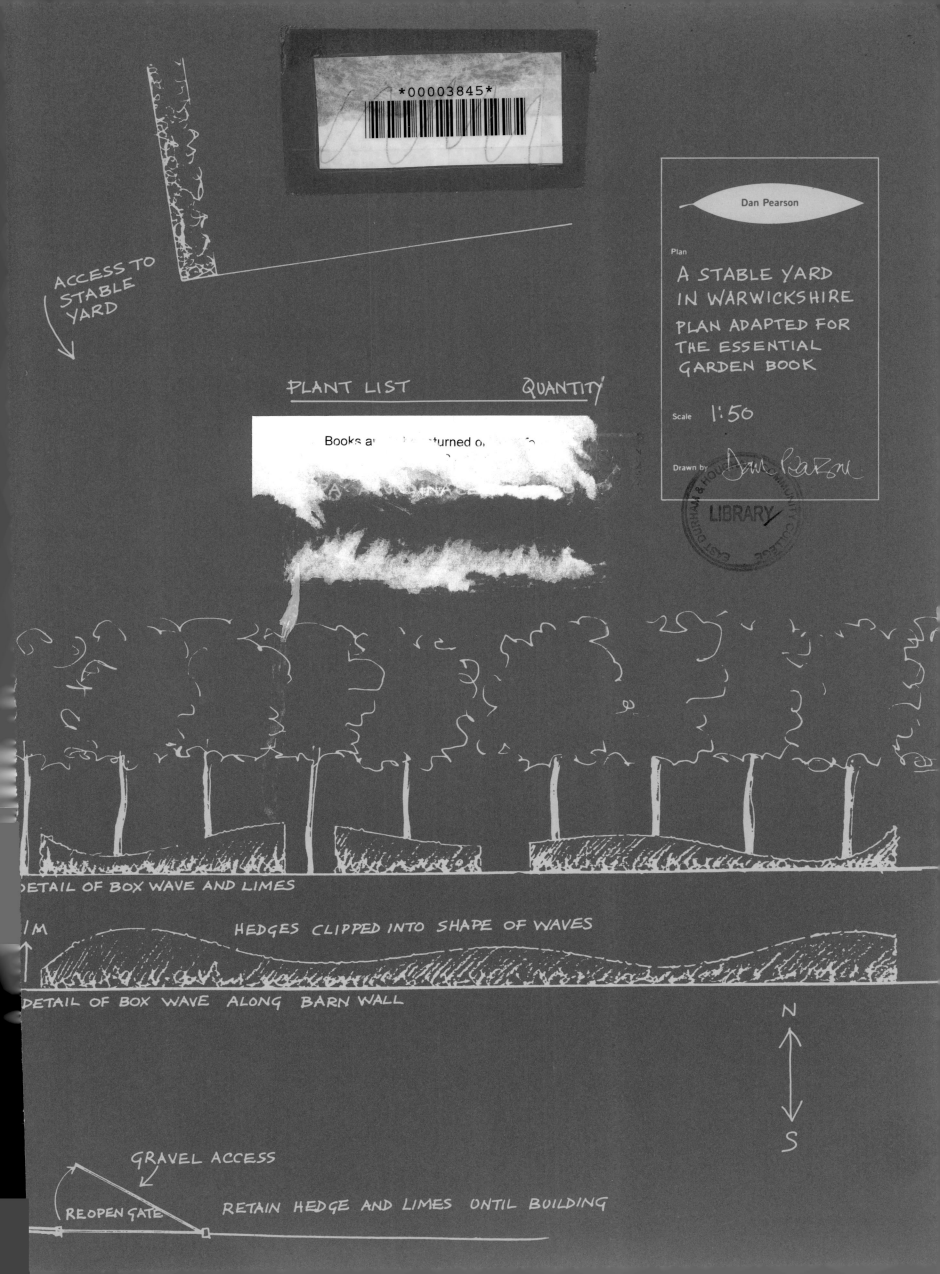

ACCESS TO STABLE YARD

Dan Pearson

Plan

A STABLE YARD IN WARWICKSHIRE

PLAN ADAPTED FOR THE ESSENTIAL GARDEN BOOK

Scale 1:50

Drawn by *Dan Pearson*

PLANT LIST   QUANTITY

DETAIL OF BOX WAVE AND LIMES

1M   HEDGES CLIPPED INTO SHAPE OF WAVES

DETAIL OF BOX WAVE ALONG BARN WALL

N
↑
↓
S

GRAVEL ACCESS

REOPEN GATE   RETAIN HEDGE AND LIMES UNTIL BUILDING

GARDEN BOOK

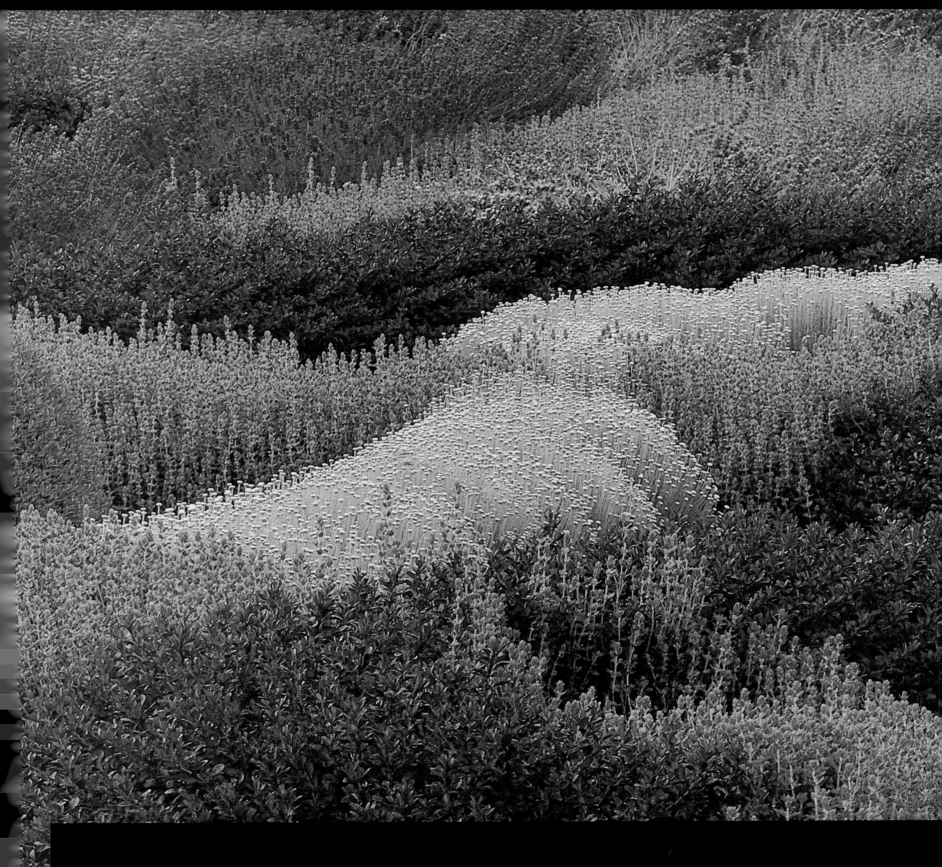

TERENCE CONRAN
DAN PEARSON

Commissioning Editor: Stuart Cooper
Project Editor: Richard Atkinson
Editors: Carole McGlynn, Barbara Haynes

Art Director: Helen Lewis
Art Editor: Mary Staples
Visualizers: Lesley Craig, Jean Morley
Illustrators: Paul Bryant, Lesley Craig, Vanessa Luff,
    Agneta Neroth, Angus Shepherd

Picture Researcher: Claire Taylor

Production: Suzanne Sharpless, Jill Beed

Contributors:
    Part 1: Terence Conran
    Part 2: Dan Pearson
    Part 3: Andrew Wilson, Jennifer Potter
    Part 4: Dan Pearson
    Part 5: Isabelle Van Groeningen, Richard Key
    Part 6: Isabelle Van Groeningen

Project Consultant: Simon Willis

First published in 1998 by
Conran Octopus Limited
37 Shelton Street
London WC2H 9HN

Design and layout © Conran Octopus Limited 1998
Preface text © Conran Ink Limited & Dan Pearson 1998
Part 1 text © Conran Ink Limited 1998
Part 2 pages 52–55 text © Conran Ink Limited 1998
Parts 2 and 4 text © Dan Pearson 1998
All other text © Conran Octopus Limited 1998

A catalogue record for this book is available from
the British Library.

ISBN 1 85029 919 6

Printed in China

Publisher's Acknowledgments
*The publisher would like to thank the following for
their help with this book:*
Jonathan Chidsey; The Conran Shop; Victoria Davis;
Lucy Gent; Leslie Harrington; Wendy Jones; Tony
Lord; Andrew Miller; Frances and Andrew Mossman;
Helen Ridge

Useful addresses compiled by Ian Christopher-Poole

Endpapers based on a design by Dan Pearson

Photographs on pages 6–7
Clockwise from top left:
'Granite Song', a sculpture by Peter Randall-Page,
along the Two Moors Way, Devon; an elevated
walkway in Philip Johnson's garden at New
Canaan, Connecticut; pots of *Agave americana*
'Variegata' lining steps in Seville, Spain; a planting
of miscanthus and pennisetum grasses; a tangle of
morning glory (*Ipomoea purpurea*) and fennel.

CONTENTS

Gardens have never been as important in our lives as they are today. In our stressful world, the garden has become a sanctuary – a place to be in touch with the seasons and elements, and in which to refresh the spirits. Indeed, with our landscape being eroded by industry and urban sprawl, the garden is the only green space to which many of us have access. This is why it is essential that we use our gardens to the full, as spaces for modern living. It may be that you have no more than a windy terrace on your roof or a green swathe around your house. But whatever outdoor space you have, its development into a place which is functional and beautiful will bring with it a better quality of life, providing you with somewhere to play, to make, to tend and to breathe.

There is at last an exciting meeting of disciplines in the world of garden design. Architects are talking to environmentalists, horticulturalists to sculptors. The result is a drawing together of professional skills which, coupled with gardening's rich history, is making garden design both more challenging and more exciting than ever before.

The Essential Garden Book sets out to prove that the design of your garden is every bit as important as the design of your home. At its heart is our belief that careful, considered planning and design are key elements behind a successful garden. Good design is about the coupling of form and function; this book marries the best of both, showing that there is modernity in garden design just as there is in any other discipline. We hope that *The Essential Garden Book* will help you to see the potential of your own garden with fresh eyes, and to seize the opportunity of making it your own.

The need to create gardens – to fashion from nature places of order and retreat – connects us to the ancient civilizations of Sumer and Egypt, Greece and Rome. Whether established to provide food, to furnish a place for contemplation or simply to satisfy a desire to nurture, the garden is an arena in which men and women have played out a drama of perpetual optimism. The gardener's plans, ripe with promise, are often foiled by nature's unpredictability, yet the sensations of colour and scent, of growth – indeed, of life – are ample recompense.

While our homes evolve in a series of distinct, controlled stages, as our priorities and circumstances alter, the garden is in a continual state of change. Gardens are dynamic, three-dimensional places which thwart our attempts to impose finite human plans on them. Yet they are often where we find harmony. This is perhaps to do with their capacity to arouse emotions on many levels. You have only to look at children playing outdoors to see how intuitively we adapt the natural landscape to human needs: climbing trees; damming streams; creating secret dens; following the progress of a ladybird across a path.

Gardens provide a forum for the meeting of different disciplines and the art of gardening is a unique combination of design and artistic skill, science and nature. In designing an outdoor space we seek to integrate the natural elements of soil, rock, water and plants with construction materials such as stone, wood, brick, concrete, metal and glass, negotiating a delicate balancing of scale and proportion, accent and contrast, rhythm and motion. In doing so, the garden becomes the focus of dreams as well as a source of heartache, and a unique expression of our relationship with the natural world.

A west-facing deck captures the last of the day's sunshine, the simple chair a perfect place from which to contemplate this meadow garden in New Jersey, burning gold in the late sun.

Past and present

'God Almighty first planted a garden. And, indeed, it is the purest of human pleasures,' wrote Francis Bacon in 1625. 'It is the greatest refreshment to the spirits of man; without which, buildings and palaces are but gross handiworks.' While the first attempts to impose order on the natural landscape were almost certainly inspired by the need for food, the inclination to 'civilize' nature has a long and continuous history. The earliest surviving example is the plan for a garden belonging to a court official at Thebes in Egypt, dating from around 1400BC. The rigidly symmetrical layout is centred on a straight path covered with a pergola that leads to the main residence. Parallel with the main axis, tree-lined avenues lead to walled enclosures, and the garden includes four rectangular ponds, complete with waterfowl, and two pavilions. These are elements it shares with the shaded water gardens of Persia, which, in turn, evolved into the model for traditional Islamic gardens. From the seventh century onwards, the Arab conquests of western Asia, Egypt, North Africa and, ultimately, Spain established these as the dominant motifs of formal garden design.

Their characteristic feature was the use of water – usually shallow, rectangular pools fed by narrow canals and fountains. Water, of course, was a luxury to desert dwellers, not only enabling plants to grow but also cooling the air and soothing the senses. The most famous of these gardens, the Alhambra in Granada, Spain, is a jewelled world of light and space and air, a cool, shady oasis in the fierce sun of the southern Mediterranean.

From the hydraulically powered automata in the gardens of Syracuse and Alexandria in the first century BC, the underlying theme of western garden design has been our mastery of nature. This continued through the peristyle gardens of Roman villas and the cloistered monastery gardens of medieval Europe to the French baroque and the English landscape movements of the eighteenth century and beyond. At the same time, the imagination has seized on the garden as an arena for indulgence, pleasure and adultery. Adam and Eve's expulsion from the Garden of Eden, the lusty exploits of the numerous lovers in Boccaccio's *Decameron* and the gender confusions of Shakespeare's comedies all take place in

a setting where, implicitly, the fecund potential of nature wreaks havoc on the rational instincts of man.

The gardens described by Boccaccio in the *Decameron* illustrate the trend during the Renaissance to open up the garden, moving away from the prevailing model based around a cloister or courtyard. Architects like Donato Bramante designed terraces and stairways to create sculpture galleries and theatrical sets whose drama derived from the tension between the controlling hand and the natural landscape beyond. With the invasion of Italy by France at the end of the sixteenth century, the Italian model for garden design was taken further north. One of its most ambitious practitioners was André Le Nôtre, whose gardens at Versailles became a paradigm for eighteenth-century garden design throughout western Europe: elaborate, baroque 'carpets' of geometric patterns were set out along vistas lined with fountains, topiary, parterres and smaller, 'hidden' gardens.

The exception to this fashion was England, where the formal garden began to take its inspiration from the natural

1 Water has been important in gardens throughout history and across cultures. This garden in Palma de Majorca is modelled on a Moorish pleasure garden: enclosed, cool and shady, the play of running water provides respite from the heat.
2 Traditional Japanese gardens symbolically express the natural landscape in miniature. Every morning, monks at the Tojuku-ji Temple in Kyoto rake the mobile sand – usually taken to signify water – around a solid group of stones.

3 The English landscape movement carved bravura vistas into parkland gardens. The water garden at Studley Royal in Yorkshire was laid out after the style of William Kent by its owner, John Aislabie, after his expulsion from Parliament in 1720. The garden juxtaposes planes of geometric order with the gently undulating swathes of lawn.
4 Intricate parterres of clipped box at Uzzano in Italy radiate out from stone statues; the magnificent cedars in the background were planted at the end of the nineteenth century.

landscape. The great champion of this 'new' design was William Kent. His plans for the gardens at Chiswick House (1734), with its meandering stream and wandering paths, were so influential that the gardens at Stowe in Buckinghamshire, on which Kent worked alongside Lancelot 'Capability' Brown, were entirely modified to make it less geometrically formal. Capability Brown – so called because he believed that the natural landscape had 'capabilities of improvement' – came to be seen as the pre-eminent designer of the eighteenth-century English landscape style, modelling his gardens in accordance with nature's harmonies. His most famous works – at Petworth in Sussex and Blenheim in Oxfordshire – dispense almost totally with statuary and include very few buildings, shaping the garden,

4

1 From 1803 to 1921, this site in Delaware housed the largest gunpowder factory in the United States. When manufacturing ended, the Crowninshield family created a garden around the jumble of abandoned industrial buildings. The result is a classically inspired ruin-garden, the derelict buildings supplemented by architectural salvage.
2 At Innisfree garden in New York State, this staggered bridge forges a path through dense ferns to the glorious expanse of meadow on the shores of the lake.
3 To western eyes, this Japanese garden at Kengo-in might appear centuries old, but it is a modern design. The spreading azalea hedges, punctuated by the stark verticals of tall tree trunks, take their lead from the landscape.

instead, across swathes of gently undulating grass interspersed with organically shaped bodies of water and clumps, rather than rigid avenues, of trees.

Brown's garden-as-park remained the dominant model for English gardens, evolving in the hands of Humphry Repton, who combined rolling parklands with more formal terraces adjacent to the house. Repton, who makes an appearance in Jane Austen's *Mansfield Park* (1814), also began to incorporate flowers into his designs, returning to a feature largely absent since the Renaissance. Though botanical expeditions had been introducing new plant species to Britain and Europe for some 300 years, the great increase in overseas trade and travel during the nineteenth century brought back plants that considerably extended the garden's season of interest.

The enlarged palette of colours available to the gardener produced results that were not to everyone's taste: 'scarlet geraniums [and] yellow calceolaria . . . are not uncommonly grown together profusely,' wrote William Morris in 1882, 'in order, I suppose, to show that even flowers can be thoroughly ugly.' As the haughty certainty of her writing suggests – 'A dahlia's first duty in life is to flaunt and to swagger,' she wrote in *Wood and Garden* (1899) – Gertrude Jekyll worked with enormous confidence in the garden. Often collaborating with the architect Sir Edwin Lutyens, she carefully structured her flower gardens, and concealed their artifice underneath the generosity and profusion of her plantings.

Her contemporary, William Robinson, carried garden design into the twentieth century, advocating a style of gardening that works with and from nature. He struck a chord with landscape architects across the Atlantic as well as with those based in Britain and Europe. In North America, the toils of forging a new world had largely relegated the garden to an afterthought and American gardens, even in the nineteenth century, usually borrowed from European models.

4

In seeking inspiration from nature, the prevailing course of twentieth-century garden design neatly dovetails western and eastern philosophies. The roots of Chinese – and, through it, Japanese – garden design derive from the animistic beliefs of early civilization: that all elements of the natural landscape, from the sky to bodies of land and water, were manifestations of other spirits inhabiting a shared world. Thus, the overriding purpose of oriental gardens was to effect a harmony with the natural world. They attempted to re-create the mood of a favourite natural landscape using symbolic forms: male and female, upright and reclining, rough and smooth, mountain and plain, rock and water.

Japanese gardens evolved into two distinct forms during the Kamakura period (1192–1333): the hill garden, which conjured up the 'perfect' spirit of Mount Fuji; and the smaller-scale flat garden, whose level surface was punctuated by small rocks, symbolic of the harmony between land and water. This essentially abstract form finds its most famous and radical expression in the temple garden of Ryoan-ji in Kyoto, covered with raked sand and set with 15 stones, divided into five groups. Alongside these meditative, religious spaces grew gardens that derived their aesthetic from the Japanese tea cult and were designed to evoke humility in the face of natural splendour. Planned according to strict rules, tea gardens are comprised of a series of settings that induce different states of spiritual contemplation – the seclusion of the mountain shrine, for example, or the serenity of moonlight through clouds.

These gardens both look back to earlier Chinese models – where the garden, like a scroll painting, unfurled to reveal new views – and anticipate western gardens of the twentieth century. Many of the most powerful modern gardens take a holistic approach to design, seeking clues from and working with the natural habitat. The exquisite placement of rocks and boulders and the interrupted vistas at

5

4 Charged with making a public park from an industrial wasteland in the Ruhr, architect Peter Latz chose not to raze the derelict site but to work with it instead. Concrete bunkers have been planted with flowering lawns and climbing plants trained to grow up their walls, breathing new life into a dead space.
5 The Waterland garden, designed by Janis Hall, sculpts dramatic, wave-like forms into Connecticut countryside. Its impact is heightened late in the day, when the low sun casts long shadows across the garden: you could be staring out across an angry sea.

Innisfree in New York State – designed by Walter and Marion Beck in the 1920s – create a rhythmic landscape that seems to echo the cyclical process of decline and regrowth. As a garden of sensations, Innisfree achieves on a grand scale the more intimate effects later created in the Netherlands by Mien Ruys, who juxtaposes man-made and natural forms, exploiting contrasts of light and shade.

But twentieth-century garden design has been radically altered by the impact of modernism and the challenge it issued to more conventional aesthetics. Roberto Burle Marx in Brazil, Luis Barragán in Mexico and Isamu Noguchi in the United States drew on the sculptural elements of planting and landscape design. At the same time their gardens became spaces for human occupation rather than places merely to behold. Facing what American landscape architect Garrett Eckbo called a 'horrible pot-pourri' of historical garden

features, the garden designers of the twentieth century have been equally keen to respect human needs and natural habitat. Thomas Church created small gardens for outdoor living in California; the English designer John Brookes later wrote about the garden in similar terms, in his book *Room Outside*. Contemporary American designers Wolfgang Oehme and James van Sweden use broad drifts of indigenous species in their plantings; Shodo Suzuki reinterprets traditional Japanese design using modern materials and technology with an affinity for the existing spirit of a place. Nowadays garden design is no longer constrained by the opposed aesthetics of man taming nature or of nature taming man. It is about balancing the natural world against our needs, respecting materials and working with the available space and prevailing conditions in all three dimensions. It is gardening as the art of the possible.

The functions of a garden

For the dedicated plantsman, gardening is a passion on which to lavish hours of attention in contented oblivion; for other people, gardening is no more than the equivalent of outdoor housework, a chore to be done to keep absolute chaos at bay. Between these two extremes fall the vast majority, squaring any gardening aspirations with the practical limitations of space, time and budget. Few people could fail to find beauty and pleasure in some form of garden, and an outdoor space provides most of us with a welcome retreat from the hectic pace of life.

A garden can be more or less whatever you want it to be. You may prefer the clean lines and minimal simplicity of a paved courtyard planted with only a clump of bamboo, or you may be seduced by the charming disorder of a scramble of wildflowers. And whether you are considering a garden space as small as a balcony or as expansive as that of a remote house on the coast without a neighbour in sight, the garden allows you to express your taste and personality just as surely as your house or apartment does. If your home is immaculately neat, for example, without a speck of dust, it is unlikely you

will want a garden running riot with self-seeded plants, climbers that smother every surface and a path fringed with overhanging grasses.

There is something enticingly restful about retreating to the garden. Even the smallest backyard has room for a couple of folding chairs where you can sit with a cup of coffee and the morning paper before rushing off to work, or unwind with a long, cool drink at the end of a hard day. You may enjoy being in the garden on warm, sunny days when the air is heavy with the familiar smells of summer, or you may prefer eating an informal evening meal outdoors, as the light dims and the temperature cools.

Sights, scents and sounds pervade a garden. The simplest water feature can provide its focal point as well as a soothing aural backdrop. Depending on where you live, a pool may also encourage wildlife, though in one of his essays, *Of Gardens* (1625), Francis Bacon warned that 'Pools mar all, and make the garden unwholesome, and full of flies and frogs'. Times change, of course, and thanks to electric pumps and modern filtration units, the static pool of dank water is largely a thing of the past. But maintenance remains important – fashioning your bucolic idyll around a pool dappled with sunlight filtering through a canopy of trees means that you will regularly need to clear the water of fallen leaves. The 'natural' look is no solution to the search for low-maintenance gardening, nor an excuse for neglect.

For most northern Europeans, the private swimming pool is a luxury, if not a status symbol. But in many parts of the United States and Australia, as well as Mediterranean Europe, swimming pools are commonplace. With their crisp lines and crystal-clear water, they import modernity into the gardens they occupy. We may think of David Hockney's *Splash* paintings, or of Esther Williams amid some extravagantly choreographed waterfest – swimming pools evoke fantasies of sunshine and carefree privilege.

1 Children need their own private places and often build secret dens. Faced with a tepee as magnificent as this one, tucked into a garden amid the Shenandoah forest in West Virginia, the children might find themselves fighting off the adults for residence. **2** From birds and insects to badgers and foxes, wildlife enters our world through gardens. Frogs have a knack of finding man-made ponds in which to make their homes. **3** Water, water everywhere. This pool in the Caribbean appears to tip over into the surrounding landscape, though from the pool itself the view is a seamless blend with the sea beyond.

4

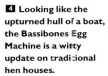 **Looking like the upturned hull of a boat, the Bassibones Egg Machine is a witty update on traditional hen houses.**

 **The grounds of a farmhouse in western Connecticut provide acres of space for play. An established tree makes an ideal spot for a hideaway as well as a sturdy anchor for the hammock.**

A clapboard shed with dovecote, a picket fence and regimented rows of lovingly tended vegetables: an idyll redolent with nostalgia. Growing your own fruit and vegetables connects you with gardeners through the ages.

5

6

1

2

3

1 Spiralling slivers of slate make a playful course for fountains of water in this specially commissioned piece by Daniel Harvey at Kew Gardens in London. The sparkling effect of sunshine on water is maximized by its organic shape.
2 Cities are not the most hospitable garden environments. This courtyard garden in Berlin challenges the forces of urban life, with nature winning the upper hand. Instead of consigning a beaten-up old car to the scrap-metal yard, a resourceful gardener has turned it into an unusual plant pot.

4

Swimming pools require careful positioning to enjoy the best of the sunshine; and, as with any water feature, safety is a priority, especially if there are young children about.

For children – and many adults, too – the garden is a natural playground. It can provide the opportunity to watch wild birds, chase after butterflies, throw a ball or play with the family pet. Many people are convinced that days were longer, summers sunnier, lawns more immaculate and flowers sweeter-smelling during their childhood, and if that strikes a chord with you, why not make your garden an emotional expression of such memories, perhaps tucking away a tree-house or a den in a secluded corner? Most of us will respond with enthusiasm to the invitation of a winding path, a door in a garden wall, a glimpse of something half-hidden further on. Such outdoor 'rooms' illustrate one of Sir John Soane's tenets of architecture, the importance of hazard and surprise, as applicable in the garden

as indoors: a garden that shows its hand on first sight lacks the magic of one that tempts you to explore further.

Quite how you choose to plan your garden will depend on its size and your own priorities. The trick is not to feel strait-jacketed by convention: some of the most enchanting gardens have evolved from ignorance or innocence, or a simple desire to push the boundaries. Derek Jarman's celebrated garden in the bleak shingle at Dungeness has spawned many lesser imitations, but it serves as a useful example not only as an expression of a personal aesthetic, but as a reminder that gardens can be created in the most seemingly inhospitable environments.

Some gardens spring from a passion for a particular plant or flower, whether it is alpines or antique roses, still others from a palette of colours, like Vita Sackville-West's white garden at Sissinghurst in Kent. You might dedicate long hours to nursing exotic plants in a hot-house. While gardens are for relaxation and for

contemplation, they are equally places for horticulture and activity. The act of gardening itself, in connecting us to nature and stimulating the senses, gives a great sense of achievement. The satisfaction of observing the first flowers of spring coming into bloom or of watching a tree steadily growing to maturity is one of gardening's chief pleasures.

Harking back to the earliest impulse to cultivate the land, home-grown fruit and vegetables brought fresh to the table have always tasted much better – and there is no need for a vast estate to grow your own. Lettuces can edge a path and runner beans be trained to flourish amid plants grown for their flowers or their scent. George Eliot, in *Scenes of Clerical Life* (1858), described the richness of such a combination perfectly as the 'charming, paradisiacal mingling of all that was pleasant to the eye and good for food. The rich flower border running along every walk, with its endless succession of spring flowers, anemones, auriculas,

5

6

3 Hi-ho, hi-ho . . .
Long dismissed as an
archetype of kitsch, the
garden gnome can be
a witty and endearing
ornament. This merry
band winding their way
through a forest of ivy
couldn't fail to raise a
smile . . . could they?
4 In the right spot,
simple pleasures are
the greatest indulgence:
a rug, a low table,
sunshine, dappled shade
and a Mediterranean
view to die for. Close
your eyes and you're
already there.
5 Founders' Bottom
in north London was
used as a decoy airfield
during the Second
World War, before two
sisters turned it into
allotments for working
Londoners. Today, it
is a labyrinth of secret
gardens tucked away
among the urban sprawl.

7

wallflowers, sweet williams, campanulas,
snapdragons and tiger lilies, had its taller
beauties such as moss and Provence
roses, varied with espalier apple trees;
. . . you were in a delicious fluctuation
between the scent of jasmine and the
juice of gooseberries.'

Gardens accommodate trial and error
much more forgivingly than our homes.
For every disappointment there is the
compensation of an unexpected surprise.
With their rich tapestry of colour and
texture, light and shade, and their fluctuations with time, season and climate,
gardens arouse the senses, refreshing the
mind and body. Their rewards are many
and varied, and not always predictable.
In the best gardens, from the most modest to those on a grander scale, mankind
works with nature to splendid effect. In
the sound-bite culture of today, gardens
remind us of a different pace of life: as
Beverley Nichols wrote, 'It is only to the
gardener that time is a friend, giving each
year more than he steals.'

6 Although it receives
very little direct sun,
this small patio garden
in Paddington, New
South Wales, feels
light and inviting.
Yellow-washed walls,
stone paving and
shade-loving plants
suggest an oasis of
tranquillity in an
urban setting.
7 Gardens are for
growing plants just
as much as they are
opportunities for
al fresco activities. You
do not need a rambling
country cottage to
cultivate a flower
garden, nor does such
a garden have to be
exquisitely polite.
Spiky agaves and
cordylines lend a bold
effect to this hillside
planting in Berkeley,
California, spiced with
the colours of annual
eschscholzias and
verbenas.

Mood and atmosphere

The Chinese and Japanese have always been masters of mood and atmosphere. From the tea room to a moss garden, they conceived settings that would create particular sensations. A spot from which to watch the dawn break, or a clearing in which to sit and listen to the wind whistling through bamboo: seats and places of shelter were carefully sited so that the sitter could best appreciate the mood of the landscape.

Though the spiritual affinities between mankind and the environment are less explicit in the West, the concept of the garden as a retreat and a place of inner fulfilment is equally familiar. At the most basic level, comfort and a sense of peace can be achieved by creating a garden that is pleasing to the eye: a palette of pastel colours, a seat nestling among a bank of grasses or a well-placed piece of garden sculpture might encourage meditation or simply banish everyday worries. Albeit on a rather more contrived level, Monet's garden at Giverny also creates a sense of peace; it modulates colour, light, texture and, with that, mood and atmosphere in what one critic has called 'a daring reinvention of his paintings in flowers'. The garden in turn became the most famous inspiration for Monet's later works, its lily pond a subject to which the painter returned again and again.

The combination of plants and still water is a particularly evocative one, keenly sensitive to changes in the quality of light: darkly bleak beneath a clouded sky, restful and reflective on a sunny day. Moving water, on the other hand, creates effects that range from the onomatopoeic babbling of a brook or the trickle of water over pebbles to more thunderous manifestations, like the cascade of a waterfall or the crashing of waves against a rocky shore. At Ninfa, a medieval town close to Rome, American expatriate Marguerite Chapin created an English-style garden in which the reeded river holds a wistful

1 Winter holds a special magic as well as particular dangers. The *jeu d'esprit* of this red bench balanced on the icy surface gains an extra frisson of delight from its unattainability as a place to sit.
2 In this Majorcan villa, by Silvestrin and Pawson, the operatic scale of the outdoor dining area commands attention and awe in equal measure.
3 Established over eight hundred years ago, the moss garden of Saiho-ji Temple in Kyoto, Japan, exudes ethereal tranquillity as dawn breaks on a new day. The central, winding lake is shaped into the calligraphic symbol for life. The mature trees and apparently endless boundaries lend the garden an almost primeval quality.

2

3

4

5

gratification: buildings, paintings and sculptures may last longer, but gardens provide a unique continuity with the past and the future. Imperfection feels at home in the garden: musty smells and worn, distressed work surfaces are rather comforting in a garden shed, whereas they would cause concern in the house. Garden structures and furniture made of natural materials acquire a patina with age which enhances their appeal. Show gardens, for all their ingenuity, seldom feel real and often lack charm because, by their very nature, they have had no opportunity to mature.

Context, as well as the passage of time, lends a garden its character and its atmosphere. Both the climate and the local landscape give important clues about the mood a garden might adopt. A rural garden can always borrow from the surrounding countryside: it may aspire to merge seamlessly with views in the middle distance, bringing nature right up to the back door or, alternatively, might create a more ordered environment in which provision is made for recreational activities – the difference, if you like, between a picnic blanket laid out on the lawn in the shade of a tree and one flung down in the middle of long grass.

The garden, or a part of it, might take its mood from one particular feature, either natural or man-made. It could focus on the majesty of a mature tree, or it might open up a viewpoint from which to watch the ephemeral glory of an early morning mist as it lifts and evaporates. In the south of Scotland, Charles Jencks sculpted a garden based on his interest in chaos theory and geomancy, while the Connecticut landforms of Janis Hall show a bold interpretation of form, harnessing the elements and using the dramatic effects of shadow. At the other end of the scale, the gentle charm and mystique of Derek Jarman's garden at Prospect Cottage derives, at least in part, from its fearless optimism set against the forbidding backdrop of Dungeness nuclear power station.

4 A mass of perennials caught basking in the sun's last rays beautifully illustrates the varying qualities of light. Over the course of a single day the impressionistic haze of colours will modulate from bold primaries to muted harmonies.
5 Messing about on the river – or, here, a duck pond – is a perfect way to spend long, lazy days. In this garden on the San Juan islands north-west of Seattle, the banks of the pond are densely planted with irises, cardinal flowers, paper birches and willows.

fascination, as if it were the setting for Millais' painting of the death of Ophelia. By contrast, at the Parc André Citroën or outside the Pompidou Centre, both places in Paris, water has been exploited with spirited playfulness.

While William Kent might famously have believed that 'nature abhors a straight line', formal gardens laid out to a strictly geometric pattern do have a wonderful air of calm. In the West, it was only with the advent of modernism in the early part of the twentieth century that an aesthetic developed that questions the rationale of orderliness; Japanese design has, in fact, always favoured asymmetry, believing the flow of energy through the garden to be blocked by symmetry.

Part of a garden's appeal, of course, is that no matter how hard we try to shape and control its appearance, there are always unexpected developments and setbacks. Gardens deny and defy instant

The ever-changing garden

No garden ever looks the same: it is always altering and evolving. During spring and summer, periods of intense growth, you can chart the changes not just on a weekly or a daily basis, but by the hour, as daisies open their petals to the dawn of a new day or sunflowers incline their heads to catch the sun as it moves across the sky. The closer you look, the greater and more varied is the drama of life in the garden. As the English garden writer Stefan Buczacki has put it, 'Beneath every leaf there is life, hiding from the sun and rain; beneath every stone, there is a miniature jungle, a struggle for existence between competing natural organisms.'

You do not, of course, have to be much of a naturalist to observe change in the broader picture of the garden. The telltale signs of the shift from one season to the next – snowdrops and crocuses pushing through the last dustings of snow, long summer evenings infused with the perfume of jasmine or sweet peas, trees laden with ripe apples for harvesting before the leaves turn colour and start to fall – are simply the most obvious manifestation of life, growth and evolution. Over the years, a flagstone terrace will acquire the patina of age, the posts and trusses of a pergola will disappear beneath the tangle of vine and clematis, and a tree planted to commemorate an anniversary will grow to maturity.

Although change is most obvious in the seasonal cycle of temperate climates, it is not confined to them. The intense heat of the sun in a cloudless desert sky demands relief in the form of shade, and in large, open areas it blurs forms and colours as the heat-haze rises; in the aftermath of a tropical downpour, as well as bringing temporary respite from the suffocating humidity, colours will become brighter, forms sharper and distances clearer. Gardens everywhere are ripe with change and mystery, with variety and surprise: observing how the elements of a garden are altered with time will help you to exploit its potential to the full.

1 As night falls, the silhouettes of mature tree trunks take on a slightly sinister quality.
2 Natural materials like stone and timber acquire a mellow patina with use and age. Here, however, it is as much neglect and lack of use that have produced this lichen- and moss-encrusted still life.
3 The fresh young leaves on the trees in this French orchard herald a new cycle of life and productivity.
4 Snowdrops push their heads above the frosted ground, their fragile flowers one of the first signs of an end to winter.
5 Sunflowers tilt their faces to follow the path of the sun, mapping out long summer days.

1

2

3

4

5

6

7

9

6 Tall trees against the night sky; gardens take on quite a different character by moonlight.
7 Though winter frost can be a menace, the way it dusts plant forms in the early morning is breathtaking.

8

8 Cloud Valley Farm in Australia sits amid the cloud-wreathed hills of the surrounding countryside in an ethereal mist of rain. A garden's magic does not have to depend on blue skies and sunshine for its best effects.
9 Just as spring reveals the true range of greens in the garden, so autumn produces a magnificent palette of browns, from golden grasses to the blazing reds and oranges of trees whose leaves turn colour before falling.

Planting and architecture

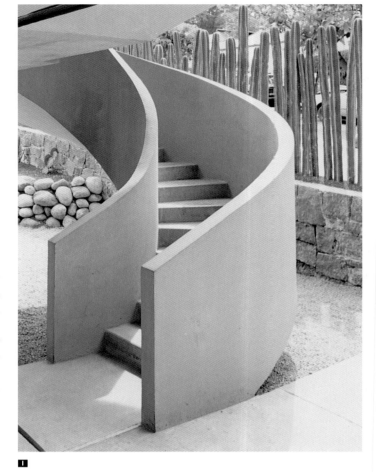

It was not until the nineteenth century that the title and profession of landscape architect came into currency. It was devised by Frederick Law Olmsted, who, with Calvert Vaux, was responsible for Central Park in New York. In coining the term, Olmsted was only making explicit the architectural principles behind an approach to garden design that stretches back to the gardens of the ancient world, all of which were formally laid out in relationship to the house.

In the fourteenth century, the central theme of Italian Renaissance gardens – that planted forms should reflect the shape of built forms – also developed from an architectural starting point. Even the English landscape movement of the eighteenth century, which sought to restore gardens to 'nature', carefully manipulated form and space, juxtaposing densely planted areas with open voids from which to view the scenery. The gothic-romantic gardens championed by Sir Uvedale Price and William Gilpin – with their steep falls, poetically rotting fallen trees and dark chasms – were as

1 In Mexico City, cacti form a witty perimeter fence to the house of artists Diego Rivera and Frida Kahlo, designed in 1930 by Juan O'Gorman.
2 A gently inclined flight of steps gains great presence and *gravitas* from bamboos framing it. The light filtered through their stems draws the eye as the winding pathway leads the visitor on.

deliberately designed to follow an architectural narrative as the formal geometric layout of André Le Nôtre's Versailles. The differences in style and approach simply reflect the prevailing aesthetic of a time and a place.

As well as taking their lead from the style of the house, gardens can also include architectural elements in their design. Along with the utilitarian garden shed, the pergola is probably the most ubiquitous of these, which is hardly surprising given the variety of roles it can perform, from framing a view or creating a focal point to providing a scented, shady retreat. The architectural potential of the garden extends well beyond its built forms, however, to planting itself. A walkway flanked by bamboo, silver birch or poplars will have a very different impact from one bordered by a neat lawn or a mixed border.

One of the most influential landscape architects of the twentieth century, the Danish-born Jens Jensen, believed that, 'We shall never produce a worthwhile art of landscaping until we have learned to love the soil . . . and to fit man's accomplishments into its infinite harmony.' Working in the midwestern United States alongside architects such as Frank Lloyd Wright and Louis Sullivan, Jensen drew on the natural landscape for inspiration while controlling his compositions to create artificial sight lines and resting points. As the gardens have matured, they show decreasing evidence of human

5

6

intervention. Though his work incorporated some formal elements – such as flower or vegetable gardens laid out to a geometric grid – Jensen slipped these surprise parcels of order into the overall informality of his garden designs.

In recent decades, there has been a conscious attempt to reconnect our urban areas with the countryside beyond them. Buildings with 'living' roofs of grass and wildflowers bring nature back to areas lost to construction, as well as cleansing the air. More high-tech in its approach,

a nine-storey office block in Osaka, designed in 1987 by the Italian architect Gaetano Pesce, imitates a bamboo forest in appearance and, by incorporating glass-fibre plant containers in its walls, brings greenery to the heart of a city in which land prices are too high to contemplate a more conventional garden.

The need to work with – rather than against – the landscape is keenly felt today by the designers of buildings as well as gardens. In France, architects Edouard François and Duncan Lewis

3 In Basingstoke, Hampshire, a hint of Babylon is brought to the world of work. Roof terraces and balconies brimful with plants provide verdant and serene relief from monochrome office life.
4 Built structures in the garden are a means of dividing space and introducing order. The opening in this exterior wall in California draws the eye through to a quiet courtyard garden.
5 This fantastic tree-house nestles in the canopy; although t has its own purpose-built supports, ladders and branches lash it to the surrounding trees.
6 At Branitz Park in Germany, Hermann Fürst von Pückler-Muskau, nineteenth-century traveller and gardener, created an extraordinary melding of architectural and landscaping styles.
7 In Iceland, workers' cottages are roofed with peat, sprouting heathland grasses.
8 Heather Ackroyd and Daniel Harvey take the English obsession with perfect lawns to bizarre new ends. Sprayed with mud and grass seed, this stairway was transformed in just a few days.

conceive new buildings which almost spring from the soil: they have designed a cluster of *gîtes* clad in hedgerow and interplanted with indigenous trees, and a school building that appears to grow out of the surrounding paulownias like some giant tree-house. 'Green' architecture connects us intimately to the world we inhabit and re-defines the garden not simply as a space to provide us with spiritual nourishment but as a life-sustaining environment in itself, on which future generations will depend.

7

8

EXTERIOR DESIGN

A well-planned garden will have the same effect on your life as a well-planned house or a beautifully cut piece of clothing: it will be a pleasure to use. A well-designed garden fulfils many important roles. As a link with the natural world, it invites you to experience the pleasure of being outdoors, with its rich spectrum of sensory delights, and to enjoy the fluctuations of the seasons. The best gardens work as an extension of your home, too: in these days of restricted room and limited free time, they have become a highly valued living space.

As with anything that works well, the key to success is good design – the marriage of practicality and aesthetics. A garden cannot function on only one of these levels: its diverse elements need to be carefully balanced so that its appearance is complemented by how well it works as an outdoor space. Gardens must also have the potential to change over time – no garden is ever the same from one year to the next.

Garden design is all about making the space work for you by matching your needs and preferences – what you want from your garden – to the fixed conditions of your plot, from its size and outlook to the type of soil and the time you have to spend in it. While designing your garden, you will be operating on many different levels: you are dealing not only with plants and hard materials, but with less tangible elements like light and shade, and the use of space. But do not be daunted by this – the diversity of factors involved makes the design process both exciting and challenging. The following pages take you through all the stages involved in the process of designing your own garden and, whether you have a tiny alley or a view over a rolling landscape, will help you create a personalized space that you want to use all year round.

A sense of place

We all know a place whose atmosphere is entirely its own: perhaps a turbulent coastline with jutting fingers of rock resisting a rough sea, where every part has been influenced by the elements; or a cool, mossy glade which, in terms of experience, is the antithesis. These may be places towards which you gravitate time and again because of their spirit and their effect on you. They are good for the soul and essential to a balanced way of life, which can all too easily succumb to the pressures of day-to-day existence and be devoid of spiritual experiences.

It is their sense of place that sets such environments apart: something which, when you try to put a finger on it, may be elusive and unfathomable, though its atmosphere is omnipresent. It can be a combination of forces which gives a place its spark of individuality, such as a bank of twisted roots or a bleached horizon stretching for ever, or it can be something simple, like the dark entrance to a cave or the colour of an exposed rock. Although a sense of place is usually thought to be governed by nature, our modern land-scapes, worked by man, have developed

a potency which sometimes sets them apart. Take, for instance, the quilted, undulating landscapes of the Yorkshire Dales in northern England, where the fields have been divided by the tracery of dry stone walls, or the adobe buildings in New Mexico, which seem to emerge from the earth itself. These environments have a strong identity; although they have been put together by man, they have developed a spirit of their own.

As our landscape is being depleted, however, a new uniformity is emerging that is a result of intensive farming and

2

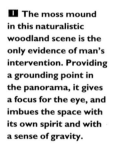

1 The moss mound in this naturalistic woodland scene is the only evidence of man's intervention. Providing a grounding point in the panorama, it gives a focus for the eye, and imbues the space with its own spirit and with a sense of gravity.

1

3

2 This fog garden in Ishikawa, Japan, employs a boldly minimal treatment designed to infuse the garden with the power of the elements.
3 The placement of two chairs next to the exposed rock gives a focus and definition in a botanic garden in Massachusetts. The simple device both acknowledges and reinforces the sense of place in this open site.

streamlining. Motorways look the same for mile after mile and modern housing developments are often unrecognizable one from the other. The landscape is being stripped of its soul and, with it, its sense of place. But fortunately a sense of place is something which can be created, and gardens are the perfect arenas for doing so. The best gardens are entirely personalized spaces; the creation of a special mood relies on the garden being set apart, visually and atmospherically, from anywhere else. The elements for creating a sense of place are all there at

your disposal – movement, light and shade, colour, texture, scent and the momentum of continual change through the days and the seasons.

The art of creating a successful garden lies in seeking out the potential, the essential clue which will give the garden its spirit and individuality, and tapping into it. A memory or simple idea may be all you need to imbue a space with a spirit of its own, by injecting something which releases what is already there. For instance, Mien Ruys, the Dutch garden designer, has captured a sense of place in

different parts of her garden by creating very specific environments. At one end of the scale, a woodland clearing has been made with a gravel path which wraps around a perfect moss circle, illuminated emerald green from the shafts of light through the trees. In another part of the garden she has created a small seating area for contemplation in the shade of a nut tree, where a small fountain gently trickles over a stone sphere nestled in foliage. The juxtaposition of man-made elements with the natural ones of growth and light and shade are the secret behind the potency of these garden spaces. The moss circle would be less powerful for being overrun with other woodland plants, and the shade under the nut tree would lack the same focus without the stone sphere and the fountain.

Good planting alone can create a sense of place: a grassy mead punctuated by the dark, static forms of yew topiary, for instance, or a shaded courtyard lifted with unadorned containers of cool, white hydrangeas. Recognizing the potential of a location, then working with it through the careful placement of garden features, may be another route. The gnarled bole of a tree could become the backrest for a simple seat, giving the space a purpose and a focus, as would the siting of a hammock between two boughs. Even in intensely urban situations, such as the alien environment found on rooftops, it is possible to create spaces that capitalize on the other-worldliness of the surroundings and harness the atmosphere. In combination with appropriate materials and planting which reinforces the extraordinary nature of the garden, the place can be given a spirit and an individuality which sets it quite apart from other rooftop sites.

Gardens are potentially very powerful places. Combining freedom of expression with the discipline of good design is the surest route to providing your garden with a unique quality and your world with a spirituality that should be an essential part of modern living.

Choosing a style

The look and feel of your garden should be as personal to you as the style of your house. Just as we go to great lengths to decide on the elements of a room – the colour of the walls, the choice and placing of furniture and objects – to create an atmosphere with which we feel comfortable, we follow the same process in the garden. And, as with an interior, it is crucial to decide on the garden's overall look before embarking on its detailed design.

Garden styles are rich and varied – yours will all depend on what kind of place you want to conjure up. Style is not just about fashion: it plays an important role in creating gardens that fit their location and provides a unity in design terms. You may already have a clear idea about the look of the space, whether it should be a leafy corner of gentle countryside, an unkempt and exciting wilderness where each turn reveals something unexpected, a tranquil retreat which has a cool formality or an exotic jungle mix, with architectural plant forms and contrasting flowers and foliage. If you are a plant collector, an informal style may suit you best, since it will accommodate an eclectic taste more easily; whereas if you like a greater degree of structure, you may prefer a rigorously minimal space where a sense of order prevails. Although there are obvious styles to choose from – formal or informal, traditional or modern – there is no reason why a garden cannot contain elements of each. Often the juxtaposition of styles is what gives a garden its vitality and its originality.

A formal style lends a precise tone to an outdoor space – it is clean, calm and uncluttered. Formality demands respect: its ordered lines and symmetry give the

1 Nature reigns in a romantic garden by Gilles Clément. The moss-covered trough and manicured hedge prevent the scene from being lost completely to the relaxed mood it is designed to capture.
2 The elements at play in this Mexican courtyard are a sense of enclosure, colour and shade. The central evergreen tree gives the necessary shady canopy while the warm ochre of the walls prevents the courtyard from looking bleak.
3 A voluptuous mix of whimsy and profusion gives the garden at Great Dixter, Sussex, its distinct style. This derives in part from the juxtaposition of order, shown in the clipped yews, and disorder, seen in the fulsome planting, which includes cortaderia, *Salvia uliginosa* and *Aster lateriflorus*, all blooming in late summer.
4 Rigorously formal, this garden by David Hicks implies restraint as well as order. The symmetrical precision of the layout lends the scene grandeur, yet its simple lines make it easy on the eye.

3
4

Informal styles of garden tell a very different story. They have a lived-in feel and are comfortable on the mind and the eye. Informal gardens tend to gravitate towards the wild and will only work for you if you are happy with a degree of disorder and an environment that is not so obviously manicured. Informal spaces often feel more restful as they demand less from the occupant, the elements being left to evolve through the hand of nature rather than that of man. But the random feel may be illusory: an informal garden may have to be as carefully constructed and managed as any formal garden. It is merely an organized chaos.

The juxtaposition of the formal and the informal is interesting because it creates tension and contrast – on one hand setting up an order and, on the other, letting it go. One way to combine the styles is to overlay the formal bones of a garden with soft planting; the most famous example of this is at Sissinghurst, in Kent, where tightly clipped hedges and directional pathways are an essential framework for, and contrast to, the relaxed tumble of foliage within them. The one would not be quite the same without the other. Alternatively, you could follow the classic design principle of using formality near to the house, with the garden becoming increasingly informal and the natural world dominating more and more the further away you go. Choosing the balance between the two styles is a pivotal starting point in the design process.

Beyond the balance of formality and informality lie finely tuned questions of taste, such as whether a garden will use one colour range or another. But these decisions can be taken one step at a time. It would be wrong to think that only one style is right for a garden: gardens are highly eclectic places and rules are there to be broken, so you can follow any route you choose. As long as the space works, ideas can be given a twist and the elements within it can be manipulated in any way you like, to create a space that is entirely your own.

eye a direction to follow and provide a clear narrative. It can be seen as an anti-dote to the chaos of day-to-day living and, to an extent, to nature itself. Its imposed order effectively tames nature by turning plants into divisions and walls, the very building materials of the garden itself. Formality is often used to smooth the transition from the order of the house to the relative disorder of the garden; it may take the form of a pair of topiary shrubs to either side of a door or a simple path lined with a sharp edging of grass. You can adopt various levels of formality, from a mown path through long grass at one extreme to the rigidity of eighteenth-century landscape gardens at the other. They suggest different degrees of order in an environment which is always pulling towards the informal.

Sources of inspiration

The gardens of history have all influenced the garden as it is today, and there is still much to be learned from the past. The Chinese were building gardens as long ago as 2000BC; their language and the philosophy behind them were taken to Japan much later by Buddhist monks and reinterpreted there. The simplicity and clarity of form of Japanese gardens, where every element is invested with significance, has influenced a lot of contemporary garden design.

Today we find ourselves in a shrinking world. Technological developments have provided us with seemingly infinite sources of inspiration from all disciplines and all cultures but, at the same time, our natural landscape is fast being depleted. As a consequence, the natural world has once again become a rich source of inspiration and elements of the landscape are being brought into our gardens. A bleached grassland, for example, may inspire a naturalistic planting which mimics the succession of plants over the season. A simple hedgerow or cool, mossy woodland glade may influence a section of your garden devoted to tranquillity. There is a huge number of good garden plants that can be used to refer back to the original inspiration yet reinterpret it on another level, by extending the season or heightening the natural effect with an injection of colour. Fine water reeds can be backed by flame- and copper-stemmed willows, heathland created with bronzed grasses and the vertical forms of brown foxgloves planted with birch trees, chosen for their dappled white stems.

Topographical forms may influence the structural elements in a garden. You could clip an area of hedging in a way that re-creates a rocky ravine. A limestone pavement could inspire the random placing of stonework in a terrace, or a stony beach might influence a free-form gravel courtyard where pebble sizes and self-sown planting dictate the pathways. A rocky steppe could be the stimulus for tiered levels of decking, or a spring trickling down from a rock face might be

Gardens are an ideal meeting place for different ideas and creative disciplines. They appeal to all five senses, they use colour and movement as well as form and texture, they draw on religion and philosophy, and they reflect the ebb and flow of the seasons and all nature's fluctuations. These dynamic living spaces could be inspired by something as simple as a conversation, or as exotic as overseas travel; or they could be driven by the memory of childhood and the desire to recapture the child's feeling of total escapism. Designing a garden brings together art forms, like painting and sculpture, as well as architecture, interior design and the science and art of horticulture, giving garden design rich resources to tap into and making its potential quite explosive.

The inspiration for garden styles, moods, individual features or planting schemes can be found all around us, both in the natural world and in a world dominated by man. A look at the history of gardens reflects this diversity and makes a logical place to start researching ideas. Many of the ancient gardens were built as a direct response to the environment, from the cool enclosures of the Moorish gardens, which sought to provide sanctuary from a harsh and desiccating climate, to the esoteric gardens of the Orient, which aimed to mimic nature itself. By contrast, other gardens – such as those of the Italian Renaissance – were built as a statement of wealth and supremacy, where man demonstrated his control and power over natural forces.

1 There are sources of inspiration everywhere. This head by Alberto Giacometti, just like the forms in the garden, plays with volume, light, shade and contour.
2 The mounds in Charles Jencks' and Maggie Keswick's garden in Scotland refer to the sculptural forms of the hills beyond. Their manipulation of the land's natural contours takes the landscape into another realm altogether.
3 This powerful slate sculpture by Richard Long forges a harmony between art and the natural landscape. Its beauty is in its simplicity.

3

reinterpreted in metal and concrete. The inspiration for your garden may well come from closer to home – the colours of a room, the layers of a textile or even the forms in a painting.

You can mould a garden's elements in the same way that a sculptor would assemble a piece of work or a painter would use a palette of colours. The multi-dimensional garden can also harness other sensory qualities, like sound, touch and smell. A garden based on movement and sound would use plants selected for their mobility and acoustic qualities; grasses and willows can almost be choreographed so that their swaying motion is seen against an architectural backdrop, such as a building or the static lines of clipped topiary.

By contrast, in the harsh environment of a city inspiration may come from the lines of modern architecture itself. You may wish to soften these lines with tumbling planting or to accentuate them with an order and architectural quality in the planting itself. You may respond to the other-worldly environment of a rooftop by taking the man-made forms of the buildings as the focus and using the sky as the frame within which to create your garden picture, as well as the inspiration for its colour scheme. At ground level, you may want to capitalize on the sense of enclosure caused by tall neighbouring buildings to create a green room, inward-looking and private, as a retreat from the noise and bustle of city living.

A practical way of discovering what kind of garden will suit your tastes and match your needs is to make a list of your likes and dislikes: not simply of specific plants and features but also of shapes, colours, buildings and landscapes, as well as more nebulous feelings and emotions. You can also bring together notebooks, clippings and mental images to create a collage of ideas which will become the focus of inspiration for the framework of your garden. This brainstorming device will serve as a freeing-up exercise and help to clarify what you really want out of your garden, besides providing you with some guiding principles for choosing plants and other elements of the design.

4 The eccentric structure of Watts Towers in Los Angeles is half-building, half-sculpture. Organic and yet engineered, it could be an exciting starting-point for the design of outdoor urban spaces such as roof gardens. **5** Dark balsam poplar trunks rising from a swathe of cow parsey, and seen against the horizontal bands of colour in this copse, could inspire a planting of your own. On a smaller scale, black-stemmed bamboo might replace the trees.

4

5

THE DESIGN PROCESS

1

Producing an overall design for your garden gives a focus to your ideas and hence to the garden. Never be afraid of tackling the design: the process is more straightforward than you might think. There are set rules and logical sequences by which the design is built up, from its beginning as a simple plot to its fruition as an outdoor retreat, tailor-made to your needs. Each situation is different and every individual will treat the space in his or her own way. But the guidelines remain the same: they will form the building blocks for a well-planned garden.

The starting point of the design process is a simple matter of assessing and evaluating your plot. This is no more complex than the procedure we go through when we meet a stranger or decide whether a book might be worth reading. It is a case of seeing how the land lies and familiarizing yourself with what lies ahead. In garden terms, this will involve such realities as the size and shape of the plot, whether it is overlooked, which way it faces, the amount of sun and shade in its different parts and the condition and type of the soil.

Once you have identified the existing conditions, you can start to make decisions about the best way to treat the space so that it really works. How do you move through it? How will you use it? Resolving the practicalities is what gives your garden its form or bone structure. The aesthetics are then applied to the elements within it, so that the garden takes on a look of its own. Everybody has – or can learn to develop – their own aesthetic sense, and the ways in which individuality can be stamped on to a garden are many and varied, from setting slate into a brick path to give an interesting texture to juxtaposing a rambling mass of climbing foliage over a simple support to provide shade in summer.

While the garden design process is essentially a creative one, it is also about making mistakes: mistakes help you to resolve your thoughts and preferences. While the plan is only on paper, you still have the chance to revise it; this saves you from making costly errors on the ground. Drawing up the design may take you just a matter of hours or it may take many months: whatever the time scale, it is a process which deserves thorough attention. The following pages will take you through all the stages in the design process, from sketching out your first thoughts on a rough piece of paper to carrying out an accurate survey of the plot in order to draw up your final plan.

1 A roof garden poses design constraints of a practical nature. Heavy planters are pushed to the perimeter of this space, giving a growing area for foliage needed to soften the hard lines of the Manhattan skyline, yet leaving a generous place to sit.
2 Here the meeting of house and garden is given extra significance by the incorporation of a tree. But what do you think of the steps?

2

3 A small terrace in the angle of this building forms an essential spill-over area from the house. Planting encloses it to create a garden room.

3

4 Climbers may be the only planting in this courtyard, but their height and soft contours give the space a sense of enclosure and well-being, as well as providing a contrast to the hard lines of the building.

5 In this garden, continuity is extended from one level to the next by the mossy green steps. The curve is sensuous and enticing.

Assessing your plot

You need to know your plot inside out before you can apply to it the design that is starting to emerge in your head. Evaluating and gathering hard information about the site is a vital part of this process, but one of the most important things to assess and record is your initial gut reaction to it. It may be that the site gives you a sense of claustrophobia; you may feel overlooked or exposed. Your first thought might be that a view is blocked by an overgrown shrub or tree, or you may have the impression that a slope is overpowering the house. In established gardens there may be features which you are keen to retain or enhance, and others which it is immediately obvious are in the wrong place and should be relocated or removed altogether. Note these reactions as they will all need to be addressed in the course of the design process.

The next stage is to make a rough sketch of your plot, not necessarily to scale, on a sheet of paper. Pace out the boundaries of the site and use the rough measurements as the basis for a simple plan. If the plot is small this should be a relatively easy process, but if it is too large to see all at once, use an Ordnance Survey map or a set of deeds, roughly scaling them up to give you a working drawing. Indicate on this the north/south orientation and the main features like buildings and driveways, as well as views and boundaries, noting whether these are fences, hedges or walls. It is also a good idea to take photographs at the beginning, setting the house or other buildings in a context and showing any dominant features. These can be used not only to chart progress later on but also to remind yourself about the volume of summer foliage during the winter months, and vice versa.

Noting down which direction the site faces will reveal the areas dominated by light or shade. A simple compass reading is enough, or a note of where the sun rises or sets. Recording areas of light and shade pinpoints the most usable spaces, which in turn influences where you locate

a terrace for sitting out and a lawn for play, as well as areas for plants and for buildings or features. Any space in the shadow of a tall object, or under the canopy of a tree, will be subject to shade: there are many shade-loving plants to choose from for these situations, but hard surfaces such as stone paving or decking will need to be treated with algicides to prevent them from becoming slippery. Conversely, on the sunny side of large features you might have to think about providing a shade-giving structure or turning them into areas which make the most of their sunny situation. Note the direction of the prevailing wind to evaluate whether you need to furnish shelter for seating or for delicate plants.

Include the house in your drawing, indicating the main frontage, the points of access to the garden and the rooms which will provide the principal vistas. Note the views beyond your boundary: there may be an interesting building, a feature such as a church steeple or even a neighbour's tree which could become a focus, or you may look out on a landscape or even a skyscape which ought to be emphasized in the design. Sometimes a view may be physically blocked by vegetation, or you may be distracted from it by an eyesore such as an ugly shed or the strong, hard lines of a garden fence. If one of these interferes with your thought process, simply hold up your hand to block out the unwanted feature from

1 Being overlooked by surrounding buildings is a hazard of many city gardens. Foliage and flowers are used in abundance to screen this New York balcony from the apartments opposite.
2 In this garden, designed by Wolfgang Oehme and James van Sweden, shade has been turned into a virtue by the use of paving, making a simple space to sit in the cool.

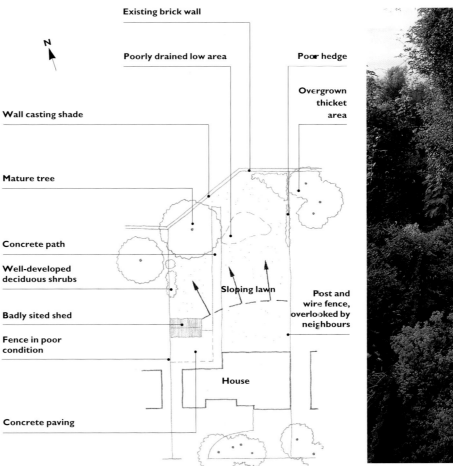

3 This site has typical problems such as a badly sited shed, a path which divides the garden in two and an overall lack of privacy. Its assets include a handsome mature tree and a mellow old brick wall.

Existing brick wall

Poorly drained low area

Poor hedge

Overgrown thicket area

Wall casting shade

Mature tree

Concrete path

Well-developed deciduous shrubs

Sloping lawn

Post and wire fence, overlooked by neighbours

Badly sited shed

Fence in poor condition

House

Concrete paving

3

5

4

your line of vision. These elements can also be scored out on the photographs by overlaying tracing paper and tracing out the scene again with the objects omitted.

The next step is to map the existing planting on to the sketch plan. If the site is entirely overgrown, chart any main trees and shrubs by drawing a rough outline to indicate their spread, and noting their type (for example, deciduous shrub) and approximate height. Where there are too many plants to map individually, indicate the area they cover, and key this to a separate list of plant names. Mark those plants you definitely want to keep with an asterisk, to help visualize what should be done with the space later on.

Noting the site's topography, or the lie of the land, is an invaluable part of the design process. A site that falls away or rises up from the house can be indicated with rough cross-sections which may have to be surveyed thoroughly at a later date. In the meantime these sketches will show where ground may need to be made up or excavated.

Finally, test the soil. Make a series of holes 45cm (18in) deep at strategic points around the site to reveal the depth of the topsoil and indicate whether your land lies above bedrock, sand, clay or gravel. These factors will affect how well the soil drains and will influence the type and positioning of plants; a boggy area, for example, is an ideal site for a bed of lush, moisture-loving species. A soil-testing kit will determine whether the soil is acid, neutral or alkaline, and how fertile it is. Get an idea of what will succeed in your situation by looking at what grows well in the surrounding landscape or neighbouring gardens. Talking to neighbours will also fill in any missing links about the climate, especially the likelihood of frost and drought, and answer your questions about who has responsibility for boundaries which block light or need repair.

Once all this information is gathered together, the design process has begun in earnest and you can start to collate all the ideas you have for your garden.

4 Checking the orientation of your plot will ensure that you put seating in the best spots. This bench is placed against the wall to capture the last of the evening sunlight. Scented planting around it will help to make this a place in which to enjoy the remains of the day.

5 In this coastal garden in the Isles of Scilly, the range of plants has been chosen for their tolerance of salt-laden air and shallow soil, as well as to create a barrier. *Amaryllis belladonna* flower in autumn, sheltered by a belt of shrubs. The landscape sets the mood.

Working with space

1

1 The division of space is treated masterfully at Sissinghurst, in Kent. Hedges and walls make enclosures or rooms, within which paths compartmentalize the space further, on a more domestic scale.
2 Trellis divides two areas of this garden. The shade cast by the bamboo overhead increases the sense of passage to the more open courtyard beyond.
3 In the wooded environment of Lake Forest, Illinois, the glassy surface of this circular pool provides a feeling of open space. The wooden deck allows access to the very edge of the scene.

A well-proportioned garden will feel calm and restful, and the key to this harmony is balance. It is vital to work towards a balance while you are structuring the garden: a common failing of gardens is their poor use of space. All too often, a garden feels cramped and claustrophobic, with an overbearing amount of foliage and elements that vie with each other for attention, leaving the overall impression muddled and confused. By contrast, gardens where all the components are pushed to the edges for fear of breaking into the centre of the canvas leave you feeling stranded and exposed.

A space that works has a balanced relationship between the masses – the 'filled' areas which give height or bulk, such as planting beds or ornamental features – and the voids, which are the spaces between them. A strong framework, with a definite demarcation of the masses and voids, provides you with a usable, comfortable space, allowing you to introduce detail – in the form of plants and features – at a later date. Positive spatial planning is a basic component of good design

and some of the best garden designs are in fact the simplest. The temptation can be to introduce too many elements that will only clutter the site; whether your space is small or large, remember the maxim, 'less is more'.

Dealing with space is fundamentally a practical interpretation of your needs and desires; aesthetics can be applied only once these needs have been resolved. This involves deciding how to use the different areas within a garden: do you need an area for play, for seating, for growing and so on? Do you want a shed or a greenhouse? Where will you locate dustbins or the compost heap? Before making decisions about how much space to allocate to these areas, evaluate their relative importance so that you can prioritize your needs and avoid placing too many demands on the garden.

Mapping out a garden which feels generous in its proportions is easier on paper than on the ground, with all the visual distractions. Good proportions and a balanced relationship between different elements will create the feeling of comfort that is necessary in the garden. For example, the dimensions of a terrace which adjoins a building should relate to the volume of the building itself in some way, so that one does not overpower the other. A useful rule to follow is to take the height of the house-front to the eaves and lay that measurement on to the ground. The relationship between the horizontal and vertical spaces will then have an inherent balance, reflected in an area which feels correctly proportioned; a terrace which is too small for a building will always feel pinched and uninviting. The terrace should then be 'grounded' by a suitable amount of foliage which should relate, in turn, to the rest of the garden.

The shapes in a garden – of terraces, lawns, planting beds, pools, structures – greatly influence the way we perceive and experience it. Rigidly geometric shapes immediately delineate boundaries and channel the view. A circle, for instance, stretches the open space to its limit, taking the eye outwards and creating an entire and complete space that does not feel constricted by the shape of the original site. It makes a space which is a resting point. A square draws the eye to each corner, providing a more rigid space which will feel man-made by comparison. A square or rectangular space resembles a room more than a clearing and lends itself to a formal garden layout.

You can manipulate empty spaces and the elements within them to deceive the eye into imagining that a small site might be larger and an expansive site more intimate. Breaking up an area into different compartments or 'rooms' is a device often employed to create a feeling of intrigue and surprise. A passage through these divisions may enhance the sense of excitement by focusing a course through the site that makes use of every corner. A more open-plan garden, which can be viewed in its entirety, will feel smaller because the boundaries are immediately obvious: in this case, the 'narrative' will have a single chapter rather than several which unravel in a sequence. But even in a tiny plot you can use trees, plantings or a seat to separate off an area and suggest that more lies beyond. A screen will provide enclosure at the same time as it reveals more of the garden, inviting us to explore further.

A space can be set up in many different ways, so that the areas within it not only work on a practical level but create a framework on to which you can 'hang'

2

4 Here the 'clearing' – a circular 'cour sel seat' in the glade – is the observation place for this naturalistic scene designed by Jens Jensen in the Lincoln Memorial Garden, Illinois. Its openness sets the space apart from the overgrown nature of the garden.

3

the body of the garden. Compartments can be divided by planting, trellis, fences or hedging. A division can even be indicated by a well-placed arch which will act as a focus as well as connecting two spaces. The juxtaposition of an open area and a fuller one will emphasize both situations. Enclosed passages through tunnels of foliage or along narrow pathways leading out into a clearing are a similar device which can work in a small or a large garden. Other visual tricks, too, can be used to create a feeling of space. Brickwork laid widthways across a narrow paved area will widen the space, and laid lengthways it will elongate a path.

At this stage of the process you must exercise your imagination to envisage the site's full potential. In an open site, erect temporary screens, such as bamboo canes and string or sheets hung on a line, to visualize the spaces that can be created. In an overgrown plot, clear any superfluities away to clarify its possibilities. Clever manipulation of space will provide you with a strong and enduring skeleton for a garden that has room to evolve.

4

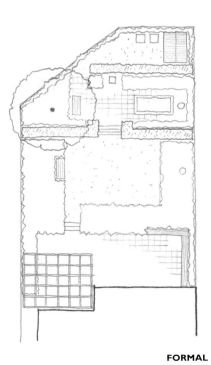

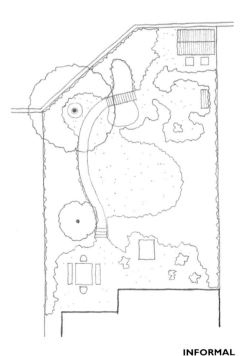

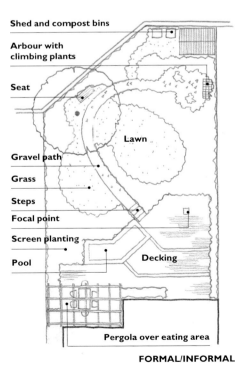

Shed and compost bins

Arbour with climbing plants

Seat

Gravel path

Grass

Steps

Focal point

Screen planting

Pool

Lawn

Decking

Pergola over eating area

5 A formal treatment of this space divides it into three main areas on geometric lines, using clipped hedges: a paved terrace, a lawn surrounded by planting, and a private retreat at the far end. The informal treatment uses more liquid shapes: a gravelled terrace incorporates planting and a sandpit, and a curved path leads down past a wildflower meadow to the lower end, where a wooden bridge and a pond give the focus. The planting provides screening and height. The third option overlays a formal layout with informal planting. The design becomes less geometric further away from the house.

5   FORMAL   INFORMAL   FORMAL/INFORMAL

Views and focal points

Just as a room needs a focus – a window or a fireplace, for example – a garden must have a point on which the eye can rest. Even in the most pared-down garden, a focal point – it could be a simple urn or a large container – gives something to catch the eye and to which it can return from different points; otherwise there is nothing to lead you away from a potential jumble of activity. Gardens are not static places: they should inspire movement, a passage through them, so we can savour fully the experience of being in them. Focal points and views act as a focus for this passage, a strategy by which people orientate themselves.

If we think of the garden in terms of a narrative, views and focal points help to create and reinforce the story, drawing the visitor through it chapter by chapter. In each situation, there is a different sub-plot to unfold. You may be on the edge of a magnificent landscape, or walled in by uniform fencing. In either case, your first task is to locate any existing focus; this may be an emphatic existing feature, such as a shapely tree, or a view out of the garden which can be 'borrowed'. If none exist, they will have to be created and incorporated into the design.

Viewpoints are just as important. They are the places you look from, and which reveal what is within the garden as well as what might lie outside it. In open-plan gardens, focal points should ideally be placed with regard to viewpoints from the house, like windows and doorways, as well as to terraces and seating areas within the garden itself.

A view from the garden may be obvious – a fold in the land or a neighbour's magnificent tree, a dramatic cityscape or the point at which the sun comes up or goes down; it might be only a sliver of the garden's horizon. But in many cases, such views are obscured by foliage, an overgrown hedge or a badly placed outbuilding. If you can clear the obstruction without opening up unwanted views, then you can break into the garden's boundaries to reveal a wider panorama,

'borrow' a view and give the impression that a confined space is larger and also more open. Incorporate your chosen view into the design so that it is revealed strategically. You might decide to make it the main focus of the garden, in which case it may lie at the end of a path or a pair of borders, or you may prefer to treat it with an element of surprise. In this case, the view or focal point might be hidden by hedging, planting or trellising, and revealed at a chosen stage in the route through the garden. On the other hand, you may want to keep a sense of enclosure, the view being an added bonus but not the main focus of the garden.

Some gardens lack a natural view out, particularly if they are surrounded by unappealing buildings or by fencing. You need to provide these enclosed gardens with an internal focal point, which will become the pivot of the route through the space and a cornerstone on which various elements might be hinged. There are many ways of providing a focal point. As these elements are often used as 'resting places' in the garden, a focal point needs to be clear and simple. It may be something very modest – a piece of topiary, for instance – or it could be a garden building

1

2

of some kind. A piece of furniture, such as a seat, is a literal resting place and so makes an ideal focal point, providing a natural draw through the garden. The view back from the seat, or other focal point, will also need careful thought; the seat could become a place from which you look at the garden as a whole, or a viewpoint into another area, which in turn should have its own focus of attention.

Garden buildings, such as gazebos, are used as a sign or a draw in much the same way as furniture. They can provide a focus in the garden or they can become a viewpoint, providing views through their windows or openings. Doorways and gates can also be used as focal points, giving an area an entrance and an exit, perhaps into another compartment of the

3 In this New York community garden, a simple *trompe l'oeil* continues the path into an imaginary distance. A device which should be used with care in the garden, the understated example here works in a down-to-earth, humorous way that does not compete with the garden's natural elements.
4 A well-placed urn provides a sense of place and a focus within this relaxed scheme, adding weight among light foliage and giving the eye a point on which to rest.

garden: a simple device, indicating what may lie ahead. Hedging is successfully used for this purpose – the light at the end of a hedged walkway is a powerful draw. Use sculpture and garden ornament with care in this role: it is important to seek a balance between the object and the garden itself, so that the focal point does not eclipse or fight with the planting around it. Use strong, well-proportioned pieces, such as a large stone trough or a simple urn, and avoid excessive ornamentation.

Whether you decide upon drama or modesty, the views and focal points are pivotal places in the route around your garden, however small that space may be. They provide at the same time the momentum for the journey and the resting places along the way.

Paths and lines of desire

Once you have plotted out the main areas of the garden, you must find the best way of connecting them. Given an open field with an entrance and an exit in opposite corners, the natural way across the space between is the shortest – a diagonal. In a garden, this would be problematic as the areas to either side would then become underused, there being no reason to venture into the rest of the space. Such direct routes are known as lines of desire. You can often see them as muddy tracks trodden across lawns in badly planned public spaces and even as direct routes through flower beds.

A good design would first identify the line of desire running directly between the main elements, then re-route it to take you round the garden in a way that uses the space to the full. Paths in this way form an important part of the garden's bone structure and clarify how the space should be traversed, so you need to work out their route at an early stage in the design process, as without designated pathways your space will lack direction and be underused.

Routes through the garden should be carefully planned so that they connect all the important elements in it, from a focal point and a terrace to a doorway and a compost heap. A well-thought-out route not only allows you to negotiate the space with ease but also reveals your garden's full potential by leading you on from, say, a terrace to the pool, via an interesting group of plants, unravelling its narrative in a logical sequence.

As well as serving a practical role, paths determine how we experience a garden. Their location, width and shape – whether straight lines or curves – as well as the materials used in their construction must all be chosen to ensure that they work within the overall design. Carefully placed, they will not only serve their purpose in the most rational way but also enhance our visual appreciation of the garden. Good design is all about balancing the logical route with more aesthetic considerations.

From a practical point of view, paths must be incorporated in the areas of a garden which will be subject to the most wear. These are the entry and exit points and the principal route through the garden, connecting its main elements. These hard-wearing areas should always be paved, using a material harmonious to their situation. Primary routes can then be subdivided, to provide access into subsidiary areas of the garden; since these secondary paths will receive less wear,

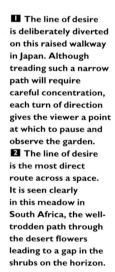

1 The line of desire is deliberately diverted on this raised walkway in Japan. Although treading such a narrow path will require careful concentration, each turn of direction gives the viewer a point at which to pause and observe the garden.
2 The line of desire is the most direct route across a space. It is seen clearly in this meadow in South Africa, the well-trodden path through the desert flowers leading to a gap in the shrubs on the horizon.

3 Instead of a direct line leading from **A** to **B**, a route has been planned which takes you on a journey round the garden; by taking a zig-zag course, the space is used fully. A path leads from the terrace, past the pool, where a bench in the dappled shade of the tree becomes visible; from there, an enticing view is revealed of an arbour draped in foliage, taking you to this quiet retreat at the end of the garden.
4 The sculpture and bench on the curve of a wooden pathway draw the visitor along a planned route through this densely planted garden; they provide a focus at the vista's end.

they can be given a different treatment. Paths must always be tailored to the situation: where they are a main route and used continually, they should never be less than 1m (3ft) wide. This will allow for tumbling plant growth on either side, for two people passing or walking side by side and for wheelbarrow access. There are few things worse than walking along a path which feels like a tightrope.

Paths are useful divisions in gardens, marking the logical end to one element and the start of another, or delineating a space with a distinct line on the ground. They work best when they are clearly defined, in marked contrast to the surrounding materials, and are often most successful when given more than one purpose. A path beside a lawn, for instance, can become a buffer for both the lawn and a planted border, dividing one from the other and providing an 'observation platform'. Lawns, which are soft-wearing, should be negotiated via paths following the line of desire as closely as possible, to prevent 'short-cutting' across the lawn. Diversionary tactics can be employed where there may be a strong urge to cut across space, by using a strategically placed tree or shrub.

In some situations you may want a path to be a powerful element in the design; in others it might be a device which should recede into the background, being merely a route from which to view a planting or a track for a wheelbarrow across grass. But any path must

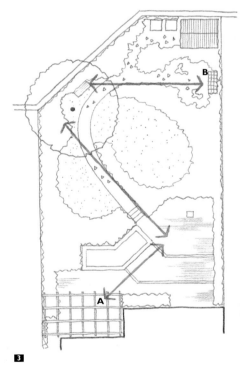

3

be designed as carefully as a planting scheme or a building. Choose an appropriate material, in terms of colour and texture, that will reinforce the garden's essential character. Using local materials will help to achieve a unified appearance, especially if you choose a surface which is sympathetic in style – old bricks for a relaxed path in a country garden, for instance, or plain reconstituted stone in a modern, minimalist environment – while an inappropriate choice, such as concrete slabs employed alongside an old building,

4

will always jar. In terms of texture, the crunch of a gravel path will engage the senses more than, for example, a solid flagstone path. The choice of pattern can be used to make us move more quickly or slowly through the garden. In visual terms a plain, untextured surface is undemanding compared with patterned brick, for example, which commands a certain amount of attention. The plain surface will play a quieter role, ideal for a path whose main purpose is as a foil for other features, such as a border.

Connecting home and garden

1 This inside–outside space partly shelters a living-room that is almost entirely open to the garden. There is a total blurring of boundaries. **2** In the dramatic treatment of this tiny Japanese garden by Shodo Suzuki, the granite waterfall fills the entire view from the window. The scene becomes part of the room, the planes of the boulders being echoed indoors with a carpeted step in a similar shade. **3** The view back to the house deserves as much consideration as the view out. The rose-clad walls of this 'shingle tower' on Long Island integrate the house with the garden, while the surrounding volumes of foliage help to ground it in its site.

As an outside room, the garden has very different parameters from an indoor one in that its ceiling is the sky and its appearance is subject to the continual ebb and flow of the seasons. However, as we have seen, designing an outside space is a similar process to that of interior design and many of the same principles apply. Both involve a choice of flooring materials, light sources, seating and decoration. If your approach is the same for both environments, with careful planning the gulf between the two can be bridged smoothly, so that there is a natural flow from inside to out. The garden will then be seen as a valuable extension of your living area, rather than an entirely separate space to be used if and when the sun shines.

As your home is your primary living space, it makes good sense to analyse how you live indoors before moving into the garden. Look at which rooms and which windows provide the principal views out and where the main access into the garden will be. This will help you to orientate the design so that the garden reveals its full potential when you look out at it from indoors. It will also provide clues

about vistas or focal points that could be created outside as a deliberate draw from one environment to the other.

The point at which you enter the garden is of great importance. If there is no direct access from a main living area – if, for example, the door to the garden is off a hallway – this may involve a radical rethink of your internal space to create an easier transition from indoors to out. French windows or a single glazed door make an immediate visual link between house and garden. If you then enclose or delineate the space immediately outside so it relates in scale to the adjacent room, this gives a sense that the floor plan of the house merely extends beyond the walls of the building into the garden. The 'enclosure' can be formed from foliage or may even be from hedges, walls or fencing. If the spill-over area from the house becomes a terrace, a balustrade might be appropriate, or simply a clear demarcation line where the terrace ends and a lawn or a planted area begins. A shelter, such as a pergola or verandah, would reinforce the illusion of this space as an extension of the house, making a gentle transition from indoors to out.

1
2

3

4 The concrete terraces in this modern garden by Isobelle C. Greene were inspired by aerial photographs of rice paddies in mountainous Asia. The angled retaining walls spill from the house into the garden while referring strongly back to the angular forms of the building.

5 Large glass doors forming one wall of the living-room break the boundary between this house and garden in California. With the doors open, the outdoor terrace becomes an extension of the room and scents as well as sights are brought indoors.

4

5

play area for young children, or as an eating area, or both? If seating is included, consider the choice of style so that it entices people to venture outside. There should be a stylistic link with seating indoors, for example in scale or colour, if not in the material itself. Just like a room, a garden can be transformed with lighting by night, providing the space with a focus once darkness falls. Even in bad weather lighting can be used to draw the eye outdoors, to serve as a reminder that there is space beyond the confines of the house. In this case you may wish to provide general background lighting for the whole garden as well as more focused lighting in areas of greater use.

The progression from inside to outside should always be fluid. A terraced area can be linked in style to that of the home, either through the architecture of the building or through a colour scheme within the home itself. Planting can set a style and a mood or reflect a particular aesthetic: a cool minimalism using bamboos and undemanding ground cover, for example, or a more relaxed style using a jumble of forms and colours. Where there is a view out, the process may well work in reverse, the view influencing the style of the garden immediately around the house and that, in turn, influencing the decor of the rooms. A view of the sea or a river may suggest a colour scheme both for the planting in the garden and for the furnishings or walls of a room.

Having created a comfortable area outside the house that integrates inside with out, it is important that the route into the rest of the garden is clearly defined, so that the flow continues beyond the immediate area of transition and, once again, there is a natural draw. A path could lead you from the terrace to the main focal point of the garden or out from the first 'room' into the garden's wilder recesses. One 'wall' of the first garden room could be punctured, by using gauzy and semi-transparent planting, or by leaving a window in a hedge or wall so that the view is not interrupted.

Treating the areas with a degree of uniformity helps to integrate the two worlds. Flooring materials are an obvious starting point. Although you may not want or be able to match them exactly, echoing the colour or texture of a floor will be enough to establish a connection. A pale carpet, for instance, can be echoed with a similarly coloured gravel, or a tiled indoor floor with frostproof tiles outside. If you are tempted to continue a tiled floor indoors with an identically paved terrace, be aware that used out of doors materials are subject to weathering and may change colour or otherwise wear very differently from those indoors.

Taking the idea of the spill-over area being another 'room', think about its function in the same way as that of a room in the house. Do you need it as a

Surveying the site

By this point in the design process you should have a good idea of the advantages and drawbacks of your site and be starting to get a feel for what you would like to achieve within the space. You are now ready to carry out an accurate survey, to provide you with an outline plan on to which you can draw all the components of the garden. Accurate plans are a vital part of the design process: not only are they essential for plotting where everything will go, but drawing them can loosen up the way you think and help to crystallize your ideas.

Find out first whether plans have ever been drawn up, either for the site or the building, as these could be used as the basis of your own site plan. If plans are available, check them for accuracy before noting any remaining details and adding them. If no plans exist, go back to the sketch plan you made at the beginning, when starting to assess your plot (see pages 36–7), and put more accurate measurements on to it.

Measuring the site is not a difficult process, but clarity and accuracy are crucial: be precise, not only when measuring but also with your notation. In cold and windy conditions, it is tempting to hurry and you may confuse numbers or write them down illegibly. Never take anything for granted and double-check all measurements. It is easy to assume that two boundary fences run parallel, for example, but they may not and your assumption could lead you to make serious miscalculations. If your plot is large you may need more than one plan, in which case divide the site into separate areas and draw a series of plans that relate to each other.

You will need a 30m (100ft) tape measure and, preferably, a friend to help you measure the dimensions and to work out the exact location of the boundaries, buildings and main features within the space. In most cases, a plan of the garden should include at least one side of the house and it is generally a good idea to begin measuring from this point.

■ Railway sleepers are used here to snake a path down this steep New Zealand lakeside garden. The descent makes a virtue of the potential difficulties of the site.

■

- Peg the tape measure down securely and run it across the façade of the house; if the building is free-standing, measure each side of it. Take running (progressive) measurements, noting on the plan the direction from which they were taken. Measure from the corner of the house to each feature on its front, like doors and windows that open on to the garden, and measure the depth of any recesses by taking a right angle off the main tape. Include the position of drainpipes, gullies and boiler flues.

- Once you have recorded the house measurements, use these as your reference point from which to plot other features. Measure and mark all the boundaries of the garden, noting the heights of hedges, fences and walls. Include gates, paths and other significant existing features, like garden buildings or trees and shrubs, that you may want to keep.

- To plot individual features, use the process called triangulation (which is illustrated opposite): measure from one corner of the house to a tree near the far boundary, for example, then measure the distance to the same tree from the other corner of the house. Write down both measurements clearly so you will be able to plot the tree's location accurately on the scale plan. Record the spread of tree canopies, too, to remind you to allow for the shade they cast.

- If you know where electric cables, water and waste pipes run, include this information on your plan, as well as the location of any inspection covers and septic tanks. Note the plot's orientation, marking north on your plan.

- Make a note of any slopes on your survey so that you can later decide whether there is a need for terracing or steps. You may want to change the levels to accommodate a sitting area, perhaps, or move intimidating banks away from a building. On downward-sloping land, running out a tape at right angles, and horizontally, from a fixed point will give you an approximate idea of the fall.

- Measuring the levels to a greater degree of accuracy than this is rather more complicated. In a small garden, it can be achieved with a spirit level, planks and pegs relatively easily (see opposite). When landscaping a larger site, you may decide to employ a surveyor to do a professional site survey in order to avoid the risk of costly mistakes; this could save you both time and money in the long run.

- Once you have recorded all the dimensions, draw up a plan of the site on grid paper, to an appropriate scale, and transfer to it all the information you have gathered. A scale plan enables you to decide how to fit all the different elements into a limited space and relate them practically and aesthetically to each other. A scale of 1:50 or 1:100 will be most appropriate for an average-sized garden, with the latter fitting comfortably on a sheet of A2 paper.

To measure the level, use two wooden pegs and a straight-sided plank 3m (10ft) long. Knock the first peg into the ground as straight as possible and put the plank on top of it. Adjust the plank until a spirit level shows it to be level, then knock a second peg into the ground 3m (10ft) away; adjust its height so that, when the other end of the plank is placed on top of it, the plank remains level. The difference between the lengths of the first and second pegs above ground will determine the fall over a distance of 3m (10ft). Continue across the site in this way, noting down data at each 3m (10ft) interval. Add these figures together to ascertain the total fall in the ground over the distance measured; this is usually expressed as a ratio (here 1:10).

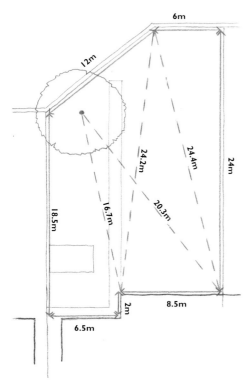

6m

12m

24.2m

24.4m

24m

16.7m

20.3m

18.5m

2m

8.5m

6.5m

TRIANGULATION

Triangulation is a good method of measuring a garden and positioning the existing features in it. Once you have recorded the house's dimensions, use this process to measure the distance to each feature from two fixed points on the same line, clearly noting both measurements. Choose two points far apart for greatest accuracy, making a wide-based triangle. Convert the actual measurements to the scale you are using, and set a pair of compasses to the first radius; make an arc from the first fixed point, then adjust the radius and measure from the other fixed point; where the two arcs intersect marks the exact position of the feature.

2

2 Planting has been integrated into the hard landscaping of this garden by Erwan Tymen, utilizing the gentle fall of the land. Plants like phlomis grow on the wider 'landings' between steps.
3 Enclosure, a gentle ramp and a degree of formality have all been incorporated in the design to make the most of this sloping site.

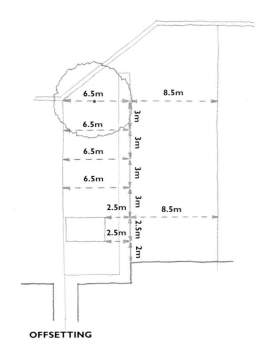

6.5m

8.5m

3m

6.5m

3m

6.5m

3m

6.5m

3m

2.5m

8.5m

2.5m

2.5m

2.5m

2m

OFFSETTING

Offsetting is another method of recording the position of garden features, based on right angles. Run out a long tape measure at 90 degrees to a set point on the building and lay it along the length of the garden; this will give a main reference point from which individual features can be mapped. (In a wide garden, you may first need to run a straight line along to continue the length of a wall.) With a second tape, take offsets at 90 degrees to the first tape wherever a feature occurs, noting the distance at which it lies from the first tape.

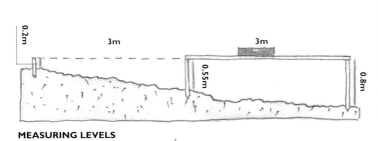

0.2m

3m

3m

0.55m

0.8m

MEASURING LEVELS

3

The concept plan

1 The simplicity of the coloured dividing wall and steps and the minimal planting in a Steve Martino garden contrast theatrically with the wilderness beyond. This powerful device is employed to make two dramatically different environments.

The outline plan you have just drawn up will give you a clear idea about the site and the relationship between the existing elements within it. The next stage is to produce the concept plan: this is a working drawing on which you will lay out the garden's main areas and features. It is the collection point for your ideas and the skeleton of the garden-to-be. Once you have the concept plan, you can draw up detailed planting plans and, if necessary, supplementary plans devoted purely to the garden's hard landscaping – the paths, paved areas, steps and garden structures such as pergolas.

Seeing the project on paper, without the clutter of visual interference, will encourage you to develop your ideas for the garden – to make decisions about how much space to devote to your terrace, for example, and how to get from the terrace to the lawn in the most logical way.

At this stage you can rework the design as many times as you like, superimposing different ideas on the photocopied basic outline plan. Use a soft pencil so as not to be inhibited by each mark; the process should be free of restrictions and hang-ups, imagined or otherwise. Include in the margin any important observations from the site analysis, like the prevailing wind, areas of shade, views out and so on, and write a checklist of all the elements you would like to include alongside.

BREAKING INTO THE SPACE

When faced with the unworked outline plan, breaking into the empty space can at first appear daunting. But never forget that the most successful gardens are often those with the simplest ideas: a strong, simple skeleton makes the best possible framework, because you can lay detail over it and introduce planting to soften it. Therefore be bold right from the start – divide up the area first into its basic compartments, starting with those elements which are of most importance to you. Having the plan on graph paper will help you to divide the space up, on a grid system, into units. Remember that, for a garden to work, it should be easy to traverse, so make the paths and terraces generous and clear.

Concentrate first on the most positive aspects of your plot and make sure they are used to their full potential. These may include a sunny corner, which could become the location of a seating area, or a wonderful view, which might dictate the way you orientate the whole garden. Once you have identified these key factors, look at other important aspects, such as the spill-over area from the house, which you may wish to make into a terrace or an eating area. Deciding where to place the utility areas should come into the early stages of planning rather than as an afterthought. Sheds, green-houses and compost bins are often placed near the boundary but they need not be; they should never be so far away from the house that they are little used. Divisions and screens can be used to separate them from the main garden, or a feature such as a piece of topiary can be placed to one side to distract attention from them.

Use the whole area. A failing of many designs is a tendency to stick to the edges, where there is a degree of security. The art of good design is to create functional spaces which are both comfortable to live in and pleasing to look at. Link them in a logical way: this is where paths and the placing of focal points play a key role. Work through your checklist in order of priority, introducing the elements about which you feel strongly and rejecting those which become inappropriate or merely optional. At this stage you are also making decisions about which of the existing plants and features you want to keep. Each element, old and new, needs to be weighed up and evaluated in the context of the garden theme as a whole.

1

2 Massed planting makes a simple foil for this secluded seating area; trees give the necessary shade. The flat lawn is a deliberate contrast within the sloping site, creating a sense of enclosure.

3

WORKING TOWARDS A BALANCE

Gardens are three-dimensional spaces which should, as we have seen, have a balance between open spaces – like clearings, lawns and terraces – and the filled spaces, which include planted areas as well as buildings and features. A border, for example, should be made deep enough to balance a lawn adjacent to it; if it is too narrow, it will be out of scale with the green expanse and its proportions will look mean. It is also important to have a balance of scale between the elements that make up the garden. Buildings are an obvious reference point: a large house façade demands a bolder treatment of its garden than a small cottage. Every garden tells its own story: the narrative should have a beginning, an end and be punctuated along the way with features and stopping points, maybe a view, or a seating area for reflection. Introducing contrasts within the space will help to give the narrative a momentum, whether through the textural juxtaposition of lawn next to a path, or the vertical form of planting against the horizontal plane.

3 Trellis makes an effective divider in a small space because it forms an open, see-through screen. The staggered hedge gives a sense of intrigue.

Getting organized

Making a new garden from scratch is a serious undertaking and it is important to be realistic about what you can achieve yourself. However ambitious the project, organization is the key: spreading the workload over several seasons will reduce the strain on your time, energy and resources. Good planning helps you to order your priorities and tailor the work so that it takes place in a logical sequence. Soil may need to be moved to make way for a terrace, for instance, but before the terrace can be laid you may need to install an electrical power circuit, or even a drainage system if you have a problem with surplus water. All building works are disruptive and need to be completed before any soil preparation or planting can take place.

To help you manage the sequence of work, use your basic concept plan to prepare a separate drawing detailing all the elements of hard landscaping you wish to include: where terraces may lie, where walls need to be built or fences erected and where paths and access routes will be located; indicate areas for lawns and for planting, too. This plan will enable you to allocate time and money in logical stages (you could possibly use a different colour for each stage of the work), and to ensure that all the hard landscaping is completed to make way for planting in the dormant season.

Any work involving earth-moving must be carried out first: this relates to changes of level, drainage schemes and the laying of water mains and electric cables. The next stage will be laying down paths to give you access to all parts of the garden, followed by any other areas which need solid foundations, including a paved terrace, boundary walls, steps or the base for a shed. Clearing the ground for areas of lawn and improving the soil in plant borders come next, followed by laying the lawn and the planting itself. This can also be done in stages, the long-term plantings – such as hedges and trees – taking priority over bulbs, perennials and vegetables.

Part of the process of getting organized to start the work is to carry out some research into the materials available. Your choice will be influenced by several factors, including cost, ease of laying and your own personal taste, but it is also important to bear in mind the prevailing local style. Where possible, use materials which help to link the garden with the house, as well as the surrounding landscape, so that it has a unity with its outdoor setting.

GETTING PROFESSIONAL HELP

Designing a garden can be a complex task and you may be completely stumped by what lies in front of you. If you feel that compiling your own plan is too daunting a process or that the implementation of dramatic changes is beyond your capabilities, you might consider employing a professional garden designer. While some of us may be gifted with an artist's eye for plant associations or the ability to conceptualize space, few amateur gardeners can combine the horticultural, design and construction expertise that a good designer offers. There is much to be gained from using a professional garden designer, whether you require him or her to plan and build the whole garden, to come up with an overall design, or just to advise on a planting plan.

In the long run, professional advice can mean tremendous economies in time and cost, saving you months or even years of trial and error. A fresh eye is often all that is required to give a new slant to something that has become over-familiar; one discussion with a designer may be all you need to unblock your vision and reveal the garden's potential. The garden designer's trained eye may well pinpoint a blocked view or detect an imbalance between lawn and borders, which will help you to go forward. You may, however, want further assistance, in which case a designer will proceed to draw up a concept plan outlining the new design and, maybe, some supplementary plans to detail the hard landscaping and

planting. A designer will help you to focus your ideas about what you want from your garden and tell you how to achieve it, will draw up schedules for carrying out the building work and planting, and will appoint and manage the contractors.

Always remember that your garden is a very personal venture, an intimate space that should reflect your personality and desires above those of anyone else.

1 Always seek the advice of a structural engineer when building a roof garden – weight is a major factor.
2 The creation of a water course through a wood requires the use of a mechanical digger to excavate the bed and the skills of craftsmen to build the stream's retaining walls.

3 Your concept plan may look something like this. It shows all the main components of the garden, in scale, enabling you to see their relationship to each other. Separate, more detailed hard landscaping and planting plans can be drawn up from it. A well-planned garden will reduce the amount of effort involved in its creation, enabling you to complete the work in stages. You may need a landscape contractor or builder to lay down the hard landscaping, for which there must be access alongside the house.

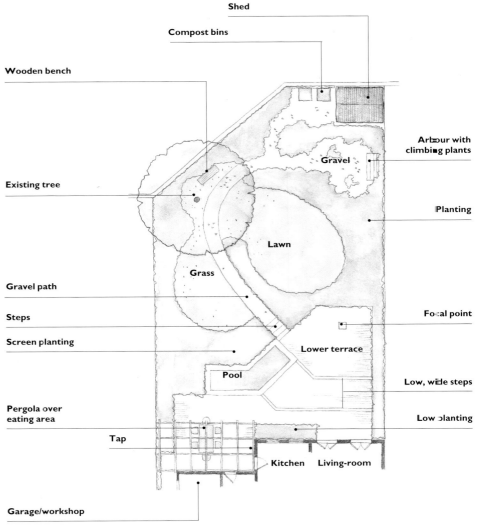

Shed

Compost bins

Wooden bench

Existing tree

Gravel path

Steps

Screen planting

Pergola over eating area

Tap

Garage/workshop

Arbour with climbing plants

Gravel

Planting

Lawn

Grass

Focal point

Lower terrace

Low, wide steps

Pool

Low planting

Kitchen   Living-room

3

A designer must be able to understand and communicate your ideas, therefore it is important to choose one with whom you share a sympathy; this will help in the amalgamation of your ideas with his or her skills. The best form of recommendation is, as always, word of mouth, but there are also professional bodies, such as the Society of Garden Designers in England, which will be able to recommend an experienced, qualified designer working in your area. Ask to see examples of past work and a portfolio of designs, and try to visit an existing garden to gain an insight into the style and quality of his or her completed projects.

After an initial meeting, involving a discussion about your requirements and what it is feasible to achieve within the space, a designer will quote you a price for the design and, if this is agreed, will supply a contract outlining terms and conditions. He or she should also give you an estimate for the works that lie ahead, including materials and plants, so that you have a clear idea of the total cost.

Once you agree, the designer will survey the site to produce an accurate plan recording all relevant information and existing features of the site. This information will then be used to produce a draft scale plan incorporating the proposed new layout: the concept plan is open to discussion at this stage. Once agreed, the plan is regarded as final and planting plans and construction drawings will be worked up from it.

You may wish to go ahead and implement the design on your own from this point; or the designer will be able to recommend a contractor and, if you wish, oversee the work. The actual process of building the garden will generally rely upon skilled craftsmen, such as builders to construct terraces and walls, metal workers and carpenters where needed, and perhaps even plumbers and electricians too. A good landscape contractor would be able to supply all these skills, in addition to having the necessary horticultural knowledge to prepare the soil and introduce the plants.

Regardless of whom you employ, and how much of the work they carry out, make sure you cover all eventualities. It is essential to have a very clear idea of what you want before work starts: schemes that evolve as they go are full of unexpected, and sometimes costly, surprises. The checklist below will help you to consider all possible aspects, including both the obvious and some hidden ones. Have everything in a written contract so you have some recourse if problems arise.

- Before any work starts, check planning regulations to ensure you are within your rights with any developments or changes of use: some local authorities have restrictions about types of railing or fence heights, for example, notably in conservation areas.
- Check with the planning authorities that there are no preservation orders on any trees you are proposing to cut down, prune in any way or remove.
- Inform neighbours about any work you are having done, especially changes to boundaries which might affect their view or lessen their light.
- Ensure that there is proper access to the site before works take place, allowing the free movement of heavy machinery and materials. In cities, where limited access through the house or across shared land makes it impossible to get the machinery on site, excavations may have to be done by hand, which will push up the price.
- Check that each contractor guarantees the standard of their work and has adequate insurance cover. Make the main contractor responsible for any sub-contracted labour.
- Agree both start and completion dates.
- Be clear and specific about all your requirements.
- Keep a close eye on developments, and speak up the moment you feel there is something you are not happy with.
- Make sure that the contract includes a clause stating that the site will be cleared and the garden left in good order at the end of the job.

Barton Court
DESIGNER: TERENCE CONRAN

1

2

3

Barton Court lies just over one hour's journey to the west of London. When Terence Conran bought the eighteenth-century house and its grounds in 1972, both were derelict. The grounds total around 20 acres, with a river to the front and a walled kitchen garden to the back. In redesigning the garden, the priorities were to restore the kitchen garden and to 're-orientate' the house so that it enjoyed an uninterrupted view down to the river. The driveway was re-routed to the back of the house and a ha-ha built, using brick and flint from derelict outbuildings, to create a formal garden area in front of the main entrance. An old terracotta urn stands on the river bank, making a commanding focal point.

Great care has been taken to create a garden on a comfortable scale, by making a number of intimate outdoor 'rooms' around the house. There is a sheltered corner for outdoor dining; an enclosed lawn with a small terracotta fountain; a cluster of topiary yews amid a daisy-dusted lawn. The garden reveals itself as a series of interconnected areas, while retaining a sense of the overall scheme.

The walled gardens behind the house, once overgrown with thistles and pine trees, have been returned to their former splendour. The central vegetable plot, with its orderly, serried rows of crops, is flanked by an orchard to one side and a walled lawn and conservatory to the other. The beds, edged by dwarf hedges, are divided by gravel paths running the length and width of the enclosure. At their central intersection, four plane trees provide a shady umbrella in the middle of summer. Beyond the kitchen garden, a potting shed and greenhouses testify to the labour necessary to support it; Barton Court's full-time gardener spends most of his time here.

While very much a working kitchen garden, the fruit and vegetables are inter-planted with flowers for extra colour and variety. Herb beds and borders create a medley of scents as you pass through. The produce ranges from tomatoes and asparagus, through peas, runner beans, cauliflowers and cabbage, to soft fruits and herbs. In addition to produce raised for home consumption, the garden also supplies Conran Restaurants in London. So successful is this semi-commercial enterprise that the kitchen garden has now been extended into the orchard.

The garden at Barton Court is a labour of love. Though certainly ambitious in scale, its execution is surprisingly modest,

1 The far corner of the kitchen garden affords a fine view of the Georgian mansion, seen through the spires of verbascum and feathery dill.
2 Set against the fringes of woodland, the topiary garden juxtaposes bold forms against a lawn dappled with daisies. Viewed from the ground, the clipped shapes in box and yew create an intimate setting that gives no hint of the expanse of land beyond.
3 A group of fibreglass deer, made by artist Nick Munro, appear to have crept from the wood for an inquisitive inspection. Their view shows the wisteria-clad front of the house and the buttressed ha-ha dividing the formal garden from the lawn.
4 The driveway bisects the garden. To either side of the house and to its front, there are separate spaces for recreational activities, including spots where people can sit and read, work, snooze or eat; the ground in front of the river is used for an annual cricket match. The potting sheds and greenhouses are beyond the kitchen garden.

working with the soil and the seasons and the whims of nature. A late spring frost in 1997 decimated the established wisteria, but its skeletal form soon gave way to a second flowering more vigorous than any seen for years. This is a garden that resists the temptations of instant gratification, instead maturing quietly, confident that the best is still to come.

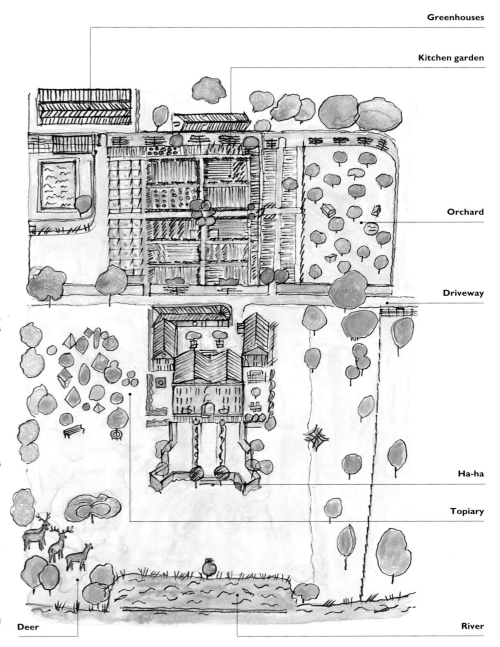

Greenhouses

Kitchen garden

Orchard

Driveway

Ha-ha

Topiary

Deer

River

4

5

5 Enclosed by brick walls, the vegetable garden has its own microclimate, a degree or so warmer than elsewhere in the garden.
6 Immediately in front of the house, the most formal garden space is contained by the brick and flint walls of the ha-ha. The porched doorway opens on to a stone terrace and looks down the grass path bordered by espaliered fruit trees towards the river.

6

1

2

3

4

5

1 A simple octagonal tree seat provides a shady spot on the edge of the topiary garden.
2 Part of the garden's charm derives from the relaxed way in which order – such as the rows of neatly planted vegetables – lies side by side with the informality of flower borders that are allowed to self-seed. Here, centaureas and euphorbias spill over on to the path.
3 To either side of the house lie small 'secret' gardens. The one here is furnished with a sofa made from terracotta brick-tiles, set among foxgloves. Designed by Tania Harvey, the sofa is so heavy that before installation the ground had to be reinforced.

6

7

8

4 The conservatory is a jungle of heat- and moisture-loving plants, like the grapevine and arum lilies. An irrigation system on an electric timer ensures that the plants do not dry out in the heat.
5 In spring, the vegetable garden gives little indication of the intense productivity in store. The ground has been sown with salad vegetables and the first shoots of runner beans start to climb their poles. Forcing jars protect young rhubarb plants from late frosts.
6 The greenhouse is used both for bringing on tender seedlings before planting them out in the vegetable garden and for the nurture of more exotic plants and flowers all through the year.

7 Fresh from the earth, these onions are organically grown and full of flavour.
8 Every year, the garden at Barton Court produces a bumper crop of juicy tomatoes. Their shapes may be rather less regular than supermarket varieties, but their flavour proves the advantages of growing your own.
9 Self-sufficiency has seldom looked so appealing. Chickens and ducks have a free range around the orchard, disturbed only when their eggs are collected or when the irascible geese get territorial.

9

CREATING THE FRAMEWORK

Strip any garden of its features and embellishments, including its plants, and the structural division of the area is revealed. Erecting or laying down this permanent structure – comprising the walls, fences, points of access, paths and steps, as well as lawn and paved areas – is the first step in making a garden. Once this is done, you have the makings of a dynamic space on which you can build and which will flourish and be enhanced with time. A garden with good 'bone structure' will have a spacious feel even when its dimensions are tiny: once you find a way of dividing the plot, there is something to traverse.

A garden's structure is most evident and clearly defined in a formal design. The great historic gardens of France and Italy succeed principally through the architectural definition of their space, using hedges as walls and creating a series of compartments or rooms, each with specific roles or commanding dramatic views. In the softer flower gardens of Britain, such as Hidcote and Sissinghurst, the idea of rooms was taken a stage further, with colour themes within the rooms, the dark yew hedges being used as a foil for dazzling herbaceous perennials. The soft planting provides a juxtaposition with the formality of the structure and introduces a relaxed character and mood. At the same time as these gardens were being created, in the 1930s, the Dutch designer Mien Ruys was using interesting new principles to give her gardens a framework: she laid a Mondrian-style grid on the ground to divide up the space and, while some areas were planted, others were left as voids; the overall look was balanced, exciting and not at all geometric.

In contemporary gardens, hedges, screens and walls are still used to define space, but a much more informal arrangement allows views and vistas to open up in surprising places. Planting may partially enclose a patio while lawns or areas of gravel or paving provide more open spaces. John Brookes has used planting to break up the garden at Denmans, Sussex. This Mediterranean-style garden, based on the principle of a dry stream bed using gravel as a surface, is divided by foliage screens. These sometimes obscure the view completely while in other parts the lack of planting allows easy access from one area to another. However informal, this garden still has a framework which gives it both its essential narrative and a sense of space and intrigue.

1 Posts driven into the ground and decorated with bottles create an eye-catching screen and an individualistic but definite border to this path. The screen is permeable yet potent.
2 Dramatic rock strata and linear planting are used in this garden to create a sense of width and division. The bamboo creates a vertical screen, set apart from the actual boundary.

3 This slate terrace links and yet divides the swimming pool in the background from the ornamental pool. Planting softens the angular lines and makes the space feel more intimate.

4

4 A wattle fence topped by a laurel hedge creates the boundary and clipped holly provides the sculptural elements that reinforce the garden's division.

5

5 Flat planes of concrete are used as sculptural elements to define and divide this space. Architectural planting acts as a counterbalance.

Boundaries and divisions

1

Garden boundaries define the extent of individual ownership, while divisions compartmentalize the space internally. Besides creating privacy and shelter, boundary structures also perform other roles, such as excluding livestock and providing physical security. These functions vary in importance depending on location; you are unlikely to need to keep cattle or sheep out of a town garden, whereas privacy and screening become an absolute necessity in an overlooked city plot. Geographical factors should play a part in the treatment of boundaries, influencing the choice of materials and the way in which they are used. The building materials available locally – the type of stone or the colour of bricks, for example – are an intrinsic part of the vernacular architecture and it is important to respect and exploit this character when creating a new garden.

Where the perimeters of a garden are defined by a physical barrier – a wall, fence or hedge – this gives a strong sense of enclosure. They may be accentuated, taking the form of high walls or solid evergreen hedges, to heighten the seclusion and privacy within the garden, or they can be so discreet they are almost unnoticed: a post and wire fence or traditional estate railings, consisting of slim metal rods with four horizontal rails, increase the sense of space by helping to merge a country garden into surrounding landscape. Where high boundaries are not necessary, ground-level forms of demarcation, such as a pathway, a slight change of level or a contrasting hard material, may be used to define ownership without screening or blocking views. The ha-ha, originally a French device consisting of a ditch and retaining wall, enables the garden and landscape to be enjoyed as one space, without a visible division when viewed from the house, but the wall is high enough to keep out cattle and to create a distinct boundary.

The physical limitations which boundaries impose on a garden are not linked to its use and can all too easily control, or

2

impede, the choice of layout. A common mistake, when setting out borders, lawns and terraces, is to reflect the shape of the site in the belief that this maximizes the available space and makes the garden appear larger. Space *is* used to the full, but, by reinforcing the site's shape, this approach may accentuate its limitations. It is often better to distract attention from the boundary by, for example, placing planting a little way in front of the boundary rather than on it, and creating spaces and areas within the garden which focus the eye internally, possibly leaving some areas out of view to be discovered and explored separately.

The Japanese have a term for this technique – *shakkei* – literally, borrowed scenery. By disguising the boundaries with dense planting, the full extent of the site is obscured and scenery or planting from other gardens, or from the landscape beyond, are exploited as if they are

part of the garden. A similar approach is possible on ground that runs downhill, away from the house. It is relatively easy to camouflage and 'lose' boundaries on ground that slopes away, to leave an open panorama and to gain a greater sense of freedom.

In front gardens, the arrival point of most properties, boundaries tend to be more in evidence, as a sense of ownership and identity are considered important, unless of course they are part of an open-plan development. While individuality of expression is possible, you may also want to think about making the front garden cohere with the wider environment, in design or materials, or both.

CREATING DIVISIONS
There is often a need for spatial division within the garden as a whole. Although it can be dramatic to see a complete garden all at once, nothing then remains to

1 This demarcation by design partnership Delaney, Cochran & Castillo juxtaposes organic and man-made forms, playfully dividing the more manicured part of the garden from the wilder area.
2 Another installation by Delaney, Cochran & Castillo creates a low division using cut stone and natural boulders, again dividing formal from informal.

3

4

5

3 This dry stone retaining wall marks a definite division and yet allows a view through to another part of this garden designed by Wolfgang Oehme and James van Sweden.
4 A beech hedge, which does not totally lose its leaves in winter, creates a semi-opaque division within a garden; its height allows views to be retained. A path through a break in the hedge links the two areas of the garden; the bench provides a focal point.
5 The magnificent organic form of this woven willow 'wall' is a focus in itself. The doorway creates a sense of expectation and is the essential link with what lies beyond.

inspire your imagination or to invite exploration. The successful division of a large outdoor space creates comfortable and atmospheric gardens on a human scale. Compartmentalizing the space also heightens the drama of moving from one space to another, each with a different character. If you divide your garden into 'rooms', it is a good idea to leave one space free of features and strong colour, relying on the static simplicity of lawn and hedge to provide respite before moving on to the next tableau.

Hedges or other internal screens and divisions need not be overpoweringly high: hornbeam, for example, makes a see-through hedge when clipped tightly, or it can be pleached – trained to be grown on stilts, carried above head height on tall, clear stems. Hedges at waist height will separate different areas while retaining views across the garden. The more solid the hedge, and the darker

its colour, the better defined are the spaces or holes cut into it. Entrances, exits and views framed by solid screens always take on a sense of importance.

The construction of walls and fences introduces an architectural quality into the garden. Choosing the material from which the house is built will link the property to the garden, especially if similar laying patterns and construction techniques are also used. Planting will soften the mass of solid walls or fences; use the soft, mobile foliage of bamboo, for example, which moves in every breeze, to alleviate the hard texture of a wall. Before designing any wall, always check local building or planning regulations as height limits are often set for free-standing and boundary walls. In many areas there are also planning regulations concerning the actual design of boundary structures, which may put restrictions on the materials you can use.

Fences in steel, aluminium or wood provide a less solid and often more transparent screen than walls, reducing the impact of boundaries and divisions. Trellis is the most open form of division and casts intriguing shadows across the garden; train plants over trellis to make it a more opaque screen. Paint or stain a fence or trellis with dark blue or dark green if you want to turn it into a discreet background against which more lightly coloured foliage and flowers stand out.

Don't feel constrained by conventional boundary solutions: try using stretched canvas, glass blocks or fine aluminium mesh for an imaginative alternative. In a small garden, there are more subtle ways of separating the space, using a change of level or an informal plant grouping as the dividing element. Perhaps the most exciting spatial division is the use of water: it creates a form of separation while keeping the visual link between different spaces and retaining a sense of openness and continuity. One of the best examples can be seen in Sir Geoffrey Jellicoe's canal with stepping stones at Sutton Place in Surrey. On a more modest scale, designer Cleve West's narrow rectangular pool runs across the width of his small London garden from fence to fence; a single slab lets you cross.

Entrances

1 This simple wooden doorway set in a stone wall offers a tempting invitation into the world beyond – maybe into a 'secret garden'.
2 Luis Barragán used strong planes of colour, both as a draw to the visitor and also as a screen, in the dramatic entrance to this Mexican garden.

By their nature, entrances offer some of the most dramatic and exciting opportunities in garden design, being linked with a sense of arrival and the experience of passing from one space to another. From grand entrances, heavily decorated and embellished, to the humblest of garden gates, there is a feeling of anticipation in passing through, in expectation of discovering what lies beyond.

The simplest entrances are gaps left in solid screens and divisions. The way light falls on different surfaces is enough to identify these openings – so the screen itself might be in shadow but the space beyond filled with light, or vice versa. Narrow entrances in architectural hedging and walls use this play of light to good effect and, when located at the top of a slope, will produce the dramatic effect of revealing nothing but open sky beyond.

Doors and gateways tend to emphasize and exaggerate these simple openings. Historically, gateways were designed to impress, usually carrying a coat of arms or a motto. At times of unrest, they also performed a protective role and many gardens, as parts of private estates, were fortified. Gates were originally made of wood, but once wrought iron was introduced they often became exaggerated in size and highly ornate. Even though the functional role of gates has altered over the years, doors and gates are significant architectural features of many contemporary gardens, in which they serve to heighten and dramatize the movement from one space to another.

Gates also have a security role, keeping children and pets in and unwelcome visitors and animals out. Security gates should always open into the garden. As a means of restricting access, they can take the form of automatic barriers, which as an added safeguard may be controlled by infra-red beams or coded entry pins. Many gates are simply designed to block off a track from public access or to stop animals straying on to private property. Cattle grids are useful in rural areas, to prevent animals crossing; they make a resounding clatter to announce every arrival – no gate is necessary.

Entrances need not be of conventional design. The element of surprise and discovery can be imaginatively contained within their design to turn them into a dramatic component of the garden. At Hat Hill Copse, a sculpture garden in Sussex, a pair of unassuming rusted iron gates set into a white flint wall open with robotic grace to give entry by prior arrangement. Elsewhere in the garden, gates and doorways designed by artists add interest and drama to transitional and entry points, including a huge, gesturing 'Gateway of Hands' by Glynn Williams marking the start of a sculpture trail through tall and densely planted trees. Antonio Gaudí created a series of spectacular gates in and around the Parque Güell in Barcelona. His use of

3

3 Living 'walls' create organic and tactile garden divisions. An opening that separates two parts of a garden can be fashioned in any way you choose; here, the yew hedge has been allowed to grow higher over the entrance, creating an arched top and a vista of classical formality.
4 An exquisitely constructed rustic moon gate acts as a focus in this informal woodland setting, channelling the view through to a new space beyond.
5 The sliding graffitied gates, which are an integral part of this building, become a colourful and eccentric division when needed. Left open, they allow one part of the garden to flow into another.

texture and natural imagery creates a strong sense of identity, using local features and vegetation for inspiration. A false section of 'wall' fashioned from metal slides opens to reveal an entrance, while a series of gates using palms as a motif introduces plants into the static elements of the garden.

The width of a single gate should be a minimum of 1m (3ft), while the opening of double gates, normally designed to allow vehicles through, should be at least 2.4m (8ft). A design guideline is to relate the width of the gate to the width of the pathway it serves; while the height of an entrance will depend to some extent on the surrounding structure. There should always be an obvious and direct link from an entrance in a garden boundary to the main door of the house.

Choose timber gates of a simple and robust design, as this will give weight and strength to the structure; the supports or piers should also be simple. Metal gates can be light and delicate in design, allowing an unhindered view through them. Wrought or cast iron will rust and deteriorate unless it is treated; though occasionally a rusted finish will produce a patina which can be used to interesting effect. Painted aluminium or galvanized steel will give a longer, maintenance-free life. Always try to relate the design, colour and scale of brackets and latches to the surrounding architecture, of which they are a part.

Occasionally, the framework of a door or gateway is all that is required to denote an entrance. Moon doors, or *di xiu*, are the famous circular or moon-shaped entrances in the walls of Chinese gardens, rarely cluttered with unnecessary gates. Portals or arches in steel or timber might just as easily be used to frame an important view or denote a significant route as they would be to contain a door. Windows cut into hedges or set into garden walls provide a tantalizing view of a space beyond which, while it may in fact never be accessible, can still act as an important part of the garden.

4
5

Paved areas

1 Cobbles suggest informality and are used to move away from the building and into this tropical garden. They are appropriate for laying with random edges, as here, which creep into planted borders.
2 Gravel throws a simple uniformity across the floor of a courtyard, providing a continuous surface that is easy on the eye and which links the organic elements within it to the walls and building.
3 Pebbles are a textured form of paving which can be fashioned into any design. In this London front garden, pebbles in two colours are laid in a geometric pattern, providing a contrast to the softer, surrounding planting.

Paths and paved areas are a crucial part of the garden's framework: in fact, without paving most gardens simply would not function. We have already seen how the direct 'lines of desire' get translated into the best route around a garden in the early stages of the design process (see page 42). When it comes to integrating paths and paved areas into the garden's overall structure, you need to think in terms of pleasing lines and proportions as well as specific materials. While paths connect different parts of the garden, the broader paved areas provide a focus for outdoor activities. Some small gardens and courtyards are entirely paved.

Quite apart from practical considerations, paving is a versatile and exciting element of the garden. Hard materials have great visual qualities; their textures and natural colours make a subtle but valuable contribution to the character of the design and provide an effective contrast with the softer, organic qualities of

planting. Indeed, the judicious combination of the man-made and the natural lies at the heart of all good garden design.

Early forms of paving were simply bedded in the earth for stability and support. The Romans perfected this technique, even creating an early form of concrete for strengthening the ground. As craftsmanship developed, increasingly elaborate schemes and patterns were produced, using finely worked stone, tiles and brick. Modern paving is now laid on to a carefully prepared base or foundations, which may include reinforced concrete to support excessive weight, or may simply be compacted sand, allowing individual paving units to move slightly under pressure (see page 222).

There is a vast choice of natural and man-made paving materials, all with a look and a mood of their own. Your eventual choice will be influenced by its cost, practical suitability and harmony with the surrounding architecture. But at this

stage you will be more interested in getting the line and shape of your paved areas right so that they complement the planting and features of the garden.

Start from the viewpoint your eye uses most, which will often be the access from the house. In determining width, it is always a good idea to take the lines of paths from those of the property, relating them to the width of doors, windows or a wall. This gives a unity which helps to make the house and garden feel comfortable. The choice of straight or curved paths will depend on the style of garden. Hard, straight edges make a precise, formal backbone which can be softened with planting. Curved lines have a more informal look; they look better for being generous and there should always be a reason for them following the garden's contours. If your setting is already very informal, like a woodland, introducing curves can almost dissipate its natural atmosphere by overworking it.

4 No diversionary tactic is used in this route to the sea. Warm wooden decking gives a chance to walk barefoot in the open air between two environments.
5 Cobbles and stone paving here visually connect the terrace and the stone-built house, and draw the horizontal plane down.

4

slate, are full of iridescent colour, while granite can be as white as snow or as black as coal. Stone is generally laid as slabs of varying sizes, called flagstones; granite is also available in small cubes or setts. Stone slabs are the paving equivalent of floorboards: you are aware of the laying pattern but it is never intrusive.

Gravel, on the other hand, creates an effect more akin to a fitted carpet because it smooths everything out. A natural material, it comes in a variety of colours and grades, from smooth, rounded pea shingle to coarse granite chippings which sparkle with crystal quartz. Gravel makes a continuous paved surface and gives an opportunity to integrate hard and soft materials since plants can be grown through it. Unless your whole garden is paved, loose gravel needs to be contained by a retaining edge to prevent the surface from spreading.

Brick can be manipulated to create relatively formal or informal effects, depending on the type of bricks chosen

and the method of laying. Engineering bricks, which are often blue or purple-black, have a smooth, formal look. They are dense and strong and, since they do not absorb water, they never get covered in lichen or moss. Hand-made bricks are more porous, which gives them a softer look; they may be wire-cut or moulded to give them a particular surface texture. The way bricks are laid will affect the garden's character: unpointed bricks can be simply brushed over with a sand mix, suggesting informality, while pointed bricks, which can readily be kept clean, have a precise appearance.

Concrete is a mixture of cement, sand and aggregate (gravel) which, when they are combined with water, produce a thick liquid. This can be poured into almost any shape, making it very versatile. If used imaginatively, the possibilities are wide-ranging. Topher Delaney and Andy Cochran, two designers working in California, mix chemical dyes with concrete to produce vivid finished colours which they use in bold abstract patterns. Interesting textures can be achieved if you expose the aggregate, by washing or brushing away the fine concrete just before it sets, to reveal the stones within.

Timber is a good choice where weight is restricted, such as roofs and balconies, and where you want to cover something up. It is a warm and flexible material, in sympathy with organic planting. Usually it takes the form of decking, the raised floor floating above uneven or unsightly surfaces. You can use softwood pressure-treated with preservative for the deck itself provided you use hardwood for the structural supports touching the ground.

For a more elaborate finish, borrow an idea from the ancient Greeks and use mosaics. Mosaics, made using ceramics, cobbles or glass, will introduce strong colours and texture to a paved area. Used sparingly with the neutral tones of slate or limestone, the effect can be stunning. Gaudí is renowned for having used cheap local materials; in his mosaics he fashioned them into something fantastic.

Another important aspect is scale, which relates to the size of paving unit as well as the area covered; the way these scales interact will contribute to the garden's overall mood as well as creating textural interest. Bear in mind that using large units in a generous expanse of paving will tend to make the space appear reduced. Mien Ruys uses traditional compact Dutch paving bricks in small spaces within her garden to give the illusion of space. Keep the texture simple in a small paved area, using no more than two materials and choosing a straightforward laying pattern.

Stone paving always introduces opulence to a scheme. Natural stone occurs in many different colours and surfaces, from limestone to granite, and the tone may vary within one kind of stone or even in a single slab. Riven stone, such as many sandstones and slates, is often made more attractive by its uneven weathering patterns. Others, like Chinese

5

Patios and terraces

■ **White mulberries provide both shade and a degree of formality in this simple gravel terrace, linked to the design of the house by a retaining wall in the same colour. The terrace runs the length of the building, creating an elevated outdoor room and direct access to the garden beyond.**

A terrace is, literally, a raised level surface with a vertical or sloping front. As an architectural feature of historical gardens, terraces afforded views across the landscape and to some extent became a symbol of power, showing how the land could be shaped and controlled, as they were often carved from or built on to the landscape. Terraces almost disappeared in the eighteenth century at the hands of Capability Brown, who swept the landscape right up to the walls of the house, but Humphry Repton reinstated them, more as a plinth on which the house sat, in effect divorcing it from the landscape.

The word *patio* is Spanish for courtyard and refers to an inner court, open to the sky, in Spanish houses; it is used to describe parts of the Alhambra and the Generalife gardens in Granada, Spain. In wider modern usage, the patio is a paved area which has become the focus of outdoor living. Its rise in importance is closely tied to the notion of the 'outdoor room' expounded in the 1960s and 1970s by John Brookes, in which the garden was first used as a living space, rather than as a resource purely for gardening. John Brookes' concept was in itself a response to the suggestion of many modern American designers, such as Thomas Church, that gardens were for living.

One of the principal reasons for the creation and inclusion of the modern terrace is to provide a sun deck, warm and full of brilliant light in the summer months, as well as a centre for outdoor activities like eating and entertaining. Paving provides an all-weather surface to support both furniture and people and to withstand relatively heavy use. Paving should always be laid with a slight slope, termed a fall, to enable rainwater to drain away rather than form puddles of standing water. In particular, it should fall away from an adjacent building, and start a minimum of 15cm (6in) below a damp-proof course, to prevent rising damp.

Link the design of a terrace with that of the house, in both proportions and the materials you use, perhaps repeating the dimensions of windows, doors or other architectural features. John Brookes proposed that the geometric grid used in the layout of the property should form the basis of a terrace layout. Making the terrace the same size as a room of the house imposes a unity between house and garden which can be further extended into the garden as a whole. If you use graph paper to draw out your concept plan, you will find it easy to lay down a regular square or rectangular grid, starting with the dimensions of the terrace but then exploiting the same grid as a basis for design across the entire garden.

In positioning the terrace, consider the orientation of the garden – look at the way the sun works round the site, creating changing areas of light and shade, and site the terrace or patio to benefit most from this. In a temperate climate, a light and warm position is most desirable – shade can always be introduced by planting or a pergola – but in a hot climate choose a location that benefits from shade. The area adjacent to the house is most practical, but, if this is unsuitable in terms of the orientation, you could have a wide pathway alongside the house, with the main area of paving some distance away. Choose a location backed by a wall rather than letting the terrace simply 'float' in the garden, or enclose it by planting. You will still need a direct link from the terrace to the house, in the form of a path, for ease of access.

■

2

In larger gardens, it is possible to have a series of terraces, each with a different purpose: a breakfast terrace might take advantage of early morning sun, a more enclosed terrace, backed by hedges or planting, might be the ideal place for reading and private relaxation, and an evening terrace, closer to the house, suitable for entertaining. In smaller gardens, a single area of paving needs to serve several purposes, from dining to play. Plan the size according to intended use, aiming to be as generous as possible. It is always better to have too much space than too little. Plan for guests if you enjoy outdoor entertaining and take into account adjacent planting, which will increase in size, overhanging the patio as it matures.

Keep the design straightforward, and avoid awkward or inaccessible corners. Incorporate interesting details if appropriate to the scale and character of the garden; sculptural elements like large containers can be used to give definition. Limit the combinations of materials to no more than two for greater harmony and ensure that at least one ties in with the character and vernacular style of the house. Lighting recessed into the paving produces an evocative night-time display or you can wash light across the floor, from fittings on the side walls, to highlight textures and laying patterns in the paved surface (see page 244).

Planting around the paving will soften hard edges and create the atmosphere and enclosure that large expanses of paving often lack; and plants will also provide colour and form. Containers and sculpture work well with paving, giving vertical emphasis and breaking up empty or open areas. Gaps may be left for plants in paving or openings created in timber decks to allow planting to grow up and through from below, linking the terrace more strongly to the rest of the garden. By opening the joints between paving units, grass, thyme or other fine-leaf ground covers can be allowed to invade in a random fashion, softening the overall effect of a paved surface.

2 Decking laid on the diagonal in this Melbourne terrace draws the eye away from the building and into the garden. The terrace is framed by jungle plants, which give it a tropical atmosphere.
3 Minimalism reigns in this Majorcan garden designed by Silvestrin and Pawson. Flat planes of earth colours are softened by the organic form of the olive tree, furnishing a visual contrast as well as essential shade for the patio.

3

4

4 Planting encloses this simple paved terrace. Foliage dominates, spilling over the flagstones at ground level and rising up to give height and an atmosphere of enclosure, while at the same time allowing views through into the rest of the garden.

Changes of level

2

1

1 A change in level
invites you to exploit
the exciting potential
of moving water. These
steps allow comfortable
ascent, while the gentle
waterfall creates a
cooling element in the
dry landscape, planted
here with olive trees,
clumps of lavender and
formally clipped box.
2 Shallow terraces
are the Mediterranean
traditional treatment
for a sloping site. The
principle behind these
terraces applies as
much to the garden as
it does to olive groves,
creating horizontal
growing areas.

Sloping sites present both problems and
opportunities. They are often described
in negative terms, but, given imaginative
and inventive design treatment, they can
be dynamic and exciting elements of a
garden. In addition to the various ways
of dealing with a natural slope, changes
of level can be deliberately introduced,
by removing soil from one part of the
garden and transferring it to another, to
give an exciting dimension to the design.
The 'cut and fill' operation required must
be considered at a very early stage of the
garden's creation.

Changes of level nearly always indicate
the presence of man and the exertion of
power over nature. The earliest remaining terraces are recorded in Egypt, built
in front of the royal tombs near Thebes.
This simple grandeur recurs in Rome,
influencing later Renaissance gardens,

which, in turn, have inspired the formal
terraced gardens of today. The stepped
pergolas at Bodnant, in north Wales, for
example, create a dramatic descent from
the higher formal terraces into the exoti-
cally wooded valley below. This garden,
together with many Italian counterparts, uses changes of level to good effect,
exploiting steps, slopes and retaining
walls to the full against a backdrop of
spectacular views.

While steps, ramps, natural slopes and
terraces could be found as individual
elements in a design, it is also possible
to use them together in more complex
schemes, as is shown at Bodnant. The
combination of organic and built forms
which express a change of level can create
a great sense of movement and energy
in the garden on a sloping site, as well as
giving it a sculptural dimension.

The play of light and shade on their
surfaces make steps a valuable tool in
garden design; where possible, treat them
as a positive design feature rather than
a purely functional element.

There are guidelines to building steps
that you should take into account at an
early planning stage to make sure they
work on a practical and safety level as
well as an aesthetic one (see page 232).
The step is made up of the riser (the vertical height) and the tread (the horizontal
surface). The relationship of these dimensions is important to comfort and ease of
use; any inconsistency here will render
the steps difficult or dangerous to use.
For guidance in designing steps, the
tread depth added to twice the height of
the riser should give a figure of about
60cm (2ft). It is good advice to use, as
minimum dimensions, a riser height of
15cm (6in) and a tread depth of 30cm
(1ft). Measure steps in other outdoor
locations, considering whether you find
their ascent or descent comfortable.
Never relate interior step dimensions to
those in the garden they will appear
awkward and out of scale, normally too
steep for the outdoor location.

These dimensions give a workable and
practical guideline but, as ever, rules are
made to be broken and steps are designed
to serve different purposes. To slow down
movement and create more gracious progression, increase the tread dimensions
and decrease the riser dimensions. At the
extreme, this technique creates elegant
terraces wide enough to be decorated
with furniture, sculpture and ornament.
The Swedish landscape architect Preben
Jakobsen demonstrated an unfettered

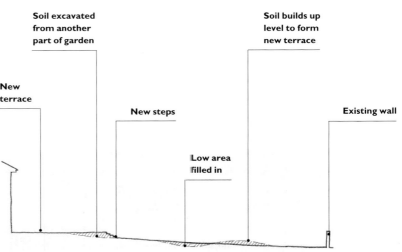

Soil excavated
from another
part of garden

Soil builds up
level to form
new terrace

New
terrace

New steps

Existing wall

Low area
filled in

3

3 The diagram shows
how the cut-and-fill
technique can be used
to change levels in the
garden. Filling in with
soil excavated from
elsewhere in the
garden has enabled
two terraces to be
made here, with steps
leading down from
one level to another.
Always keep topsoil
separate from subsoil:
never mix the two.
4 This carefully built
series of small terraces
with retaining walls of
natural stone provides
neat planting bays
and links the building
to the garden.

4

approach to changes of level at a horticultural show in 1982 with a stunning
garden in brick, consisting of shallow
paved and planted terraces and including
pools of reflective water.

Steps are potentially dangerous and
need to be made obvious. If regularly
used at night, consider lighting them for
safety (see page 244). It is good practice
to use at least two steps together – never
a single one, which can easily be forgotten
or overlooked. A slight overhang on the
riser will create a shadow line which
draws attention to the physical change of
level. With steep slopes, where many
steps are required, it is good practice to
incorporate landings, or level spaces,
between every eight steps. Where steps

are prone to being slippery or there is a
big drop, or if they may be used by the
elderly or infirm or by young children, it
is a good idea to incorporate a handrail.

Steps can also be used as built-in seats,
rather like a series of terraces, for which a
height of 35cm (14in) is necessary – this is
difficult to negotiate but comfortable to
sit on. It would be usual to incorporate a
flight of more functional steps alongside,
in the style of an amphitheatre. There are
several ways of dealing with the edge of a
flight of steps. If space permits, steps can
be taken into the surrounding slopes,
allowing paving and planting to merge.
Otherwise, the architectural quality of
the steps might be emphasized by walls
constructed alongside them. A slight
gradient on each step will allow water to
run off the surface easily. It is also useful
to build a drain alongside longer flights of
steps; this in itself can provide a suitable
way of edging them.

Steps are the most efficient way of
managing level changes in the garden but
they are impossible to negotiate with a
wheelchair and difficult for the elderly.
Ramps provide a gentler means of ascent
but occupy a much greater area than
steps. Ramps should not have a gradient
steeper than 1:12 (the gradient describes
the slope and expresses the height
climbed over a given distance: a gradient
of 1:12 means that one metre in height
is gained every 12 metres). Like steps,
ramps should not be continuous over
long distances: break the slope with a flat
landing every 10m (33ft) or so. In smaller
gardens, where ramps can be difficult
to accommodate, a combination of steps
and ramps might be more appropriate.

The greater the change of level, the
more exciting the results in design terms.
Retaining walls accommodate dramatic
changes of level, effectively holding back
the earth when new levels, terraces or
pathways are created. Retained earth
can exert a great deal of pressure on a
vertical structure so the wall must be
strong enough to hold back the earth
effectively and safely. Walls that are over
1m (3ft) high need to be reinforced; you
may need a structural engineer to help
design them. Retaining walls are normally
constructed of brick or stone, but new
modular units, resembling modified bricks
with a pocket at the back, allow planting
to be incorporated into the fabric of the
wall. Cascades of alpine, ground-covering
or climbing species can look spectacular,
harmonizing often large structures with
the surrounding landscape. Water also
works particularly well in conjunction
with level changes: its vigorous movement, in cascading streams or gushing
spouts, will introduce noise and sparkling
activity to the garden scene.

To alleviate the architectural qualities
of steps, ramps and retaining walls, plant
the sloping ground with shrubs and
ground cover or lay it to lawn to provide
a softer and more organic contrast.
Gradients of up to 1:3 can be accommodated with mown grass but the transition
from flat to sloping ground must be
achieved gradually to prevent awkward
and difficult mowing. There is so much
more visual stimulation in undulating
ground than in a flat plane: contoured
ground can become a dynamic element in
the landscape, catching the light which
expresses its form.

Lawns

All gardens are a combination of open and filled spaces and whether you treat the open spaces with hard materials or plant them with soft will depend on your intended use as well as personal taste. While the use of hard materials over any large expanse can become harsh and bland, grass is a much softer, more 'user-friendly' surface. A lawn provides a restful quality in a garden, giving much-valued greenery as well as a space for relaxation and recreation. The emerald-green lawns of Britain are the envy of the world, and the balance of smooth green sward contrasted with textured border planting has been extensively copied. The smooth, uniform texture of lawns makes a perfect foil for planting. Both the tactile quality of grass underfoot and the delicious smell of newly mown grass give pure sensual pleasure.

Most lawns are made up of a combination of different grass species, selected to suit the lawn's use. Finer grasses, known as bents or fescues, are generally used for high-quality, ornamental lawns and for sports surfaces such as golf greens and tennis courts, where precision play is required. Lawns that will be subjected to regular use, perhaps for children's play, require heavier-wearing species such as meadow grass or ryegrass. These tend to have a coarser leaf and their habit means that they cannot be cut short enough to give a precision surface. There are new cultivars constantly under development, however, and it is now possible to find these grasses with a much finer leaf. In many parts of the world, this choice is not available and indigenous species giving a homogenous 'lawn' quality may be used instead.

Before committing yourself to a lawn, bear in mind that they need very regular maintenance, including watering in dry spells. Britain and Western Europe have in recent years experienced higher temperatures and drier summers, which has led to some concern that lawns are not wholly appropriate if climatic changes are under way. Alternative solutions are being considered seriously, for example 'lawns' using ornamental grasses or low-growing herbs such as chamomile. While their textures and scents offer refreshing alternatives to the traditional lawn, they

1

2

1 The circular pattern brushed into the dew on the grass is a magnificent but transitory addition to this early morning scene in autumn. By 10 o'clock, there will not be a trace left.
2 A weed-free lawn would appear bland against this daisy-studded sward. Left untreated, the broad-leaved 'grass weeds' will bring another dimension to a lawn.

3

can never really take its place. With even limited use, these communities would suffer and they therefore become another form of decorative planting. Gravel or shingle has also been used as a substitute for lawn, usually in small city gardens, and while it is one of the most suitable hard materials for an open space, the safety and softness underfoot are lost.

SHAPE AND SIZE

The shape of your lawn will be affected by the style of your garden. Bold, clean shapes like squares or rectangles work well in contrast with associated soft planting and will also make mowing and maintenance more straightforward. The spaces created even in small gardens are often larger than any interior room, and this scale needs to be appreciated. Avoid minuscule areas of lawn as well as complex shapes which incur disproportionate upkeep; when thinking about lawn size, always bear in mind the maneouvrability of a mower. A mowing edge, normally a flat trim of paving around the perimeter of the lawn, is a practical addition as the lawn mower will simply trim over the

edge of the grass. This will affect the visual quality of the lawn, however, formalizing its shape to a certain extent.

Remember that lawns are a living surface and will suffer from excessive wear and tear. Keep the access points as wide as possible, perhaps running grass along the edge of terraces and pathways. Narrow or restricted routes will soon cause wear in one part of the lawn, leading to the invasion of weeds and soil erosion. Sloping sites may prove to be unsuitable for the establishment of lawn grass and on steep slopes mowing can be dangerous as well as difficult; a 1:3 slope is the maximum recommended for mowing.

In areas of restricted use, wild meadow communities (see page 180) can be established. It is often assumed that these habitats require no upkeep, which is certainly not the case. However, once the maintenance regime is in place, they will need less attention than a traditional lawn. Their establishment and success rely on creating a balanced environment in which wild flowers and grasses can live in harmony. The contrast between long and short grass presents interesting

design possibilities. The English designer David Hicks used this to good effect in his own garden in Oxfordshire, where formal lawns, cut and rolled with precision, are set against long vertical stalks of shimmering meadow grasses. It is also possible to cut pathways through longer verge or meadow grass, perhaps even changing the route each year.

Lawns can be treated in very individual ways: they can be left long or mown short; they can have patterns cut into them; they can be studded with daisies or planted with naturalized bulbs. Among the most stunning lawn effects are those in which the early-morning autumn dew is brushed away to form fabulous geometric patterns, seen only fleetingly in the period between sunrise and mid-morning, before the rising temperatures evaporate the moisture. This magical approach to the lawn gives a welcome new lease of life to a familiar feature and the opportunity to create a new work of art each day. How you manage your lawn is entirely up to you; but your treatment of it will help make your garden into a very personal statement.

3 In a hot climate the texture and colour of greenery is calming and restful. In this garden in Auckland, New Zealand, an area that is part-terrace, part-lawn uses clover instead of thirsty grass.
4 Varying lengths of cut have been used to delineate formality on this green expanse. Textural juxtaposition of two heights of grass is a simple yet potent treatment; here it has been used to create patterns reminiscent of medieval knot gardens, but the 'design' could be changed from month to month in the growing season.

4

Installing power

1

2

3

1 Uplighting adds an exciting element to this Sydney garden at night-time, illuminating the vertical bamboo canes and throwing moving shadows on to the walls.
2 Electricity has been used here to drive a fog machine and to illuminate the pool area of this Australian garden designed by Vladimir Sitta.
3 Mechanized blinds are essential to keep this low-maintenance conservatory cool and well shaded.

Electricity has transformed the modern garden. The capacity to supply power to work spaces, greenhouses, summerhouses, water features, lawn mowers and irrigation systems, as well as to lighting around the garden, literally at the flick of a switch, greatly expands the scope and use of the garden. Bearing in mind that the installation of electricity and electrical appliances within the garden is a specialized and potentially dangerous activity, you may wish to seek professional help and advice at the design stage and always when installing them.

The supply of power is all too often an afterthought. It makes much more sense to consider mains electricity right from the initial planning stage since it needs to be laid in protected or armoured cables, which are, for safety reasons, buried at least 60cm (2ft) underground. The cable should have been laid through a standard protective sheath as an extra precaution. Excavating trenches to this depth is disruptive once the garden is in place and may cause damage to the roots of plants and areas of paving. But if you install electricity prior to laying out the garden, trenches can be excavated in the most convenient positions before the garden is created. Try to route cable trenches along the foot of boundaries or the edges of a lawn, avoiding areas of the garden that will be subject to regular digging and cultivation. It helps to record the route of the cable on your garden plan.

Think carefully about where you will need power points for a lawn mower and any other mobile appliances, and for an electric pump if you have a water feature.

You can then plan a logical power circuit round the garden. Locate switches for outdoor lighting within the house if possible; lighting and power for sheds or other enclosed structures can be located inside them. Fit all outdoor wiring with a circuit breaker for additional safety.

LIGHTING
There are many different kinds of outdoor lighting (see page 244) and using a combination of them will enable you to bring the garden to life at night. Low-voltage lighting systems are cheaper and simpler to install than the mains-voltage alternatives, yet the output and impact of this lighting is dramatic. The fittings and fixtures are small and can easily be hidden or disguised within the garden. Low-voltage systems are fed through

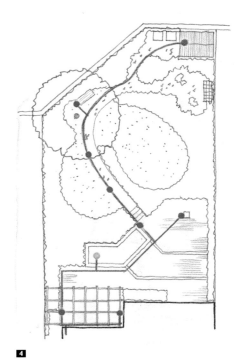

● Lights
○ Water feature
● Power points
——— Route of cables

4 Route a power circuit to follow a logical course around the garden. Bury the cables alongside paths for safety, so that they are not disturbed by cultivation. It is a good idea to have separate cables for lighting and for the provision of electric power. All electrical installation must be undertaken by a qualified electrician.

4

a transformer, which you should either locate indoors or within a weatherproof structure outdoors. The cable serving the system does not have to be buried deep in the ground but it is good practice to run the cable in a protective sheath. It is still useful to mark or record the routes.

One disadvantage with a low-voltage system is the reduction or loss in voltage over long cable runs. The maximum working distance is approximately 30m (100ft), which, for gardens of any size, can be restricting, especially if the lighting is fed from a transformer within the house. In such cases, it is best to locate the transformer centrally within the garden, fed by mains electricity. Several low-voltage lighting circuits or cable runs can then operate in shorter lengths from this central outdoor location once you have decided where to place your lights.

Voltage loss is also related to the number of fittings linked to the system and to the size of conductor cable. The acceptable loss is 5 per cent, resulting in a voltage drop of 0.6 volts on a 12-volt system. In addition the capacity of transformers needs to be within 10 per cent of the operating load of all the lights put together. Externally sited transformers should be placed at least 10cm (4in) above ground level, making them suitable for vertical mounting on walls; their positions can easily be disguised with planting. Consider the upkeep of your lighting system before installing it. There is no point creating interesting effects which can only be achieved by placing lights in positions that are impossible to get to when you need to replace a bulb.

5 Electric power allows a central pump to drive the slim water jets, adding playfulness and dynamism to this small public garden in Japan; the design is by Shodo Suzuki.

5

WATER

In addition to powering lighting, lawn mowers and irrigation systems, the other chief use of electricity in the garden is for running fountains, jets and other moving water features. As water and electricity are a potentially lethal combination, safety in installation and in use is of paramount importance. Most underwater pumps and underwater lighting fixtures are now supplied with cables attached; always allow for some excess cable to prevent stress and stretching should any of the fittings move during use.

Junctions or connections should be made outside the water feature itself, which presents the problem of taking the supply into the water. Most features are man-made and therefore contained by either concrete or butyl. Since butyl

liners must not be punctured, it is easier to bring the cable up to the surface, along with the liner before burying it underneath, or running it alongside, paving. The cable has to run over the edge of the waterproof layer, which makes it easily visible and potentially prone to damage. Disguise the cables wherever possible, perhaps with a planted container, but for additional safety also run them through a protective sheath.

Submersible pumps are most appropriate for very small water features and they are easily hidden at the bottom of the pool. Surface-mounted pumps need to be housed separately and disguised, but, since they tend to be noisy when in use, you should site them well away from the main entertaining areas or routes through the garden.

Drainage and irrigation

The water in your garden is a precious resource: in some parts of the world there is too little, in other areas too much. Historically, farmers have tried to control the level of water saturation in the ground in order to grow crops and this approach has been followed in gardening to enable a wider range of plants to be grown. The threat of global warming has made once-dependable climatic patterns difficult to predict, though, and it is now considered better to work with the climatic conditions you have rather than resorting either to drainage systems or artificial irrigation. But sometimes one of these is the only solution, if you want to avoid waterlogging or to grow more than a very limited range of plants.

DRAINAGE

In areas of high rainfall, you may have to consider some form of drainage if you have poorly draining soil. Clay soils, which hold moisture naturally, are prone to waterlogging, especially if they have been compacted by heavy machinery during the construction of a house. In other soils, hard layers (pans) may form which can prevent the soil from draining properly. Water is also held naturally within the ground at a level termed the water table. In certain areas this may be deep underground, but elsewhere it can be at or just below the surface and here flooding can occur, with the ground almost permanently waterlogged. The water table can fluctuate seasonally, creating standing water in wet periods and disappearing completely in dry seasons. Observe your soil over a period before drawing conclusions about whether you need to provide drainage.

A range of drainage systems has been developed, from the simple French drain – a gravel-filled trench – to sophisticated grid or herringbone schemes. Most work using gravity, each length of drainage pipe being laid in a trench to a shallow gradient to carry water away. Pumped systems are particularly suitable for low-lying ground. The clay tile land drains

1 A standpipe performs an essential function in a large garden, where a hosepipe will not stretch from the wall of the house. This one has been masked by low hedging.
2 In Terence Conran's garden in the south of France, water is channelled off from a water course to irrigate the terraced beds alongside as and when it is needed. In a hot, dry climate it is worth having artificial irrigation on an automatic system.

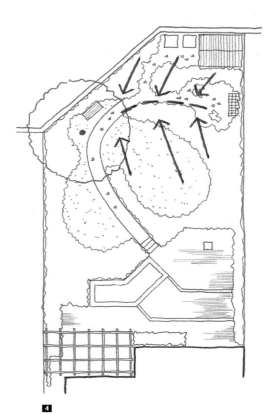

3 A catchment grille has been discreetly installed alongside a shallow step to channel the water run-off after rain. The terrace, which has been laid to a slight fall to help water drain away, appears to continue uninterrupted.

4 You may need to install a simple drainage system to prevent waterlogging. Here, a gravel-filled French drain runs below the gravel path and a gentle fall in the lawn directs excess water into it.

3

4

traditionally used to channel water have now been superseded by corrugated, perforated plastic rolls of pipework that are easier to install and more resilient. Geotextiles (non-rot, woven fabrics) are often used in conjunction with a drainage system to screen out the fine silt and sediment which can impede the free flow of water. These below-surface drainage systems, hidden below lawns, beds and paving, have to be installed before any hard landscaping takes place.

Surface drainage deals with the simple removal of water from an area of paving. Although paved areas appear flat, they should always be laid with a gentle fall or gradient, an almost imperceptible slope which allows the water to run off into a gully or channel and then to a soakaway or surface water drain via a grilled drain opening. Slopes of 1:60 are most usual. The gullies may be quite inconspicuous or may form a distinctive feature in the paving, if material of a different colour or texture is used. With smaller terraces or pathways, water can simply be allowed to soak into the ground alongside, as long as the soil is free-draining.

Soakaways are an alternative to a complete drainage system. They are basically large gravel- or stone-filled pits,

from which water seeps into the surrounding ground over a period of time. Site them well away from structures and buildings; never use a soakaway in a clay soil area as its drainage will be impeded.

IRRIGATION

A basic water supply for your garden is best provided from an outdoor tap. This can be located on the house wall or you could lay a pipe to carry the water supply to a convenient part of the garden.

The provision of irrigation is normally associated with arid areas, where the lack of moisture causes severe problems. However, the artificial watering of gardens has become common even in wetter zones, and the improvements to plant growth and health resulting from an effective irrigation system are marked. A wide array of systems is available, from a simple perforated pipe which lies on the soil, letting water seep slowly into the ground, to computer-controlled sprays and sprinklers, and undergound pipes which dispense water at the flick of a switch, popping up during the night and disappearing during the day. Any sophisticated system should be put in place before a lawn is laid so its installation does not cause too much disruption.

The use of irrigation is increasingly under question. Many designers and gardeners prefer to work with the natural conditions of the landscape rather than trying to change or modify them to suit taste or convenience. In Essex, a relatively dry county in the south-east of England, Beth Chatto has created a garden on the site of a previous car park that requires virtually no water. Plants grow in textured groups through a layer of gravel, providing colour and visual interest throughout the year. They are watered once, when they are planted, then left to take their chance; any failures are removed. By contrast, at Black and White Cottage in Surrey, the garden designer Anthony Paul has exploited the site of his garden, a damp river valley, to plant dramatic herbaceous foliage plants that thrive in the moist conditions.

German designers pioneered the use of massed perennial plantings suited to their situation and chosen for their compatibility with each other. In the late twentieth century, these designers mark a change of attitude towards planting design, combining their horticultural artistry with a more sensitive ecological approach to the garden.

GARDENS FOR LIVING

Gardens have always mirrored the needs of the people who create them. From the tightly enclosed 'flowery meads' of a medieval castle, and the sumptuous terraces of Renaissance Italy, to the comfortable outdoor rooms of Edwardian England and country-house America, we have moulded our domestic landscapes to our own image.

Today, pressures on time and space mean that gardens are more precious to us than ever. Yet as the available space shrinks, so the activities we seek to perform there grow ever more diverse. How we accommodate potential conflicts owes much to the inspiration of Californian designers like Thomas Church, one of the first to design gardens for modern living that also work as compositions in space and meet the unique requirements of site, too.

The garden now fulfils a multitude of roles: a place to grow plants that can be admired for their texture, scent or form, but also vegetables and fruit for your table; space for quiet enjoyment and noisy games; a place to sit, cook, eat, talk, potter or swim; a refuge from nagging obligations; a point of contact with the natural world. These are just some of the demands you may bring to your own private paradise.

The starting point is always to gain a clear idea of what you want your garden to do. Planning a garden is just the same as planning a house, whether a bedsit or a mansion. The most important difference is that garden rooms are outdoors, so you have to take account of elements like sun and wind. As you start to plan, imagine how you will move through the space and how the different activities link up. Clarifying your intentions at this early stage will help to produce a garden with a strong narrative, the essence of good design.

Evening sunlight gilds a circle of rustic chairs in a woodland setting. This simple view satisfies many of today's conflicting expectations of what a garden may bring: escape and retreat, solitude and good company, a meeting between the tamed and the untamed, a deeply private peace.

FEATURES AND FOCAL POINTS

Features and focal points give the garden much of its drama. From sculpture, statuary and urns to seats, summer-houses and garden buildings, ornamental features punctuate the design, leading the eye into the best views and creating a sense of movement and discovery. Well-chosen features also add a 'texture' to the garden's narrative and stamp your undisputed authorship on the garden you seek to create.

But where to begin? Even though clutter has its charm, the best advice is always to work from the simple, adding layers to a single idea that expresses the garden's main purpose. The same feature can create very different moods. Water may rush excitedly down channels and cascades, like the glorious crayfish cascade at the Villa Lante, near Rome, that hurtles down towards the Fountain of the Giants; or, blackly still, it may pluck clouds from the sky to shine in dark reflecting pools. A summer-house may act as focal point or secret space. Likewise, a seat may be placed to enjoy the view, or itself to close a vista.

Perhaps above all else, ornament carries an echo of other times, other places: a hint of Spain in glazed Moorish tiles, *azulejos*, used to decorate fountains, tanks and pavilions; a playful reminder of the garden's classical heritage in a massive stone urn adorning an urban courtyard; a memory of California in the simple loggia used to frame a view. But though we may look to the past for guidance, most urban and suburban gardens of the late twentieth century cannot accommodate too much magnificence. The challenge is to develop a new design language using materials that speak to us today. A carefully placed container or topiary shape, a small fountain, a bench, a simple wooden summer-house, the stones and driftwood to be found in Derek Jarman's garden at Dungeness in Kent – all these features play their part and deepen our enjoyment of place. They also link us to the gardens we make.

In all but the most enclosed space, locality should guide the way a garden looks and 'feels'. A formal English garden will have a very different character to a formal American one, and a contemporary French garden will differ from a modern Japanese one. Within the context of a strong design, features and focal points can take the lead in reinforcing this sense of place without letting the garden's own individual voice be compromised.

Focus in a garden – like photography – can be long or short. Seen in close up, the feature draws the eye into its heart. Viewed from a distance, it lifts the spirits and the eye. Either way, if properly scaled and chosen, features add the vital breath of life.

Conservatories

Conservatories are for show, for style, for exoticism, for people who yearn to invite the garden inside the house all year long. Dedicated primarily to the culture of plants, they also extend the house into the garden, allowing you to control the climate and therefore to grow the plants you want, rather than the ones you must. Garden rooms, by contrast, are more obviously part of the main house, but they share in the atmosphere of the garden through windows and doors and an airiness associated with outdoor living.

Originally called 'orangeries', the first conservatories were strictly for those wealthy enough to indulge their passion for exotic fruit and were popular across the courts and grand estates of northern Europe from the mid-sixteenth century onwards, reaching deep into Russia. With the advent of new technologies in ironwork and glass, the Victorian imagination soared to create immense glass palaces like the Great Conservatory at Chatsworth, Derbyshire, by Sir Joseph Paxton. The same passion for horticultural display lives on in the humbler structures of today.

Conservatories are either free-standing or, more usually, attached to the living areas of the main house, creating a natural progression from inside to outside. Careful planning can emphasize this unity of house and garden by using the same paving materials inside and out and by echoes of similar planting.

A conservatory should be sympathetic to its parent building in style, scale and detailing. Usually this means matching architectural styles. An Edwardian-style conservatory will look out of place on most modern houses, but a modern conservatory may complement a period house. You can commission a custom-made structure from an architect or builder, or turn to one of the many companies offering off-the-peg designs. New technology and construction materials have produced glass structures without any obvious support, discreet enough to blend with all ages of buildings.

2

4

1 A sympathetic conservatory corner: tropical planting set directly into the floor enfolds the sitting area, excluding the sparsely planted exterior.
2 This conservatory at Mount Vernon, Virginia, connects inside with outside through tall 'orangery' windows and mellow paving. Old garden tools, cloches and a simple wooden planter create a mood of ordered restraint.

3 Jungle foliage in a converted Parisian factory contrasts with the clean lines of painted metal railings and wooden decking.
4 The relaxed enjoyment promised by this artist's studio comes from placing people close to plants.
5 Conservatories need not adjoin the house. This aluminium, polycarbonate and wood pavilion hovers at woodland's edge.

5

6
8

7

Always try to face the conservatory away from prolonged midday sun, as hot, dry conditions cause plants to wilt and encourage pests and diseases. Dramatic temperature fluctuations between day and night call for effective ventilation, particularly at roof level. The use of blinds and tinted or partially reflective glass will prevent excessive heat, while double glazing and heating systems will moderate low night-time temperatures. The design must take account of chores like watering, feeding, spraying and occasional potting. Unless the conservatory is very small it will need a permanent water source, and the flooring material must be able to withstand leaks and spillages.

Your choice of plants will depend on the climate you want to maintain. If your taste runs to jungle but you dislike its sticky humidity, try temperate plants like vines and sparmannia, introduced in pots or containers. Tiered stands will give your plants maximum light while trellis or wires fixed to the wall can support curtains of climbers. Lush planting will also benefit from deep troughs sunk into the ground to give the plants greater depth. Or you may prefer minimalist space that leads the eye 'outdoors' without the distraction of too much foreground.

Water in a conservatory exaggerates the changing quality of light as it mellows during the day. Still, dark pools have the reflective qualities of glass; moving water throws back shimmering reflections on to surrounding surfaces such as plants, pavings and furnishings.

A garden room lies half-way between a conservatory and the house proper. Its atmosphere can be heightened by using outdoor furniture in cane, rattan or metal, and by grouping plants in containers as you would on a patio or terrace. How you plan the room depends on how you intend to use the space. Russell Page, for example, dreamed of a ground-floor room that would be part workroom, part library, part studio and part tool shed for 'all the odd extensions and aids to the gardener's two hands'.

6 An energy-efficient conservatory: vented at the apex to provide fresh air for the house, warm air is recirculated from a heat exchanger.
7 The best garden rooms take their cue from outside. In the Mexican jungle, a living tree shades the upper terrace; jungle encloses the space below.
8 In place of lush planting, this cuboid room pushes weird geometry to extremes.

Summer-houses and gazebos

A summer-house or gazebo introduces a hint of playfulness and romance into the garden. Often built of lightweight materials, they encourage the imagination to play with forms and ideas. The eerily fantastic gardens of the Désert de Retz, created by Baron de Monville in late eighteenth-century France, included a pyramidal ice house smothered by weeds, and other follies in the Chinese style. (The main house itself was built to resemble the broken shaft of a gigantic column.) But for inspiration you can look equally to contemporary themes and materials.

Style and treatment depend on what the building is for. A secret retreat to talk and eat with friends suggests a very different setting to a focal point intended to draw the eye along a vista. Always think how the space will be used and enjoyed: a ramshackle summer-house can look picturesque or plain neglected.

The traditional view on designing all garden structures is to match the style and materials to nearby buildings. While such advice is clearly right for most formal gardens, it *is* possible to be bolder, provided you know the kind of effect you want to achieve. Gardening shows and magazines are crammed with off-the-peg designs you can adapt to your own mood and vision. Such pattern-book gardening has illustrious precedents: some of the most delightful books of summer-house designs were produced in the eighteenth century in styles ranging from the gothic and the Chinese to rustic grotesque and Palladian severe.

You may prefer to slide the summer-house into its setting, with echoes of architectural details like window shapes or roof lines from the house. Allusions like these give the same satisfaction as harmony in music. Study masters like the American designer Thomas Church, whose airy poolside loggias and lattice-work pavilions snuggle into their sites, California style. For a summer-house that is intended as a private place, dark materials and a simple structure blend easily with the garden, especially if it is wreathed with planting. A focal point permits greater flamboyance, using bright paintwork, perhaps, or stained wood. Glass, concrete and steel can be combined to produce a modern pavilion that is both simple and elegant.

A gazebo, strictly speaking, is designed to provide views across the garden and beyond, like the Jacobean turrets at Montacute in Somerset. The name comes from joke Latin (*gazebo*, I gaze); it means the same as a belvedere or mirador. Many cultures have a tradition of viewing pavilions: Ottoman kiosks overhanging the Bosporus, for example, and Japanese stands built specially for moon-gazing. Gertrude Jekyll wrote about her raised brick gazebo in west Surrey, known as the Thunder-house, used to track storms across the fields and distant chalk hills.

To gain full advantage of their site, gazebos often have open sides, sometimes trellised with wood or traced with ironwork. Some are quite open to the skies. Alternatively, a retractable tent or canopy offers daytime shelter that can be opened at night to reveal the stars. In a large or country garden, a gazebo placed on the boundary can provide a perfect 'frame' to the landscape. Viewpoint and focal point: the roles are intertwined.

1 Not quite a gazebo, not quite a summer-house either, this open, wooden structure melts into its site, providing a charming area to sit between wood and wild flower meadow. A tarpaulin over its roof would give some weather-proofing, if required.
2 As work patterns change, garden buildings are finding a new role as office-from-home. Hidden away behind tree ferns and glazed on all four sides, this solid wooden summer-house is an ideal writer's retreat.

3 Known as 'Conran's folly', this modern gazebo stands 6m (20ft) high in the Berkshire countryside. It was commissioned from Tom Heatherwick as a garden hideaway for cigar smokers, and the twisting shape was made from 500 pieces of identical plywood.
4 The open wooden frame and overhanging deck of this waterside viewing pavilion slide unobtrusively into the landscape. Colour, materials and line enhance the serenity of inky still water and natural planting.

5 Vernacular in style and construction, a pepperpot gazebo rises from misty woodland. Its sense of belonging to the environment comes from the stones repeated in steps, retaining walls, roof and dry-stone walling, rooting the structure into its grassy mound.

4

5

6

7

6 Open-backed chairs and a sturdy circular table perfectly match the trellis walls of this circular retreat, blurring the distinction between inside and out.
7 Sharp lines and white walls offer an uncompromising focal point in a woodland setting. Here, the summer-house is used like sculpture, isolated from its environment.
8 This womb-like structure achieves the opposite effect: going beyond shelter, it expresses an affinity with natural form that makes it come alive.

8

Arbours, pergolas and arches

1

2

3

1 The dripping racemes of hardy wisteria have made it a favourite climber across the world. Solid beams give it support.
2 The living structure of this ivy-clad arbour echoes the geometry of clipped box, a perfect match for the scrolled stone bench. Looser background planting offsets the formality.
3 A tunnel created from twisted deciduous holly suggests contrast: of darkness moving towards light, and of organic growth framing the hard edges of the distant hedge doorway.
4 Yves St Laurent's walkway at 'Majorelle', Marrakech, echoes the blue used throughout the garden. Even at midday, the shade cast by its canopy makes the heat bearable.

Good design flows from a good, simple bone structure. Arbours, pergolas and arches can play the role of skeleton, linking, separating, giving your garden mass and height. In hot climates especially, they let you manipulate light and shade, producing dark tunnels that thread towards a pinpoint of light or weave through patches of watery green shade.

An arbour usually refers to a shady retreat formed by trees or climbers grown over a framework of wood, metal or trellis. The French and Dutch of the seventeenth century were especially keen on arboured pathways or *berceaux*; an outstanding example is the restored Queen's Garden at Het Loo in the Netherlands, where hornbeam trained over wooden arches has created an intimate, enclosed maze, away from the open formality of the court. Arbours can make entrancing focal points, like the trellised arbours at Villandry in France, providing shady seats around bubbling water jets.

Tracing their origins right back to the vine-laden structures of ancient Egypt, pergolas are continuous arbours built to carry climbing plants for shade and food. Still used to give welcome shade in summer, they have also been adapted to colder climates. Late nineteenth- and early twentieth-century designers in Britain and America produced bold designs using local materials that exude a sense of place. Frederick Law Olmsted's design for the Vanderbilt family in North Carolina, for instance, used side panels of trellis cut with oval 'windows' that made portraits of the garden beyond.

'I do not like a mean pergola,' wrote Gertrude Jekyll in 1899, 'made of stuff as thin as hop-poles.' Her advice holds true today. Make sure the supports are wide and tall enough for any climbers you plan to grow, and for people walking underneath. At first the height may seem excessive, but climbers soon drape and fall. Timber, brick, steel, aluminium and staunch trellis all make suitable material for the uprights, with cross-beams of timber, steel or aluminium.

Place the pergola on a pathway, or use it to emphasize a vista or focal point at one end (a seat or sculpture, perhaps), or to entice the eye along a main axis. On terraces used for entertaining, a pergola helps to create an intimate atmosphere and acts as an overhead screen; in new gardens, it provides instant presence. Free-standing structures will elegantly frame a view; if left unplanted, they become almost sculptural.

Marking a point of entry or transition, arches, like pergolas, should be bold and imposing, generous enough to permit free passage. Planted arches should let climbers dominate. Or you can strip the structure bare, choosing materials and finishes – timber, iron, steel, aluminium, brick, textured concrete – that will create an architectural accent in counterpoint to the garden's softer greenery.

5 Cut bamboo canes installed by Japanese landscape architect Hiroshi Teshigahara create a tunnel that twists out of sight. A floor of pine needles picks up the theme of natural materials.

6 Pergolas work best when they are strong in design and build. Steel supports like giant croquet hoops follow the mirrored water's curve. As each support stands freely, wires are used to train the wisteria into an overhead canopy.

7 A pole 'tent' for climbing plants, this rustic arbour erected over grass is sculptural in its own right and could be left unplanted. Structures like this have a relatively short life, so anticipate their renewal or eventual disintegration.

4

6

5

7

Water features

1 Clustering water-lilies, abundant marginal planting and swirl of goldfish give a natural air to this 'designed' pool. Children in particular will be drawn to its teeming life, so it is not for areas where the very young can stray.
2 Still waters capture and inspire reflections. Here, a skin of water stretched across a terrazzo marble slab projects a moving sky overlaid with tree-shadows, adding depth and movement to quietude. The dancing figure at the far corner is surely unnecessary.

A garden without water is a place that lacks soul. Drama, depth, excitement, mystery, the lure of the natural world – even the simplest pond or birdbath can hint at water's expressive qualities. Underwater life, such a magnet to children, also plays a part in its appeal.

The symbolism of water can be traced back to the desert gardens of Islam, walled paradises dissected by the four rivers of life. The Moors introduced these symbols to eighth-century Spain, where they were later transformed into the channels, basins, jets and water court-yards of the great gardens of Granada, the Alhambra and adjacent Generalife. Further east, from the early sixteenth century, the Moguls took the Persian desert traditions into Afghanistan and the dusty plains of India, then up into the verdant hills of Kashmir, where they elevated the use of water into the highest art form, with tumbling chutes or *chadars* faceted to catch the light and to amplify the sound of falling waters.

For sheer exuberance, though, nothing can match the gardens of the Italian Renaissance, that surge of confidence in man's ability to control the natural environment. The gardens of the Villa d'Este at Tivoli, near Rome, continue to resound with water splashing and thun-dering from magnificent fountains and cascades. Much quieter are the gardens of Japan, where rocks and sand sometimes imply water in its absence.

The search for new forms of expression draws inspiration from these earlier cultures. The swirling moon ponds and sculpted earthworks of the Scottish gar-den created by American architectural critic Charles Jencks and his wife, the late Maggie Keswick, recall the early eighteenth-century formal water gardens at Studley Royal in Yorkshire. Mexican designer Luis Barragán drew on Moorish Spain to create shimmering, minimalist pools and reflecting water channels, while Renaissance Italy and Kashmir find their echo in the work of the late Sir Geoffrey Jellicoe, the English designer.

1
2

3 Designed by
Wolfgang Oehme and
James van Sweden,
this modern cascade
is constructed from
natural stone and sited
close to the house,
providing the constant
sound of tumbling,
falling water.

3

4

5

6

4 Bringing water into
the garden is the best
way of increasing its
wildlife. Pebbly stones,
self-seeded perennials
like *Alchemilla mollis*,
sedges, grasses,
bog-garden plants and
wildflowers re-create an
entirely natural-looking
habitat. In gardens
with no running water,
similar effects can be
achieved with pumps
and recycled water.

5 A projecting lip
of stone transforms
a channel of water
into a thin, translucent
curtain in this shady
corner. Mind-your-
own-business (*Soleirolia
soleirolii*) and hart's-
tongue ferns (*Asplenium
scolopendrium*) casually
green the walls.
6 These fountains
were designed by Alain
Provost for the Parc
André Citroën in Paris.

1

2

3

1 Water gives life to everything that grows and endless enjoyment to the gardener. A water staircase or *levada* in Madeira, taking you with its flow, conducts water around the garden while healing the soul with its cool, musical cascade.
2 Quietness is just one of water's qualities. You can also spray it, spurt it, shoot it any way you please, as here in an exuberant and anarchic water sculpture by Japanese landscape architect Shodo Suzuki.
3 Water in a grid-shaped paradise garden is given a thoroughly contemporary treatment by the American designer Martha Schwartz. Alternating with crab-apple trees set in white stones, the fountains are linked by coloured tile-lined channels. At night, lights recessed into the basins create a brimstone glow.

New materials and modern technology allow us to control and contain water in almost any form. Even in today's smaller plots, it is possible to distil traditional elements, bringing much-needed refreshment into our stressful lives.

Formal pools are geometric in shape, with clean, hard edges: circles, oblongs, squares, ellipses or narrow channels. As planting has a softening effect, most formal pools are sparsely planted, if at all, though water-lilies and plants with dramatic architecture can suit formal surroundings. Spiky iris gives vertical emphasis, for example, in contrast to the water's smooth plane.

Still, reflective pools add depth to the garden, bringing the sky down to earth and introducing a mood of contemplation. Aim for a depth of approximately 75cm (30in). The base must be dark to catch the best reflections: you can do this by using a black pond liner. The influence of canals or pools is especially soothing in town gardens, where reflected light can relieve the oppression of high walls and tall, enclosing buildings, and can even help to brighten the interior of the house. Think carefully where to place your pool

4

5

4 Modern materials meet naturalistic planting to create new harmonies. Here, water constantly recirculates, dropping from a steel-girder water spout into a concrete basin set in drifting lavender.
5 Water brings life to the smallest corner. Bubbling out of copper pipes to drain away through stones, this miniature fountain can be safely enjoyed by all, even the very youngest children.
6 The reflective pool in this formal water garden shows how water can capture and intensify the mood of its surroundings – in this case, greenly mysterious.

6

in order to create the best reflections. A wider oblong pool placed across the view will let your house rise from its mirrored image, hung upside-down in the manner of a French château.

Informal pools are more organic in shape, often edged with rocks and stones and deliberately 'natural' in planting. But beware of cliché – in particular the ubiquitous kidney shape. And however wild you intend your planting to look, be prepared to keep it under control, like a planted border. Aquatic plants are quick to colonize and choke small features. Use planting shelves and baskets to restrict the spread of marginal plants and to accommodate their different needs. Plant the edges in a way that relates the pool to its wider environment. Willows, coloured winter stems of dogwoods, ferns like the royal fern (*Osmunda regalis*), bamboos, ligularias and perennial clump-forming grasses all give a 'watery' effect.

By planting the various water depths, you can develop specific habitats for wildlife. Submerged, emergent, marginal and bog planting all offer different food sources to satisfy a range of fish, frogs and other creatures, also attracting birds and dragonflies. Keep the water clear with oxygenators, but avoid rampant plants like *Elodea canadensis*: in many parts of the world it is a notifiable weed.

Moving water adds vivacity and sparkle, whether arched in jets, backlit by sunlight, or sluicing over rocks as at Fallingwater, Pennsylvania, where Frank Lloyd Wright boldly merged the jutting house with rock, stream and wood. Alternatively, water can be misted, sprayed, bubbled, or used to create harmony, like Sir Geoffrey Jellicoe's musical cascade at Shute House in Wiltshire.

Don't be discouraged if your space and resources are limited. Small basins, fountains and birdbaths work perfectly well; and where water must be recycled, electric pumps bring fountains, cascades and waterfalls to life, aerating the water at the same time. Water flowing through or across paving is another of the effects you can achieve. You will need a reservoir, such as a small pool or underground tank, as well as an automatic feeder mechanism and an overflow outlet. Features like these can safely introduce the excitement of water to the smallest child, as well as humidity to the surrounding plants.

Sculpture and ornament

1 A potent, wild landscape provided the inspiration for Derek Jarman's garden on the Kent coast. Beachcombed objects (twisted metal, rusting tools, driftwood and stakes) quickly took on the role of sculpture amid the tufty planting.
2 Sculpted stones by Peter Randall-Page repose like fallen fruit at the edge of a frosty lawn. Their smooth surfaces demand to be touched, adding extra sensuous appeal.
3 A giant ornamental jar sitting under a fruit tree in Sir Frederick Gibberd's garden in Harlow, Essex, shows the importance of placement. To keep the soil surface bare, unplanted, and opt for the jar only, is genius.

When properly employed, sculpture and ornament can capture and express the essential spirit of a garden. A gargoyle peering through the undergrowth at the Villa Aldobrandini, Frascati, recalls the Renaissance splendour of the water garden, long since reclaimed by creeping scrub. William Kent's nubile Venus at Rousham, Oxfordshire, projects an early eighteenth-century Arcadia. The artist Barbara Hepworth's standing stones and hollowed bronzes in her Cornish studio garden proclaim her affinity with landscape and place. 'The sensation has never left me,' she wrote in her autobiography. 'I, the sculptor, *am* the landscape.'

The Western tradition of using sculpture in the garden goes back as far as the Romans, at least. During the second century AD, the Emperor Hadrian scattered sculpture like trophies around his Tivoli villa to show off his travels. From the Renaissance onwards, sculpture told complicated allegories: with the right

education you could 'read' gardens like a book and experience the required emotions. But then landscape itself became expressive with the English landscape garden of the eighteenth century, and statuary slipped out of fashion, until reclaimed by the Victorians with their taste for pomp and formality.

Today, after a period of uncertainty, sculpture and ornament are again finding their place in the garden. The American Thomas Church, for example, promoted the use of sculpture because 'it survives the changing seasons yet is not unchanging'. Natural materials in particular gain a patina of age and change their appearance in different lights. He also advised playing with convention. 'The old concept that statuary should dominate the area or should be at the end of every main axis and cross axis doesn't apply any more,' he wrote in *Gardens are for People*. 'It can be used casually on a wall or to brighten a corner of the garden.'

A few of the old rules should still be borne in mind. As simple, bold elements generally work best, always choose sculpture with restraint. Large pieces can exert their power even in restricted spaces; and even small gardens should not as a rule be cluttered with small artefacts. But misjudged scale can feel threatening, so you may need to experiment before buying or commissioning a new piece for your garden. Sir Geoffrey Jellicoe's outsize urns in the Magritte walk at Sutton Place, Surrey, provide a fine visual joke for a public space, though not necessarily one you would wish to repeat in your own backyard.

Outdoor sculpture can be the most tactile of art forms, inviting close inspection and contact. Or you may wish to highlight the contrast between solid mass and living matter, between permanence and evanescence. Sculptors like Richard Long and Andy Goldsworthy use natural forms and elements that rise out of the

4 In Japanese gardens, ornament is used precisely and sparingly for its symbolism. Lanterns and water basins, *tsukubai*, are strategically placed to take advantage of special views revealed when guests humble themselves by bending down to wash.
5 Ben Nicholson's sculptured wall created for Sutton Place in Surrey stands at the opposite extreme. Bold in conception and monumental in scale, it dominates the formal pool and continues to reverberate through its reflection. The edges of the pool repeat the lines and curves of the wall's geometry.
6 The simple plinth of polished slate saves this small flint statue from its wild surroundings. The sculpted figure, by Peter Gough, shows a man performing a shoulder stand.
7 Outdoor sculpture parks are increasingly popular throughout the world, with a growing emphasis on 'natural' forms and materials providing valuable inspiration. These charred oaks by David Nash can be seen at the Goodwood Sculpture Park in Sussex.

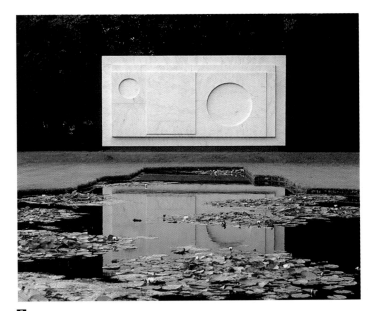

landscape, encouraging a re-evaluation of 'art' and 'environment'. Film-maker Derek Jarman achieved the same effect with the holey stones and driftwood of his seaside garden in the windswept shingle of Dungeness, Kent, framed by a squat and brooding nuclear power station.

Placement is all-important. Since your garden may already be well furnished with plants and other features which define its character, any sculpture you choose will need to interact with its surroundings. For a clear, bold outline, consider highlighting a statue against the bitter green of a yew hedge or an ivy-clad wall. A sculpture as focal point is best appreciated in isolation. One well-placed and carefully chosen piece will always have more impact than several objects haphazardly strung together. You could, in contrast, construct a series of sculptures to tell your own 'story', like the journey of Aeneas through the grottoes and temples of Stourhead in Wiltshire.

1. Birch plywood twisted into a simple seat gains colour and texture from the warm, honey-coloured gravel and a spiky background of late-summer grass.
2. Standing stones like these convey a strong sense of place. Covered in lichen and echoing the vertical lines of conifer and birch they exude a quiet power reminiscent of the sacred groves of the ancient Greeks.
3. Found objects like this tree-trunk alligator bring playfulness into the garden – and welcome surprise.
4. The quiet presence of 'Spires', a slate sculpture by Herta Keller, comes from the juxtaposition of architectural form and natural setting. Its bold outline and intricate texture make the leaves appear fresher, softer, greener.
5. Like a giant child's abandoned toy, this painted steel sculpture by Gary Slater lies beside an equally uncompromising swimming pool.

Alternatively, you might wish to tempt your visitors to explore further by using half-hidden statues and ornaments as signposts on a secret trail.

Whether your sculpture needs a plinth depends on its context. Some pieces can stand directly on grass or paving; heavier pieces need a simple, reinforced base. Choose materials that either complement the sculpture or manage the transition from the sculpture to the surrounding ground. A neutral material like stone or smooth concrete usually works better than a decorative or textured surface.

Statues and sculpture are not the only form of garden ornament. Boundaries, gates, plant containers, tables, chairs and benches, sheds, paths, sundials, birdbaths and lanterns can all combine purpose with aesthetic appeal. American designer Martha Schwartz even used bagels preserved with marine lacquer for a Boston garden, while Topher Delaney and Andy Cochran planted a hillside with the jagged remains of a stone table and concrete terrace destroyed for a client's 'Garden of Divorce'. The cardinal rule is to think simple and think bold before you think anything else.

6 Constant levelling with a stonemason's trowel preserves the pristine shape of this Japanese sand cone. Though frequently seen in temple and shrine gardens, the cone's origins are obscure. Its truncated top recalls the volcanic outline of sacred Mount Fuji. Or it may have evolved from the piles of gravel designed to replenish the raked 'waves' of dry sea.
7 A mound of granitic sand in a Melbourne backyard reintroduces into suburbia a sight common in Australia's arid heartland: the termite nest. Drawing their inspiration from Australia's landscapes, the designers of this space have created a modern backyard where people can play without the usual trimmings and chores of a suburban garden.
8 Coloured bottles (and a few cans) strung along a metal fence take ornament to the boundaries and declare their creator's highly personal tastes.

5

6

7

8

As with sculpture and statuary styles, tastes in garden ornament change and recur in response to deeper undercurrents within societies. Egyptian and Roman obelisks were popular on the balustraded walls of Jacobean England, later staking the boundaries of Georgian estates. Arts and Crafts architects such as Sir Edwin Lutyens masterfully carried through a consistent design to the smallest detailing of gate and latch; while the Spanish architect Antonio Gaudí built fantastic sinuous walls for the Parque Güell in Barcelona that dramatically reproduce the flowing forces of nature.

Ornaments such as containers, urns or boulders can be grouped together to good effect. Symmetry works best for formal designs, using even numbers to create an easy balance. A pair of urns, for example, will perfectly frame a flight of steps or entrance cut in a hedge. Odd-numbered groups create a dynamic asymmetry that better suits an informal style. For groupings of terracotta pots, use different sizes and designs to enhance the effect.

Select generously sized containers to give plants plenty of root space and to prevent rapid evaporation. Always make

sure materials can withstand the climate; some pots are not frost-proof. Urns take on a sculptural quality when placed well so consider leaving them unplanted as an architectural feature. English designer John Brookes used tall, shapely oil jars effectively in a lushly planted border of his garden at Denmans in Sussex.

Reclaimed materials and architectural salvage make a personal statement at a fraction of the cost of commissioned sculpture. Old containers like lead or zinc water tanks or antiquated sinks can become planters, and raised gardens can be created from old chimney pots. Look at the gardens and landscapes of Scottish poet and sculptor Ian Hamilton Finlay for inspiration on incongruous mixtures of materials. His 'Sacred Grove' in the Kröller-Müller sculpture park in the Netherlands uses classical bases to turn trees into columns with unnerving effect.

A garden needs seats to be properly enjoyed. Sometimes these are best placed out of sight, offering seclusion; or they may be angled to reveal an unexpected view. Seats that close a vista beckon with their promise of rest. As with all forms of garden ornament, placement is all.

Lighting

1

2

3

Lighting reclaims your garden from the night and turns it into theatre. Like a stage director, you can manipulate space and mood, cleverly altering perspectives and giving texture, form, even colour new meanings. Flickering candles, flares and fairy lights will further heighten the theatricality for special occasions. Or you can strive for the magical effects of the Moguls, who placed lighted candles in niches behind waterfalls to create curtains of shimmering flame.

As people get busier, some gardens are now used almost exclusively at night. Lighting is essential to make these spaces come alive. And night-time gardening (when the slugs come out to feed) is a way that some city people unwind. So, when designing any garden, it is worth considering how light might extend the use of space instead of planning only for day use and adding lights at the very last minute.

Spotlighting creates drama by picking out the main characters of your garden: a statue, bench or architectural planting. Always provide additional background lighting unless you wish your feature to 'float' in complete darkness, and avoid the glare that comes from placing lights too close. Side-lighting best reveals three-dimensional form, creating an interplay of shadows while hiding the light source.

With water, direct the beam at plants or features grouped around the pool, throwing dramatic shadows across the dark surface of the water itself. Strong architecture looks particularly arresting when viewed upside-down in still water. Underwater lighting must be carefully placed to avoid exposing the mechanics of liners, plant containers and other fittings. But below a waterfall or a fountain – such as the glorious Trevi fountain in Rome – the effect is exhilarating.

Uplighters and spread lights placed at ground level can identify routes and produce dramatic patterns when seen from above. You can also use uplighters to wash light across vertical surfaces like walls or fences and to pick out rough textures like brick or flint. An uplighter

directed through plants in front of a wall will project silhouetted patterns that shift in the wind. Decorated screens and trellis benefit from similar treatment, as do trees with bare, wintery branches. Trees in summer may need more than one light source, because of the density of their leaves. If lighting groups of trees, place the lights at different angles unless you want uniform lighting for an avenue.

For roof gardens, uplighting through glass block screens set in the flooring will produce an atmospheric glow, while light thrown up through skylights can be incorporated into planting schemes.

Many city skylines are most vibrant at night; your own lighting could try to complement the panorama.

Downlighting gives the garden depth and perspective. It works especially well when a narrow-beamed light is mounted in or above a tree to simulate ghostly, soft moonlight. Downlighting is also used for security. Put sensor lights on a separate circuit, though, and activate only when the garden is not in use, as the harsh lights create an uncomfortable glare.

Softer background lighting creates a mood of mystery, transforming familiar plants and features into unknown

1 Natural light brings a wintery morning glow to Dean Cardasis' translucent screens. Similar effects could be achieved by discreet back-lighting.
2 Lighting reinforces the magical properties of water, but make sure the fittings are hidden. In this dripping fountain bowl by Delaney, Cochran & Castillo, lights are concealed underneath the outer rim, creating a skirt of flowing icicles.
3 A combination of lighting types changes a tree-fringed lawn into an unknown space. In the foreground, laser lights make natural stone brim with strong yellow beams. Whiter spotlights at different angles pick out trees, which rise mysteriously out of the darkness.

4 Uplighting is most effective with trees that have strong, visible trunks and branches. For trees with full summer leaf-canopies, reserve this form of lighting for winter. In summer, experiment with downlighting to achieve the effects of moonlight: garden lighting is a flexible art.

5 A meandering path leads to the entrance of the Villa Zapu in California's Napa valley. While the architecture is straight-edged, the landscaping is based on the spiral and the serpentine. Lighting helps to hold the two together.
6 Lighting works best where the light sources are hard to identify. Seats look good when lit for effect, but make sure the sitters are not disturbed by the glare.

shapes. For outdoor entertainment, aim for a low level of illumination around the table. The glow from fittings directed at nearby features and plants will give a soft, subdued light overall, enhancing the pleasures of sitting and eating outdoors on long summer nights. Candles on the table provide additional mood lighting.

Flares and candle lanterns heighten the excitement and lend romance. One low-cost idea for a party is to put candles in brown paper bags weighted with sand, the tops turned back into collars to stop the bags catching fire. Dotted around the garden, they produce an ethereal glow.

In small spaces mains-voltage lighting has only limited use. Low-voltage lights are more practical for the garden: safer to lay and to use. The low heat output also reduces the chance of scorching plants. As fixtures are compact and unobtrusive, they are easily hidden. When you bury cables in the ground, make sure you allow enough cable to reposition the lights, if necessary, and mark their position on a garden plan for future reference.

As lighting effects vary, you should ask for a demonstration before you buy. The white light of low-voltage halogen bulbs picks out focal points effectively.

For background light, consider the softer yellow glow of tungsten: other colours, such as mercury's cool mint green, should be used with extreme caution. Coloured filters can turn foliage a surreal black or blue, best reserved for special occasions.

New fibre optic technology is taking garden lighting into new territories because it is not directly connected to electric current, as in Gilles Clément's Parisian pool that glints at night with illuminated pebbles. In America, the designer Ron Wigginton used fibre optics to light up perspex rods in his boardwalk re-creation of the night sky.

THE WORKING GARDEN

Gardening is a hard-earned pleasure. Planting, weeding, pruning, digging, watering, tending the soil — all reap visible rewards as you watch your garden grow. And if occasional pottering is more your style, you can plan your space for minimal maintenance: the idea of a garden accommodates many degrees of toil. Whatever garden you have in mind, each needs its own working area: a place for sowing and potting on, for propagating cuttings and storing tools and equipment.

In the large estates of Britain in the eighteenth and nineteenth centuries, whole armies of staff worked behind the scenes to support the elegant extravagance of the pleasure garden. Potting sheds, greenhouses, cold frames, melon yards, pineapple pits, compost heaps, bee boles, dipping pools and gardeners' cramped cottages sprawled into small villages tucked out of sight. Many estates had underground tunnels and trenches to let their workers pass unseen, maintaining the illusion of a natural Eden. But now our plots have shrunk in size and the 'armies' are usually ourselves.

In small gardens especially, where much of the space is constantly on view, these areas must be planned to work well and to look good, too. Don't be afraid of bringing a compost heap into your design or ending a vista with a garden shed. Greenhouses, too, can be brought out of hiding, along with cold frames and stockbeds. Well-thought-out layouts, imaginative structures and a sensitive use of materials can integrate the working area into the garden, making a feature out of the virtues of good husbandry. Always sketch your proposed layout first to evolve the most efficient flow between tasks. And think about how much space you will need for each activity. Main paths, in particular, should be wide enough to take a wheelbarrow. Working space that is well organized will bring rewards in the years to come.

For kitchen gardens, the choice lies between creating separate areas for vegetables, fruit and herbs, or mixing productivity with visual enjoyment — scattering herbs around a terrace, for example, or planting fruit trees in a border. 'Potager' gardening means designing a productive garden that is also ornamental, adding flowers and features more commonly found in gardens intended just for show. But as every vegetable grower knows, even the most humble kitchen garden can gladden the eye, the heart – and the stomach.

Growing your own produce appeals to the most primitive of human instincts: nature and nurture, the pride of planting, tending and harvesting the fruits of your labour. The beauty of form brings its own sensuous pleasures, too.

Sheds and storage

1

2

3

4

A well-ordered garden shed is immensely satisfying. Part of its appeal looks back to the great working kitchen gardens of the past; and it encompasses the full range of gardening activities, from energetic digging to quiet sowing and potting. But the well-organized shed is practical above all else, simplifying your garden management and giving storage space.

Traditionally sheds, compost heaps and storage areas have been tucked away behind trellis, fencing or planting. With good design and sympathetic materials, this should not be necessary. Decorative paintwork or staining can give new life to the simplest structure. Thomas Church painted a *trompe l'oeil* door on to a blank shed wall that dominated a courtyard garden, turning a problem into a feature. The imaginative gardener might build a folly for tools, or Claes Oldenburg might build a folly out of a tool.

1 Compost-making needs insulation and air, provided here by breeze blocks and slatted wooden sides that can be removed for easy access. A cover will maintain a stable environment.
2 A working shed needs to be organized properly. Here, hooks save space and pots hang like a garland from the roof.
3 The well-made shed proudly takes a central role in the garden's design. Trellis for climbing plants adds an ornamental touch.

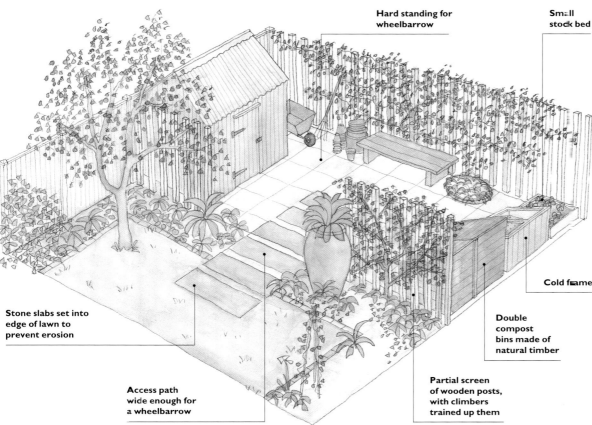

Hard standing for wheelbarrow

Small stock bed

Stone slabs set into edge of lawn to prevent erosion

Access path wide enough for a wheelbarrow

Cold frame

Double compost bins made of natural timber

Partial screen of wooden posts, with climbers trained up them

4 A reclaimed railway carriage finds a final resting place. The division of space into compartments is perfect for a gardener's many different tasks.
5 This typical Australian outhouse shows that well-built sheds in good materials need not hide away.
6 Partially screened but not hidden from the rest of the garden, shed and working area demand careful design, good materials and tidy habits to work well.
7 Very small spaces call for ingenuity. This dog-kennel of a shed provides just enough space to store tools and potting equipment. Anything larger might feel rather oppressive.

Where you site your working area will depend on functional demands and security. A lawn needs a mower within easy reach and a shed to house it securely. Potting sheds and compost heaps need access. Storage areas for activities that link indoors and outdoors should be close to the house: a log store near the back door, for instance. If you plan a single working area, you may need to compromise between conflicting demands.

Timber is the material most often used for garden buildings because it is light and relatively cheap. Concrete, brick and stone may suit you just as well. Basic sheds can be bought off-the-shelf: a size 1.8m long by 1.2m wide (6ft by 4ft) holds the minimum tools needed for a small to medium-sized garden. Anything smaller will force you to crouch. Larger gardens need bigger sheds, which come with windows and workbenches for potting.

Tiny backyards call for ingenuity. Try attaching small storage compartments to boundary or house walls, like outdoor shoe tidies. You can buy these in rather utilitarian materials or make your own out of timber, painted or stained to blend in with their surroundings. For extra storage, incorporate custom-built box seats into terraced garden walls or make use of empty spaces below timber decks, fitting a hinged trapdoor to reach watertight storage boxes below.

Good compost is one of your garden's chief treasures. 'In American gardening,' writes Michael Pollan in *Second Nature*, 'the successful compost pile seems almost to have supplanted the perfect hybrid tea rose or the gigantic beefsteak tomato as the outward sign of horticultural grace.' Lawn clippings, soft prunings, cuttings, dead leaves and flowers, and kitchen waste all help to improve soil structure, giving back to your garden the nutrients it needs. The simplest compost bins are often best: slatted boxes made of sustainable hardwood or treated softwood. Two bins are more practical than one, and three are ideal: one for fresh waste, one for rotting down and one for garden use.

Greenhouses and frames

The smell of a greenhouse is rich and musky, instantly evocative. While they are usually considered the province of keen plantsmen, greenhouses in temperate climates allow all gardeners to extend the growing season and experiment with a wider range of plants. Early crops of salad, fruit and vegetables, and enriched plant stocks through propagation, are among their many uses.

Greenhouses were traditionally put up in walled gardens, backed against a sunny wall. As structures became plainer they found their way to the bottom of the garden, but the wide choice of attractive contemporary styles has brought them back into view. For smaller gardens, the standard greenhouse size is 2.4m by 1.8m (8ft by 6ft); while polygonal models are economical with space and look more like summer-houses. In tight corners, mini- or lean-to greenhouses can be erected against a sunny house or boundary wall.

Siting is crucial. A greenhouse needs a sunny, sheltered position away from shade canopies, wind tunnels or frost pockets. If the entire garden slopes, site the structure some way uphill, away from solid barriers like walls that catch the cold air as it flows downhill. To gain the most light in spring, orientate the ridge from east to west. You will need to consider heating: the usual choice is between electricity, gas or paraffin. Many modern greenhouses incorporate solar panels to reduce running costs. Shading, insulation and good ventilation are also vital to control temperature and create a healthy growing environment for your plants.

Frames can be made of timber, plastic-coated steel or aluminium. Timber is the classic choice: always seek suppliers using a sustainable source. Hardwoods are long-lived and need little attention; rot-resistant cedar can be treated each year to retain its colour. Softwood frames should have been pressure-treated with preservative and need regular painting. The narrow glazing bars of metal frames admit more light than timber ones. While aluminium alloy needs minimal maintenance, plastic-coated galvanized steel should be checked regularly for rust and painted every few years.

Cold frames are useful for hardening off delicate young plants before planting on in the garden. Usually built of brick or timber, they have a glazed lid which can be removed during the warmer days and replaced at night when temperatures drop. They can be free-standing (but site them away from areas used by children)

1 Some climates need shade-houses rather than greenhouses. Climbing plants and blinds will provide further screening.
2 Green and earthy in atmosphere, this well-stocked greenhouse closely resembles a conservatory – a place to sit as well as work.

3 This lean-to greenhouse absorbs heat from the house. Unless a lean-to is situated against a sunny wall, however, the light may not be sufficient for activities like propagation.
4 Good ventilation helps to control pests and diseases as well as temperature. Staging provides much-needed storage space.
5 Constructed against the boundary wall, a classic, white-painted greenhouse blends easily with informal, cottage-garden style planting by the house.

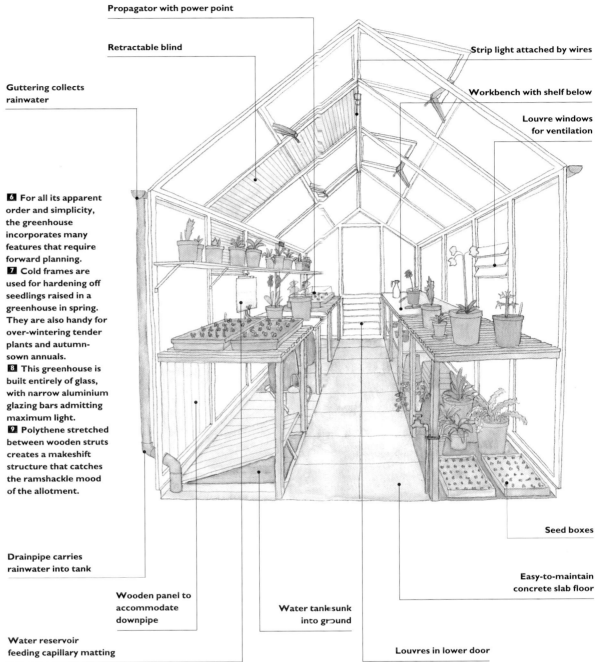

Propagator with power point

Retractable blind

Strip light attached by wires

Guttering collects rainwater

Workbench with shelf below

Louvre windows for ventilation

or, more usually, built against the solid wall of your greenhouse. As they are used mainly in late winter and spring, place them on the sunniest side of the greenhouse for maximum light, being prepared to shade them on sunny days. Raising their height may make access easier, and provide useful storage space beneath.

Planting cuttings, sowing seeds and pricking out all require adequate space in your greenhouse. Pathways to the door should allow a minimum width of 1.2m (4ft) for wheelbarrow access. Make sure that all surfaces can be cleaned and sterilized easily to prevent the spread of pests and diseases. Concrete is the most appropriate flooring in a greenhouse, but cold frames can have gravel or sand for a free-draining base.

Traditionally sited close to the working garden, stockbeds contain plants used to obtain seeds or cuttings for propagation. They are also useful in observing how new plants perform before giving them a central role in any planting scheme. With pressures on space, it is now more usual to blend stockbeds into the garden proper. A simple layout with rectangular borders recalls the 'order beds' of the old physic gardens; or you may prefer more informal planting.

6 For all its apparent order and simplicity, the greenhouse incorporates many features that require forward planning.
7 Cold frames are used for hardening off seedlings raised in a greenhouse in spring. They are also handy for over-wintering tender plants and autumn-sown annuals.
8 This greenhouse is built entirely of glass, with narrow aluminium glazing bars admitting maximum light.
9 Polythene stretched between wooden struts creates a makeshift structure that catches the ramshackle mood of the allotment.

Drainpipe carries rainwater into tank

Wooden panel to accommodate downpipe

Water reservoir feeding capillary matting

Seed boxes

Easy-to-maintain concrete slab floor

Water tank sunk into ground

Louvres in lower door

6
8

7

9

Fruit

Crisp apples, fragrant strawberries, sun-ripened peaches and apricots: these fruits represent some of the most highly prized treasures of the productive garden. But individual specimens look equally good in an 'ornamental' setting. The architectural forms of many trained species fit well with formal layouts. You can grow free-standing fruit trees as the shapely centrepiece of a border where they will contribute a froth of spring blossom and glorious autumn colour, as well as fruits for your table. Even tiny yards can accommodate pot-grown cultivars: tubs of apples and pears, for example, or planters brimming with strawberries.

Fruits are classed in several different categories: tree fruits (which are also known as top fruit); soft fruits (bush and cane fruits, and strawberries); vines (grapes and other woody climbers, like kiwi fruit); tender fruits (such as lemons, oranges and pineapples); and nuts. Whatever type of fruit you choose to grow, there are certain basic cultivation rules to observe. Fruit needs a sunny, sheltered position, with protection from the wind (provided by hedges, permeable fences or trees). Never plant in hollows or depressions where frost may bite the buds and inhibit growth. For efficient harvesting and maintenance, grow fruit in rows: a regular planting pattern lends itself to square or rectangular beds, perhaps enlivened with herbs and ornamental paving. Or you can incorporate vegetables into the design to create a doubly productive garden.

Provide plenty of space around larger fruit trees and bushes to allow good air circulation and to give room for expansion as they grow. You must also allow easy access for pruning and harvesting, so avoid planting a fruit tree at the back of a large border. Some species, such as apple, resent competition from ground-covering plants, which is the reason why any surrounding grass is removed in commercial orchards. Pathways provide practical surfaces as well as introducing extra pattern and texture into dedicated

1 A warm sheltered wall provides ideal support for tender fruits such as this fig. Restrict the roots in a concrete or slate box, approximately 60cm (2ft) square, to encourage fruiting.
2 Espaliered apple trees grown as 'step-overs' make attractive edging in the kitchen garden. Correct pruning, and a dwarf rootstock, is necessary to keep their shape.

1

fruit areas. Main routes need to be 1.2m to 1.5m wide (4ft to 5ft) to accommodate a wheelbarrow. Lesser paths for access to beds and rows can be reduced to 90cm (3ft) or less, if necessary.

Of all the fruits, tree fruits occupy the most space. If grown on any scale, apples, pears and nuts usually require a separate orchard, but most gardens can include one or two orchard trees. Free-standing forms of bush, half-standard and pyramidal fruit trees usually work best in small spaces. Choose trees grafted on a dwarfing rootstock for the smallest gardens: these crop well and their mature size will be much restricted. Fruit trees can also be pruned and trained into ornamental shapes. Espaliers, cordons and fans may be grown against a supporting wall or held within borders and beds on a wire framework. Their slender, elegant silhouettes provide strong form in the winter garden. Trained as 'step-overs', they make an attractive edge to a productive bed. More dramatic forms such as fruit arches give important vertical emphasis.

Tree fruits like peach will need protection in colder climates, restricting the sites on which they can be grown. In the

2

3

3 Grapes trained along wires form a graceful arch that gives shade as well as fruit. In cooler climates, vines can be grown in a heated greenhouse.
4 A peach tree in mown grass keeps its shade away from the kitchen garden. Peaches flower early and must be protected from frost; they also need plenty of sun.
5 Forcing pots for rhubarb produce an early crop of temptingly tender pink stems and make showy borders for either fruit or kitchen gardens.
6 Cages protect soft fruits and small fruit trees from predatory birds. For the cage, use wood or metal supports covered with small-meshed netting in plastic or nylon.
7 Training fruit trees as cordons saves space and looks good. Here pear cordons grow against a wall at Barrington Court in Somerset, where Gertrude Jekyll gave advice on the planting.

4

5

6

northern hemisphere, a sunny south- or west-facing wall will store residual heat overnight, which may be enough to save the early blossom from frost damage and encourage fruits to ripen. Nectarines, peaches, apricots and dessert plums are all good wall fruits, as are pears and figs.

Although the plants of soft fruits are relatively small, they are still greedy for space: rows of raspberry canes should be set about 1.5m (5ft) apart, for instance. To save space, gooseberries and currants can be trained as cordons on wire. All these fruits benefit from the protection of cages to stop birds eating your crop. Finding well-designed cages is not always easy; and you will need to consider where to store temporary structures over the winter, or design and build structures that will withstand winter weather.

Since Roman times, vines have been valued for shade as well as fruit. Trained over a pergola, a grapevine will give shelter from the summer heat and a good crop of grapes as summer draws to a close. In cooler regions they need temporary or even permanent protection: with careful planting and maintenance, a vine will grow happily in a greenhouse or conservatory. Plant the vine at one end of the greenhouse, then train it up a side wall on supporting wires and along the apex of the roof. In lean-to greenhouses, the vine will benefit from heat absorbed through the wall of the house.

Strawberries are perhaps the most versatile fruiting plant. As well as providing decorative ground cover and edging to pathways, they make excellent container plants for terraces and small courtyard gardens. They also bear one of the prettiest fruits, with attractive small white flowers and three-lobed leaves. Figs also grow well in large pots. Their handsome foliage is a bonus in any garden. In Mediterranean climates, citrus fruits grown in tubs have long been appreciated for the heady scent of their flowers and their ornamental fruits. In temperate climates, however, they must be brought under glass to avoid winter frosts.

7

Vegetables

1

2

3

4

Growing your own vegetables is simple, fast and immensely satisfying. This is especially true today when intensive farming has driven choice and flavour out of much shop-bought produce. But before you take up vegetable gardening, think carefully how much time and space you want to commit. The goal of self-sufficiency demands more of both than most gardeners can spare. Many people will find it more worthwhile to concentrate on the more unusual or attractive species for an occasional treat.

The tradition of growing vegetables for food stretches back several millennia. In Europe and America, many of the great old vegetable gardens from more recent times have been lovingly restored to give continuing inspiration. In the early nineteenth century, the American President Thomas Jefferson surrounded his Virginia country estate of Monticello with fine terraces for vegetables and fruit, proving that beauty can also reside in utility. Recent restorations in England include the Lost Gardens of Heligan in Cornwall, with nearly two acres devoted to over 300 varieties of fruit and vegetables.

Growing vegetables for their looks as much as their taste is called 'potager gardening' in Britain, or 'edible landscaping' in the United States. A potager arranged as a separate enclosure will usually incorporate ornamental features like seats, arbours, fountains and containers. Beds are kept small and attractively edged with lavender, low-growing box or herbs.

Perhaps the most sensational showcase for ornamental fruit and vegetables is at Villandry in the Loire valley of France. Here, in the twentieth-century re-creation of a much earlier *jardin potager*, geometric beds edged with box display neat rows of celery, swiss chard, cabbage and ornamental kale, all with richly contrasting colours and textures. Although this is gardening on the grandest scale, there are lessons for the private plot: not least that imaginative design can make the humble kitchen garden rival the most showy herbaceous border.

1 Well-kept paths and narrow beds make this an easy vegetable plot to work. Neat edging, graceful pots and jars and an old-fashioned water pump help it to look good, too.
2 Rows of onions and brassicas encroach on the house. Dwarfing rootstocks mean that nowadays even apple trees can grow in pots.
3 In temperate zones, vegetables need plenty of sun, but some shade can also be welcome in periods of intense heat. Many brassicas and lettuces, for instance, are cool-climate crops.

4 The tidy geometry of stone walls and low box hedging contains a mixed planting of vegetables, herbs and flowers, in classic potager style.
5 Sturdy wooden tepees support fast-climbing beans, giving instant height to this 'homestead' planting scheme. The chipped bark of the path is also used to mulch the beds.
6 Gourds trained on arches, a path of close-mown grass and a sculptural seat create an unexpectedly exotic vista in this Sussex vegetable garden.

5

6

Even if you do not want a separate potager, many vegetables are attractive plants in their own right and make good partners for perennial flowering plants. The waxy blue-green leaves of cabbages; the tall, shapely forms of globe artichokes; and the fern-like, feathery foliage of carrots all look good in borders. For colourful edging try leaf vegetables such as ruby chard with its richly red oar-shaped leaves, or salad crops like frilly lettuces; and courgettes can be used to fill any gaps in a border. And if space is really limited, you can even crop a window box by planting new dwarf species of lettuce, tomatoes, broad beans and peas.

In larger gardens, more committed vegetable growers will want to create a working kitchen garden. This area can be screened by walls and hedges or enclosed with ornamental planting: trained fruit trees, perhaps, or trellis planted with hops, beans and other climbers such as roses, passion flowers or fan-trained figs. Enclosure allows you to introduce a formal layout in contrast to more informal planting elsewhere in the garden. Beds with crops planted in short rows and organized in squares or rectangles, are now taking over from the old allotment style of long, regimented rows. A square bed of 1.2m to 1.5m (4ft to 5ft) is ideal: this allows you to reach into the middle of the bed without treading on the soil. To soften the formality, you may want to

vary the bed sizes and style of planting. But above all, a kitchen garden must be practical; ease of cultivation comes first.

The geometric patterns of brick or other small units such as setts make good paving in the kitchen garden. Keep the design simple, allowing a minimum width for main paths of 1.2m (4ft) to allow wheelbarrow access. Pyramids of runner beans trained up bamboo tripods will give almost instant height to a newly established area of the garden. Because of the shade they cast, arches and pergolas are less suitable in a vegetable plot. Pots and urns provide colourful planted features, as long as they are watered regularly, and are good for 'cut and come again' vegetables such as lamb's lettuce, radiccio and other Italian salad crops that will soon regrow after picking.

All vegetables need well-prepared soil with good drainage, plenty of sunshine and protection from damaging winds. A convenient water supply is essential. As well as enriching the soil, a liberal use of compost, well-rotted animal manure and mulches help to conserve moisture and control weeds. Except for perennials such as asparagus, globe artichoke and seakale, you will need to rotate crops to prevent a build-up of specific pests and diseases by regularly replanting beds or rows with vegetables from the different plant groups (legumes, alliums, roots and tubers, and brassicas).

7 Stone flag paths in a French potager complement an architectural planting of cabbage, artichoke, onion, orache and bronze fennel.
8 The modest scale of house, garden and wooden picket fence produce a design of great charm that is also easy to work. Beds for flowers, vegetables and fruit are raised and edged with treated wood.

7

8

Herbs

1 Though growth can sometimes be leggy, herbs make attractive additions to any part of the garden, while late summer sunlight throws into relief their varied textures.
2 'Knots' of santolina and lavender were common in Europe from the late fifteenth century. Here, a seat squeezed between yellow spikes of evening primroses invites quiet (and scented) pleasure.
3 Planted in the gaps between paving, a mass of creeping thyme, sage and rosemary brings the scent of aromatic herbs almost to the window.
4 No garden is too small for a collection of herbs. Silver-variegated thyme, rosemary and parsley varieties are among the herbs crowding into this terracotta planter.

Everyone has space to grow herbs, even just a few aromatics on a windowsill or in pots on a terrace. The most sensuous of plants, herbs should be planted where they can be easily touched: by doorways and pathways, for instance, or sown among raised turf seats. Touching or crushing the leaves releases their scent, so redolent of the Mediterranean climate from where many herbs originate.

The term 'herb' refers to any plant used for medicine, flavouring or perfume – a huge range that extends to shrubs and trees as well as herbaceous perennials and annuals. In addition to the wild species still widely grown, cultivars bring even stronger scents or more striking foliage. Purple or golden sage, golden-leaved marjoram, and many varieties of thyme will grace a mixed planting scheme just as well as a proper herb garden.

Herb gardens have come down to us from the kitchen gardens of the Greeks and Romans, and from ancient physic gardens dedicated to healing. Many herb gardens today repeat patterns familiar from medieval woodcuts. Their tight

geometry gives structure to the loose, often straggling plant forms, creating shape even in winter when annuals and herbaceous herbs die back. Edged with box or small-leaved evergreens such as rue or cotton lavender, formal beds make a tapestry of planting subdivided by paths. Alternatively, you can mimic the interlocking designs of seventeenth-century knot gardens, tying low hedges of box or santolina into rectangular, square or diamond-shaped beds. Siting a knot garden close to the house means that you can best appreciate its intricate patterns from upper windows.

Many modern designs are geometric, too, based on squares, circles and more unusual figures, intersected by paths. Where space is limited, a raised circle can accommodate several varieties in separate segments edged with brick. At the other extreme are wilder plantings that look like meadows or rampant cottage gardens, with herbs spilling over paths and in all directions.

The traditional herb garden is not the only place to grow herbs. Though colours are generally muted, their varied foliage effects make them ideal border plants: purple fennel, for example, wraps its neighbours in a gossamer screen while frilly parsley neatly fits an edge like a ruff. You can use herbs to enliven rows of duller vegetables in the kitchen garden, or to fill gaps in brick and stone paths. Tiny, neat leaves of thyme contrast well with plump spikes of chives or feathery grasses, or you can experiment with a limited palette of leaf colours and textures to achieve a chessboard effect.

Because of their origins, most herbs prefer full sunlight and free-draining soil. Mediterranean species such as rosemary,

5

6

7

8

thyme and sage respond particularly well to a gravel mulch. Taller herbs will need shelter against the wind from walls, fences, trellis or hedging. Some herbs will tolerate at least light shade and a few – for example angelica, feverfew and chives – will grow in damp shade. In colder climates, use frames to grow basil if it is needed in any quantity. Mixing annual and perennial herbs is a good way of letting one 'cover' for the other to maintain interest throughout the year. Herbs in frequent use may be best planted in a vegetable garden: chives, for example, which can look ragged when cut often.

Growing herbs in containers increases their versatility. Mediterranean species are traditionally grown in terracotta pots, but any container will do as long as it gives adequate drainage. Shiny surfaces complement the rough silver and grey texture of many herbs, for instance. Group a collection of pots near the kitchen door. And if you lack a garden of your own, windowboxes and hanging baskets allow you to enjoy the scents and beauty of a herb garden in miniature.

5 A spectrum of greys and greens and the neatly clipped forms of santolina and lavender cleverly reflect the shapes and shades of the pebbled path.
6 The exuberance of herbs and perennials (including betony, yarrow and larkspur) is firmly contained by wooden edging.
7 Culinary and medicinal herbs mix with scented flowers that would also have belonged in the apothecary's garden: roses, poppies, lilies and columbines.
8 Soft fruit, herbs, shrubs and roses spill into drifts that enclose a private sitting area in this French potager – an ideal place in which to enjoy their scent and restful greens.

ENTERTAINING AND PLAY

Play is serious business. Just as our indoor living space gravitates around kitchen and hearth, so outdoor areas for eating, gathering and family enjoyment provide a focus for design, like the 'honeypot' areas in recreational planning. And yet the garden must still work well aesthetically, providing sufficient growing space for trees, shrubs and flowers, for vegetables and fruit – a place where you can reach out from the closed spaces of work to recapture an affinity with the soil, and with living things.

In designing gardens for entertaining and play, think how you want the space to work – for you and all the other people who will use it. Ask children what they want most, too, and be prepared to change your plans. Above all don't rush: possible conflicts should be thought through in advance, or your idea of paradise will be tainted by the stresses you seek to escape. In even a smallish plot it is possible to provide both pockets of quiet and larger areas for more boisterous games. It is equally possible to make play areas look good: a circular path bordering a lawn, for example, will provide a satisfying curve and a merry-go-round for small cyclists, while still allowing for easy mowing and maintenance.

When you know how the spaces will flow together, then you will begin to see the kind of setting and props you need to gain the most enjoyment. Sets and setting: gardens have long enjoyed an element of theatre – as backdrop to the courtly masques of Inigo Jones, for example, or as massive earthworks borrowed from the stage, like the eighteenth-century turfed amphitheatre at Claremont in Surrey. In New South Wales, the Czech-born designer Vladimir Sitta even added a fog-making machine to a folly feeding a swimming pool with filtered water, creating an aura of mystery.

For most domestic gardens the scale is rather more intimate. The aim is to create settings that will enfold actors and spectators, doers and watchers, giving them a space that actually works. This means thinking about where you might want to sit and the kind of seating that will match your mood; about shade and sun and sheltering from wind or rain; about swimming pools and games; about cooking and eating in the open air, and just as crucially, about bringing food to the table. Get these details right and your garden will repay your efforts with the rest and enjoyment you seek.

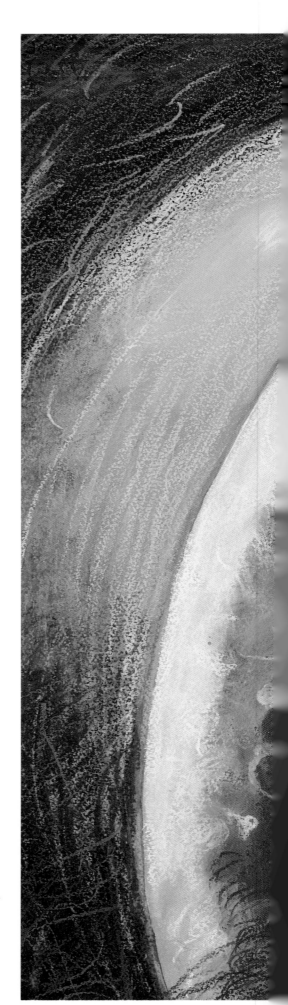

Gardens are meant to be enjoyed; only the most fevered gardener can spare no time to use the garden for the pursuit of other pleasures. As Samuel Johnson might have said, when a man is tired of his garden, he is tired of life.

Furniture

Garden furniture spells immediate enjoyment. Imagine sitting in the speckled shade of a twisted tree or with a group of friends around a terrace table. A single empty seat glimpsed in the distance beckons with its promise of gentle ease; two empty seats invite intimacy.

Seats can be functional, designed and placed to help you sit, eat, rest, talk and quietly enjoy a view; or they can play a central role in design, ending a vista, perhaps, or linking the architecture of house and garden. Many forms of garden furniture achieve both aims. Arts and Crafts designers like Sir Edwin Lutyens created seats and benches that admirably developed the crafted chunkiness of their houses. And throughout the garden's history, fantasy has inspired many designs, from the Villa Garzoni's winged lions of Ancient Rome to Antonio Gaudi's serpentine benches in concrete and mosaic in Barcelona's Parque Güell.

Style, materials and placing all depend on purpose. Most gardens benefit from a scattering of relatively permanent, weatherproof seats in places where they will be best enjoyed. These can be supplemented by lightweight pieces moved around as necessary and stored indoors or in sheds. Deckchairs, canvas or cane chairs, or painted café tables and chairs, are ideal for picnics, adding a touch of colour and summer exuberance.

1 A hammock strung between two stout trees promises long lazy afternoons under filtered green shade.
2 Made of moulded terrazzo, this six-foot bench by Tom Heatherwick makes a sculptural statement in a woodland setting.
3 Water attracts people like a hearth in winter. The natural wood of steps, decking and well-crafted loungers deepens the mood of longed-for peace and seclusion.
4 Careful matching of bench and tree has created an organic seat that appears to 'grow' from between its buttressed roots.
5 Enjoying a position both sheltered and open, this starkly simple set of table and benches illustrates how contemporary styles can fit into a traditional setting. The reverse is harder to achieve.
6 These elegant, free-flowing chairs by Luke Pearson were designed specially for a city roof garden and perfectly reflect the clean lines of decking, grass and steel planters.

7 Kenzo's wooden table with sunken leg space draws on the economy of traditional Japanese design. Setting the slatted lines at right angles to each other makes the table appear to 'float'.
8 These lightweight chairs made of modern materials harmonize well with their surroundings, echoing the criss-cross trellis and blue planting.
9 Wicker chairs, even in a modern setting, suggest a certain Edwardian ease. Arm rests also carry bottles, a thoughtful touch.

Resilience, long life and good looks make timber a favourite for more permanent garden furniture; always select renewable sources. Hardwoods like teak attain a silvery-grey patina that blends gracefully with foliage: re-treating or oiling every few years will restore the warmth of younger wood. Softwoods such as pine are usually painted or stained and require greater maintenance. Metal is extremely versatile: generally painted, the light wirework of reeded wrought iron contrasts with heavier cast iron. The Victorians favoured elaborate flower patterns such as ivy, nasturtium, fern and blackberry, but today, iron is usually replaced by a lighter cast aluminium. Contemporary designers of furniture also use galvanized chrome and brushed aluminium in their natural states. Off-the-peg plastic is cheap, light and fairly long-suffering, but is rarely exciting. Woven willow or wicker can be used indoors and out, though it needs protection from wet weather.

You can also adapt structures to take built-in seats: for instance, making low dividing walls double as seats. An ideal height is 35cm (14in), with a width of at least two bricks. The walls of raised planting beds, steps and changes of level can all be treated in this way, especially on terraces and small seating areas, to welcome a sudden influx of friends.

Shade and shelter

Religions born in the desert promise a paradise of spreading trees and cool fountains, protected from the fierce winds and burnished sun of a hostile environment. Stepping from light to shade can be a transforming experience, like entering a cave. Shade and shelter continue to cast their spell, even in colder latitudes.

Many large gardens of the Italian Renaissance contained a *bosco* or dense grove of standing trees, planted mainly for shade in contrast to the magnificent formality of the rest. Versailles had its *bosquets*, ornamental thickets enclosing features and walks, and even the formal gardens of late seventeenth-century England, like Ham House in Richmond, had clipped woodland walks or 'wildernesses'. The Frenchman André Mollet recommended these in 1670 'either for studious Retirement or the enjoyment of Society with two or three Friends, a Bottle of Wine and a Collation'.

Tree canopies give the most natural shade, filling the garden with shifting silhouettes as the sun moves slowly round the sky. Luis Barragán used 'shadow walls' like giant screens to catch their restless movement. Whitewashed garden walls achieve similar effects. Delicate birch or ornamental thorns work well in profile. Good trees for spreading shade include apples and Japanese cherries, such as *Prunus serrulata* 'Shirotae'.

Roots near houses, however, can cause cracking and subsidence, and many city gardens have no trees. Trellis screens and canvas awnings offer protection from sun and give privacy from upper windows. Slatted shadows cast by an overhead screen of wood or bamboo laths recall a Mediterranean or Californian sun. A stout pergola draped with wisteria, fragrant jasmine, honeysuckle, the crimson glory vine (*Vitis coignetiae*) or climbing roses performs a similar function.

Parasols of lacquered or plain-coloured canvas give temporary shelter to smaller terraces and eating areas, while tents are rather more flamboyant. Curtained, swagged or screened with muslin like an

1 Mediterranean climates demand differing degrees of shade according to the sun and the season. The canvas awning may one day be replaced by vines trained between the supports.
2 Improvised tree-stump seating in a Dutch garden benefits from a 'living' wind break that also holds back the wilder planting beyond.
3 Continuing the rustic theme, a structure of wooden poles supports a spreading wisteria growing at the edge of a meadow. Site and shelter are here perfectly attuned.

4

4 Tightly enclosed
by a semicircular
hedge and wearing
its clipped shade like a
hat, this private space
is practical as well as
delightfully unexpected.

old-fashioned mosquito net, they must
be anchored with ropes or wires attached
to pegs driven into soft ground or fixing
points built into the house or terrace.
Rain may need a more robust solution.
Open pavilions are perfect for summer
showers, offering protection but also
magnifying the drumming of rain on the
roof and the smell of fresh, damp earth.

Many gardens need shelter from the
wind, which creates problems for plants
and people. Roof gardens, balconies and
coastal gardens are especially vulnerable,
as are areas with fierce prevailing winds
like the *meltemi* in the northern Cyclades
and the *mistral* in Provence. Permeable
wind breaks and shelter belts are better
than solid barriers, which create further
eddies. Hedges, planted trellis panels,
balustrades, palisade fencing and decorative brickwork with empty spaces
worked into the pattern all help to provide a semi-permeable barrier that will
reduce wind speed and avoid vortexing.

Views out across windy spaces can be
protected by glass screens built into
walls. The effect is often surreal, like a
Magritte painting. A similar approach
works well in a roof garden, using clear
reinforced glass to take advantage of
views out or backlit frosted glass to
create an other-worldly glow at night.

Screens within a garden create extra
pockets of privacy and shelter, making
you feel comfortable and enclosed yet
teasing with glimpses of the surrounding
garden. Such niches humanize the scale
of the garden and add to your enjoyment
of it. Contemporary gardens can harness
treatments ranging from the modern to
the more traditional; a range that encompasses coloured perspex screens and
materials like whitewashed or rough-cast
concrete, but also crowded topiary yews
or pleached limes spaced like soldiers on
parade. For a garden at a recent show,
three young English designers devised a
scaffolding of stretched canvas and glass
'bricks' that could be moved around the
garden like room dividers, creating new
spaces according to mood and need.

5

5 Skimming a
hillside in Queensland,
Australia, this steel-
frame tent house by
architect Gabriel Poole
is shielded with canvas
blinds that adjust in line
with the tropical light.
6 A small corner of an
urban garden provides
a canopied retreat.
Whitewashed walls
brighten the shade
while the pergola
gives shelter from the
sun and privacy from
upper windows.
7 If all else fails:
innovate. A yacht sail
provides shelter at
midday – and a triangle
of bright white light as
shadows lengthen.

 6

7

Cooking and eating

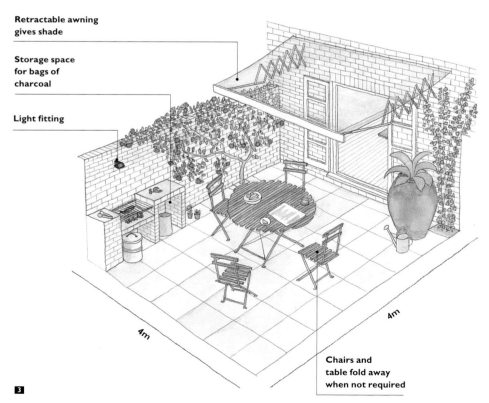

Retractable awning gives shade

Storage space for bags of charcoal

Light fitting

4m

4m

Chairs and table fold away when not required

1 A barbecue needs only good food, good company and a patch of outdoor space to be a success. A gilding of evening sunlight adds special effects.
2 For the table, placed to take advantage of the panoramic views, metal grille and boulder combine natural and man-made materials.
3 The smaller terrace must be adaptable. Furniture can be folded away, and an awning gives temporary shade.
4 Outdoor eating can benefit from sun or shade, depending on the season. This intimate, leafy eating area faces south and grows shadier with the summer.
5 Sited away from the house, this private outdoor dining room has space for more permanent features.

Food tastes better out of doors – even food cooked indoors. A sandwich in the park is better than a sandwich at the desk. Eating out in the open air turns a simple meal into a celebration: a candle-lit meal with friends under the stars has a magic rarely found within four walls.

If tastes today veer towards the informal, we follow a long tradition of dining in the garden. Banqueting houses were common in princely gardens from the seventeenth century, as recommended by Sir Francis Bacon in his famous essay, *Of Gardens*, published in 1625. Later in the eighteenth century, Horace Walpole wrote a very funny account of alfresco dining at the landscape park of Stowe, where the elderly guests stumbled about in the dark, wrapped in blankets. Only recently, in Provence, a grand dinner party was in progress when the watering system came on. Nobody knew how to turn it off; the guests in all their finery were drenched and the wine watered.

For most of us, dining outdoors is a summer affair, to be enjoyed on warm evenings when the air is scented by tobacco plants, jasmine, wisteria, lilies, or tropical blooms like frangipani. Most eating areas are located beside the house, but a terrace at the end of the garden may give more privacy; and, depending on the orientation of your house, this is where you may receive the best evening light.

Give yourself and your guests enough space to eat and relax without crowding. Measuring your dining room and relating the dimensions to your garden space may give you a better idea of how many people will be able to sit comfortably around a table there, bearing in mind that built-in barbecues, storage space and work surfaces will need extra space. Shield the barbecue from winds that might otherwise engulf your guests and neighbours in smoke. Any work surfaces should be easy to clean and weather resistant.

If all this seems too much, buy a portable barbecue you can trundle round the garden to catch the best sun. Sometimes, impromptu meals give the most pleasure.

Seasoned timber benches and table can be left outside

Folding chairs provide additional seating

Built-in seat with storage underneath

Climbing plants on pergola provide screening and shade

Planting encloses the space

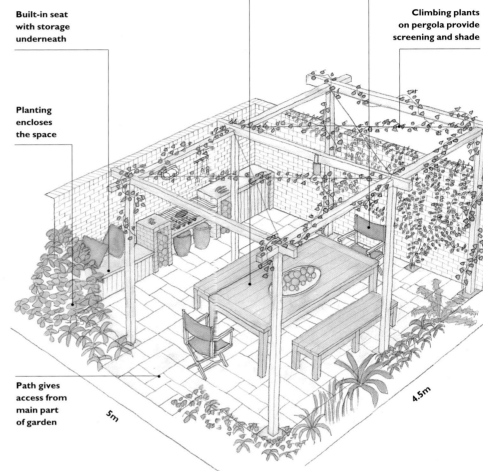

Path gives access from main part of garden

5m

4.5m

4

5

6 Shaded by thin bamboo, this terrace mixes built-in elements with indoor furniture and furnishings to give a 'lived-in' air.
7 Geometric surfaces and grid planting make a shady formal outdoor dining room. Food can be brought from the house or cooked on the built-in barbecue.
8 Repeated slatted lines hold the design together, and throw welcome shadows on the eating area.

6

7

8

Family gardens

'I was always a passionate gardener,' wrote the late Derek Jarman, 'flowers sparkled in my childhood as they do in a medieval manuscript.' It's not just children who turn to the garden to play: adults, too, welcome green space in which to sit, play games or quietly read a book.

In principle a 'family garden' sounds fine, but it can lead to conflict. Children should be seen and not heard. Or heard but not seen. Or both? Or neither? Parents must balance safety precautions with a child's need to explore the world – and where better to venture first than the private, protected world of the garden, with its real and imagined spaces?

Some conflicts are inevitable: between noise and quiet, for example, or between play space and planting space. Those with larger plots can create separate areas in the manner of an Edwardian country house, each with its tennis court, croquet lawn, bowling green, pond, flower borders and wilder woods. But most people today want space to work in several ways at once (often at the same time), and expect it to look good, too.

Very young children's play areas are best sited close to the house so they can be both seen and heard. Sandpits are great for the under-fours; temporary models come in bright, lightweight plastic, or you can include a permanent area in a terrace or in decking. All sandpits

1 Growing children need their own space for wilder games and imaginative play. This adventure camp set among the massive tree trunks of a Cornish garden is ideal.
2 Concealed in the trees like an oversize nesting box, this robust Californian tree-house provides a hideaway for the child in all of us.
3 The best structures are versatile. Dan Pearson's open tepee caters for both children and plants; tarpaulin could just as well turn it into a tent.
4 A permanent paddling pool attracts a cluster of younger children, though babies and toddlers should never play near water unsupervised. A frame of planting creates the illusion of privacy within adult sight.

6

5 A gravelled
Australian courtyard
provides space for a
game of boules. The
French expect a special
kind of surface; other
players may be less
demanding.
6 This tree-house
perched above a wall
creates an exciting
lookout while also
sheltering the sandpit
at ground level.
7 An intriguing stone
path disappears into a
hollowed trunk that is
curtained with climbers
to form a jungly den.

7

should be covered when not in use to
prevent fouling by animals; a waterproof
cover also keeps the sand dry. Most
children adore paddling pools and water
fights on the lawn. But even relatively
shallow ponds hold dangers for toddlers,
so ornamental water features should be
banished or well guarded until the children get older. Then a wildlife pond can
be introduced to exert its quiet fascination on children and adults alike.

As children grow up, their play takes
them further from the house. Brightly
coloured slides and climbing frames can
easily dominate the garden, spatially and
visually. To lessen their impact, choose
forms in natural materials such as wood;
or make a statement with their boldness.
Gardens evolve, like people, through
different ages; you won't have to live
with them forever. A compromise is to
introduce minimal screening, giving you
and your children at least the illusion of
privacy. A deciduous hedge such as hornbeam can be trimmed into a thin line
until it is almost transparent. Trellis
screens, threaded with delicate climbers
or unplanted, will let you see the children
without making them feel policed.

Older children (adults, too) are great
builders of camps, dens and tree-house
retreats. Ladders and tree swings of stout
rope are ideal, or you can turn to one of
the specialist companies offering custom-

made climbing-frames. Far better than
expensive equipment is to give children a
space to call their own, if you possibly
can: perhaps a wilder fringe with trees to
climb and clumps of tall bamboo. Shady
corners and secret routes will stimulate
play and bring children closer to nature.

For most family games, grass is hard to
beat, especially for football, volley ball,
cricket, short tennis and badminton. The
newly developed fine-leaved rye grasses
provide a resilient surface. For croquet,
luxury grasses give a better play if mown
short. Boules requires a rectangle of compacted sand, perhaps under shady trees
to re-create the atmosphere of a French
town. For life-sized chess, create a chessboard by alternating squares of different-
coloured materials such as concrete,
gravel or paving slabs.

And don't forget that the gardening
bug can bite early. Gertrude Jekyll, the
grande dame of Edwardian gardening,
was given her own little garden as a child
'in a nook beyond the shrubbery, with a
seat shaded by a "Boursault Elegans"
rose'. And the American garden writer
Michael Pollan remembers as a four-
year-old escaping the adult radar to the
'garden' he shared with his sister and
their friends: a strip of unplanted ground
squeezed between hedge and fence. At
that age, he said, 'there is room enough
for a world between a lilac and a wall'.

Swimming pools

A near essential in hot southern climates, still a luxury further north, the outdoor swimming pool mixes health with hedonism in a symbol of contemporary life.

While English gardens have offered 'cold baths' since Georgian times (such as William Kent's chilly octagon at Rousham, Oxfordshire), outdoor swimming pools crept into use only after the First World War. The English designer Russell Page – himself a great builder of pools – particularly admired Sir Philip Sassoon's square pool at Port Lympne, Kent, which placed the water line almost at the level of the horizon.

The swimming pool's stylized glamour only arrived with 1930s Hollywood and the extravagantly choreographed films of Esther Williams, which promoted a sleek, modernist design. In 1947, Thomas Church created a powerful icon with the now-famous pool at El Novillero, Sonoma, in California: a dream of curved blue water, spindly oaks in redwood decking, weightless sculpture and distant salt marsh. The modern pool was born.

But pools need space: more than many town gardens can afford. An average-sized pool is 7m to 10m long by 4m to 5m wide (up to 33ft by 16ft). You will also need an area for sitting and sunbathing, housing for filtration and heating, storage space and perhaps a pool house.

Shape will depend on the lines of your garden. Formal rectangles remain popular for small pools, but free-flowing forms can also work well. Consult the work of designers you like to see how they match client needs to site. Russell Page – who disliked circles – announced a particular fascination with the oval, 'which has a mysterious charm and always looks easy'. Lap pools are for serious exercise; their length and narrow width share the elegance of an ornamental canal.

Whatever shape and materials you choose, make sure they fit with the landscape. In northern regions, turquoise tiles can look alien under all but the bluest skies. Dark greens, blues or even battleship grey may merge better with

1 Inspired by the spare geometry of Mexican designer Luis Barragán, a sheet of water sluices playfully into a shower at the edge of a Californian pool.
2 Low planting and a high water line create tufty reflections and give swimmers an exciting eye-level view of the garden. Shaped like a giant punctuation mark, the pool is entered down gentle steps.
3 A ramp leads down to a secluded 'island' in a sixteenth-century Tuscan watering place, creating a peaceful and shady seating area in the middle of the pool.

4 Coherence and contrast slip house and pool into an open site, playing the hard edges of architecture against the sinuous lines of mown grass. Low-level lighting draws guests down towards the pool.
5 A spa pool refreshes a Melbourne garage roof with the soothing sounds of recirculating pool water. Rendered concrete and recycled decking catch the tone of the city skyline.

4

5

the surroundings. The darkest pools give the sharpest reflections, but many people find their black waters forbidding.

Paving and coping materials help to connect the pool with the architecture of house and garden. Choose from textured concrete, stone, brick or timber decking, but take care with slate, tiles and surfaces that may become dangerously slippery when wet. Where a pool is set high against a backdrop of sky or sea, the coping can be omitted on at least one side. This lets water cascade over the pool edge to a drain below, blurring the line between water and sky, or pool and ocean. Planting, too, can ease the pool into its setting, screening the mechanics of filtration and pump room. Hedges may be necessary for privacy: enclosed pools make especially secret spaces.

Heated to much higher temperatures and aerated for massage or therapeutic use, hot tubs or jacuzzis can be used from early spring into autumn. They are often linked to swimming pools, partly for ease of maintenance. Like plunge pools, they fit into gardens that are too small for anything else, positioned on a terrace or recessed into nearby ground.

And don't forget lighting. If the pool is some way from the house, you will need lights to guide your way. The pleasures of a moonlit swim are heightened by the milky iridescence of light underwater.

6

7

6 Set in the roof of a contemporary house in Majorca, this watery shoebox invites guests to swim above the olive trees, but sunbathing requires strong nerves.
7 Organic shapes bring pool and setting together. The rows of clipped santolina hold off the encircling trees.

SMALL-SPACE GARDENING

Size is altogether relative. A small garden in Europe would probably be judged huge by Japanese standards; and yet few Australians or west-coast Americans would want to squeeze their gardens into an average-sized European plot. But it is universally true that for many garden-owners today, space is at a premium and a lot of accepted design advice simply cannot apply. Gardens in towns and cities, particularly, are often little more than yards or back alleys overshadowed by tall buildings. And if you live in an apartment, your 'plot' might extend no further than the window-ledge or balcony.

This need not spell failure. Listen to Vita Sackville-West, planter of Sissinghurst's generous acres: 'Every garden-maker should be an artist along his own lines,' she says firmly. 'This is the only possible way to create a garden, irrespective of size or wealth. The tiniest garden is often the loveliest.'

A fertile imagination can work miracles with limited resources, transforming yards, alleys, porches, verandahs, even ledges and doorways into exuberant miniature gardens. All you need are a handful of pots, some climbers and a few well-chosen features. Success means making the limitations of site work for you, not against you. Many small spaces are enclosed and shady, for example. Choose shrubs, grasses, perennials and ground-cover plants that thrive in these conditions; and foliage plants like ivy, castor-oil, hostas and ferns with their infinitely varied textures and shades of green.

If you don't have a yard to call your own but have access to a roof, consider taking your garden up into the skies. For it is here, among the aerials and chimney stacks of our cities, that many of the most adventurous small gardens can be found. The only rules that must be obeyed are those of the structural engineer and town planner, and the courtesies of the neighbourhood: you make your own aesthetics. By 'greening' your corner of urban rooftop, you are bringing life back into a world dominated by hard-edged concrete and wearing your 'green' credentials proudly on your sleeve.

The flame-red pelargonium perched on the top-floor balcony of a high-rise block proclaims the same belief that gardens are good for us. Creating even the smallest oasis will nourish your spirit and, for the wider community, bring benefits to the street and neighbourhood in which you live.

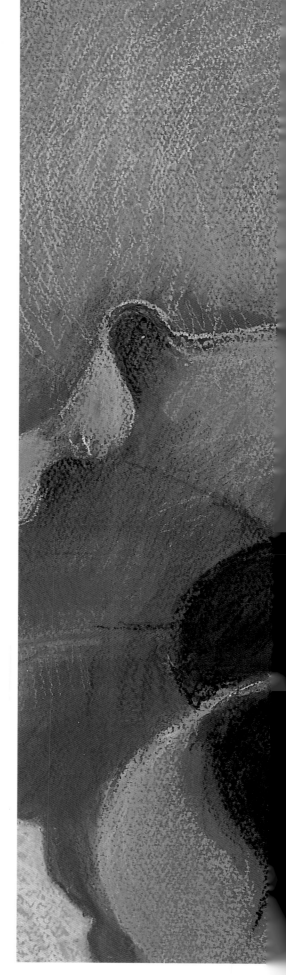

A bucketful of ivy and daisies and a pot of pansies turn a window-ledge into a garden. Creativity feeds on boundaries and limitations; the sonnet brings as much joy as the epic poem.

Front gardens

1 A wooden ramp leads to the front door across a sandy planting of grasses, spiked and feathered and crowned like discarded toupees.
2 Low planting allowed to creep between paving stones softens the harshness of the car-parking space. The path's whiteness directs first-time visitors to the hidden door.
3 This elegant city garden is English to its core. A granite path set within cobblestones indicates the car has given way to people and plants. The gate implies privacy without compromising security.

The front garden is where private meets public, an encounter that different cultures treat in very different ways.

In *Second Nature*, Michael Pollan saw the front lawn in America as 'the collective face of suburbia .... In the back, you could do pretty much whatever you wanted, but out front you had to take account of the community's wishes and its self-image.' Much of Europe prefers private, defensible space, with obvious boundaries and a statement of personal taste. But as the front garden opens out to public view, it often hovers uncomfortably between the two spheres.

Small front gardens do present design problems. Security demands the house should be visible from the street; yet robbed of privacy, the front garden offers little scope for leisure use. As car ownership increases and parking gets harder, more front lawns succumb to asphalt.

Clarity of purpose can usually resolve some of these conflicts. Thomas Church, as usual, offers sound advice: 'In making

4 A house in colonial Williamsburg, Virginia, welcomes the visitor with its seamless transition from public to private space and bold declaration that it has nothing to hide.
5 Cacti and other succulents grouped around a magnificent *Fouquieria splendens* lead the eye towards the wide, shallow steps that curve round to the entrance.

the entrance a place of welcome,' he wrote in *Gardens are for People*, 'simplicity and harmony are the most important ingredients.' Vita Sackville-West put forward a different approach that still maintains a clear, guiding idea. 'If I were suddenly required to leave my own garden and to move into a bungalow . . .' (you can almost hear her aristocratic tones), 'I should have no hesitation at all about ruffling the front garden into a wildly unsymmetrical mess and making it as near as possible into a cottage garden.' Somewhere between these two extremes you may find the design that works best for you, ferrying guests to your door and complementing the architecture of house and street.

If you must have your own parking area, use dark paving materials to hide oil spillage and staining, and soften the drive with low planting strips to fit the space between wheels. Gravel is attractively crunchy underfoot and thoroughly disliked by burglars. Where space allows, use different paving for cars and people: granite setts and brick, for instance, or brick and gravel. In larger areas, try to provide a turning circle or reversing bay to prevent dangerous manoeuvres on the road, but don't let the car dominate your approach to the front of the house. Use restrained lighting to illuminate the front door for guests at night – and to help you find your key and the keyhole.

Doorways often cry out for planting. A formal pair of evergreens grown in tubs, such as bay or oddly clipped box, gives a focus to the entrance and clearly identifies the front door. More informal groups of containerized plants also work well, especially on wide porches and pathways. To provide an unexpected touch, you could use a plant with which you would not normally associate your climate: for instance, Australian bottle brushes (*Callistemon citrinus*) could be used in temperate Europe, and further north, to give a Mediterranean feeling, *Magnolia grandiflora*.

Climbers and shrubs relieve the dullness of blank walls. Ramblers, climbing roses and clematis will need support from a frame; or use self-clinging ivies, Virginia creeper and climbing hydrangea. To give greater mass, bulky deciduous or evergreen shrubs can be used. Tiny front lawns are often a bother to mow: so opt for low-maintenance ground cover and shrub borders instead. Simple, bold blocks of textural planting work well in restricted spaces, breaking up the paved expanse and softening the outline of the house. Plants can also be used to screen dustbins stored at the front.

Aim to keep the house in view of the road. Tall hedges, walls or fences give greater privacy but they also shield unwelcome intruders. Walls or hedges at waist height will identify boundaries without screening the front garden, or you might introduce more informal boundary planting, again kept low.

For open-plan estates and shared front gardens, the first requirement is to make the space look and feel cared for. Michael Pollan called it democratic landscaping. 'To maintain your portion of this landscape was part of your civic duty,' he wrote with a sly smile. 'You voted each November, joined the PTA, and mowed the lawn every Saturday.' But if tidy lawns (to you) spell democratic gloom, find other ways of pursuing the communal ideal – with shared planters, perhaps, and matching horticultural themes.

6 Clean lines, sparsely planted bamboos and gravel beds suggest a Japanese influence on this Sydney garden by Vladimir Sitta. Boxes of still black water further add to its calm.

Balconies and window-ledges

1 A first-floor balcony can just squeeze in table and chairs that happily borrow the colour and greenery from nearby.
2 Table and benches are built into the structure of a sheltered verandah, positioned for its sweeping views across forest and distant hills.

3 Secured by panelled glass, a barely furnished Australian verandah takes the house into the trees, dissolving the usual boundaries between inside and out. Struts in the decking encourage the eye to look outside.
4 Every city-dweller longs for a corner of outdoor space. Here, plants in graduated rows bring shelter, privacy and life to this suntrap balcony.
5 Pot-grown bananas and spikier exotics invite the jungle up on to the verandah of this wooden house – an opposite approach to the merging of boundaries. Here, the decking takes the eye along the verandah.

Narrow spaces do not restrict the urge to garden. In Germany, groups of neighbours often coordinate planting displays; while in southern Europe, individual plants are used extensively to create façades awash with foliage and colour.

Householders in Britain have been tending their windowboxes for centuries. In his classic of 1722, *The City Gardener*, the London nurseryman and author Thomas Fairchild recommended oranges and myrtles for balconies, and elaborate waterworks modelled on Versailles, 'to be fixed at Pleasure to the Water-Pipe, and changed for others if we saw convenient'.

Some balconies need little or no planting: their attraction lies in their detailing, or in the graceful sweep of climbing foliage against the façade. A balcony can equally enclose an intimate garden or, in modern buildings especially, offer scope for ambitious planting that relies for effect on both plants and planters.

Choose containers for either harmony or contrast – terracotta against a cast-iron balcony, for instance, or polished steel against stone. Use plastic or fibreglass for any larger, unseen containers, as these are generally lighter than other materials and hold water well.

Most plants, including climbers, can adapt to pot conditions: check their rooting needs when you buy. Larger containers give your plants more of a chance to survive adverse conditions such as wind and drought (itself made worse by wind). Seaside species often adapt well, as do grasses, bamboos and small-leaved plants that lose less moisture. Large-leaved herbaceous perennials and plants with delicate flowers may succumb to wind damage and scorch. An irrigation system or tank will make watering easier.

Often restricted to summer annuals, windowboxes offer scope for seasonal planting: winter and spring bulbs set among neatly trimmed evergreens, perhaps, or more permanent evergreens. Include scented species such as lavender for open windows. On a kitchen window-ledge you can grow vegetables to provide

4

5

6

at least a small crop – many dwarf varieties have been developed expressly for this purpose. Try herbs for a sunny windowsill in the kitchen, both for picking and for their aromatic qualities. When arranging plants in windowboxes, think about the view from inside as well as out. Remember that sunlight shining through petals can fill your room with colour.

Windowboxes come in timber, terracotta, or nearly maintenance-free plastic, concrete and aluminium. You can paint wood or terracotta to harmonize or contrast with the woodwork of your house. Fix the box securely to the ledge or – in houses with little or no ledge – attach it to brackets. Allow a minimum compost depth of 20cm (8in); and spread a bottom layer of gravel or small crocks over the drainage holes in the bottom.

Balcony pots and windowboxes have traditionally used peat-based compost as their growing medium. Environmental concern about peat extraction favours the use of alternatives: loam-based composts have a good structure and retain moisture and fertility. A number of alternatives, like coir, are still being tested.

6 A German turfed roof gives ecological insulation. Bamboos and trellised roses soften the cleanly modern lines of the architecture on the balcony below.
7 The flaming red pelargoniums repeated on balconies across this hill-top village are a classic image of southern France.

7

Courtyards and alleys

Two traditions in particular inspire the smallest gardens: the Japanese courtyard and the paradise gardens of Islam. From Islam the tiny modern courtyard has borrowed the sight and gentle sound of splashing water. And, like paradise, it turns its back on the world outside. But spatial constraints have also produced some of the most striking contemporary designs that owe their success to innovation rather than tradition.

Japanese simplicity and restraint fits well with a modernist approach to design and planting. Instead of disguising the boundaries, walls are brought into the design; and views or scenes created from a simple combination of foliage texture, paving patterns and surfaces. Often, these back- or side-alley gardens are kept behind glass; Shodo Suzuki created such a viewing courtyard consisting only of quarried stone blocks, cascading water and a single ivy. Another courtyard by the same designer has a chessboard flooring of gravel, marble and dumpy moss, planted with spindly, multi-stemmed *Stewartia pseudocamellia*.

Your choice of plants will depend on growing conditions – sunlight especially. Shade-lovers are most likely to survive dark, cramped spaces: they offer exciting foliage textures and a restful mix of greens. If possible, plant directly into the ground, otherwise use containers and raised beds to create rooting depth. Even tallish shrubs and trees can be used, as long as the effect is not claustrophobic. Any unsightly structures can be masked by climbers, checking first that they are suitable for your light conditions.

Such small, inward-looking spaces can be theatrical in their effects and changed as often as you wish. Mirrors and *trompe l'oeil* add unexpected depth; try something else when they lose their ability to surprise. Jaded walls can be painted, or whitewashed for tree and plant shadows (limewash also keeps the bugs at bay). Warm reds and orange advance, making a small space shrink further; blues and greens recede, adding depth.

Fencing materials like bamboo screens or woven willow hurdles have exciting textures. Light, natural or artificial, adds a mysterious density if shone through patterned or frosted glass; small spaces should be lit subtly. Avoid direct glare by washing the surrounding walls with a background glow or directing lights into the planting. Lighting focal points from the side gives better shadows.

As always, the soundest advice is to stay simple. A single paving surface, for example, unites the space, while small-scale units like stone setts, cobbles and brick will increase the illusion of space. Gravel adds textural interest, is easy to lay and relatively cheap. Use it to cover existing hard surfaces, or to hide eyesores like drain covers. Concrete can work well if used sympathetically, and will gain a patina fairly quickly if washed over with yoghurt or unpasteurized milk.

1 A palm-fronded modern courtyard combines the virtues of an Islamic paradise with an outdoor living room.
2 Low box surrounds a hardy trachycarpus in a walled garden by Anthony Noel.
3 Bold good humour inspires Johnny Woodford's backyard. Yucca and steel carrots hover over ferns, phormium and sinister lily turf. A chain deters neighbours' cats.

4

5

6

4 Basement wells are often shady. Here, even the tree trunk has been whitewashed to refract light. The delicate metalwork of chairs and ornament adds line without mass.

5+**6** A Moorish-style courtyard in south Melbourne, owned by tile-importer Jurgen Plecko, transplants the essence of paradise into the heart of a contemporary house: a shady palm, splashing water, a patch of greenery. Wall lights create a different energy at night.

7 A wildlife pond and natural planting bring the wide outdoors to a family backyard in Haarlem, the Netherlands. Changes in paving break up and enlarge the space.

8 This small London courtyard re-creates the jungle with strong foliage shapes and plants that grow up towards the light. Flowers add tropical reds and oranges: pastel shades would look out of place here.

7

8

Roof gardens

1

2

3

4

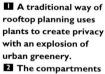

1 A traditional way of rooftop planning uses plants to create privacy with an explosion of urban greenery.
2 The compartments of this New York rooftop re-create an entire formal garden with sheltered seating, clipped shrubs and climber-clad walls.
3 Designers Delaney, Cochran & Castillo bring the jokes and shocks of the avant-garde to a commercial rooftop in San Francisco, with assorted boulders, painted concrete and regimented planting.

Roof gardens revel in extremes – of light and space and climate, of cluttered roofscapes and wide open skies. And because they are so unexpected, they offer freedom from earthbound conventions.

First, establish your design concept. Is this a garden that happens to be on a roof, or a roof space that 'gardens' with skylights and chimneys and sweeping city views? Will your garden be visited or simply viewed? Do you want to bring wildlife and greenery back to the city? In Stuttgart, Germany, roofs are planted with grass, ground cover, climbers and creepers, for the environment's sake as much as aesthetics: vegetation insulates the buildings, and helps the city breathe.

The most famous early roof gardens were the Hanging Gardens of Babylon, reputedly built by King Nebuchadnezzar II in the sixth century BC. But the roof garden's widespread appeal came only with the new building technologies of the last century or so, especially advances in waterproofing and wide-span structural supports. Some of modern design's greatest names have created roof gardens: the robust geometry of Le Corbusier and Frank Lloyd Wright; the fluid flamboyance of Roberto Burle Marx; the walled emptiness of Luis Barragán. More recent designers like Topher Delaney and Andy Cochran have also been captivated by the roof garden's aerial spirit.

Safe construction relies upon solid structural support, the use of lightweight materials and a dependable waterproofing and drainage system. For new houses, the roof area can be strengthened during construction. To convert an existing roof, consult a structural engineer: the roof may be strong enough to take waterproofing, draining layers and paving laid directly. Alternatively, the parapet walls may be able to support timber decking, at the same time disguising ugly or uneven surfaces and aiding drainage.

Good enclosure is crucial for safety and comfort. Balustrade or perimeter fencing must always conform to local building and planning regulations. Wind breaks

5

6 The symmetry of chessboard gravel planted with potted foxgloves echoes the shape of windows in surrounding blocks. A whitewashed chimney hung with miniature shrub balls adds a touch of humour.
7 Here is a Japanese rooftop created for show: organic topiary forms that flow into each other, reminiscent of cloud forms, which are of course entirely appropriate for a garden in the sky.

6
7

will probably be necessary, though you won't want to block panoramic views. Solid barriers cause turbulence; use semi-permeable screens instead, like stretched canvas, trellis or woven wire. Glass can deflect modest winds, but needs cleaning.

Planting must usually be contained within raised beds or containers, using lightweight aggregates as a drainage layer below a relatively shallow compost. With all shallow, free-draining growing media, plan for an irrigation system, or at least a rooftop water tank. For purpose-built roof gardens, planting tanks can be sunk into the structure so that trees and shrubs seem to grow directly out of the roof, like a crown of hair.

4 Inspired by the serenity of Japanese gravel gardens, a Santa Barbara rooftop by Isobelle C. Greene creates its inward focus with the sparest means: gravel, grass, stones, concrete, low-level seating and beautifully shaped pots.
5 Shallow-rooting birch trees give this New York rooftop a mad haircut, declaring that out on the roof, the imagination reigns.

PLANTING DESIGN

Plants are the very essence of a garden, fleshing out the bones of its basic framework to create a mood and convey a particular style. Along with the hard landscaping, the plants we choose and the way we put them together define a garden's overall character. The plants are your garden's living element: you must always take their needs into account, choosing only subjects that fit their environment and selecting partners that are compatible in every way.

Acquiring plant knowledge takes time, but understanding how best to use our plants greatly enhances the pleasure we derive from them. It also lets us move more confidently and freely through the design process, knowing, for example, that a selected plant will flower at the same time as its neighbour and will not overwhelm it, or will, perhaps, provide a lustrous foil for it all year round. Like any other art form, good planting relies for its effects on the creation of harmonies or contrasts of form and shape, colour and texture. And, as the plant palette is so immense, whether you are a first-timer or an old hand, planting design is a never-ending process of discovery.

In designing with plants we join our practical knowledge with our aesthetic appreciation of their characteristics. If you select plants first and foremost for their suitability to the environment, and then for their individual characteristics and their compatibility with each other, you can finally weave them together in such a way that their colours, texture and movement sing out. The seasonal aspect is one of the greatest rewards of putting together a garden: the best planting designs are multi-layered, providing a succession of seasonal effects and an ever-changing cloak of foliage all year round.

UNDERSTANDING PLANTS

Plants are some of the most tenacious and adaptable life forms on earth. On a vertiginous mountainside or in the bowels of a swamp, some kind of plant life will have found a niche for itself: their desire to grow against all odds is encapsulated in the phrase 'nature abhors a vacuum'. Good gardening is the ability to harness this tenacity, and good planting design the skill to piece the elements together, reinterpreting nature in the garden setting. Knowing something of plant biology – their habits, needs and life cycles, and the habitats in which they naturally grow – will help you to use them and care for them better.

Plants are divided into several groups: woody trees and shrubs, bulbs, perennials, climbers, annuals and biennials. These groups perform very different roles in a garden and it is essential that each should slot into the garden dynamic in the right place. For example, the wrong choice of tree can plunge a small garden into shade, just as the right tree will revitalize a space previously devoid of foliage. Understanding plants will help you sift through the many thousands there are to choose from, which can often seem overwhelming; we are spoilt for choice, with species gathered from around the world as well as native plants, and improved varieties being introduced every year. It is all too easy for an unruly eclecticism to develop in the garden, with plants from wildly differing altitudes and latitudes competing for space and attention.

If possible, garden with nature, not against it. With water increasingly scarce, it is more important than ever to take plant habitats into account so that, for example, in a site prone to drying out in the summer months, you group drought-tolerant plants together. The days of high-maintenance schemes, grouping plants with wildly differing needs, are numbered. Plants are fairly adaptable, however; once you understand their habits, you can push the boundaries of planting schemes to combine your carefully chosen ingredients, complementing and contrasting to maximum effect.

A garden should work on some level every day of the year; an understanding of the life cycle and seasonality of your plants will let you orchestrate your plantings so they look good from spring to winter. As in a musical symphony, in a carefully planned planting scheme the seasonal cycles have no beginnings and no ends, each movement linking seamlessly with the next.

1 Nature is given the upper hand in Gilles Clément's garden, where cool, leafy conditions promote the growth of mosses, ferns and wood sorrel.
2 Late-flowering *Deschampsia cespitosa* and *Phlomis russeliana* strike an effective textural balance in this monochrome drought-tolerant planting for a sunny situation.

3 The banyan tree's buttress roots provide a sure footing for any plant that can tolerate the dry, dense shade of its canopy.

4

5

4 With its powerful, upright growth, bamboo will immediately furnish a garden with a distinct atmosphere, provided the conditions are fertile.

5 Growing from seed in just a few weeks, red cabbage can be grown for food or for the appeal of its glaucous, crinkled foliage.

Plant types and characteristics

An understanding of plants is a vital part of good planting design and will prevent you from making unsuitable choices and combinations. Reading books, visiting other gardens and observing what grows together in the wild will help you to focus your choice of plants more clearly. And knowing about their characteristics is made easier by a broad classification system which breaks plants down into groups with shared attributes and life cycles as well as roughly similar needs.

TREES AND SHRUBS

The largest plants, trees and shrubs, make up the most stable and enduring element in the garden. They provide the scheme's three-dimensional framework, contributing permanent form, acting as a foil and providing screening, shelter and shade for other plants – and people.

Wherever you are gardening, you will be able to use something from this wide group, whether you need shelter from salty sea winds or shade in a sunny court-yard. However, you should do some research at the planning stage to avoid choosing the wrong tree or shrub. It is vital to choose plants of an appropriate size and rate of growth for their position, although if necessary they can be pruned to keep them within bounds; young saplings can all too readily lose the elegance of youth and become unruly. Their placement is also crucial: make sure they do not block out valuable light or cast unwanted shade. Keep trees at a reasonable distance away from buildings, to prevent their roots from damaging walls and their leaves clogging gutters.

Trees and shrubs will provide many different effects. Evergreens like the glossy-leaved hollies and the strawberry tree (*Arbutus unedo*) bestow a solid form and constant presence on the garden, in contrast to deciduous plants, which look altogether lighter once they have shed their leaves. Deciduous trees and shrubs, including fruit trees, will open up views in winter, allowing light to flood down to ground level. They also bring an essential element of seasonal change to the garden: freshness, and sometimes blossom, in spring, and rich colour in the autumn. A combination of evergreen and deciduous plants is ideal, lending both a constant anchor and a lighter, fluctuating element to your planting.

Trees and shrubs tend to be viewed as slow-growing, but their ever-enlarging bulk can soon create a strong impression. In gardens that have plenty of space you can incorporate slow-growing trees and shrubs, like *Magnolia grandiflora*, with faster growers, like *Buddleja davidii*; the latter will provide initial shelter and bulk but can be removed once the magnolia is established. While buying larger trees and shrubs will give immediate impact, younger plants establish quicker in the long run, outstripping the initially larger introductions. A sapling will outgrow a semi-mature standard within three to four years, because the older tree takes much longer to acclimatize to its new environment and to recover from the shock of root disturbance.

CLIMBING PLANTS

Climbers are a large and disparate group, defined by their habit of growth. Most are woody plants, although some are perennials and a few, like the morning glories (*Ipomoea*), are short-lived annuals. The main way in which climbers differ from trees and shrubs is that their habit leads them to rely on something other than their own woody stems for support; most climbers are opportunists and, given support, will grow indefinitely. Without it, they will sprawl on the ground and, although they can be used as ground cover, their dominating nature means that they will scale anything put in their way. In the wild they are often found in woodland, with their roots in shade and their heads in sunshine; this is also how they are happiest in gardens, where they are an invaluable softening element.

The group can be further sub-divided according to the way in which they climb. This influences the form of support you give them, as many need initial help to set them on their way. Twiners, such as honeysuckle and wisteria, will wind around any vertical support narrow enough for them to encompass. The creepers, like ivies and Virginia creeper, have aerial roots or suckers which cling to a solid surface like a wall or a fence. Clematis have developed modified leaves that twine around stems or other leaves, twigs or wires, and passion flowers (*Passiflora*) have tendrils which, once attached, act like springs, coiling and hauling the plant skyward. The ramblers, which include brambles (*Rubus*) and a

1 Spanish broom (*Spartium junceum*) and annual wild poppies live side by side in a hot, dry position: inspiration indeed for a domestic planting.
2 Olive trees, grasses (*Stipa tenuissima*) and lavender have been used in bold sweeps across this hillside in California, framed by the strong vertical forms of cypress. The olives screen the building, accentuating the height of the mound, while in the foreground the grass provides movement and drama.
3 A mixed planting of shrubs and aromatic herbs densely planted as ground cover protect the soil all year round. The distinct shape of the stone pine's canopy dominates the planting, taking the eye upwards.

1

2

3

number of roses, use thorns like a grapple as their method of securing themselves. There is also a group of lax shrubs like *Solanum crispum* or ceanothus which do not actually climb, but which have an unwieldy nature that benefits from the support of a wall. Many climbers need regular maintenance to keep them within bounds and flowering their best.

PERENNIALS

In the wild, where there is enough light and water, a level of non-woody plants will form an 'understorey', or lower layer of planting, to smother and protect the soil surface. These include perennials, bulbs, annuals and biennials, but it is mostly perennials which occupy this level as soon as there is a gap in the shrubby layer. This adaptable group can be found in wetlands, drylands, shade and burning heat. Perennials differ from the woody plants, which store energy in their bark, in that they rely on their thick, fleshy

roots, or a collar of foliage at ground level, to replenish their growth from year to year. Some perennials have evergreen foliage, which gives year-round effect, but most are herbaceous, dying down to below ground level in winter.

As a group, the perennials vary from close-matted ground cover like lamiums, periwinkles and herbaceous geraniums, to bulky foliage plants like giant rhubarb (*Gunnera manicata*). In between, there is a range of herbaceous plants grown for their foliage, including herbs themselves, valued for their form and texture as well as their fragrance and culinary use. One of the joys of perennial leaves is that they are constantly being replenished and renewed. Some foliage plants may go through a complete metamorphosis during the seasons; the moisture-loving *Darmera peltata*, for example, rises from a tight knuckle of growth to unfurl plate-shaped leaves 1m (3ft) across in a matter of days. The same can be said of many

Tree

Multi-stemmed tree

Climber

Shrub

Trees, shrubs and woody climbers give a planting scheme its initial three-dimensional quality, also drawing the eye upwards and capturing the breeze. Evergreen or deciduous, they give the garden its permanent structure. It is important to be aware of the ultimate size of woody plants before introducing them into the garden.

Perennial

Sub-shrub

Bulb

With lower-growing sub-shrubs, perennials provide the bulk of the understorey in a scheme, covering and protecting the soil below loftier subjects. Bulbs contribute flowering interest in a single season before dying down completely.

flowering perennials, which provide the predominance of colour in the garden. Whereas a shrub will take about five to seven years to mature, the perennials can start to work in the first season. They are ideal for providing visual links within the garden and for covering the seasonal changes, so there is always something fresh and interesting to look at.

In gardens, perennials have traditionally been used in isolation in borders and flower beds. But more recently there has been great interest in their ability, when planted *en masse*, to clothe the entire soil surface, which reduces long-term maintenance as well as providing a modern garden aesthetic. Interest has also developed in the ornamental grasses, which bring movement, grace and informality into planting schemes.

Perennials are now being bred for resilience, with the need for staking being replaced by self-supporting varieties that are also able to extend the seasonal interest by drying, where they stand, into architectural skeletons: fennel, the eryngiums and many grasses have an intriguing winter outline. Although some perennials still require frequent division to keep them vigorous, the modern approach is to use varieties that are longer-lasting and less labour-intensive. For example, the tall, purple-flowered *Verbena bonariensis* will flower for five to six months. No longer confined to the herbaceous border, today perennials are even being used as a replacement for park bedding in public spaces, while in city plots many perennials, such as *Festuca glauca*, can be confined to containers.

1 Early in the season drifts of bulbs – here, winter aconites (*Eranthis hyemalis*) and snowdrops – make the most of high light levels before the tree canopy develops, bringing sheets of colour to dark corners.
2 Planting should be designed to provide long-term interest and seasonal fluctuations. Here clipped box gives formal structure to the summer informality of perennial hostas and shade-loving ferns.
3 Drought-tolerant perennials – aloes, agaves and echeverias – are juxtaposed for their textural and sculptural qualities. This planting by Ruth Bancroft brings interest to an arid part of the garden throughout the year.
4 A drift of annual *Cosmos bipinnatus* makes an effervescent contrast to the weighty tree trunk, flowering from midsummer until the first frosts.

BULBS

Bulbs, along with corms and tubers, occupy a unique niche. Their underground storage organs enable them to grow rapidly, beating the competition before leaves emerge on the trees in spring or before conditions in hot, dry sites become too harsh for growth; they then survive dormant underground for the remainder of the year.

Spring bulbs such as tulips, narcissi and the tuberous erythroniums play a vital role in the garden, enlivening shady corners which, in the summer months, are too dark for a lower level of growth. You can use bulbs under shrubs in the 'dead' area left exposed by the deciduous plants that die down in winter; and in spring, bulbs will enliven grassy areas. Planted among perennials, bulbs can extend the season of a planting both at the beginning of the year and at the end, using the valuable space among other growth. As long as their leaves receive plenty of sunshine, *Amaryllis belladonna*, colchicums and nerines will provide flashes of autumn colour at the front of a border that is flagging at the end of the summer season.

3

ANNUALS AND BIENNIALS

Grown from seed and completing their whole life cycle within one or two seasons, annuals and biennials encompass border and container plants, climbers, herbs and vegetables. Their vivid and immediate flowers will provide interest among long-term plantings, or they can be used as a more mobile element within a perennial scheme. They can be sown either *in situ* or in a protected situation before being planted out for an early display, or to inject colour into an area where it may be lacking. Eschscholzias and nasturtiums, for instance, will self-seed among perennials, making a new garden feel 'lived in'.

Although most vegetables fall into the same category as annuals and biennials, because of their specific horticultural requirements they tend to be grown separately. However, many can be used to provide impact in planting schemes: take, for instance, the rich foliage of ruby chard or the red flowers of runner beans. Gourds can be used to clothe arches or fences with their rapidly growing foliage; globe artichokes, with their architectural form and silvered leaves, can create dramatic accents in the border.

4

Planting and ecology

1

Gardening has taken many different forms over the centuries, from the manicured parterres of Renaissance gardens to the naturalistic garden settings of today. To some extent, the garden has always represented man pitching his energies against nature . . . and nature resisting. But attitudes are changing, and today we are living in one of the most interesting periods of gardening history, in which our rich heritage is being coupled with concern for our increasingly vulnerable environment. The more ecologically sensitive approach to gardening that has developed over the past few decades looks to nature for its inspiration as well as its answers. By combining the diversity of plant resources and modern horticultural expertise, we can develop garden schemes that are entirely appropriate to their environment.

PLANTS IN THE WILD

In nature, plants are entirely governed by the climatic conditions and local microclimate in which they are growing. There is no helping hand to supply extra water when it is needed, nor any additional protection when the weather turns cold. Plants have to survive where they are – or die. There is an indigenous flora in all but the harshest environments, whether in the dark recesses of a canyon, or on the wind-blown, shifting dunes of a coastline. Only seriously damaged environments, such as man-made deserts created by drastic alterations to the landscape, are devoid of plant life.

Across the range of habitats, plants form communities which can become the model for the planting in our gardens. Observing and learning from nature will pave the way to a more measured approach to gardening. This does not necessarily imply that the garden has to take on a wild appearance; it merely requires you to respect the existing conditions and work with, not against, them. The result will be a lower-maintenance form of gardening, since you will not be spending hours battling with acid-loving plants in an alkaline soil, for example, or watering moisture-loving perennials on a dry site. Instead, there are many alkaline-tolerant plants, from lilacs to pulsatillas, from which to choose, as well as a vast range of perennials, such as achilleas or Jerusalem sage, which flourish in dry conditions.

At a basic level, there is a natural succession of plants that, over time, will colonize any piece of land left untouched by either agriculture or urban development. The derelict land will initially be taken over by grasses and robust perennials but, as time moves on, other plants will start to colonize the grassland. Bramble seeds, for example, will be dropped by birds, and those of scrubby species like buddleja blown in by the wind. In their turn, fast-growing pioneer woodland trees like silver birch will invade the brambles and shade out the grasses. The shelter they provide will be home to a new set of shade-tolerant species like ferns, mosses and foxgloves. Forest communities, such as oaks and ivy, represent the 'climax' vegetation, the tree-clad environment that is the final stage in this ecological cycle. Although this succession is based on competition, its development illustrates the communal nature of plants: to take plants out of their ecosystem – whether grassland or woodland – is to remove them from a balanced community where like grows with like and protection is offered at all levels by other plants.

With a little lateral thinking, garden sites can be matched to similar conditions found in nature. A windswept roof garden, for instance, has parallels with conditions at the seaside or those on exposed hillsides, and plant communities growing there can be used as inspiration for what may survive on a roof. Choose from any of the drought-tolerant grasses, which roll their leaves along their length to prevent unnecessary exposure to the wind, or the low, mound-forming plants like thyme and thrift (*Armeria maritima*), which have reduced their stature and

2
3

4

leaves to an absolute minimum. The silver-leaved plants, such as *Convolvulus cneorum*, which are commonly found in exposed situations would also be ideal, their leaves providing a reflective surface to deflect the sun's rays.

Faced with an entirely different situation, like a dark and dingy alley, you can use the forest as inspiration. The forest floor is home to many plant species, including ferns, epimediums, tellimas, pulmonarias and hellebores, which are entirely appropriate to the confines of a shady passageway. The microclimate here is based upon shelter, the walls of the buildings providing the equivalent of a forest canopy, so shade-loving plants that have developed light-catching, broad leaves are ideal: as they are less prone to dry out, they can afford to be larger. Indeed, in an exposed situation they would act like sails in the wind and fail to cope. If your land is wet, it is sensible to look at wetland species adapted to moist conditions, rather than attempting to drain it. Suitable plants might be any of those you see round the margins of ponds and lakes in the wild, including willows, dogwoods and irises.

NATURE AS INSPIRATION

Looking to the environment for ideas makes good sense visually as well as horticulturally. A more relaxed, naturalistic approach allows lawns (or parts of lawns) to be turned into meadows whose close-knit communities are, by nature, mixed. You could let your borders mingle and merge naturalistically, growing plants together in such a way that they build up communities that support each other rather than stand in isolation, exposed and vulnerable. You might juxtapose this informality with a more rigorous attention to order elsewhere. A mown path through long grass will appear planned rather than random, and a clipped hedge will bring order and a focus to a relaxed planting.

Nature should be a constant reference point when designing with plants: a scheme that works has a settled and enduring quality, setting up patterns and rhythms that imitate those found in the wild. Wherever you are gardening and whatever style you adopt, planting for natural conditions is the surest route to a balance – which is, after all, what good planting design is all about.

1 In all but the most inhospitable of environments, growth will colonize the ground. Here, wet conditions allow mosses and horsetails to proliferate.
2 This desert flora is dependent on little more than night dews for its moisture, proving that there is a plant for even the most arid situation.
3 Any shafts of light penetrating the dense canopy of beech will sustain the understorey that has evolved to inhabit this woodland's cool conditions.
4 The meeting of earth and water is bridged by the invasive rushes which have colonized the shallow mud around this lake. They encircle the wetland zone between water and the shrubby growth of the oaks on higher ground.

PLANTING PRINCIPLES

A planting design has to work on many levels. First and foremost, the plants should be happy in their environment, but other aspects must be taken into account for a scheme to reach its full potential. It must be a truly three-dimensional composition, working from the very top level – the canopy – through every layer, right down to the surface of the soil itself.

Time adds a fourth dimension: a scheme should be viable not only from day to day, but from season to season and year to year. Building in room for change is an integral part of planting design; understanding the life cycles of plants is a vital component of this.

Armed with information about how plants behave and what they need, you can think in broad terms about how to use them. Planting principles are based on a combination of practical knowledge and an awareness of the aesthetic values of colour, form and texture. In a garden, good planting has the same effect as a well-chosen fabric laid over the bare bones of an interior: it sets a style and creates an atmosphere for the space. The style may be formal or informal, traditional or modern, controlled and minimalist or lavish and abundant: planting that suits a country cottage will not necessarily sit happily in a roof garden or a city courtyard, and vice versa.

Planting as an art form combines elements of painting and sculpture, relying for its effects on the creation of harmonies or contrasts of colour, form and texture and the setting up of patterns and rhythms within a scheme. Certain guiding principles have evolved, like the colour wheel. But once these are understood, rules can – and should – be broken; often the most exciting plant combinations are the most unexpected. One way of trying out plant associations is to make posies of flowers and foliage to test what works well together, just as an interior designer might experiment with fabric swatches.

By following the guidelines for planting design outlined in the following pages, you will create a garden that works in both the short and the long term, and that allows for surprises. When it is based on a sound set of principles, good planting works like a harness, rather than a manacle, applied to nature. The skill is to juxtapose plants in a scheme that works in its environment and breathes life into the garden. It is the intimate meeting of man and nature – an alchemy that is never the same for any two people or situations.

1 The soft, feathery growth of bronze fennel is a foil for the strong form and colour of the day lily (*Hemerocallis lilioasphodelus*).
2 A birch copse on the edge of a woodland breaks the darkness of the trees beyond. The flowery meadow has been encouraged to spread right up to the edge of the wood.

3 *Euphorbia × martinii* is an example of a plant that is as good in foliage as it is in flower. A dependable perennial for a hot, dry position, its rosy young growth is enhanced by early-morning dew.

4 The opulent flowers of *Papaver orientale* 'Beauty of Livermere' make it well worth incorporating into a planting for its impact, though it flowers for three tantalizingly brief weeks only.

5 The leaves of red-veined *Begonia grandis* subsp. *evansiana* have a clear outline and beautiful colour detail.

4

5

Creating style and mood

Style is as much a factor in planting as it is in the architecture or ornament of a garden. You may have laid out strong lines with the hard landscaping, but it is plants that clothe the garden, creating its atmosphere. Deciding on a style – it may be clipped formality, oriental simplicity, romantic overflow – will shape (and restrict) your plant selection, giving the design cohesion. Remember that less is far clearer than more: a plant list should always be pruned by at least half early on if a coherent style is to develop.

Having selected the plants, it is the way you use them that will give your garden its direction. The planting style will depend on the overall look you have chosen for your outdoor retreat and on matching it to its location. Combinations of plants can influence a space to such an extent that they either lift the spirits or dash them. Fortunately, the planting is one of the most mobile, adjustable elements in a garden and, with judicious plant combinations, sombre areas can be enlivened within a few months. For

example, juxtaposing the bright foliage of Bowles' golden sedge (*Carex elata* 'Aurea') with *Galium odoratum* will very effectively bring life into a shady corner.

FORMAL STYLES

Formality in the garden is best achieved with a pared-down collection of plants, allowing the eye to concentrate on their form, rather than the distraction of varied colours and textures. Symmetrical placement reinforces a formal style, while clipped, manicured planting creates a mood of control that is entirely appropriate for a minimalist scheme or as a link with the hard, structural elements in or adjoining the garden.

Hedging makes an excellent formal element, but it is a good idea to alleviate dark hedges like yew by planting something lighter in front, such as kniphofias, if you do not want the effect to be too sombre. Emerald-green box and deciduous hedging such as beech and hornbeam appear less heavy. Hedging has brought a mood of restrained formality to gardens

1 Using nothing more than clipped box, a contemporary Japanese courtyard garden makes a graphic, minimal composition. Order and formality are rigidly imposed on organic plant forms.

4

through the ages. From the Zen gardens of the Orient to the clipped architecture of Versailles, plants have been used to represent mountains, rooms and figures. Formality need not necessarily be all hard lines and architecture, though: it could, perhaps, take the form of a fantasy lunar landscape carved in topiary, or hedging planted in waves and serpentine sweeps. The wildly eccentric yew topiary of Levens Hall in Cumbria is another extreme example of our desire to control nature; but today's attitude to even highly stylized formality is more relaxed.

A formal style works best when static forms are juxtaposed with plants that have a degree of informality, to provide maximum contrast as well as essential balance. The result is an exciting meeting of order and disorder.

INFORMAL STYLES
Many people's ideas of gardens are highly romanticized, with plants playing a key role in creating a sensual, indulgent atmosphere. A romantic style demands an acceptance of the haphazard way in which plants grow, and a certain 'organized chaos': this can be implied by letting wisteria twine through rambling roses on a pergola, a bough overhang a path, or self-sown plants like alchemilla or verbascums remain in paving.

An informal garden is multi-layered, one level of plants being supported by the next and elements working together and against each other with some degree of abandon. But behind the relaxed, even random mood will be a highly ordered

2 Lotusland, in California, has an atmosphere all its own. It is a fantastical wonderland combining flights of fancy with a celebration of natural forms. In the hot, arid conditions of these gardens, the shape and texture of plants predominate.
3 The pale trunks of silver birch and the carpet of ground cover at their feet create a scene of cool sophistication.
4 An informal tangle of *Crambe cordifolia* and oriental poppies evokes an air of slight abandonment and the sense that nature rules.

approach to the planting; though such schemes look informal, the plants still have to be carefully chosen to work in harmony, rather than in competition, with one another. In recent years, the relaxed approach has been taken a stage further with the development of the wilder garden, using nature as inspiration. You can put together a planting scheme that feels like a wild meadow on the edge of woodland but is, in fact, made up entirely from ornamental plants like thistles, including eryngiums and *Cirsium rivulare* 'Atropurpureum'. Ornamental grasses such as stipas have been a huge influence on this form of gardening, evoking a mood which is reminiscent of an open landscape, like meadowland.

TOWN GARDENS
In urban situations the influence of the surrounding landscape is usually far less important; designing the planting is more like creating a theatre set, since you are working within already constructed man-made boundaries. So, if conditions allow, you can create a jungle, where the planting is exotic and suggests another place entirely, or perhaps evoke a shady glade or a garden from the Orient. Plants are powerful signatures of place and it may take only a single plant – a bamboo, perhaps – to set up a sequence of associations. You can imply water and a cool atmosphere with leafy subjects like angelica and ligularias, and the mood of a sun-baked environment with sculptural succulents like agaves and echeverias. Colour themes, too, will lend atmosphere, from cool contemplation to invigorating heat. Though it would be possible to create such effects in a rural setting, they tend to work best in confinement.

Above all it is your personal vision that determines the garden's mood, and since gardening is a stylized interpretation of nature, your use of plants will greatly influence its atmosphere. A garden can even contain various different styles and moods within its boundary, provided you are bold and clear in your intentions.

Layers of interest

A good planting scheme is like a collage or a tapestry. It is a sophisticated, multi-layered composition, all the elements of which are dependent on each other for practical support and protection as well as visual contrast. A successful planting design will convey an inherent order and harmony, as it does in nature.

If you look into the waters of a pond or the inner recesses of a wooded glade you will discover this natural hierarchy and order, each component having its own niche within that order. For instance, in a wood the main canopy protects the whole world within the woodland: there is ivy on the tree trunks, and layers of progressively shade-tolerant species occupy every strata. In a clearing made by a fallen tree, a shaft of sunlight allows further species to flourish in the dappled light, each competing with the next but, at some point, striking a balance. When extra light floods into deciduous woodland during winter, a further layer – the bulbs – capitalizes on the brief growing period before new leaves start to appear on the trees and the forest floor is once again plunged into shade.

A garden works on much the same principle as a woodland, with the body of planting consisting of different layers. In creating a planting scheme you move away from the horizontal, introducing some bulk or height to take the eye upwards and also providing a degree of surprise. Once you have height, lower areas will immediately be influenced by it and, at least partially, cast into shade. This gives you the opportunity to create multi-layered effects, not only to add interest in the areas underneath, but also to provide a protective 'eiderdown' for the soil. In nature, you rarely find bare soil: it would be eroded by winds and rain, which would blow away the essential humus content and pummel the surface, leaching it of valuable nutrients. Instead, the earth is generally colonized by a close-knit community of ground-hugging plants, which help the soil to retain its nutrients. Ideally, you should aim to have no exposed soil in your garden: after all, bare soil merely acts as a weed-reserve, meaning extra work for the time-conscious gardener.

PLANTING IN LAYERS
Different plants like to grow at different levels, ranging from those that prefer their heads in sunshine, such as clematis or honeysuckle, to those, including ferns and hellebores, that are happiest at ground level, requiring the protection of their companions and the comfort of dappled shade. The middle layer or, to borrow a term from natural history, the understorey, can also act as a valuable foil to the layer above it. Planting in layers not only works on a practical level: it also allows a wider range of plants to flourish and provides the opportunity to associate plants, allowing the creation of interesting harmonies and contrasts that would not be possible if each plant was grown in isolation.

Striking a balance between plants in the different layers is all-important: each plant will have to get along with its neighbour. There is no point, for example, in placing a sun-lover like catmint in the shade of something taller and more expansive like a buddleja. Often layers must be planted up in stages, as those

1

3

2

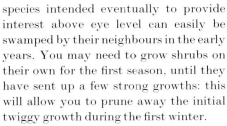

species intended eventually to provide interest above eye level can easily be swamped by their neighbours in the early years. You may need to grow shrubs on their own for the first season, until they have sent up a few strong growths: this will allow you to prune away the initial twiggy growth during the first winter.

Giving the soil underneath roses a protective and nourishing mulch in their first season will allow you, by the second, to plant in it a lower level of perennial ground cover, like geraniums, which can act as both a foil and a contrast, as well as a weed-smothering blanket to protect the soil. Subsequent layers can then be added among the perennials, including spring and summer bulbs. In later years, as the shrubs grow to form a strong enough

3 The flower spikes of *Echium candicans* link with the loftier backdrop of shrubs and are echoed by lower-growing lavender in the centre and succulent kalanchoe flowers in the foreground.

4 In a cool glade, layers of planting have been used to take the eye from the tree canopy through the tall astrantia and mid-height rodgersia right down to ground level, with the grass *Hakonechloa macra* 'Aureola' and the fern *Adiantum pedatum*.

structure, you might introduce climbers such as clematis to weave through early-flowering subjects and take the flowering season further into summer.

Even in perennial plantings that at first appear to be all on one level, there are always opportunities to add interest, perhaps with bulbs or a layer of ground-hugging plants to provide a collar of greenery around the slightly taller perennial subjects. Introduce both tall and short perennials to vary the height, and make the best use of the space so that, for example, autumn-flowering grasses rise through early-flowering hemerocallis as the summer season progresses, providing interest and a vital seasonal continuity.

Over the years a garden will evolve, most schemes becoming progressively dominated by shade. From time to time you will need to reduce or remove some plants; species that have colonized the shade will then suddenly be opened up to sunshine, as happens when a tree falls in woodland. Far from being troublesome, these adjustments are an opportunity to inject new interest into the garden.

Fitting the requirements and habits of your plants to each other can be likened to putting the pieces of a jigsaw puzzle together. The complete picture may be the result of fine tuning, but a garden which works on several levels will enrich your outdoor world.

5 On the edge of woodland, plantings of miscanthus and pennisetum grasses are boldly used as an understorey, integrating the cool expanse of lawn with wilderness beyond. The planting allows views into and through the wood, yet also maintains the intrigue.

Planting for succession

The way a garden fluctuates from season to season is one of its magical qualities: it is never quite the same place from one day to the next. In nature, the process of change is a rich experience, and the quiet moments can be just as interesting as the bursts of activity. In creating a planting design, making the most of the life cycles of plants provides a further challenge and opportunity. In a garden setting, you can manipulate the pace of change so that nature's tidal movements, or surges of growth, like the explosion of blossom in spring, are meted out against a backcloth of garden plants selected for their longevity of flower and continuity of interest. Meanwhile, the troughs between the main surges can be made enjoyable by planting that provides the garden with a quiet succession of flowers or fruits throughout each season.

Planting for year-round interest is an art in itself; unless you want a predictable garden of evergreens, you must orchestrate the planting carefully to create a succession of seasonal effects. A scheme that has a magnificent crescendo at one point in the year – often midsummer – but then slumps back into being a green backdrop, may well have a place in a garden large enough to accommodate several areas of planting, but does not belong in a small garden. Where space is limited, planting schemes have to work hard to provide interest all year round.

In any scheme, there will usually be a main season of interest, depending on the key plants in a particular grouping, but there should be something to fascinate at every time of the year. By including some ornamental grasses, for example, you will enliven the late-summer lull common to many gardens, because this is when the grasses come into their own. Even in the smallest space, provided you have a strong framework of durable plants, you can weave among them species whose interest is more ephemeral, whether it is the appearance of spring bulbs or the winter skeletons of perennials. When drawing up your list of plants, choose a range that covers the four seasons so that, when putting together a particular combination, you know there will be a natural focus at each point of the year.

Giving a durable structure to the scheme means selecting a plant or combination of plants which will have merit for as many months as possible. Some form of evergreen ground cover is a sure way to ensure a stable continuity, but you may prefer to choose a perennial such as *Eryngium agavifolium*, which metamorphoses over the year but retains interest at each stage, or perhaps a shrub which provides a presence in both its summer and winter forms, like the bulk of cistus or lavender. The understorey can either be a dynamic combination of plants which weave together to provide year-round change – like *Euphorbia cyparissias* mixed with black-leaf clover (*Trifolium repens* 'Purpurascens') – or it can create a seasonal focus, remaining quieter for the rest of the year: for example, the russet tones of bergenia and *Tellima grandiflora* will enliven the lower level in winter. At this time of year the upper storey is denuded, revealing once again what lies underneath. Other more ephemeral elements can then be incorporated, including coloured stems for winter, berried shrubs for autumn and bulbs to push through in spring.

Climbers play a special role in providing a succession of interest, as they may be used in a vertical or elevated position which cannot be clothed in any other way. Clematis will also clamber up shrubs or trees which otherwise have only a brief seasonal interest, like spring-flowering cherries. Many twiners and creepers flower in late summer and several, such

A well-planned planting can take on many different incarnations over a year. In this planting scheme the elaeagnus forms the framework, even when denuded in winter, while a succession of compatible perennials provides seasonal variations.

Winter/Spring

Summer

as ampelopsis, with its distinctive china-blue berries, are at their best in autumn, bringing interest into the garden with their foliage or fruits.

The idiosyncrasies of each site present a particular challenge, and the most successful plant combinations for it will be revealed by experimenting. You will – obviously – put together plants that are suited to each stratum of the scheme (shade-tolerant plants in shade, sun-lovers in sun and so on) but another part of the equation is to keep an open mind about what is seen as 'seasonal interest' in the garden. Many plants hang on to their winter forms as a matter of course, and if you cut them down for the sake of tidiness you will rob the garden of winter interest. Some plants, like sedums, form

cinnamon skeletons, their brittle winter growth providing a perfect outline to be enhanced by frost, while many other perennials, such as thistles and grasses, come into their own in winter. The stems of willows and dogwoods bring colour to the winter scene and many other trees have coloured and textured bark which, along with their shapely outline, are then revealed to great advantage.

The best planting schemes will be both multi-layered and will reflect seasonal change, so there is always something happening. If the plants are sensitively combined in a close-knit and balanced community, their cycles of growth and dying down will furnish you with an ever-evolving garden environment that has contrast, pace and harmony.

A *Elaeagnus* 'Quicksilver'
B *Leucojum aestivum*
C *Helleborus foetidus*
D *Clematis tibetana* subsp. *vernayi*
E *Foeniculum vulgare* 'Purpureum'
F *Papaver orientale*
G *Sedum* 'Herbstfreude'

Autumn

2

Plant colour

1

2

Colour enriches our whole world. Used well, it is one of the gardener's most powerful resources: it will bring a garden to life, infusing it with a special atmosphere. Intensely emotive, a colour may soothe or refresh the spirit, excite or shock our sensibilities – but it rarely fails to affect our mood in some way.

Colour gives us a unique means of expressing ourselves. In the garden, you can exploit and manipulate it to suit your own taste, whether bold and uncompromising or subtle and modest, just as you would use colours in the decoration of a room. But, of course, in a garden colour is far less static: it appears to change in different weather and at different times of day, and it can metamorphose over the course of a season as well as a year.

Be aware of the effect the quality of light has on colour outdoors and always take your climate into account when choosing plants for colour. In the wild, it is mainly the tropical plants that have flowers of brilliant and intense colour; in the sun-filled gardens of California or the Mediterranean, strong, bright colours look perfectly at home under a blazing sky. Pastel and muted colours tend to appear pallid and bleached out in strong sunlight, but they reveal their subtle beauty in the softer, diffused light of temperate regions.

COLOUR PRINCIPLES

Since colour has such a significant impact in the garden, it is worth learning how to use it well. Some people have a natural eye for colour, but most need to understand the art of associating colours so as to make the most of their potential and avoid combinations that are either too weak or too confrontational.

The colour wheel, based on nature's colour spectrum, the rainbow, is a useful starting point when exploring colour relationships in a garden. A planting scheme based on harmonious colours uses those which are adjacent or close to each other on the colour wheel, whereas one based on contrast puts together colours from opposite sides of the wheel. The most intense contrasts are between those colours lying directly opposite each other, such as red and green, blue and orange, yellow and violet. Rather confusingly, these contrasting pairs are known as complementary colours; used together, they make combinations that zing.

There is a further reason why the colour equation is less simple in a garden than it is in interior decoration: because there is colour in every part of a plant – petals, anthers, leaves, stems, bark, berries and seedheads – you should consider all these parts when designing a planting scheme. You might link the petals of one plant with the anthers of another, whose leaves provide a further variation on the theme.

FINDING INSPIRATION

Colour influences can be found all around us, and the natural world is a particularly rich source of ideas. You may be inspired by the bronzes, browns and dull purples of rough moorland, or by a vibrant collection of blues and greens in pebbles on a beach. You might wish to conjure up the atmosphere of a place you have visited – the rich oranges and pinks of India, or the vibrant paintwork of a seaside town. A textile, print or painting may suggest a combination of colours that you can reinterpret through plants in the garden.

What is acceptable and unacceptable in terms of a colour scheme is a matter as personal as the way you dress or decorate a room: one person's notion of harmony may be another's idea of confusion, while 'artistic' contrasts may be seen as vulgar, and 'tasteful' combinations dismissed as safe and insipid. Experimentation is by far the best way to find out what works for you: treat the plants in your garden as paints on a palette, combining them to create the effects you desire. Just as you might compare fabric swatches for decorating a room, you can work out planting schemes by assembling different permutations of flowers and foliage in posies. In this way unexpected successes, which you could never have calculated using a purely theoretical approach, may be revealed quite by chance.

USING COLOUR THEMES

Themed colour schemes group colours together in a broad sweep based upon temperature: the hot colours from one side of the colour wheel include reds, oranges and yellows as well as stronger pinks and purples, while the cool colours group calming blues and greens from the other side of the wheel together with white and soft pink. Each group has its own characteristics and uses. Hot colours tend to be stimulating and energetic; they put themselves in the forefront of your vision. The cool colours are more tranquil and less demanding; they recede rather than project. Additionally, there is yet another colour group – the 'noncolours' and the bleached-out pastels – which tends to be more complex and is dealt with separately.

Breaking colour down into these two temperature-related groups is quite a crude device, but a useful one when considering how you want to interpret colour in the garden. Choosing a colour theme or series of themes is the most reliable way of making sure that your planting design is clear and focused. Grouping only harmonious colours together is one way of avoiding the uncomfortable confrontations that can occur when groups are mixed. However, more adventurous gardeners can combine and interweave the groups for contrast and excitement, manipulating colour into a stimulating and entirely different scenario.

1 A violet-blue lacecap hydrangea; shade and twilight will make cool blues appear to hover.
2 In an energetic combination, the purple of *Liatris spicata* sings out against the pure blue of *Perovskia* 'Blue Spire'.
3 Coolest of all, white provides luminosity in shade, shown here by the flowers of foxgloves and roses.
4 The saturated colour of *Geranium psilostemon* is thrown into relief against the dark contrast of yew.
5 Here, *Cornus alba* 'Aurea' is the backdrop to yellow-flowered tree lupins and the lime-green froth of *Alchemilla mollis*.

4

COOL COLOURS

Green is the predominant colour of all gardens, since it is the colour of the backdrop and often of the ground, either in lawns or the moss and lichen on rocks and paving. Though it can easily be taken for granted, green is in fact immensely variable: pick a selection of leaves and you will see that there are blue-greens, acid greens as well as greens with a flush of purple, bronze, even brown. The choice of greens can, and should, provide the basis for most planting schemes as the foliage will dominate for most of the year.

Green is a calming and refreshing colour, and one which does not need the addition of anything else to make it work. Foliage gardens can be intensely therapeutic, as there is less to challenge the eye and more to soothe it: think of the traditional temple gardens found in Japan. However, the choice of greens becomes more important once other colours are included.

Blue-greens, as found in rue (*Ruta graveolens*) or *Hosta sieboldiana* var. *elegans*, will set a strong precedent in a planting, being cooler and less flexible than mid-greens like that of hornbeam. The darker greens, such as yew, provide weight and depth but sink back, acting as a foil for strong colours and endowing pale hues with luminosity. Their major disadvantage is that, in combination, dark greens can create a sombre mood. The bright greens, as found in beech, are the perfect antidote: they give the illusion of sunlight, particularly against a dark background, and provide levity and sparkle. Even fresher, the lime-greens and

3

5

Within the hot and cool groups, the main colours can be broken down still further, according to nuances of shade and tone. Shade concerns the saturation or intensity of individual colours, while tone affects the degree of brightness. Saturated colours project out of more muted, foliage-dominated surroundings, while the further a colour is diluted by white or muddied by darker hues, the more it will recede into the background. Harmonious colour schemes are created either by combining near-neighbours on the colour wheel, like yellow and orange, for example tangerine eschscholzia with rusty-red *Hemerocallis* 'Stafford', or by choosing colours from opposing groups but with an equal level of saturation, as when partnering china-blue *Viola cornuta* with magenta *Geranium sanguineum*. Many gardeners will choose to limit themselves to a small, clearly defined range for a sharper picture.

1 The rich, dark colouring of the parrot tulip is an out-of-season treat in springtime.
2 The velvet flowers of *Clematis* 'Niobe' complement the red-tinged dark leaves of *Cotinus coggygria* 'Royal Purple'.
3 The vivid flowers of the annual Californian poppy (*Eschscholzia californica* 'Orange King') suggest sunshine.
4 Colour is present in all parts of a plant, seen here in the contrast between the scarlet petals and black-purple stamens of *Papaver orientale* 'Curlilocks'.
5 The almost ultraviolet colour of coleus foliage gives both depth and impact to a planting, focusing the eye and bringing a weightiness to the scheme.

emerald greens of the golden hop (*Humulus lupulus* 'Aureus') and *Cornus alba* 'Aurea' can appear almost yellow. In all their hues and shades, the greens are completely dependable: they are clean, clear and uncomplicated, an essential part of every planting scheme.

While greens are often used to provide the darkness in a planting, white will, quite literally, introduce light into the garden. White also has poetry: of her white garden at Sissinghurst, in Kent, Vita Sackville-West wrote, 'I cannot help hoping that the great ghostly barn-owl will sweep silently across a pale garden, next summer, in the twilight – the pale garden that I am now planting under the first flakes of snow.'

The lightest colour, white provides a tonal contrast with most foliage and with almost every flower. Whereas green is one of the first colours to ebb away at dusk, white will be the last; this makes it ideal for use as a tonic in shade, where other colours would be lost. As the colour of purity, white should be used to some degree in every garden for its calm, clean and sobering effects: it will impart a measured atmosphere to any scheme, while as a highlight white is invaluable. Even when it has been used sparingly, white gives an essential lift and a shine to a planting scheme which might otherwise be in danger of becoming leaden.

3

The range of whites is more complex than would first appear; grouping whites together can often be problematic due to the varying degrees of cream, green and pink in them, which may not register from afar but which make up a significant component on close observation. The pure white of arum lilies (*Zantedeschia aethiopica*), for instance, can make the creamy-white of the umbellifers, like cow parsley, look dirty, and the two should never be placed too close together.

4

The blues bring luminosity and calm to the garden. The colour of the sky, and of its reflection on water, blue evokes space and refreshment. One of the last colours to leave the spectrum, it is, at dusk, all the better for occupying the twilight. In a cool and shady corner, the blues almost hover, while in the harsh light of the midday sun they are bleached out and lost. As some of the coolest colours, most blues tend to recede in the garden rather than push to the forefront, and are often used

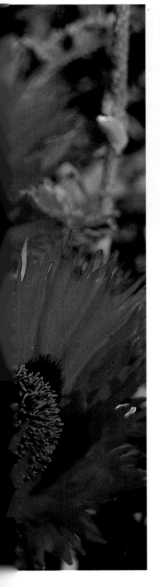

5

in a planting for that reason; planted at the end of a garden, blue-flowered plants like *Caryopteris* × *clandonensis* give the illusion of distance.

Like blue and white china plates, blue-flowered or blue-foliaged plants can be relied upon for their clean, crisp, uncomplicated presence. True blue, as can be found in *Meconopsis betonicifolia* and *Anchusa azurea* 'Loddon Royalist', is one of the rarest colours in the garden, but blues are found in a wide variety of hues that tend towards red, purple or green. Those with a higher component of green, such as gentians, tend to be more electric and, to an extent, appear purer; their vitality and energy enliven a scheme. Blues with more red, moving towards mauve, as seen in bluebells, seem softer; in certain lights they vary dramatically. Blue is a strong component in some foliage, of which *Melianthus major* is a prime example, and blue-green foliage makes a good foil for most other colours.

Pink is a colour that can appear in both temperature groups. The vibrant cerise-pink has an energy and vigour that puts it with the hot colours; *Lychnis coronaria*, with its grey foliage and carmine flowers, can wield a punch in a planting scheme. But pink is more often used for its gentleness, from the soft shell-pink of many roses to the warm, peachy pink of the foxglove *Digitalis purpurea* 'Sutton's

Apricot'. Though too much of it can cloy, pink associates well with the blue and silver of both flowers and foliage.

HOT COLOURS

The hot colours imbue a garden with energy and warmth. Many people shy away from using them at first, because their stimulating nature makes them intrusive and in consequence hard to incorporate successfully. But they are an invigorating group, adding spice to a planting and saving any scheme from blandness; when well placed, they give the boost that many gardens need. The antithesis of the receding blues, the hot colours will jump out and alert the eye to their presence in the garden. An inject on of orange into a blue and purple scheme – for instance, a clump of alstroemeria with *Buddleja davidii* 'Black Knight' – immediately gives the planting a flash of excitement and vitality.

The reds, associated with power and immediacy as well as danger, are often seen as difficult to use. But they can be incorporated into a garden with almost any other colour and, when used in the right place, the red of scarlet poppies or the bright vermilion dahlia 'Bishop of Llandaff' infuses a scheme with warmth as well as giving a strong focus. The reason why red is such a potent garden colour is that it is the complementary

opposite of ever-present green, providing a vibrant association. Though it is often relegated to its own area due to its confrontational nature, if you look closely, red is all around most gardens. It is a significant component of many plants, including the young foliage of roses, the mature leaves of berberis and cotinus, and perennials like *Heuchera micrantha* 'Palace Purple'. Red is also present in the browns of bark, earth and fallen leaves, to which it can be anchored.

Never be afraid of using red; its permutations are so rich and varied that there will be a shade for any situation. Dark ruby reds are the most easily used; they tend to sink into the background and furnish a rich, velvety relief to other colours. Purple is a fusion of red and blue, and is often more readily accommodated than pure red. While the reds allude to vigour, the purples feel opulent, as in sumptuous aubergine and the liquorice-purples of the darkest hollyhocks. With these rich, saturated purples you may be the closest you come to black in the garden.

One of the hardest colours to use in the garden is yellow, which can be tricky to place because it reacts fiercely with other colours and can seem vulgarly intrusive. It is often poorly used, being placed with the blues for contrast, a combination which can look rather crude; it works much better with other hot colours, like orange, or with more neutral tones, such as bronze foliage. A close look will reveal yellow all around in young, fresh foliage in meadows and hedgerows; it is a joyous colour, with connotations of sunshine, harvest and vigour, and this is how it should be employed, to brighten up a planting scheme. In shade, yellow has the welcome effect of artificial sunlight.

When used sparingly, yellow injects energy into a scheme, while planted *en masse* it creates a strong and weighty impact in a way that no other colour will, as you can see in a swathe of golden-yellow daffodils. Spring yellows often have a green influence and are cool and compromising, quite unlike the warm

yellows, which provide a cheerful splash of hot colour in late summer. At the warmer end of the yellows are the oranges, found in plants like eschscholzia and nasturtiums, which approach the immediacy of the reds and are best used to contrast and to highlight.

THE 'NON-COLOURS'

The 'non-colours' are less definable. These are colours which have been bleached of their strength or infused with a combination of other hues. They include pastels and earth tones, and can range from the cool end of the spectrum through to the warm. In a planting scheme they occupy a special position, needing to be handled with care to prevent them from drifting into a nondescript, perhaps lifeless mass. It is important to incorporate a level of contrast: try to include a pinpoint of strong colour, like a saturated hue from the same colour family, perhaps orange *Potentilla* × *tonguei* with bleached-out coppery grasses. Due to their gentle nature, these tones harmonize well with grasses and silver foliage, making good foils and support for the richer colours. Many of the russet-coloured grasses, such as *Stipa arundinacea*, can be used as a foil for almost the whole colour spectrum. Despite their modest impact, the pastels contain some of the most tonally interesting colours, and can be manipulated to produce schemes which may be 'off-centre' but have a certain magic.

FOLIAGE

It is easy to think that putting together plants for colour is all about flowers, but, in reality, they are a relatively ephemeral part of most combinations. The leaves provide the foil and the foundation in the best planting schemes. Foliage does not necessarily have to be green – it can take on many permutations, from brown through red and purple to a myriad of greens, grey, gold and even silver. White or cream variegation extends the range further, but can introduce an element of confusion when the foliage is being used

1 In this border, the curious flowers of bergamot (*Monarda*) are set against the dark, earthy background of red orach (*Atriplex hortensis* var. *rubra*).
2 Broad swathes of *Miscanthus sinensis* and *Eupatorium purpureum* subsp. *maculatum* 'Atropurpureum' resemble painterly sweeps across an abstract canvas.

as a foil for other colours. In this role variegated leaves, which may theoretically seem invigorating, are best avoided.

Dark green foliage provides a deep, rich foil for lighter flowering subjects, while pale foliage brings darker colours into relief. Black irises, for instance, are rendered far more dramatic by an interplanting of something like Bowles' golden grass (*Milium effusum* 'Aureum'). Silver is not as straightforward as it may seem, ranging from white- and cream-silver, which have some yellow in them, through blue-silver to grey. The variety of silvers restricts the range of plants that can be used alongside them. A truly blue-silver plant, being from the cooler end of the spectrum, will look magnificent with its opposite, such as *Elymus magellanicus* or *Hosta sieboldiana* with vermilion lobelia; for a more harmonious partnership, the hosta can be enhanced by interplanting cool forget-me-nots.

COMBINING PLANTS FOR COLOUR

As you have seen, the garden picture depends less on individual plants than on how they are combined. Since each colour has an influence on the way you see its neighbours, it is the colour association which commands attention. Creating a monochrome planting scheme is not the safe option it may appear to be. While a puritanical eye may appreciate the restraint of a successful example, like that of the white garden at Sissinghurst, such a scheme is difficult to put together as you have neither the range of plants available in a mixed scheme, nor the element of contrast to play with.

Combining colours for maximum effect is your opportunity to give the garden a new dynamic, and can be one of the most exciting parts of designing a planting scheme. You may create electricity and energy, or harmony and calm – or even a combination of the two, provided there is

3

4

5

3 Brittle parchment-coloured seedheads of *Papaver somniferum* show up against the colourful late-summer background, a haze of solidagos in flower.
4 This foxglove, *Digitalis ferruginea*, has distinctive rusty, earth-coloured flowers.
5 The dried brown heads and prickly bracts of *Eryngium giganteum* bring a ghostly beauty to the autumn garden.

a neutral element in between. Although it may seem daunting at first, combining colours is a matter of experimentation and trusting your gut reaction the key factor is keeping an open mind. Putting together plants for colour should always take second place to their horticultural compatibility, of course; if two plants will not grow happily together, you will never have the chance to see the full effect of their juxtaposition.

COLOUR HARMONIES

There are various ways to combine colours, and many gardeners choose to theme their schemes by using colours that are adjacent, or near-neighbours, on the colour wheel. Some of the combinations that work most harmoniously are those with a similar tonality; in colour terms, tone refers to how bright or muted a colour is. Plants from different colour families but within a similar tonal range can also be grouped so that they move through the spectrum progressively, rather than jumping from one side to the other. A dark red may be backed by maroon, the maroon in turn by purple, the purple by dark blue, and so on. It is important to make sure that there are surprises as well as subtleties: this red/maroon scheme may not necessarily need an opposite colour to provide the spark – a shot of orange or vermilion from the warm side of the colour wheel would be enough to bring it to life.

Cool colours may be grouped together to produce an effect that soothes rather than stimulates, by way of contrast. To prevent cool colours from becoming too gentle, add a strong, saturated base-colour to give weight to the planting and to provide it with a resonance – a strong sky-blue flax (*Linum perenne*) among pale blue *Camassia cusickii* and mauve-pink limonium, for instance. Though pure white can be combined with more or less anything, pink-whites should be kept with the warmer colours and whites with a cream or green tinge used with colours from the cooler range.

COLOUR CONTRASTS

Perhaps the most stimulating effects are made by placing complementary opposites together. Although it takes courage and may not be to everyone's taste, this device can be useful when the scheme is beginning to look just a little too safe. In fact, most complementary opposites are close in tone, and some work together better than others, but when they do combine successfully the effect can be electric. Take, for instance, the marriage of the tomato-red of *Euphorbia griffithii* 'Fireglow' and the acid-green of shuttle-cock ferns (*Matteuccia struthiopteris*), a partnership so vibrant that the red and the green can at first appear to shimmer. A similar effect can be created with the strong carmine-pink of *Lychnis coronaria* and a golden-yellow solidago – not the most easily digested partnership, maybe, but one which will shine out, relieving the potential monotony of too many yellows grouped together.

Indeed, whenever a scheme begins to look as if it needs an injection of energy, the introduction of an opposite will provide the necessary spark. You do not need to use much of the complementary colour – just a smattering will prevent the introduction from looking too contrived. Much of what gives a combination its greatest impact is the volume of one colour against the next. At Hidcote in Gloucestershire the Scottish flame flower (*Tropaeolum speciosum*) is allowed to scramble through a dense mass of dark yew hedging, its small vermilion nasturtium flowers adding spice to what might otherwise err towards sobriety.

Working with colour becomes easier and more instinctive with experience. Once you understand the characteristics of each colour group and have experimented with putting them together, you should have enough confidence to use colour successfully in the garden. At the same time, the endless permutations made possible by different combinations of plants mean there is always a new, exciting colour partnership to discover.

Plant form and texture

Plant form and texture are essential to the framework of a garden, making it a truly three-dimensional composition. While the form of evergreen plants is the most sculptural component of a planting scheme, shaping its structure and giving it body and volume, the texture of their leaves provides an enduring foil for other more fleeting attractions like flowers. The way you use the outline and the form of different plants, as well as how you juxtapose their contrasting textures, gives a garden its distinctive look.

PLANT FORM

Each plant has an outline and character of its own, and you should use plants like a set of building blocks, putting them together to create harmonies and contrasts. Although the form of evergreen trees and shrubs is fairly constant, some plant forms, such as those of bulbs and herbaceous perennials, are almost as ephemeral as flowers, dying down at the end of their season; other plants change their form dramatically as they grow or, like deciduous trees, alter their appearance through the seasons.

Plant forms are incredibly varied, ranging from skyscraping forest trees to ground-hugging creepers such as the periwinkles. There are static forms to halt the eye and hold it, like hummocky mounds of lavender or pyramidal conifers, and others to lift it skyward, like the spires of foxgloves, eremurus or alliums. Some plants can inspire a mood, whether through the emphatic, energetic spikiness of sword-shaped leaves, found in yuccas and phormiums, the wispy outline of feathery foliage plants like fennel, or the grace and sobriety found in the profile of a weeping willow.

All forms are structural to some extent, but some are simply more potent than others. There are no rules for using plant forms, but their juxtaposition should provide the planting with a clear framework, to be embellished by texture, flowers and colour. Even the most relaxed schemes are held together by

paying attention to form. Look at the vertical stems of grasses which rein in the potential chaos of a wildflower meadow: without these, there would be little to hold the eye, and a tendency towards visual confusion. Form should always take priority when selecting plants for a scheme; without it, further ornamentation will be lost or squandered.

Some designers have developed a strict philosophy for putting planting schemes together, categorizing plants into broad groups according to whether their form is vertical, spherical or horizontal. These are then combined in such a way that they create the layers of a planting: the horizontals cover the ground, the spheres occupy the middle tier, and the verticals take the eye upwards. But you do not have to put planting schemes together in such a formulaic way. A site that feels broad and expansive may need a greater proportion of vertical plants to take the eye away from the horizontal. In another situation you may want to hold the eye at one level, creating a quiet, contemplative space by grouping together a selection of spherical plants like hebes to suggest, perhaps, a cluster of boulders.

PLANT TEXTURE

While form should be seen as the structural basis of the planting, plant texture might be viewed, quite literally, as the surface. It provides another level of interest – that of touch. Watch anyone wander round a garden and you will see the significance of texture: plants will be subliminally brushed or fondled, to experience the soft hairiness of grasses, the felted grey foliage of lamb's ears (*Stachys byzantina*), the roughness of pitted tree bark or, underfoot, the soothing sensation of a cool lawn. The most textural plants benefit from being used beside paths to enrich the journey through a garden; they are especially valuable in gardens for the visually impaired.

Texture is not simply about tactile qualities. Visually, too, it provides us with both the rough and the smooth, the

1 The ribbed leaves of *Hosta plantaginea* create a clean, well-defined outline which would become a focus in a lush planting.
2 The pointed-needle foliage of pine and the softer, upright growth of heather are juxtaposed prominently here, exploiting the rich diversity of plant form.

4

matt and the gloss. Texture creates the depth and density of matt foliage, like that of yew; it equally gives sparkle to the shiny, reflective surface of holly leaves. Nature even provides contrasts within a single plant. Look at the leaves of *Magnolia grandiflora*: the felted, light-absorbing down on their undersides is a sharp contrast with the polished lustre of their upper surfaces. Glossy leaves are the product of smooth texture and they can be used as subtle foliage highlights. In sunshine the leaves of evergreen holly or *Acanthus mollis* act like a series of light-refracting mirrors, deflecting gloom and lifting matt foliage adjacent to it. With texture, juxtaposition is all; shiny leaves can be overused, in which case some matt foliage nearby will bring relief.

Textural variations contribute another important level to the plant association process, and many of the most enduring schemes rely heavily on the different textural qualities of leaves, stems and fruits. Foliage gardens have a particularly rich tapestry of interwoven surfaces. Leaves can be soft and satiny, puckered, ribbed, smooth or reflective. Others will be leathery or hard and brittle to the touch. The bark of trees may be as sleek as satin or scored and pitted, and while some fruits are dry and grainy to touch, others feel waxy and dull. Exploit this textural

3 In a loose planting clumps of miscanthus grass have been used for their rounded form, providing a resting point for the eye amid the upright tree trunks and strap-like foliage of perennials.

4 Plant form can be manipulated to bring a sculptural element to the garden. The dense growth of *Santolina chamaecyparissus* has here been clipped to create an effect like the waves of the sea or the undulations of hills.

diversity in the same way as you would put together a selection of fabrics: juxtapose them to seduce, confront, startle or soothe the eye. Used in conjunction with colour and form, texture can be relied on to bring a valuable dimension to any planting scheme.

FORM, TEXTURE AND COLOUR

The form and texture of plants is all you need to work with in many planting schemes. Foliage plants alone can be used to furnish parts of the garden, especially shady areas, which are intended to be calm and contemplative, to provide a resting point for the eye and a respite from more interactive colour and floral distraction. Such oases of calm can offset areas of more flamboyant planting, or may become the foil for a more ephemeral display of flowers. The endless permutations of form and the subtleties of foliage texture can be harnessed and juxtaposed to prevent a scheme from becoming dowdy – tufty grasses emerging from a soft, russety mat of acaena will inject a planting with lightness and pace. Alternatively, the contrasts can be orchestrated towards drama, perhaps by planting a clump of black-stemmed bamboo (*Phyllostachys nigra*) alongside the spiky form of silvery astelias.

When putting plants together, you will juxtapose their individual characteristics either for emphasis or for harmony. You might combine the satin bark of *Prunus serrula* with a ground-covering understorey like *Geranium macrorrhizum*, whose matt, light-absorbing leaf will draw the reflective bark into the foreground. The principle will work just as well in reverse. In a shade planting, the matt-green foliage of the oak-leaved hydrangea (*Hydrangea quercifolia*) could all too easily be lost in low light against the leaf litter of a non-reflective forest floor; but by placing a plant with shiny foliage next to it, such as *Asarum europaeum*, the coin-shaped, reflective leaves of the ground cover would lift the foliage of the hydrangea.

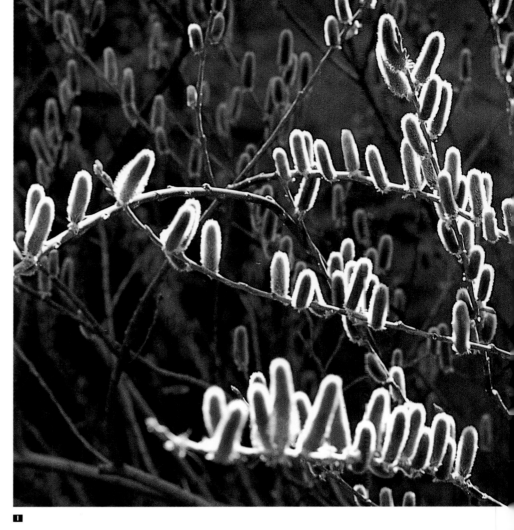

1 The furry softness of pussy willow catkins invite touch.
2 Bark can be as craggy as it is in this monkey puzzle tree (*Araucaria araucana*), or as satin-smooth as it is in *Prunus serrula*.
3 Dried seedheads of *Allium cristophii* add a brittle, spiny quality to the late-summer foliage of perennials.

Although between them form and texture provide the structure and the surface interest of a planting scheme, colour automatically enters the equation because it is present in all plant material, whether in flower or not. It is intrinsic to the fabric of plants, as clearly evident in the trunks of trees and the stems of shrubs and perennials as it is infused into the leaves of all plant subjects. As we have seen, there are endless permutations of brown and green, in addition to the diversity and magnificence of all the different flower colours.

The art of good planting is to keep a watchful eye on everything, never losing sight of the fact that plant form is the fundamental building block. Since you see the surface colour of a plant at the same time as you see its form and texture, to some extent you must consider all three elements together. However, while you will inevitably keep desired colours firmly in your mind when you select the plants for a scheme, colour should always take a secondary role until you know that your plants will work together in terms of shape and texture; this is simply a question of disciplining your vision.

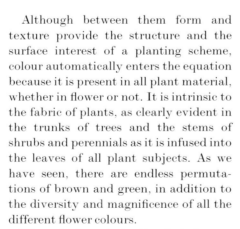

4

5

4 The cactus thorns of opuntia are used as a defence mechanism. Its inclusion in a planting draws the eye but sends out a strong 'Do not touch' message.
5 Texture can provide a planting with another dimension beyond that of form and colour. Here it catches the light that slants across the granular surface of tree bark.
6 The smooth, matt leaf of nasturtium repels water droplets, which bead and sparkle in the sunlight.

6

DESIGNING SCHEMES

There are few things in life more intimidating than a blank sheet of paper or, in gardening terms, a bare patch of earth; finding yourself a starting point is therefore crucial. The design of a planting scheme should always begin with a session involving brainstorming and a notebook, a process which will encourage you to collect together all your ideas about plants and commit them to paper. If you are stuck for ideas, this far-reaching exploration of your aims should unblock them; if you are swamped by conflicting notions, it will help to unravel your thoughts and provide them with a focus.

When you assemble plants to create a scheme, you put into effect all the principles of planting design just described, starting by matching the scheme to its environment, then choosing a range of plants that cover the seasons and embrace a variety of forms, textures and colours – so that the scheme works in terms of time as well as space. Once you have drawn up a list of plants fulfilling these requirements, but before you buy or order any of them, it helps to break down a planting scheme into its component parts, and then to build up the design on paper, creating a planting plan.

Putting together a planting scheme is a little like writing a short story or a musical composition: all need weight and substance as much as rhythm and pace. The keynote in a piece of music sets its mood and creates its framework and the most successful planting schemes are those with the clearest ideas. Certain plants will become your key, both in terms of the composition and the atmosphere you wish to create; they will serve as the anchor points around which you weave the different layers as well as the final embellishments. Where the key plants give a scheme its structure and character, the ground cover plants lay down its foundations and provide infill, and the accent plants inject the planting with rhythm and energy.

Designing a scheme is only the starting point, since no planting ever remains static and instead will develop in ways that may not tally with your initial vision. In this sense, planting design is concerned with a continual process rather than a finished product, and gardeners need practical know-how, as well as design skills, to guide the garden's development. Monitoring a scheme as it progresses is all part of the creative process and the excitement of gardening.

1 Planting schemes may be strongly led by colour. Here, *Crocosmia* 'Lucifer' sets the agenda for a hot scheme.
2 In this garden by the Belgian designer Jacques Wirtz, planting provides both architecture, in the form of hedging, and gauzy screens, with the water reeds.

3 Certain plants, such as phormiums and grasses, can become the key ingredients of a scheme, setting up a potent reference point and imbuing it with a specific atmosphere.

4 Mosses have been encouraged to grow in the Japanese temple gardens of Ryoan-ji, where they help create a mood of peace and tranquillity.

5 *Miscanthus sinensis* blooms, incandescent in low sunlight. At its best late in the season, it will continue into winter as a bleached skeletal form.

Key plants

In the process of drawing up your first plant list and subsequently refining it down to the final selection, certain plants will emerge as the linchpins of your planting design. These are the 'key' plants, which give the planting scheme its personality or structure, or both.

DRAWING UP A PLANT LIST

Use plant catalogues, photographs in magazines and books, and notes taken from garden visits to help compile a shortlist of possible plants. Then edit this list severely, initially to remove any odd men out, and later to give the scheme a stronger focus based upon the overall garden style and the mood you wish to evoke. You might want to re-create a woodland setting or introduce a colour theme, in which case the plants you select should be appropriate – first and foremost in their ability to flourish in the environment, but also for their look.

In the early stages of planning, expect to pare down your plant selection by as much as half again. When only the essential plants remain, annotate the final list with the colour and season of interest of each one; you should also have an idea of the relative sizes and growth rates of all the plants. This may involve some further editing out of incompatible plants, but the malleable nature of planting schemes will enable you to add further detail either later in the season or in a series of stages over the years.

The key plants on your list should have clearly identified themselves. Often the tallest in a scheme, key plants also tend to be the most distinctive and enduring. They are usually trees and shrubs, although not necessarily: in an all-perennial border, the key plant would be the most striking, and perhaps tallest, of the perennials. In an analogy with furnishing an empty living-room, the sofa would be the equivalent of the key plant, placed first because its weighty presence influences the room's character more than anything else; it is the point around which the other elements pivot.

THE CHARACTER OF THE SCHEME

Since key plants usually have the most personality, they will dictate the direction a scheme takes. When grouping together a collection of plants for a foliage garden, for instance, something as distinctive as bamboo will identify itself as an oriental element and swing the association in that direction. But if you were to replace the bamboo with an evergreen magnolia (*Magnolia grandiflora*), this would make the scheme suggestive of the southern United States or of the Mediterranean. Dark, columnar cypresses conjure up an Italian landscape, while bananas or palms evoke the jungle, even in a cool, temperate climate. Always select key plants for their charisma if you want your planting to have definite connotations.

Key plants do not have to dominate a scheme in such an obviously dramatic manner, however. They can be plants

with a more subtle appearance, as long as they have enough character to hold a planting together. You might choose one of the ever-shifting perennial grasses for a naturalistic planting, for example, or the laciniate elder (*Sambucus nigra* 'Laciniata'), with its fringed leaves, for a shady woodland scheme.

THE STRUCTURAL FRAMEWORK

Since key plants will give your scheme its structure as well as its greatest impact, they need to be placed first, to provide a cornerstone on which the rest of the planting will turn. This structure can take several forms: you may need the solidity of a dense evergreen, or even the informal bulk of a species shrub rose, to ground more effervescent, flowering plants; in a perennial scheme whose interest will surge and retreat over the seasons, the clipped form of topiary will

1 *Yucca gloriosa* '**Variegata' is the key plant in this succulent scheme in Tresco Abbey Gardens on the Isles of Scilly. Its powerful form creates the drama and energy which hold together the smaller details.**

give a constant volume. In these cases, it is the very modesty of the anchor plants which is pivotal to a scheme. Though vital to prevent the planting becoming an amorphous mass, these key plants are not necessarily its stars. Visually they will retain a strong presence and provide a background to other more showy subjects. They will also help to shape and divide up the land, taking it away from the horizontal plane and creating niches and corners for less bulky plants.

When plotting your scheme – on paper or on the ground – always position the key plants with care so that they make the most of a space, endowing it with form and structure, and commanding attention where it is needed. They are the most important part of the planting and, once you have identified and plotted them, you will find that the remaining plants slot comfortably into place.

2 A cherry tree forms the starting point for this informal planting, anchoring the surrounding drifts of perennials.
3 Sculpted box mounds are here the touchstone, adding weight and bulk to the looser, less defined planting around them.

2

3

Ground cover

1

2

Ground cover provides the softer, less definable element in a planting scheme, filling the gaps among larger shrubs and perennials and providing a foil for the short-term performers like spring bulbs. Ground-cover plants present you with the opportunity to create an 'under-storey' layer to contrast with the upper storey of trees and shrubs, giving the eye something to focus on at all levels. Once you have identified the key plants in your planting design, you should select ground-cover plants that will tolerate the same conditions as well as work with them visually. This lower planting layer is the foundation of a scheme and can be one of its most enduring, year-round features, though it really comes into its own in winter, when deciduous trees and shrubs have shed their leaves.

When choosing plants for the lower storey of growth, select species and varieties that are compatible with each other as well as with the environment. Include a range of plants with complementary habits of growth: those that create a ground-smothering mat of foliage and others that will emerge from it to supply height where it is required. The understorey need not be all ground-hugging plants – it may well include taller perennials, like rodgersias, rheums and geraniums, which provide the bulk of a garden's summer foliage; although they disappear completely in winter, their leaves still protect the soil for the majority of the year.

THE PROTECTIVE LAYER

On a practical level, ground cover is essential to the success of any planting scheme as it protects the earth with an 'eiderdown' of growth that prevents the invasion of weeds. It also stops the soil drying out and being baked hard and lifeless by the elements, or being eroded by the combined pummelling of wind and rain. As bare soil is both unnatural and undesirable in a garden, all planting schemes should seek to avoid it. Ground cover is the perfect answer.

Providing a layer of ground cover is not, however, the easy answer to all your problems. It is still necessary to prepare the soil carefully prior to planting, to help the plants perform the task which has been assigned to them. Perennial weeds will easily push through a ground-cover layer, however carefully designed, rendering it useless, unless you have given the plants a totally clean start. This may mean a period of several fallow months to make sure that weed clearance has been successful. The soil should then be thoroughly improved by the addition of well-rotted organic matter; to thrive, ground-cover plants need nurturing.

Try to include at least a proportion of evergreens, including lower-growing plants like acaenas, in the understorey. These can be woven together with herbaceous perennials, which come and go throughout the seasons, to produce a tapestry of growth that holds interest through the whole year. Ground-cover planting can be pushed right up under the skirts of overhanging species, and will thrive in conditions which may at first seem inhospitable. Think about the conditions that will prevail as the garden develops: where newly planted trees and shrubs will eventually give shade, choose your ground-cover plants accordingly.

PERENNIALS

A large proportion of your infilling ground-cover subjects will be perennials. This group of herbaceous plants has several different means of growth and expansion; a knowledge of individual habits will help you to put suitable plants together. The clump-formers, like lady's mantle (*Alchemilla mollis*) and catmint (*Nepeta*), grow from a central rootstock to form a clump which spreads outwards as the rootstock expands. Look up their expected diameter – *Alchemilla mollis*, for example, has a spread of 40cm (16in) after three years – and plant them in a group, spacing plants sufficiently far apart that the foliage of neighbouring clumps will eventually meet and cover the ground. Mat-forming perennials, such as *Geranium macrorrhizum* and symphytum, which increase by a creeping rootstock, make perhaps the most effective ground cover, forming an interwoven carpet which entirely covers the soil surface. Runners, such as *Euphorbia griffithii*, move through the soil with subterranean growth. Since they disappear in the winter months, leaving bare earth, they are best combined with evergreen clump-forming and mat-forming plants which will give some permanent cover.

1 A velvety emerald carpet at the Saiho-ji Moss Garden in Kyoto creates a minimal and softening contrast with the craggy tree trunks emerging from them.
2 Before the leaves unfurl on the trees in an English woodland, opportunistic bluebells make the most of the higher light levels to clothe the ground with a haze of blue – inspiration indeed for an ornamental woodland planting.
3 A dense covering of growth can be achieved with a combination of creeping plants such as *Geranium macrorrhizum* interplanted with taller, clump-forming infill plants such as *Stipa arundinacea* and *Sedum* 'Herbstfreude' to make interest at all levels.
4 Aromatic evergreen ground cover for an exposed rooftop: a carpet of thyme is densely interplanted with the sedge *Carex comans* 'Bronze Form', French lavender and a random scattering of Iceland poppies.

The optimum combinations of ground-cover perennials are those which use the characteristics of each of these three groups to build an interdependent plant community. While clump-formers can furnish weight or volume in a planting scheme, the mat-formers will fill in the spaces, with runners moving randomly through the planting. The faster the ground cover knits together, the better; this layer can then be relied on to provide interest while the slower-growing woody plants are establishing.

Always try to link your ground cover plants closely to the larger and more striking 'key' components of a mixed scheme. Being the most fluid level of planting, it should be plotted last – both on your plan and in the ground – so that it can spread into the nooks between other plants and help to 'swallow up' bare areas of earth. Think of this lower storey not as a separate layer, but as one which is integral to the whole planting, and in many ways creating the foundation of a planting scheme.

5 The lush ground cover of golden thyme extends the verdant look of the lawn beyond. *Liatris spicata* and *Liriope muscari* punctuate the horizontal layer.
6 Dense shrubs such as *Potentilla fruticosa* give protection to the soil by producing an impenetrable cover.

Accent plants

An accent in a planting composition is used in much the same way as an accent in language, to give an emphasis which punctuates the scheme rather like an exclamation mark. Indeed, the accent plants in a scheme are often those with a strong vertical form that lifts the eye skywards, like foxtail lilies (*Eremurus*), alliums and veronicastrums. Otherwise, like horizontal hebes, they may have a definite lateral form, creating a powerful sideways emphasis for a planting.

Unlike key plants, which work effectively as individuals, accent plants are better used in multiples, woven in among other plants to inject a planting scheme with momentum and pace. Though not necessarily remarkable in themselves, when accents are placed in a group their definition can bring life to even the most formless planting around them. They will direct a planting scheme which needs some sort of visual discipline: the strong lines of *Salvia* × *superba* for instance, can be used in drifts through a cloud-like planting of perennials to give the eye a well-defined form to rest upon. The verticals provide useful emphasis, especially when a planting is prone to billowing, and they will hold together a loose scheme that is lost in a tangle of growth or lacking a direction of its own.

VERTICALS AND HORIZONTALS

Accent plants are often repeated or echoed in a scheme to give it unity; used in this way, they tie disparate elements together, providing a visual link from one area of planting to the next. The upright form of salvias, for example, can be echoed elsewhere by the strong vertical leaves of iris or the powerful upward movement of grasses like *Calamagrostis* × *acutiflora* 'Karl Foerster' or *Molinia caerulea* 'Heidebraut', giving the eye an easy reference point to follow.

Horizontal accents may be employed in much the same way. When used alone, horizontals may create a layered or tiered effect which can 'set up' key plants, making them look as if they have been lifted on to a series of plinths. The horizontal form of plants like *Cotoneaster horizontalis* or fastigiate yews will provide a powerful contrast to a vertical accent; indeed, when the two are combined they create a sense of drama, exploiting the friction between the earthbound horizontals and the skyward verticals. Imagine, for example, fastigiate yews emerging from a layer of *Genista lydia*, or *Cotoneaster horizontalis* growing sideways through a clump of *Miscanthus sacchariflorus*.

A good source of horizontal accent plants can be found among perennials. Used *en masse* the flower heads of sedums or achilleas immediately take the eye above ground level. By definition, however, the horizontals also make some of the best ground-cover plants because of their spreading growth; it depends on the role you have allocated a particular subject in your planting scheme. In one of his designs, the American designer A. E. Bye used prostrate junipers in banks on either side of a flight of steps to create both a strong link with the outline of the steps themselves and a contrast to surrounding outcrops of rugged boulders. Even ground-hugging plants such as the acaenas can be used to create dramatic contrast with more lofty subjects, the contour of the earth in this case providing the powerful horizontal.

■ Red-hot pokers (*Kniphofia*) and *Persicaria amplexicaulis* thrust dramatically upwards, giving a strong accent to this mixed planting at Powis Castle in Wales.

■

In terms of scale, accent plants should always be in keeping with the key plants that form the backbone of a planting. Although powerful when used in large quantity, they should not compete with other plants in the scheme. While the key plants provide its anchor and the ground-cover layer is its foundation planting, the accents inject a flow and movement around them. The characterful key plants may have already given the scheme a strong form which can be picked up and continued with the accent plants. The tall verticals of foxtail lilies, for instance, may be repeated with drifts of vertical foxgloves and red-hot pokers (*Kniphofia*) or may be contrasted with the powerful horizontal line of the flattened flowerheads of *Sedum* 'Herbstfreude'. Strong statements such as these need to be contrasted with the softer and more fluid ground cover layer of the planting in order to ensure that a scheme has the required balance.

Accents are a vital part of any scheme: without their emphasis, plants can merge visually and a planting metaphorically collapse in on itself, there being nothing for the eye to rest upon. Accent plants provide the focus that is essential to a composition and the energy which comes from orchestrated contrasts.

2 The strong forms of *Allium giganteum* growing above this soft planting of grasses contribute line and rhythm to the planting.
3 Seen here at their best, *Agave americana* inject a powerful, if aggressive, accent against a lower ground cover of succulents and the uncompromising lines of the building.

Drawing planting plans

■

A planting scheme can take many forms, but a plan is invaluable whether you are planting a small corner beside your house or a large expanse of land. And although drawing a planting plan can appear to be a complicated, if not distancing, exercise – symbols representing plants being very different to the real things – the plan enables you to visualize the scheme as a whole, whereas a linear planting list tends to focus attention on one plant at a time. Although some of the greatest garden designers, such as Beth Chatto, cast plans aside, preferring to assemble their schemes from lists and experience, planting plans have a definite place in the design process for the inexperienced. They encourage you to think about the effects you are trying to achieve, they help you to strike a balance between the different components of the scheme, and they are the best place to make mistakes. They also help you to quantify the number of plants, work out their cost and, if necessary, draw up a schedule of work.

FROM PLANT LIST TO PLAN

Putting together a planting scheme takes foresight, as the plants will all develop at different rates. So first, before transferring the plants on your final list to your plan, you need to research the ultimate spread of each one. This will enable you to work out how close together to place individual plants; usually a perennial reaches its ultimate height in three to five years and a tree or shrub in five to ten, so this is what you should allow for. Noting its ultimate height and spread alongside the name of each plant on your list will be useful when you come to plot the plants on to the plan, so that you work in layers; any notes about seasonality and colour you made earlier will also be helpful.

Break the list down into the main groups so that it is clear what role each plant plays in the scheme, whether key plant, ground cover or accent plant. As discussed earlier, always start with the key plants as they will form its structure and cornerstone: they will reveal them-

selves, quite naturally, as those plants with the greatest weight and presence. Group the ground-cover plants into clump-forming, creeping and running varieties, if you wish, and separate out the accent plants so that they can be used in their role of highlights in the scheme.

Refer back to your original concept plan for the whole site (see page 48) and use it to make a separate scale drawing for the planting areas; if you find it helps, use paper divided into squares. Think of your planting plan as a working drawing: it will help you to work out not only how many of each plant you need for the space, but the right proportions of key plants, ground cover and accent plants. The exact number of each plant will depend on the size and the overall look of the scheme, but generally plants look more naturalistic in odd-numbered groups. Drawing up a plan also clarifies the design, enabling you to chop plants out, move them around and refine the scheme as it starts to piece itself together in your mind. When it is finally committed to the ground, the planting scheme can be further fine-tuned so that the plants work together to optimum effect.

PLOTTING THE PLANTS

Place the key plants on the plan first. These will normally be trees or shrubs, and they should be positioned where you can make the best use of their volume. You may want them to screen, to channel the eye, or to create pockets among which other plants can nestle. Sometimes trees and shrubs can be deliberately grouped very closely so that their individual spreads merge into a single mass, giving more impact; in a large garden shrubs can be grouped together to form thickets, and trees can be grouped into small copses. In perennial schemes, the key plants will be those that have the most enduring presence. To make sure your plan holds together, always remember the maxim 'less is more'. A rigorously edited plant list will have far more impact than a jumble resulting from too

many different forms, varieties and colours. Keep the key plants in particular clear and uncluttered. These are the backbone of the planting, and too much variation will only result in confusion.

Next, plot the accent plants: these are the plants which have an emphatic form and can be used to create movement and points of rest. Although they may recur throughout a scheme, you should always link them to the key plants in some way; for example, the volume of the key plants could provide a contrast to the horizontal and vertical nature of the accents. You can redraw or move the symbols around like coins on a table until the scheme starts to have a balance and a flow. It is then that you can add the ground-cover plants – those with less structure or a more ephemeral nature – linking them in turn to the accent plants.

■ Succulents from Australasia and South Africa create a hot colour theme in the arid conditions of a Californian garden. Key-plant aloes have been set afloat on a drift of lampranthus.

 **This symbol denotes a large shrub or tree, its scaled-down diameter representing the plant's eventual spread. In this scheme, the tree is an oak.**
 **Groups of key perennials or smaller shrubs can be joined on a plan by drawing a line between them to avoid individual labelling.**
4 Symbols drawn to scale and differentiated by colour or in some other way mark the exact placement as well as the eventual spread of smaller plants or perennials.

Place the ground-cover plants last, as this level of planting can be allowed to surge underneath the shrubs and spill into the spaces left between other plants. This is perhaps the most fluid level of the planting, whether you are designing a formal or an informal scheme; it protects the surface of the earth and serves as both foil and contrast.

Give every corner of the planting plan equal attention, keeping a sense of the space as a whole. Try to position small epicentres of detail and excitement at strategic points within the scheme, and make sure it has a solid foundation comprising enough plants to create interest throughout the entire year. A successful planting scheme is tidal, in the sense that as one highlight fades it is replaced by another, each surge and ebb of growth or bloom revealing something new.

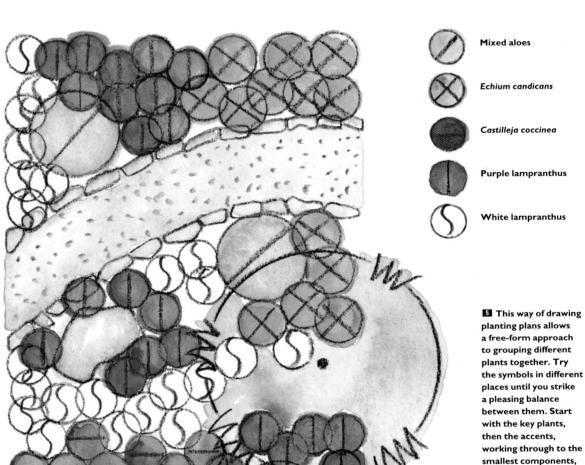

Mixed aloes

Echium candicans

Castilleja coccinea

Purple lampranthus

White lampranthus

5 This way of drawing planting plans allows a free-form approach to grouping different plants together. Try the symbols in different places until you strike a pleasing balance between them. Start with the key plants, then the accents, working through to the smallest components, the ground-cover plants.

The developing scheme

Planting schemes need continual monitoring and adjustment, both to achieve balance and to maintain the health of the plants. A sensitive gardener is constantly on the lookout for developments, good or bad; your role is to steer the planting along the lines chosen for it. The beauty of plants is their mobility, so your composition can be altered from season to season and year to year as you appraise its strengths and its faults. No gardener gets everything right the first time; do not be afraid to move plants about, as you would the furniture in a room, until you find the ideal position.

GETTING ESTABLISHED

Different plants develop at very different rates. Shrubs and hedges generally take three years to make an impression, and five before they attain a substantial volume, while trees take even longer. But perennials can start to mesh together and look established by the end of the first season. What may work in the first year after planting might not work, though, in year three: the *Verbena bonariensis* that overwhelmed a scheme in its first year may be crowded out later on. In mixed schemes, therefore, make sure that the perennials do not overshadow young shrubs in their first three years; it is wise to delay underplanting shrubs until the second season, or at least to keep young perennials in check with a summer cutback until the shrubs have lifted their heads above the competition.

In subsequent years the relationship may well be reversed: perennials will have to be moved as they become overshadowed by woody material, or the shrubs will need pruning to let in enough light for the perennials. Unruly climbers will need guidance or support in the first year or two after planting to steer their growth in the right direction.

However carefully you plan a planting, there will always be unexpected results. Some plants will die, some will grow faster than you thought, and others will seed themselves around with abandon.

1 A vegetable plot will require hours of dedicated growing and tending, but it is a rewarding form of gardening.
2 In a pared-down garden by partnership Delaney, Cochran & Castillo, grass and a few climbers demand little maintenance from the time-conscious gardener.

Even over a relatively small area, a range of conditions, like shade cast by the house, or a seam of bedrock just under the soil surface, can cause a plant to behave uncharacteristically. Keep an eye on the growth rates in mixed schemes: while the more vigorous perennials may start to behave like thugs which need to be curbed, plants that take time to establish will have to be given breathing space to do their best. It is also essential to keep all planted areas weed-free, as weeds are tenacious and greedy, and will compete with more choice subjects to extract nutrients and water from the soil.

MAINTAINING THE SCHEME

Maintaining the balance of the scheme may mean nurturing it or taking drastic action; it is generally better to give attention little and often than to let things get out of hand. If you see the balance tipping in the wrong direction, for example if a shrub is starting to block light from

3 The juxtaposition of the tamed and the wild is a design device which can be used to keep the garden on the right side of disorder. It gives valuable visual contrast and reduces the labour in a garden; the clipped topiary probably needs less time (two clips a year) than the managed wildflower planting.
4 Containers are labour-intensive but ideal for a small patio where you want an excuse to potter. Using large pots will reduce the time you spend watering.
5 In Gilles Clément's garden, the occasional clipped shrub among its rough grass is a reminder that this is a maintained, gardened space, saving it from an atmosphere of neglect.

plants around it, or a climber is beginning to choke a young shrub, intervene while plants are young. You can probably resolve the situation by pruning the more vigorous subject, but if you have to remove it entirely, it is still better to have a hole than end up with two misshapen plants. You may want to move a shrub to a new place because something has died, leaving an ugly gap, or a scheme has become unbalanced. Successful areas may benefit from being extended; unsuccessful plantings will need revision. A new introduction can change the entire look of a planting scheme and you must reappraise it as the planting develops.

Certain kinds of planting scheme demand more input than others. Fruit and vegetable gardens require the most effort, in order to make them productive. Shrubs grown as topiary need regular clipping, as do formal hedges. Clumpforming perennials eventually outgrow their space and should be divided every two or three years; some of the divisions

could be introduced into a different area, to provide continuity and strengthen the overall character of the garden. Autumn and late winter are good times to evaluate planting schemes, as shrubs can be moved in the dormant season. Winter is also the appropriate time for a thorough clean-up, for spreading a mulch of organic matter and for late-winter pruning.

Be open-minded about how you treat plants: a 'perfect' lawn can be allowed to develop ragged edges for a more relaxed style, and self-seeding annuals which randomly scatter their seed can be selectively removed to leave only those you want. But if you decide that you dislike a plant, or that it does not work in your scheme, be brave and take it out or move it. Never live with a compromise; there will always be something you would rather see in its place. Above all, do not be too rigid about how much time you wish to invest in your garden, since your ideas may well change as you become more involved in its development.

Home Farm
DESIGNER: DAN PEARSON

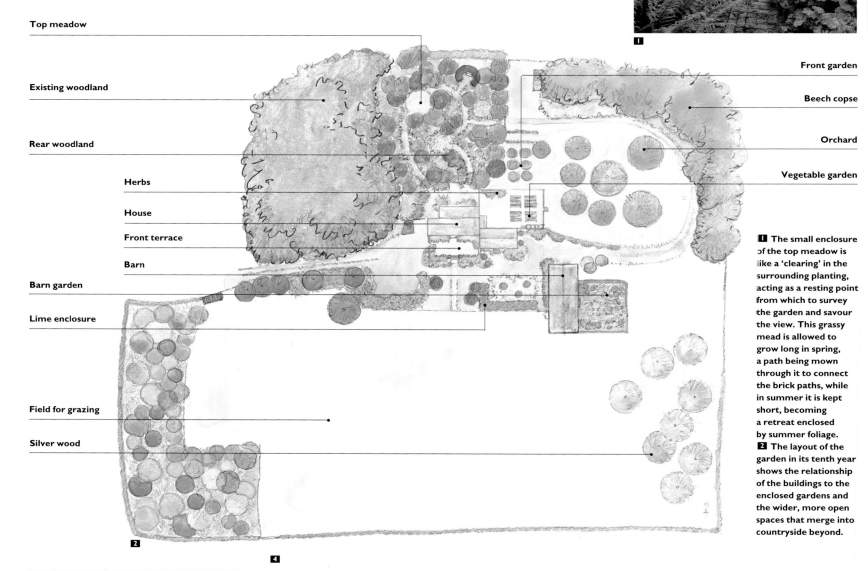

Top meadow

Existing woodland

Rear woodland

Herbs

House

Front terrace

Barn

Barn garden

Lime enclosure

Field for grazing

Silver wood

Front garden

Beech copse

Orchard

Vegetable garden

1 The small enclosure of the top meadow is like a 'clearing' in the surrounding planting, acting as a resting point from which to survey the garden and savour the view. This grassy mead is allowed to grow long in spring, a path being mown through it to connect the brick paths, while in summer it is kept short, becoming a retreat enclosed by summer foliage.
2 The layout of the garden in its tenth year shows the relationship of the buildings to the enclosed gardens and the wider, more open spaces that merge into countryside beyond.

5

3 Like a woodland track, the brick path picks a way through the seemingly random planting. It is jointed with sand so that seedlings and moss soften its surface. The planting is designed to integrate the copse into the rear garden, blurring the boundaries between them.

6

4 *Astrantia major* subsp. *involucrata*, *Alchemilla mollis*, *Cirsium rivulare* 'Atropurpureum' and *Salvia* x *superba* are integrated into relaxed drifts in the rear garden. *Clematis* 'Bill MacKenzie' softens the back of the house.
5 The barn is linked to the main house by a lime enclosure. *Stipa tenuissima* and *Molinia caerulea* subsp. *arundinacea* 'Windspiel' provide movement amid pools of blue rue. *Eryngium giganteum*, *Linum perenne*, *Aster divaricatus* and sea lavender add modest colour bursts.
6 Luminous greens bring artificial sunlight to the rear of the house. Alchemilla drifts through angelica, and *Cornus alba* 'Aurea' illuminates the bank.
7 At the front of the house, ox-eye daisies sown into the drive add an air of informality.

Home Farm lies on a gently sloping, south-facing site in the centre of England. Originally the home farm to a larger estate, the eighteenth-century buildings were sold off with four acres of land in 1987. Although the property was almost derelict, it had a potent atmosphere and, surrounded by ancient farmland, a strong sense of place.

The owner, a friend and long-standing client who works in textiles and fashion, has a passion for plants and landscape. We felt that the garden should be a celebration of the rural environment; while parts of the strategy were immediately clear, others unravelled over the years as the atmosphere of the place asserted itself. My brief was to work as freely as possible with nature, using ideas about natural plant communities; the garden should feel as if it had arrived almost by itself. Plants would provide the garden's organic structure, with hard landscaping restricted to paths for access and seating: the stone walls of the building and the scenery were framework enough.

THE REAR GARDEN

A bank to the rear of the property was excavated, creating a dramatic change of level and a shady, secluded area at its base. This garden, enclosed by the mixed woods behind and by clumps of elder and holly, was then developed to feel like a clearing within the wood. The planting is designed on a grand yet relaxed scale,

using informal species with a feel of the wild about them. The green and yellow theme brings a sense of artificial sunlight, counteracting the gloom predominating on the north side of the building. Aralias and bamboos give structure near to the house, with slate-grey *Geranium phaeum* and angelica interplanted with *Iris foetidissima*. On the garden's shady side, the golden foliage of *Humulus lupulus* 'Aureus' and *Cornus alba* 'Aurea' link the areas. Closer to the wood, the planting style is more naturalistic, using varieties of native plants such as the copper hazel, guelder rose, sweet briar roses, white-stemmed bramble and pink cow parsley.

The planting has been simplified over the years, clearing unnecessary detail and working in broader sweeps, one group of plants drifting and merging with the next. The paths now pick through the 'random' planting like a woodland trail.

THE BARN GARDEN

The easterly aspect of the plot beside the newly converted barn is different from the rest of the garden. Its view, over furrowed fields that appear corrugated in low morning light, prompted a treatment that would connect the garden to these fields and beyond. The natural colours came out of the summer landscape – bleached and bronzed grasses, the russet of seeding docks – lifted here and there with injections of crimson, scarlet, rust, orange and cream. The predominant

planting of grasses is interspersed with massed perennials which ebb and flow between clumps of cinnamon-stemmed *Arbutus uneco* and red-hipped *Rosa moyesii*, while self-seeding wild poppies (*Papaver rhoeas*) and eschscholzia move randomly among the perennials and grasses. Tall verticals provide accents, the foxtail lilies (*Eremurus*) followed by brown foxgloves later on in the season. Colour is used in bold, painterly sweeps, while the swathe of countryside beyond reconnects the garden to the landscape, reinforcing its sense of place.

7

1 In midsummer, foxtail lilies (*Eremurus* 'Moneymaker' and *E. × isabellinus* 'Cleopatra') rise up through the barn garden's grasses, which will perform later in the season and take the planting through into autumn.
2 A view of the garden from the barn in late summer. The *Stipa gigantea* has turned gold and the vertical spires of *Digitalis ferruginea* have replaced those of the eremurus.

3 Flowering from midsummer until mid-autumn, *Achillea* 'Lachskönigin' will change from brick to salmon, to buff and then brown. *Euphorbia dulcis* 'Chameleon' and ground-smothering clover (*Trifolium repens* 'Wheatfen') occupy the lower levels.
4 *Rosa moyesii* 'Geranium' is under-planted by *Papaver orientale* 'Marcus Perry'. By autumn the rose's colourful hips will emerge through ruby *Panicum virgatum* 'Rehbraun', interplanted to replace the poppies. Over the seasons the planting is designed to transform as a meadow would.
5 A splash of colour from *Eschscholzia californica* self-sown among *Stipa gigantea* gives the young barn garden an immediate 'lived-in' feel.

4

5

6

7

8

6 *Hemerocallis* 'Stafford' is planted among *Potentilla* 'Gibson's Scarlet', while *Monarda* 'Cambridge Scarlet' extends the fiery colour to the barn garden's rear corner.

7 In midsummer *Digitalis ferruginea* towers up amid *Molinia caerulea* subsp. *caerulea* 'Moorhexe' and *Knautia macedonica*. *Stipa gigantea* catches the low light in the barn garden and contributes luminosity to the planting.

8 In early autumn the grasses in the barn garden come into their own and will continue, bleached of colour, until felled by snow. Here *Stipa brachytricha* captures the breeze.

FEATURE PLANTINGS

Plants offer you the chance to create a garden full of variety and interest, and there are certain planting styles that will give it a very distinct flavour. These styles have evolved either as a result of a popular fashion for a particular scheme, from the herbaceous borders pioneered by Gertrude Jekyll to the plantings of massed perennials currently in vogue, or by matching the characteristics and the requirements of plants to a specific environment, as in meadow or water plantings. It is necessary to look at each type of feature planting separately as every scheme has its own particular horticultural needs.

The diversity of potential planting styles means that you can manipulate them to give the garden a defined focus, whether you are creating a woodland environment with leafy, shade-loving subjects or embellishing a small paved courtyard with distinctive but minimal planting. It is also possible to design your planting so that it defines the different areas within a garden, making each one distinct from the next. Architectural plants, with their strong, sculptural forms, may be appropriate around a paved terrace, where they will help to tie it in with the building, but will be less in keeping in a part of the garden dominated by softer growth. A massed perennial planting, on the other hand, can be used to integrate an ornamental terrace with an informal woodland planting, by introducing a feel of the wild while including some perennials with strong form to echo the architecture. Through good design, all these elements will sit comfortably together and yet expand the potential of the garden. Different types of feature planting can also be used to blend one area gently into the next: static topiary, for instance, will anchor a mobile, ever-shifting swathe of wild poppies and ox-eye daisies.

By employing feature plantings you will give your garden a clear identity. Of course, there is always a place for the plant enthusiast's more eclectic garden, where various styles are intermingled with the emphasis on plant variety, but for clarity it is best to group together plants that are similar in character. Using them in a mixed grouping will only dilute their defined look. Remember, too, that feature plantings are not just about appearance: they are also about practicality. In the first place, they must be appropriate to the conditions of the site, and for continuity of style they need proper maintenance.

1 Here, a cottage atmosphere is fostered by informal planting of old-fashioned plants like geranium, iris and aquilegia, which are allowed to intermingle and spill over.
2 In Logan Gardens on the west coast of Scotland the climate has allowed tree ferns to flourish, creating a lush jungle feel.

2

3 This garden in the south of France uses tightly clipped topiary as sculptural forms. Like green boulders, they separate the garden itself from the thickly wooded surrounding landscape.

3

4

5

4 Massed perennials bring a feeling of the wild to the ornamental garden, with naturalistic sweeps of salvia, nepeta and foxgloves.

5 Cacti flourish in a hot, dry environment, and evoke a desert atmosphere.

The mixed border

Borders as we now know them date from around the mid-nineteenth century and epitomize the English planting style. If carefully planned, they provide for a variety of plants, a colourful display and a succession of interest.

The word 'border' was first applied to beds around the fringes of a garden in medieval times, perhaps because early examples were edged with boards. In the borders of the early-eighteenth century, flowers were grown well apart from each other for close inspection of their blooms. As the century progressed and gardens came under the influence of the informal landscape style, flowers were relegated to a walled flower garden. But gradually formal flower gardens were established near to the house and free-form beds, filled with herbaceous flowering plants, made their appearance.

The earliest herbaceous borders were packed with colour and variety and it was only at the start of the twentieth century, with the garden designs and writings of Gertrude Jekyll, that they became more sophisticated. She showed how to exploit colour, foliage texture and form, usually designing her borders around a colour

1 A combination of *Rosa* 'William Lobb', oriental poppies and *Crambe cordifolia* creates a fulsome effect and a relaxed atmosphere in these mixed informal borders.
2 Shrubs and perennials help to integrate the ornamental garden with the more naturalistic woodland beyond.
3 A mixed border of desert shrubs, cacti and succulents blends the more ornamental confines of the garden with the surrounding scrubby hills.

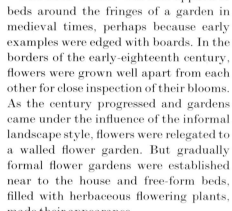

1

2

theme. The availability of species from abroad and new hybrids led to further refinement and development of the border. Now that gardens are smaller, the concept of separate planting areas for shrubs, roses, herbaceous perennials and annuals is, for most people, no longer viable. Instead, we have moved towards the mixed border.

Having such a broad range of plants at our disposal enables us to juxtapose subjects with different characteristics to stimulate the interplay of volume, height, movement, texture, form and colour. Though a mixed border is more contrived than, say, a meadow or massed perennial scheme, there is good reason to find inspiration in nature: in all but the most harsh environments plant communities are composed of woody and non-woody, perennial and self-seeded annual material. The inclusion of shrubs gives our mixed borders solid form as well as texture and foliage interest over a long season, while perennials contribute wonderful colour effects, set off by foliage plants, including grasses. Climbers use shrubs and trees as well as walls for support, spring bulbs push through under shrubs and annuals and tender perennials can be interplanted for added interest. Picture, for example, dark blood-red dahlias among a froth of bronze fennel and the cinnamon trunks of *Arbutus unedo*, or the lime-green bells of *Nicotiana langsdorffii* showing through the scarlet spears of *Crocosmia* 'Lucifer'.

Whereas early borders would usually have been at least 3m (10ft) wide, allowing for several levels and generous tiers of plant groups, now they are often no more than 1m (3ft). This should be regarded as a minimum, since under this depth you cannot fit in enough different plants to create layers and develop worthwhile contrasts. The traditional rules whereby border plants are graded, with larger plants at the back and smaller species in front, can and should be broken to create a more sculptural composition and more intrigue in the planting. In an informal border clumps of plants can be broken up and scattered, with some tall plants brought to the front for added depth. In a more formal border, the repetition of a key plant or an accent, like the vertical of veronicastrums or the clump forms of hemerocallis, will give it an intentional rhythm. Such repetition will also give cohesion to a long border that tends to be viewed in sections. Try to give your border a clear direction through a strong sense of style and a disciplined plant list: it may be colour-themed, given a loose structure or conceived more formally. It should also have balance: too many evergreens will make a border look heavy in the summer, while too few shrubs mean it will lack form in the winter.

Today's mixed border makes an ideal way of integrating areas of the garden that have different atmospheres. You could use an informal border to blend a

4 Annuals such as these nicotianas and rudbeckia extend the season of interest in a mixed border, ensuring there will be colour and performance until the autumn.
5 Grasses add grace and a naturalistic quality to the mixed border, persisting in their winter forms until their colour is finally drained.

3

4

wooded area into a more formal part of the garden, using plants that appreciate conditions of half-sun, half-shade, such as apricot foxgloves and the copper hazel (*Corylus maxima* 'Purpurea'). Interplant the hazel with the starry white *Clematis flammula* and underplant it with wood sedge (*Carex sylvatica* 'Marginata'), chocolate-leaved cow parsley (*Anthriscus sylvestris* 'Ravenswing'), martagon lilies and hellebores, all of which will merge happily into the ornamental garden. In a more Mediterranean environment, the plants, and the mood, would be different: *Viburnum tinus* can spill over from woodland and be interplanted with wild single hollyhocks, with *Rosa* 'Mermaid' allowed to scramble and sprawl. For a more exotic theme, phormiums and cordylines might be mixed with euphorbias, helichrysum and wild-sown eschscholzias.

Gardens have generally become more eclectic in the way they are put together and many innovative gardeners since Gertrude Jekyll have made entirely different use of plant form and colour, inventing a new concept for the border. The Dutch designer Piet Oudolf, for example, gives his borders a distinct character and a softer aesthetic by integrating perennial grasses into them. Whether formal or informal, designed to peak in the spring, summer or winter, the mixed border's greatest potential and challenge is to bring year-round interest to a relatively small space.

5

Massed perennial planting

In recent decades, the traditional vision of the herbaceous border has been turned upside down with the development of new longer-blooming and self-supporting plant varieties and the recognition that it is important to work with nature, not to defy it. The conventional herbaceous, or perennial, border operates on a purely aesthetic level, with plants from wildly different habitats placed alongside each other for effective contrast. Order predominates, with elaborate staking of tall species and regular division to keep the scale under control. Although perennial borders remain a wonderful thing, the traditional concept has been replaced by a new style of perennial planting whose look is altogether more relaxed and whose maintenance much less intensive.

This new approach was pioneered in the 1930s by the German nurseryman Karl Foerster, who selected herbaceous perennials for their compatibility with the site and each other, so as to produce a stable community. His work resulted in plantings which can take many forms, from a wild naturalism resembling an enhanced meadow, using grasses and drifts of perennials, to a more contrived and stylized look, which, although closer to tradition, is eminently more practical. Where a traditional perennial planting would rely on using small numbers but a wide variety of plants, a massed perennial scheme works with greater numbers in less variety, choosing subjects for their communal nature. For example, a low, ground-covering herbaceous geranium might create the framework through which scattered grasses and irises could be injected. If well planned, a massed perennial planting will take less time to maintain than a lawn.

Massed perennial schemes can be made to suit any kind of site, from low-lying wetland which, in a previous era, would have been drained, to thin, free-draining dry soils which would have been wastefully irrigated. The range of perennial plants now available is so wide that even the most hostile situations can be clothed with herbaceous growth. Take, for instance, an exposed hillside smothered in thrift, apricot yarrow and blue-green lyme grass (*Elymus magellanicus*). This planting will look good all year round, as a colourful mass from early summer to the late autumn frosts, then in its bronzed and bleached winter form; and, in a temperate climate, it will need no artificial irrigation. Such a planting also requires very little maintenance as it smothers the soil surface with growth which inhibits weeds and protects the soil from both erosion and desiccation.

1 The compatibility of site and plants in this massed planting of echinaceas and solidagos is inspired directly by the balance to be found in nature. It simply needs an annual cut at the end of the season to prevent the invasion of scrub. **2** The free spread of annual eschscholzias across a landscape in Arizona depends entirely upon their suitability to the environment. The seemingly effortless drifting is inspiration indeed for more contrived schemes in the garden.

2

4

5

In a shaded spot a different treatment could be put together using the same principles, looking at the conditions first, then choosing from a range of plants that would suit low light levels and dry soil. Here, hardy ferns can be interplanted with hellebores and *Geranium phaeum* 'Album', underplanted by a protective, ground-smothering mat of the starry sweet woodruff (*Galium odoratum*). This scheme, which will be predominantly in focus from late winter to early summer, can be extended into the late summer with the tapering spires of *Persicaria amplexicaulis*. An area that may once have been put down to shrubs can thus be given a new, more interesting lease of life.

There are perennials that can be integrated to suit any situation; the choice of style is very much open to personal interpretation. The designers Wolfgang Oehme and James van Sweden, who have worked on small private gardens all over the world and projects as large as New York's Battery Park, have made perennials their main planting tool. Their style is always bold and sculptural, placing, for example, vast clumps of miscanthus grass amidst rivers of rudbeckia to create a version of the American prairie. The Brazilian designer Roberto Burle Marx used perennials in an even more stylized way, painting the landscape with rigid forms and swathes of colour, always choosing plants which were compatible with the environment.

One criticism sometimes levelled at massed perennial schemes is the room needed for them to be successful. In fact, you can apply the principles to even the smallest space, provided you select and combine perennials to cover each season. If you choose species and varieties that have a good skeletal form in the dormant

3 An ordered drift of sedum and coreopsis by Wolfgang Oehme and James van Sweden ties the simplicity of this planting to the calm expanse of water beyond. Random clumps of *Molinia caerulea* 'Transparent' introduce an incidental element to the imposed order.

4 Massed perennials and grasses provide the informal element within the confines of formal hedging. Teasel has been allowed to seed into the scheme, its presence introducing a naturalism to the planting. The same effect could be achieved with other 'mobile' perennials that self-seed such as *Verbena bonariensis* or *Verbascum chaixii*.

5 Perennials have been used in this small-scale planting to link the shrubby elements of the garden. Echinacea and thalictrum drift through perovskia, linking it to the fluffy flowerheads of cotinus behind.

season, they will provide not just another colour range but also a strong winter outline to be enhanced by frost. *Sedum* 'Herbstfreude', which dries to cinnamon-coloured skeletons, is a good example: placed alongside the wiry forms of fennel and bleached-out grasses, the planting will continue to be a focus of interest until levelled by snow or late winter winds. There is then a brief period when you should clear the plants and weed the site before the fresh new growth of spring starts to push through.

In a domestic situation you might favour a more relaxed approach to the massed perennial scheme, one which meets nature halfway. If you contain the informal planting within a rigid, formal framework, the juxtaposition of the two will provide an exciting friction. The framework may be the confines of hard landscaping, such as paths, or the rigid lines of clipped hedging, or you can even use free-form topiary as an 'anchor'. The massed perennial scheme is perhaps at its best merging the ornamental with the wild. You can mass perennials together so that they form drifts of liquid movement that sweep among shrubs and over contours in the garden. More robust perennials like the eupatoriums and *Inula magnifica* can even be injected into areas of grassland and cut back once a year, as a meadow would be.

The most important element of massed perennial schemes is to choose plants that are suitable for the site; you should also make every effort to combine species which will not dominate each other. Although every situation is different, the principles remain the same – compatible planting is the key ingredient.

Grasses

1

1 This American massed perennial planting is inspired by the prairies, now a rarity in the greater landscape. Ornamental grasses have been planted to drift through stands of eupatorium and solidago.
2 In their bleached-out winter incarnation, water reeds have an ethereal quality. Planted *en masse*, they provide a strong vertical form, reflected in the horizontal plane of the water. They introduce movement into the garden when they capture and rustle in the breeze and they give shelter to wildlife.
3 The majestic grass *Miscanthus sinensis* is seen at its best in late autumn, when its plumage becomes almost incandescent in the low light.
4 Used here in the confines of a small border, *Miscanthus sinensis* can be relied upon to stay within bounds while supplying both bulk and grace.

Along with a more naturalistic approach to our gardens there is a developing interest in the ornamental grasses. Although not every garden has enough space to make a meadow or even to allow part of the lawn to grow long and soft, everyone has the chance to invite the grasses into their plot. This could be at the back of a border, where they will provide movement against more static planting, in containers on a terrace, or where their distinctive form is seen in isolation.

Grasses cover a vast area of the earth's surface, providing a rich, varied range of adaptable perennials and annuals. They can be used on the driest of hillsides, in moist hollows and even in the shallow waters of ponds and rivers. The inclusion of grasses introduces a softer aesthetic into your garden; their gentle growth has an affinity with the natural world. Their graceful habit captures the breeze and their light gauziness can be used in a planting like a series of semi-transparent veils. On a larger scale, some grasses have a more powerful presence. Take, for instance, the drifts of toe-toe (*Cortaderia richardii*), illuminating river banks in New Zealand with their arching flower plumes, or the fountain-like growth of *Miscanthus sacchariflorus* on Japanese hillsides. American designers Wolfgang Oehme and James van Sweden have used the impact of these grasses to provide bulk in their large-scale perennial plantings, while in Europe the Dutch designer Piet Oudolf has made grasses a significant part of his naturalistic style.

In habit grasses vary from tight, ground-hugging species to those with lofty, arching growth over 4m (13ft) tall. They are just as diverse in terms of colour, and range from cool greens, bronzes, browns and silvers to the steely blue of *Helictotrichon sempervirens*, the acid-yellows of *Deschampsia flexuosa* 'Tatra Gold' and even the blood-red of *Imperata cylindrica*. They may be plain, variegated or striped, and their flowering can take many forms, varying from the rigid, vertical emphasis of a plant such as

Calamagrostis ×acutiflora 'Karl Foerster', to the delicate, mobile seedheads of the quaking grass (*Briza media*) or the veil of the panicums and stipas. Miscanthus, with its silvered flower plumes varying in shade from smoke to flamingo pink, is one of the most spectacular sights of autumn. Many grasses look good in early spring and can be a foil to summer growth, rising to their zenith in autumn. Drained of colour in winter, they look altogether different, until they are cut down late in the season to start the cycle again. Some grasses are evergreen and can be used as ground cover, providing infill in a mixed planting scheme.

The adaptability of grasses may sound like the answer to many gardening problems, but their strong though subtle influence is not appropriate everywhere. A rose garden would not be the right place for *Stipa gigantea*, for instance. But the distinctive, unconventional look of grasses makes them suitable key and accent plants in a scheme. Whether you choose the strong outline of an arching miscanthus or the gauziness of *Panicum virgatum*, grasses tend to look best used repetitively. They can appear rather out of place seen alone, unless you have them in a pot, which deliberately sets them apart. Those grasses with a neat but slow habit of growth, like hakonechloa and festuca, make the best candidates for containers, where their clear form is revealed. In massed perennial schemes grasses are best used in clumps among 'rivers' of more colourful perennials.

There is an art in placing together species which complement each other aesthetically and do not compete for attention. Study their individual features in the grass collection of a botanic garden, preferably at the end of the season, and you will see that their forms can be broadly divided into formal and informal. Formal-looking grasses have a strong presence with their neat but powerful outlines. Like bamboo, they immediately influence the atmosphere of a place, which can be used to advantage when treating

2

them as key plants. The informality of the more gentle growers, such as the panicums, comes from their gauzy flowering panicles. Used among other plants, they create a gentle haze, blending together a scheme that needs unifying.

Grasses have two distinct habits of growth too, affecting their compatibility with each other and with neighbouring plants. The creeping species should be carefully watched or given a space among strong-growing shrubs, which to some extent will shade them out and compete with any potentially invasive growth. Their colonizing growth habit can be harnessed to stabilize banks or loose soil. In contrast, the clump-formers increase slowly from a central knot of growth: use them for their strong, defined contours, but note their diameter to avoid placing them too close together or where neighbouring growth will crowd them.

3

4

5

6

5 Here grasses are combined so that their naturalistic qualities will help to blend wood with garden.
6 Wolfgang Oehme and James van Sweden, among the pioneers of ornamental grasses in gardens, here use them in broad sweeps in place of shrubs and more conventional perennials. Grasses form three layers of this planting: the lawn at ground level, a swathe of pennisetum and calamagrostis on the other side of the path, and *Miscanthus sacchariflorus* behind.

Meadow planting

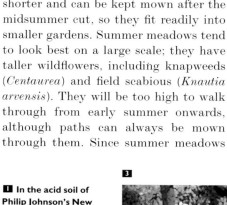

Meadows conjure up romantic ideas of hot, lazy days, surrounded by gently rustling grass and the diffuse colour of wildflowers. They are reminiscent of an era long since past; the 'flowery meade' praised by medieval writers was an early appreciation of the beauty of wildflowers.

By no means a natural environment, the meadow originated in the farming practice of using fields for grazing and making hay. Through the continual removal of the top layer of growth, woody species are unable to establish themselves on agricultural land and the fertility of the soil is constantly reduced. As fertility levels drop, the more vigorous grasses, which form a protective foil on the surface of the soil, become less dominant, giving other flowering species the opportunity to flourish.

Creating a meadow is not simply the result of letting a rough piece of grass run wild – the planting has to be tailor-made to the site, using suitable wild plants. You can either be puritanical and introduce only native species, or include appropriate species imported from other countries. Start by dividing off an area of grass, letting it grow long to see what will come up: it could be full of wildflowers or choked with weeds. This will give you an idea of how to treat the meadow area. If there are perennial weeds like docks and thistles, these will have to be sprayed off before sowing any wildflower seed. Or, you may simply need to introduce plugs of young plants into an existing piece of grass. Whether sowing or planting, remember that wildflowers do not grow neatly spaced but in a scattered, drifting way. As the meadow grows, their self-seeding will help reinforce the informal, naturalistic effect.

Meadows should be placed where they will receive direct sunlight for most of the day. They tend to look best at the far end of a garden, which usually has a wilder feel. A meadow will also make a good transitional area between, say, a lawn and larger shrubs; their soft appearance makes boundaries seem more gradual.

Introducing perennials into grassland is another option in garden areas which are inaccessible for regular cutting or where grass is too rough to be developed as a proper wildflower meadow.

Spring meadows, studded with bulbs and followed by cowslips, ragged Robin, buttercups and fritillaries, are generally shorter and can be kept mown after the midsummer cut, so they fit readily into smaller gardens. Summer meadows tend to look best on a large scale; they have taller wildflowers, including knapweeds (*Centaurea*) and field scabious (*Knautia arvensis*). They will be too high to walk through from early summer onwards, although paths can always be mown through them. Since summer meadows

1 In the acid soil of Philip Johnson's New Canaan garden the russet red of *Rumex acetosella* proliferates among fine-leaved grasses. Poor soil conditions are ideal for meadow gardening as the grass is reduced in vigour, making way for other, flowering plants.
2 Blue lupins and anthriscus are sown as a meadow that will need to be scythed or rough cut once the lupins have seeded.
3 The juxtaposition of cut grass and meadow keeps a wild area from feeling like overgrown wilderness, and also provides paths that can be moved from year to year.

4 Before agricultural herbicides were widely introduced, this would have been a familiar scene. Poppies need freshly turned soil to flourish and will quickly vanish in undisturbed soil, letting perennial weeds take over.
5 Cornfield annuals such as a mixture of corncockles and field poppies can be sown in autumn or early spring onto newly turned soil. Here, rotovating after seeding would cause perennial weeds to be stifled by cultivation and annual seeds to regenerate in autumn.

4

tend to look untidy after the flowers have finished, they are best placed away from the more orderly parts of the garden.

You do not need a sweep of land for a meadow to be successful: even small areas of grass can be allowed to grow long in parts. Indeed, the juxtaposition of the formal and the wild is a satisfying device in garden design. A weed-free lawn is about the most unnatural environment there is and, since weeds are only wild-flowers in the wrong place, you can encourage plants like self-heal (*Prunella vulgaris*), daisies (*Bellis perennis*), bugle (*Ajuga reptans*) and clover (*Trifolium*) to stud the sward with their flowers. Wildflower lawns may still be mown short enough to use as a lawn, though too much treading will damage the flowers.

Choose plant species that are suitable for the site. Beside a pond, for instance, larger-leaved perennials can be introduced to give the impression of wetland, including varieties of moisture-loving plants like kingcups (*Caltha palustris*), purple loosestrife (*Lythrum salicaria*) and meadowsweet (*Filipendula venusta* 'Rubra'), with the more robust sanguisorbas among grasses. In rather drier, but still quite moist areas, many of the American prairie species will create a

5

colourful late-summer meadow in a relatively large garden. Their lofty, vigorous growth can be used for its volume; the Joe Pye weed (*Eupatorium purpureum* subsp. *maculatum* 'Atropurpureum') and the large-leaved *Inula magnifica* will outstrip rough grasses if a small area of soil is cleared around them during the first season. Day lilies (*Hemerocallis*), comfrey (*Symphytum*) and even some larger-growing grasses make dramatic effects. In the Parc André Citroën in Paris, this planting feature is used in deliberately marked contrast to the surrounding order, to blend a small area of rough grass into shrubbery.

Once established, meadows are quite low in maintenance since wild plants thrive in poor soil and are used to surviving competition. Routine operations like cutting help to maintain a balance, but to flourish they need regular attention (see page 253). Today's meadows can be 'enhanced' with species introduced to extend the season, needing only one cut a year at the end of the summer. Meadows make glorious additions to any garden; with their gentle informality, they give the impression that a part of the garden, now wild and wonderfully overgrown, has reverted to nature.

Woodland gardens

1

2

3

The woodland garden has a strong sense of place: cool and still, its tranquillity derives from its green, shady environment. The conditions are dramatically different within the canopy of foliage, with its low light levels, and at the edges, where dappled shade plays over flowers and foliage. In the heat and flattening light of high summer, the woodland garden provides a welcome retreat.

The shaded area of your garden may be natural woodland, in which case you might need to thin out some of the vegetation before introducing other plants. If you are planting a woodland garden from scratch, beware of choosing forest trees. If you wish to have large trees, use species like oak that do not cast too much impenetrable shade; beech casts much denser shade. On a small scale, use sorbus and field maple (*Acer campestre*) or, for a more showy, ornamental effect, magnolias and blossom trees. Woodland plants can take a long time to establish, particularly the less vigorous species that do well in deeper shade. You may need to build up the layer of organic matter in the soil, importing materials like well-rotted garden compost, composted bark or decayed leaves. In a small garden, where a full-scale woodland area is not possible, the principle can be scaled down to a planting of ferns and spring bulbs underneath a single shrub or tree.

Since most plants that flourish in shady conditions have finished flowering by the time the leaf canopy is fully expanded, woodland gardens tend to be at their best in spring. Plants that survive and flourish in shade have adapted themselves to lower light levels in several ways. Bulbs appear in late winter, using the light which streams down to the ground through the bare branches of deciduous trees; many have flowered and completed their life cycles before the leaves of the trees emerge. There are also many North American, European and Asian rhizomatous species that take advantage of light early in the year, like trilliums, arisaemas and Solomon's seal

1 *Galium odoratum*, one of the best ground covers for dry shade, forms a protective eiderdown around an upright clump of *Disporum flavens*.
2 In Beth Chatto's mixed planting for moist ground, the buttercup-relative trollius provides pale highlights against the *Kirengeshoma palmata* and ferns behind.

4

5

3 Foxgloves produce tall spires of colour even in dry shade. The white form (*Digitalis purpurea* f. *albiflora*) will remain pure only if the true form is rigorously weeded out – far from desirable in this case.
4 Growing to jungle-like proportions in shade, the giant hogweed (*Heracleum mantegazzianum*) must be carefully controlled if it is not to become a problem. It is beautiful but also dangerous, and its sap should be avoided. Hogweed is seen here with cow parsley (*Anthriscus sylvestris*).
5 Young silver birches, with their luminous trunks, have been introduced as a small copse at one end of this garden to add a woodland feel. Their light foliage provides a softening cover for the shed.

(*Polygonatum*). Other adaptations include broad, light-catching leaves, like those of bergenias and hellebores, often shiny to refract the light.

Once the leaf canopy has closed over in a woodland garden the atmosphere will become cool and mysterious. There are ways to lighten the mood: gaps can be left between the trees at certain points to allow light to flood to the ground, widening the range of plants that can be grown there. In nature, falling trees temporarily open up the canopy, creating luminous, dappled glades that are bright enough to permit woodland-edge or glade species like bluebells, foxgloves, primroses and tussocky grasses to invade. Around the

woodland periphery, where there is half-sun, half-shade, is another area in which a greater variety of species can be grown, including campanulas and monkshoods (*Aconitum napellus*).

Try to keep a feeling of airiness and space to avoid the cave-like appearance that develops when an understorey is too dense. Leave a distinct space between the ground-level planting and the canopy of foliage above, so that the vertical trunks of the trees are revealed, like the inside of a cathedral, and vistas allowed through. Channel the view with a lower, infilling storey of shrubs. Try to make sure that there is not a predominance of evergreens: woodland gardens are often made heavy by the use of too many pieris, rhododendrons and other woodland evergreens. Include lighter deciduous glade species such as enkianthus, corylopsis, hazel (*Corylus avellana*) and *Rhododendron luteum* to provide a balance.

Plant the clear areas between the trees with a ground-covering perennial layer, in drifts so the planting feels naturalistic. Choose species that are compatible with each other but which provide contrast of form and texture to sweep through the trunks. Clump-forming plants, such as *Iris foetidissima* with its light-reflecting leaves, can be used as key plants scattered throughout the planting in large groups with smaller, isolated satellites, and with softer ground cover such as pulmonarias, *Lamium galeobdolon* and *Tiarella cordifolia* merged underneath. Fill in gaps with randomly interspersed

flowering plants like shade-loving hellebores, trilliums and arching Solomon's seal. Inject the scheme with accent plants to pick up on the vertical form of the tree trunks: plants such as foxgloves and cimicifugas, with their tapering flower spikes, catch the light and look wonderful in a woodland setting.

Cool colours are most appropriate in a woodland. White flowers will shine out in dim light, such as the white-flowered form of *Geranium macrorrhizum*, the white *Lilium martagon* var. *album* and *Pulmonaria officinalis* 'Sissinghurst White'. Meanwhile, blues are positively luminous in shade: a woodland floor covered with bluebells or camassias will appear to hover in the half-light, while blue-flowered corydalis and aconites will take the effect later into the season. Golden or pale lime-green foliage such as that of creeping Jenny (*Lysimachia nummularia* 'Aurea'), *Hosta fortunei aurea* and *Symphytum ibericum* 'All Gold' can give a sense of sunlight. Drifts of cream and yellow flowers – primroses, uvularias, acid-green *Euphorbia amygdaloides* and *Epimedium* × *perralchicum* – may be used to flood the dark conditions with their luminosity.

Use informal, organic materials such as wood or stone for seats and bark for paths. The planting should be relaxed and naturalistic enough to feel almost incidental, but a shady seat will allow you to contemplate the delicate forms of an environment that deserves to be savoured at close quarters.

Architectural plants

With their powerful forms and distinctive outlines, architectural plants provide a striking contrast to the softer growth elsewhere. Such plants lend themselves particularly well to an attention-stealing role in the garden. They will provide a focus, even at a distance, or will act as a strong accent to hold a diffuse planting scheme together. They tend to be larger than, and slightly out of scale with, other garden plants, and will introduce an element of the exotic into cooler temperate climates. But many architectural plants, such as *Fatsia japonica* with its shiny, lobed leaves and *Acanthus mollis*, whose shapely leaves adorned so many Roman Corinthian columns, are in fact perfectly hardy. Nor are architectural subjects necessarily merely foliage plants: many, such as sunflowers, have remarkable flowerheads and others, like euphorbias or eryngiums, have striking bracts.

In the garden, architectural plants are best used singly, either as a focal point or as a feature plant in a minimal scheme for a paved or gravelled courtyard; or they may provide the key for a planting scheme, being powerful enough to sway it in a definite direction. The jagged growth of yuccas, for instance, gives a planting an exotic air, evoking the desert or the seaside. (Gertrude Jekyll was famed for using yuccas as a full stop in many of her herbaceous borders, although the eclectic nature of her plantings might confuse today's more purist eyes.) Similarly, the thrusting, sword-shaped leaves of phormium, a native of New Zealand that can soar up to 3m (10ft) in height, instantly conjures up foreign climes when it is used out of context.

As focal points, architectural plants will rival garden ornaments or topiary and their placing needs to be as carefully considered. Choose the plants as you would sculpture, to draw the eye or to create drama. Their bold forms can easily dominate other more delicate plants and their arresting nature may foreshorten a vista, perhaps undesirable in a confined space. Even if this effect is deliberate, care should be taken over their positioning with regard to scale.

Architectural plants do not have to be used in a brazen, attention-seeking way. 'Architectural' also implies order, and there are many plants with a more demure habit whose clarity of line and classic simplicity still strike a strong note. Irises are a good example, with the rigid, vertical growth of their sword-like leaves, as are the textural, puckered leaves of rhubarb. Acanthus provide order, through their sculpted foliage and strong, upright flower spikes, while thistles, such as the silvery *Onopordum acanthium* and many of the eryngiums, and tall, powerfully sculpted verbascums, will add an architectural note to a scheme without making it exotic. All make useful accent plants, with well-defined, upright growth; their presence in a planting scheme provides a focus among more fluid, organic plant forms.

Growth tends to be more exuberant in warmer temperate and tropical environments and here architectural plants are a more common sight. Since large leaves are less likely to suffer from desiccation or the cold, they can expand to their maximum size. The work of the Brazilian landscape architect Roberto Burle Marx demonstrated the extraordinary juxtapositions that can be achieved with such powerful forms as the giant elephant's ear (*Alocasia*) with its lengthy, glossy, arrow-shaped leaves and the screw-pine (*Pandanus veitchii*), whose foliage arches out, palm-like, at the top of a stem. He was one of the first designers in Latin America to use native tropical plants in an architectural way. In contrast, desert environments produce strong, thrusting plant forms like those of agaves, yuccas and aloes, as well as bizarre cacti. Plants like these create a very strong look for dry climates, particularly in California and Mexico, where adobe buildings provide the perfect backdrop.

1 Agaves, yuccas and palms give Ruth Bancroft's garden in California the potent atmosphere of a painting by Rousseau.
2 Architectural plants demand attention and can be used, as these aloes, phormiums and agaves have been, in bold sweeps to fit in with the environment.
3 Large leaves conjure up exotic environments. Hardy if covered in winter, the moisture-loving giant rhubarb (*Gunnera manicata*), with its broad, leathery leaves and spiny stems, will bring an adventurous mood to the cooler temperate climes of the north.

3

One design approach in cooler climates over the last few years has been to use the hardiest plants of the warmer temperate zones to push the climatic boundaries of the garden and, in doing so, change its whole direction. Depending on where you live, these boundaries can be nudged towards either jungle or desert. A group calling themselves the New Exoticists has developed an uncompromising look designed to transport the viewer to another place by using tropical, jungly plants to give maximum contrast. The splayed leaves of hardy trachycarpus palms become foil to the jagged growth of yuccas and the lofty, arching grass *Miscanthus sacchariflorus* towers over the dark, paddle-shaped leaves of cannas. Such schemes can be designed around foliage of jungle-like proportions, with the cool greens of bananas (*Musa basjoo*) and the clambering growth of large-leaved *Vitis coignetiae*, or around the more gentle foliage of the Antipodean tree ferns and silvery astelias. As the look of this planting feature depends so much on the sculptural forms of the plants, their flowers and colour have become far less important; indeed, many Exoticists believe that there is no place for either.

Attention to scale is paramount in an architectural scheme. All perceptions of space change as soon as larger leaves are used and, like putting a double bed in a tiny boxroom, the effect can easily look out of place. But if the planting is planned with care and kept simple, the element of drama will be unparalleled. In a small garden all you may need to create impact is a clump of black-stemmed bamboo (*Phyllostachys nigra*) and one of giant rhubarb (*Gunnera manicata*). If you are planning to treat just part of a larger garden in this way, separating off an area clearly defined by hedges, walls or trellis will give you the most freedom. On the whole architectural plants work better close to the house, where their forms will complement the lines of the building or be advantageously set off by the hard landscaping of a terrace or courtyard.

4 Strong forms should be used with a bold hand for greatest effect; here, a line of feathery-topped papyrus is seen against a solid garden fence.
5 In the Huntington Botanic Garden, Los Angeles, an arid-land environment is devoted to cacti. The golden barrel cactus has made its own community; with their robust, rounded forms, these are 'personality' plants.

4

Topiary

1

2

Topiary is an ancient art, representing the desire to control and manipulate plants. It has featured in gardens of all traditions, from the clipped box, myrtle and bay used in the gardens of the wealthy at Pompeii to the sculpted hedges of the Alhambra and, later, the formal pyramids, cones and obelisks created from yew or box at Versailles and the grand gardens of the Italian Renaissance. In the nineteenth century Horatio Hunnewell laid out a pinetum in Italian-style terraces on the shores of a lake in Massachusetts, trimming conifers such as white pines and Japanese yew into cones, globes, pyramids and extraordinary layered tiers. And in traditional Japanese gardens throughout history, clipped evergreen azaleas have been used to represent mountains and hills.

Usually associated with formal styles of garden, topiary may be used in pairs for symmetry, in regimented lines or at the corners of a square to emphasize the geometry of a layout. As a focus, it can equally well be used on its own or among other plants, adding weight to a planting scheme; a piece of topiary may be all that is needed to transform an open area into a garden. The outsized, dark yew cones on the lawns at Parnham Hall in Dorset, for instance, create a powerful atmosphere through their juxtaposition with the horizontal lawns and the naturalism of the tree line beyond. On a much smaller scale, a topiary sphere in a container by a front door conveys the impression of a groomed outside space

Topiary is as close to living sculpture as you get in the garden, and the shapes created are entirely in the hands of the maker. As with all features and focal points, clarity of outline is vital: topiary should provide a calm, solid form, like a hill or a boulder. Used as a focus among more relaxed planting, it will pull a scheme together, giving the eye a solid, manicured element to rest upon, and acting as a foil to the natural disorder of plants. When used in this way, it should take the simplest of outlines – a cube, sphere, cone or pyramid. Like a rock among waves, a piece of topiary can be used to great effect in a meadow or among the unstructured forms of a wild perennial planting, the juxtaposition creating a magical effect. More amorphous forms may refer to distant hills or be shaped simply so that their planes catch the light. In Belgium, Jacques Wirtz has clipped box into an intriguing landscape of cloud-like forms.

More representational topiary has its place, but should be kept simple to avoid looking contrived. The stylized birds at Great Dixter in Sussex work well set against the background of the Lutyens house, and the famous jockey and horse jumping a front hedge, which died in the early 1980s, worked because it was artfully crafted and there was little to

3

4

5

6

compete with it. But simple forms work best: gardens are full of fascination without features that are too clever. Much successful topiary is in fact outsized, the scale distorted to give the piece *gravitas*.

Evergreens make the best topiary, as they retain their leaves and therefore their volume all year. Topiary comes into its own in winter, when its framework is enhanced by frost and it casts long shadows over the garden. Keep the texture as refined and plain as possible for a clear outline, particularly on smaller pieces; small-leaved shrubs work best. Dark green yew is effective because its matt leaves absorb light, allowing you to concentrate on the planes and volume of the clipped shape. In terms of vigour, the less frequently a piece has to be clipped the better defined its shape. Box and yew,

needing clipping only once or twice a year, are ideal for temperate climates. Japanese privet (*Ligustrum japonicum*) and cypress (*Cupressus macrocarpa*) are preferred in warm climates for their heat-tolerance and slow growth. Though not evergreen, beech and hornbeam retain their coppery winter foliage when pruned regularly and can be used for larger pieces of topiary. Aromatic bay and rosemary can be clipped into shapes, too. Speed of growth might affect your choice of plant; box and azaleas grow 10–15cm (4–6in) per year, whereas bay, yew and Japanese privet grow 15–30cm (6–12in) and common privet 30–60cm (1–2ft) per year; the latter will require constant clipping.

The creation of simple topiary forms is relatively easy, but for complicated shapes you will need a template. Make a

heavy-duty wire frame to represent the basic shape, or take your idea to a blacksmith, who will fashion something more sturdy. Place the shape over the top of a young box or yew plant and encourage its growth to fill the frame, trimming away any growth that strays outside the framework. Alternatively you can train ivy over the outside of a wirework frame to make 'false topiary'. Plants need light and freedom from competition to grow into strong, well-balanced pieces.

Developing pieces from young plants is a long-term project, but you can start with more mature specimens. Box and yew tolerate hard pruning: cut back into old wood in spring, keep them well fed and watered, then clip the new growth into the desired shape. Topiary is made all the better with time and fine tuning.

1 A simple metal frame twisted into the form you require can be placed over a young plant to provide clear definition for the ultimate topiary shape. The plant is simply trimmed to fill the frame.
2 Box clipped into cloud formations at Jacques Wirtz's garden in Belgium adds a surreal understorey to the apple orchard.
3 Topiary can bring humour into the garden. An asymmetric window-surround of box here makes a curious green extension to the building.
4 In Japan evergreen azaleas are clipped into forms that echo distant hills or mountains. These organic topiary shapes are voluptuous and inviting, a tactile framework for the narrow path.
5 Topiary forms at their clearest and finest. These hedges catch the light and provide the garden with perennial volume.
6 A geometric parterre clipped into a latticework pattern creates a sense of order and control.
7 An arc sculpted in this hedge adds an architectural dimension to the garden. The order of the clipped form is enhanced by its juxtaposition with the freer shapes of nature.

7

Climbing plants

Grown against walls and fences, climbers and wall shrubs make living boundaries, and supported by trellis they create rapid screens and divisions. Tenacious and vigorous, climbing plants will clothe any structure that needs softening and can cover an area much more quickly than free-standing shrubs. They lure the eye up to a higher level with their foliage, flowers and berries; they may also be worked into planting schemes to clamber up stems and trunks, bringing a second period of interest to trees and shrubs.

Climbers use various ingenious means to make their way into the upper levels of the garden. Some need help to get started and others need restraint, or at least regular maintenance, to hold them back. Always match the vigour of the climber to its allotted space or support, to avoid overwhelming parts of the garden; a tide of ever-increasing bulk and growth will choke other plants or cast them into shade. If you are training a climber to grow through another plant, make sure the host is strong and large enough to take on the additional weight; with artificial supports, see that trellis, wires and framework are suitably robust.

In a planting scheme, the role of climbers is usually that of vertical infill. Try to give them similar conditions to those they enjoy in the wild, with their roots in the cool, protected environment beneath trees and shrubs; plant them on the shady side of a tree so they can make their way up into the light once they have gained a purchase, making sure that their flowering growth is not wasted on a neighbour's garden. Keep their roots free from competition and in the early years ensure they have plenty of light to help them get established; use a cane to train young growth in the intended direction.

You can use climbers in many ways in the garden. As a form of disguise, they will soften ugly brickwork and camouflage man-made objects; sheds and garages, concealed beneath a cloak of greenery, can be given an entirely new impact. They are traditionally used to conceal or adorn boundary fences, but if you plant several climbers together, you may instead concentrate too much variation and floral impact in one area, so that the boundary you are trying to hide becomes a focus of attention. It is better to use fewer plants on a boundary, preferably more modest ones that will attract less attention. Reserve the more showy climbers – like clematis, roses and others with eye-catching flowers or coloured leaves – for the heart of the garden, leaving its periphery less definable.

Climbers make an essential backdrop for other plants, the best subjects being those that are primarily green, such as ampelopsis, *Parthenocissus quinquefolia*, *Trachelospermum jasminoides*, the non-variegated ivies and several vines. Larger-leaved vines like *Vitis coignetiae* make a wonderful foil, too, but their large leaves demand attention and they can make a space seem smaller. For a foil all year round, use the evergreens or semi-evergreens as foundation climbers and then interweave more fleeting, deciduous climbing species through them to add variation. The dark green leaves of Boston ivy (*Parthenocissus tricuspidata*)

1 The vigorous climbing rose *Rosa filipes* 'Kiftsgate' is a magnificent sight when it is in full flower, but it needs ruthless control when grown against a house wall or it will romp across the whole building.
2 Creeping Boston ivy clings tightly to masonry and will cover any edifice. Here the modern building has taken on a Gothic charm.

5 Garden divisions are softened when hidden with planting. *Clematis* 'Bill MacKenzie' and the everlasting pea (*Lathyrus latifolius*) provide interest and a gentle froth of foliage, masking the hard form of fencing underneath.

5

make an excellent background for paler flowers. Ivies and the semi-evergreen *Akebia quinata* and *Lonicera japonica* 'Halliana' will maintain interest once deciduous subjects have lost their leaves. Use variegated ivies with care, as their multi-coloured growth can easily be brash and distracting; if you wish to use variegated species, balance them with plain green forms.

CLIMBERS AS FEATURES

There is a range of situations in which climbers take the role of feature plants. In a garden where you do not have the canopy of a tree, you can clothe arbours with twining plants to provide shade and a green ceiling. A grape vine looks wonderful in a sunny situation, with its lobed leaves and its abundant fruit, or choose *Wisteria floribunda* 'Multijuga' for its racemes of scented flowers hanging down as far as a metre from its support. When trained over an arch or a pergola, climbers will give shade and some shelter as well as immeasurably enhancing these features; smothered with dense growth, like that of the potato vine (*Solanum crispum* 'Glasnevin'), these structures provide a cool passage, a sense of enclosure and a prelude to a revealed view or a new environment. Use scented climbers such as rambling roses, honeysuckle, jasmine, and clematis like *C. flammula* or

C. rehderiana against a wall or lifted on supports around a seating area to bring fragrance to nose level (see page 192).

The more showy climbers, including roses, clematis and, in warmer climates, bougainvillea or *Campsis radicans*, can be interwoven among trees, shrubs or hedges as embellishment. Let rambling roses scramble through fruit trees, or grow *Vitis coignetiae* through silver poplars for the rich flare of its autumn foliage. You can also train climbers up small-scale ornamental supports like pyramids, tripods or obelisks to give rapid vertical emphasis in a bare young garden; remove them once the surrounding trees and shrubs have caught up.

While most climbers are sun-lovers, flourishing only if their heads can bask in sunshine, some woodland climbers use forest trees as support. For instance, the climbing hydrangea (*H. anomala* subsp. *petiolaris*), *Parthenocissus henryana* and the wild honeysuckle (*Lonicera periclymenum*) will all flourish on a cool wall, as will several clematis, such as *C. tangutica* or *C. montana*, as long as they have an hour or so of sunshine each day. There is a climbing plant that will thrive in all but the most windswept situation – and, even here, a climber will survive, adapting to the adverse conditions by stunting its growth. Without climbers, the garden would be a less three-dimensional place.

6 Vertical gardening is both space-saving and adventurous. In a Mediterranean or tropical climate, a bougainvillea can be trained into a living wall of colour.
7 Climbers will utilize the space above head height, softening buildings and taking the garden onto another level. *Vitis coignetiae* and *Rosa* 'Gloire de Dijon' here decorate the rooftops.

6

7

3 Walls provide a hospitable, sheltered microclimate for tender subjects such as this *Clianthus puniceus* 'Albus', protecting them from both the wind and the frost.
4 The scented racemes of *Wisteria sinensis* cover a pergola. Given sturdy support, such climbers can be used to create verdant tunnels that offer shade in summer.

Water planting

Water in the garden offers you the chance to grow a range of fascinating, dramatic plants. While wiry reeds and white water lilies may be all that is needed to link a formal, geometric pool with the garden, for a naturalistic pool large-leaved ferns, lush grasses like miscanthus, and the strong vertical growth of bamboos and irises will help to relate the surrounding area with the water itself.

The planting in and around ponds falls into three main groups: aquatic plants, whose roots grow underneath the water; marginals, which live in shallow water and in the mud immediately around the waterline; and bog plants, which occupy the moist ground surrounding a pond. If a garden pond occurs naturally, this area will be boggy and will readily support moisture-loving plants. If your pool is man-made, unless you have artificially created a boggy margin by extending the liner outside the pool, this area will be as dry as any other part of the garden and you will need to plant it with lush-looking but drought-tolerant species so the pond feels as if it is in the right setting.

Aquatic plants keep the pond water from stagnating. Oxygenating weed lives beneath the water and provides a home to water snails and other fauna that keep the pond clean. This weed is needed to oxygenate the water and maintain a balanced environment in which wildlife can flourish, even if nothing else is planted. Floating aquatics, such as shade-giving water-lilies, must be sited carefully: they vary greatly in vigour. A vigorous lily planted in water that is too shallow will rear above its surface and eventually choke a small pond, whereas a less vigorous plant may fail to make it to the surface of deep water, perishing as a result. The wonderful lotus (*Nelumbo nucifera*) and the spectacular regal water-lily (*Victoria amazonica*), which also float on the surface of a pool, need warm water and sunshine to flourish; they will thrive in a tropical pond but should not be grown in a cool or temperate climate.

Marginal plants tend to be vigorous and are restricted only by winter cold. Select your marginals carefully, choosing moderately vigorous species such as the reedmace (*Typha laxmannii*) in place of the more invasive bulrush (*T. latifolia*), which can travel as much as a metre per month in the growing season, swallowing up ponds in the wild. More vigorous species can always be contained by planting them in large pots, provided you can keep an eye on them; otherwise strong runners, once they find the mud, will spread rapidly and freely.

Planting the marginal area of a pond will reduce the water surface area considerably during the growing season; it is often best to keep this planting to the rear of a pond so that the viewpoint is not interrupted. In more naturalistic ponds, marginal planting should be restricted to native species that may occur in the area, perhaps spearwort (*Ranunculus lingua*) and marsh marigold (*Caltha palustris*). A formal pool can be planted with showy species like irises, arrowhead (*Pontederia cordata*) and the arum lily (*Zantedeschia aethiopica*), which will thrive in mud submerged by several centimetres of water.

1 Nymphaeas are beautiful and useful additions to water gardens. Their floating foliage provides shade for submerged aquatics and fish and they produce exotic flowers on calm waters.
2 *Iris laevigata* introduces gentle vertical contrast and a shot of colour in the shallow waters of this Japanese garden.

Large, leathery-leaved ligularias and the umbrella plant (*Darmera peltata*) add drama to any pond and, in areas that are moist and big enough, the spectacular giant rhubarb (*Gunnera manicata*), with its deeply lobed leaves and prickly stalks, cannot be bettered for impact.

Planting around artificially retained water is more problematic as the species which look most appropriate tend to thrive in the damp and will not flourish in dry conditions. Here you can suggest water by selecting close relatives of water-loving species or other plants which simply look right. Species of mis-canthus, particularly *M. sacchariflorus*, can be used to suggest reedy growth. If there is room, planting in bold, repeated clumps will provide anchors for other plants, like the less moisture-dependent *Iris sibirica* or the ornamental rhubarb (*Rheum palmatum*) as well as the pokers of loosestrife (*Lythrum salicaria*) and the froth of meadowsweet (*Filipendula ulmaria*). Shrubby growth will furnish a more permanent presence and help to integrate the pond area with the rest of the garden. The silvery *Salix exigua*, with its graceful wand-like growth, and even the brilliantly coloured forms of *Salix alba* and *Cornus alba*, are all suitable. In a sheltered, more ornamental situation,

bamboo is ideal around a pond, creating the necessary visual association even in fairly dry conditions.

The planting of formal water gardens needs to show restraint. Large clumps of arum lilies, arranged formally, with delicate clumps of the smaller bulrush (*Typha angustifolia*) will provide effective contrast with the horizontal plane of the water. A solitary planting of iris will look lovely when in flower; in a warmer climate you might use lotus or *Papyrus alternifolius*. Limiting the range of plants allows you to concentrate on the smooth expanse of the water itself.

3 Water margins should be furnished with plants that match the look of the environment. Pollarded willows and arum lilies (*Zantedeschia aethiopica*) are naturalistically planted in the moist ground along the banks of this watercourse.
4 Even around artificial water features, it is important to create an appropriate feel. The reed-like foliage and large-leaved plants surrounding this water-filled stone vase help to create a watery atmosphere.
5 The lotus (*Nelumbo nucifera*) imports opulence to warm waters. With its shapely blue-green foliage and attractive flowers, it is calm and sophisticated.

Try to integrate the marginal area with the surrounding planting outside the water's edge. Where a pond has natur-ally boggy edges, the water planting will blend easily with species that have watery characteristics like large leaves and abundant growth. Groupings should be bold and free: there is no point trying to restrict naturally exuberant plants. The vertical leaves of irises cast shapely reflections into the water and provide a strong accent in loose, informal plantings: with its large, exotic flowers, *Iris ensata* is wonderful in bloom and its bronzed seedheads provide continuing interest.

The scented garden

1

Scent is capable of provoking strong emotions and evoking vivid associations; yet its inclusion is one of the most neglected aspects of a planting scheme. There is a wide range of fragrances among garden plants, from the delicate scent of primroses to the thick clove perfume of viburnum: it is possible to choose some fragrant subjects for all levels of planting, from scented hedges, shrubs and climbers to ground cover and even lawns, considerably enriching your outdoor experience.

Scent is present not only in the flowers of plants but also sometimes their leaves; the essential oils in their foliage can give plants protection against attackers. This is a particular feature of species from arid lands, where heat vaporizes the oils and releases them into the air. Scent has the power to evoke moods or landscapes: certain shrubs of hot, dry climates, such as cistus, sage, thyme and lavender, are all reminiscent of the Mediterranean. By contrast, scents activated in a humid, still atmosphere, like those of datura, lily-of-the-valley, *Tellima grandiflora* Odorata Group and *Pittosporum tobira*, evoke the damp, fecund environment of a wood.

Through careful planning, you can provide an environment which exploits scent fully. The air must be still for perfume to be 'captured', and while a gentle breeze will waft perfume around, a strong wind will quickly disperse it. An area that is protected by walls or hedges provides an ideal enclosure for scents to be savoured. The heat generated from a sunny wall will also tease the fragrance from climbing plants such as *Clematis armandii*, honeysuckle and many roses.

The inclusion of scented plants at strategic points will draw you through the garden, bringing it to life and establishing a sense of place. A small clump of balsam poplar (*Populus balsamifera*) at a gateway will greet you with its spicy fragrance in spring, as the resinous buds unfurl. On a smaller scale, the eglantine rose (*Rosa rubiginosa*), long cultivated for its aromatic leaves, needs to be placed where the wind will carry its light scent. The spicier incense rose (*R. primula*) releases a powerful yet enigmatic perfume, particularly after heavy dew and summer rain. At an entrance, scent conveys welcome: a containerized *Skimmia japonica* or *Viburnum × bodnantense* by

the front door will be enticing in winter, while in summer an enclosed porch will trap the smell of honeysuckle or jasmine.

Seating areas are usually sheltered and provide the ideal location for scented plants. Wisteria, honeysuckle or other fragrant climbers may be trained over trellis and arbours; clumps of lavender or rosemary could furnish a scented backrest to a low bench seat. Position tactile, aromatic herbs so that you can fondle them as you sit. Place a large, flat dish of the prostrate mint (*Mentha requienii*) at hand level to brush across it, and place mobile pots of lilies, lemon verbena and even basil close by to delight visitors with their seasonal variation. Encourage creeping thymes to grow in the cracks of paving: they will release their aroma when crushed underfoot. Even more hedonistic environments, such as a raised chamomile bed for reclining, can be contained by low walls or railway sleepers. Far more effective than an expansive, labour-intensive chamomile lawn, it will become a focal point in the garden.

Some floral scents are emitted during the heat of the day to attract pollinating insects, while others are given off only

1 Sitting areas are ideal places in which to appreciate scent. This seat has been sited under a bower of sweetly scented *Clematis recta*.
2 Aromatic herbs such as lavender give off their essential oils if massed together in a sunny position. Shelter from wind helps to ensure that the air is still enough to capture their fragrance.
3 The distinctive resinous scent of pines pervades a secluded corner of this garden next to a pine wood.

2

3

4 Plants with scented foliage can be raised so that passers-by can brush them without stooping. Scented-leaf pelargoniums provide an aromatic boundary in this garden.

4

once night descends. The flowers of night-scented stock and nicotianas look limp and withered by day and the individual flowers of one of the 'morning glories', *Ipomoea alba*, which last for only a night, remain as a tight bud in the daytime. Cooling temperatures at the end of the day activate the scent production of such plants to attract moths and any other nocturnal pollinators. If you plant them around windows, their perfume will drift through in the evening, bringing the garden into the house.

Many of the headiest scented flowers hail from humid temperate climates and the tropics, where their perfume is carried on moist, warm air. Plants such as citrus trees and tender daturas (*Brugmansia*) will need to be brought into the protected confines of a conservatory for the winter. Here, in the still indoor environment, their scents will be at their most potent: where the datura's perfume will take you by surprise when caught on a breeze in the garden, it will smell sickly and heavy when trapped, and even the exotic scent of citrus can be overwhelming without a free flow of air. Gentle fragrances, like those of scented-leaf pelargoniums, are more suitable for those who want a less pungent sensory experience. Even outside in the garden, some of the more strongly fragrant plants need to be carefully placed so that their scent does not become overpowering. The intoxicating scent of *Lilium regale* is wonderful if it is given enough space; growing it in a pot will enable you to control its proximity to people. Other plants need to be grouped *en masse* before they have any effect. A glade of bluebells emits a sweet, delicate scent which would be lost in a small planting, and the same is true of tree lupins (*Lupinus arboreus*) and brooms (*Genista*). In a small garden, where there is no room for planting on such a scale, careful placing becomes crucial.

Perfumed plants can be woven into a scheme whatever its composition and whether it is in sun or shade. Take a little extra care to select not only the obvious scented roses and aromatic herbs but also some subtle surprises, like Christmas box (*Sarcococca humilis*) and clove-scented pinks. These will enliven a planting scheme, providing invisible but potent associations which will stay with you long after the view has faded.

5

6

5 A clump of *Lilium longiflorum* fills the garden with a heady scent in high summer.
6 Make sure you include plants for scent at different times of year, and intersperse them throughout the garden. This lilac flowers in late spring and later on in the season it could provide support to scented clematis or roses.

Container planting

Containers bring focus and an injection of concentrated colour into the garden. Where space is at a premium, they allow you to garden in confined conditions: you can use them to furnish a dark alleyway with shade-tolerant plants, to embellish a rooftop with greenery, or to provide a seasonal welcome beside your front door. Growing plants in containers sets them apart, both visually and horticulturally. Architectural plants look better placed in isolation, where their sculptural form is used to focus the eye; other plants prefer to live in containers for practical reasons, either because they are not hardy and need to be moved indoors in winter or because they require soil conditions not found in the garden. Most plants are quite adaptable, and containerization lets us manipulate them to even greater lengths, timing displays for maximum effect by grouping plants and containers to give an intensive performance.

All plants in containers need constant care, and are dependent on regular water and food, supplied manually or via an automatic system. The key to success lies in choosing the right plants: a plant which is happy with a limited root run will flourish in confinement, retaining a good form or rewarding your care with a continual display of flowers or handsome foliage. It is also important to select plants which are eye-catching enough to merit the spotlight: this could mean the handsome, overlapping leaves of hostas, the shapely form and the extravagant flowers of a datura, or the reserve of a phormium, singled out for its simplicity of outline. Not all plants suit containers, though. Limited room means that greedy feeders fast outgrow their allotted root space and exhaust their supply of nutrients, becoming etiolated despite all the care expended on them.

Your pots or windowboxes must hold enough compost to supply water and nutrients to sustain healthy growth for at least a season. It makes sense to choose as large a container as possible, since small ones are prone to drought and exhaustion

and the soil in them will need replacing frequently. Apart from their greater visual impact, generous-sized containers need to be watered less frequently and support better plant growth. But if you wish to use them for their mobility, filled pots must be light enough to be lifted without damaging your back.

Positioned appropriately, containers belong in both formal and informal gardens. In formal gardens they can reinforce the geometry of the layout while relieving its severity; topiary box or bay, or other plants trained as standards, make especially suitable features. Placed at the end of a vista, a single large container may become a focal point; used in pairs, containers frame an entrance or a view, or will lend visual weight to a garden feature; repeated at regular intervals, perhaps lining a path or a flight of steps, they establish a rhythm. Clustered in a more random way on a patio, pots of foliage and flowering plants lend a relaxed feel to an informal garden.

As they set plants apart, containers allow a freedom that may not be appropriate elsewhere, providing the chance to create unusual effects. A display of lilies may be set on the edge of calm woodland for a touch of opulence, while an eclectic show of annuals, such as fiery 'Empress of India' nasturtiums mixed with carmine-pink petunias, will create an explosion of colour in a cool courtyard. Architectural plants bring drama to an outdoor space: the form of *Melianthus major*, with its crimped grey foliage, adds immediate elegance, while the 'fibre optic rays' of the yucca-like *Dasylirion* or the shapely foliage of the castor oil plant (*Ricinus communis*) act as an exclamation. A paved outdoor room otherwise devoid of foliage is given a sense of place by a large pot of bamboo or a lemon tree, the one contributing an oriental feel, the other evoking the Mediterranean.

Containers allow you to include plants that may be inappropriate for the garden in terms of hardiness. Fragrant oranges or a banana plant (*Musa basjoo*) can be

grown in a pot outdoors to provide an exotic association during the summer months, and moved into a conservatory for the winter. Other fruit trees on dwarfing rootstock can be containerized and used as specimens: figs, valuable for their large, attractively lobed leaves, will fruit more freely if their roots are contained. Alpine strawberries can be used to underplant container-grown apples, standard

1 *Pelargonium* 'Lord Bute' is worthy of being singled out in the garden, as it has been in this pot at Jenkyn Place in Hampshire.

3

4

5

6

grapes and currants; and invasive herbs like mint and tarragon are prevented from spreading when grown in pots.

A mixed planting within a large pot, or a variety of containers of different shapes and sizes intended to be viewed as a group, should be designed in exactly the same way as any other planting scheme. Select a key plant to take visual precedence, with other plants chosen to give the scheme's infill or its accents.

It is important to match the proportion and the form of a plant to that of the container, and to make sure that their colours and texture are complementary or create interesting juxtapositions. Your combinations of plants and their effects can be colour-themed, modified or completely altered from season to season or year to year. The medium's beauty is its flexibility. Whether the focus of your whole garden is just one container or whether that container is simply part of a greater scheme, a bold approach always has the greatest impact.

2 This large, sturdy galvanized steel planter has been designed to accommodate trees on a city rooftop, in this case multi-stemmed birch underplanted by *Festuca glauca*.

3 Large containers provide ample room for mixed planting. Here *Melianthus major* has an understorey of bulbs and *Erigeron karvinskianus* to provide an enduring display where space is limited. A layer of gravel over the hole in the base ensures good drainage.

4 Pots allow the plant enthusiast to indulge in a specialist collection, here succulents. Individual containers can be moved and arranged as specimens come into their own over the year.

5 Small-space gardening in the hands of an improviser. All that is needed is soil and tender loving care.

6 Salvaged oil drums bring life and colour to this central London community garden. Surfinia petunias and cosmos will be replaced by wallflowers for winter. A large volume of soil reduces the need for continual watering.

A city roof garden

DESIGNER: DAN PEARSON

1

2

3

4

4 Looking across from a neighbour's roof, the wooden planters mounted on the parapet wall give privacy; the hedge of lavender, interplanted with *Antirrhinum* 'Black Prince', provides scent around the boundary.
5 Dry-climate plants *Stipa barbata*, blue-green *Festuca glauca* and thrift (*Armeria maritima*) emit 'smoke' from the metaphorical chimney pots.

1 Custom-made, galvanized flower buckets are grouped to echo the cluster of chimneys all around. A planter uses the flat roof above the door, but, to maximize space and reduce weight, all other planting is kept to the periphery.
2 The view out from the door shows the datura, placed to provide shelter and for the benefit of its night-time scent.
3 A topiary bird in a nest of willow twigs, surrounded by fiery red-hot pokers (*Kniphofia*), orange eschscholzias and crocosmia, occupies the loftiest point on the roof garden, seen here in midsummer.

A top-floor apartment in a city might seem anathema to a committed gardener, but the use of containers gave a small, flat roof measuring 3m by 4.5m (10ft by 15ft) the potential to be a garden in the sky. Embracing the alien environment, this central London roof garden takes the surrounding cityscape as its inspiration. The view over the rooftops reveals a scene never glimpsed from the street – rakish chimney pots, a gasometer to the east, sunsets to the west and a distant glimpse of the Houses of Parliament. The aim was to create a verdant space that would extend the apartment during the summer, providing a place to sit, eat and enjoy the greenery as well as the scenery.

A structural engineer recommended that, although the flat roof was load-bearing, weight should be kept off it due to the age of the property. The parapet walls were raised from 60cm (2ft) to 90cm (3ft) with the wooden trough, planted with a hedge of lavender. Brackets were attached to the wall itself, 10cm (4in) above the floor, to support cantilevered plant-bearing 'shelves'. All the weight is transferred down into the wall. An artificial irrigation system was installed and a gutter erected to collect any surplus water. A wooden deck was built on top of the asphalt roof to protect the surface, spread any weight and continue the wooden floor of the apartment outside.

A group of containers was improvised from galvanized flower buckets and several larger metal ones were produced at a local duct works to house shrubs. Exposed, windswept conditions and high light levels meant that plants would be subject to winds and desiccation. It was vital to select small-leaved plants tolerant of dry conditions, like dune grasses, thrift and succulents from coastal areas, as well as plants from dry steppes and the Mediterranean, like thyme, lavender and silver-foliaged, light-reflecting species. These suggested a silvery and dusky purple theme to complement grey London skies and urban rooftops. Flashes of red and orange were introduced to echo the sunsets and to add vibrancy, while the lavender hedge provided a scented windscreen around the perimeter.

The shrubby material is grouped to give protection against the wind. Spanish broom (*Spartium junceum*), *Elaeagnus* 'Quicksilver' and, in the sheltered corner, a group of *Melianthus major* contribute dramatic foliage as well as bulk at the house end. At the far end, the dune grass *Leymus arenarius*, the graceful, silvered Coyote willow (*Salix exigua*), a *Buddleja fallowiana* and some *Convolvulus cneorum* create a gauzy screen.

Smaller, mobile pots house plants for seasonal change: in some years they are filled with scented heliotrope or ivy-leaved pelargoniums, and in others with night-scented tobacco plants (*Nicotiana alata*). The topiary bird nestling in a giant woven nest of willow twigs is, meanwhile, a constant reminder that this is a garden in touch with the sky.

5

DIRECTORY

A garden is like your own personal theatre, a stage set by the walls and floors of hard materials, with plants as its players. The walls and floors are often already in position, but you can adapt them to create a different scene. You may, however, have the luxury of choosing your own framework to blend in with the surroundings. The choice is wide and the following directory outlines the options and their merits, as well as giving you advice on construction, maintenance and cost. Some of the elements might not fit into your immediate budget, but if they are planned at the beginning you will avoid expensive mistakes later.

Trees and shrubs, both evergreen and deciduous, give permanent structure, set against the backcloth of a wall, fence or hedge. Containers can be used as a permanent focal point, planted or left empty, or to hold seasonal displays of brilliant bulbs, annuals, shrubs and perennials. Pools, rills and fountains bring water in all its different moods into the garden.

All types of flowering plants bring to life the structure and space set by the hard landscape. They change constantly, and each season has its theme. It is this continual seasonal change which makes garden design so fascinating. Some plants are eye-catching for their exciting form or their overwhelming beauty, but to provide a foil for them the modest herbs and evergreens are also essential. The choices are hard to make, but this directory aims to give a balanced assessment of the qualities of the different plants.

Finally, do not forget to include a seat from which you can enjoy your creation, whether it is hidden in a private arbour, on a terrace beneath a shady pergola, or just a hammock slung between two trees.

Walls create the backcloth to the garden. Here, brightly painted masonry is used in sharp contrast to the green plants, climbing fig (*Ficus pumila*) and Virginia creeper (*Parthenocissus quinquefolia*), which grow upon it.

PLANTS

Choosing plants is one of the most exciting aspects of garden making, but the choice is huge and increasing all the time. To help narrow it down, some of the best trees, shrubs, perennials and annuals are described on the following pages. The selection of herbaceous perennials includes grasses, some choice aquatics, ferns and bulbs. Vegetables and fruit have been chosen not only for their flavour, but also for their ornamental value and, where possible, for their ability to resist disease. Traditionally banished to a separate kitchen garden, often hidden behind high walls, many vegetables and fruit deserve space among the flowers where they can be appreciated for their decorative foliage. Blossoming fruit trees, free-standing or carefully trained, can form part of the structure of the garden as well as supplying a delicious harvest. Intermingling crops with ornamentals is a means of reducing the risk of spreading pests and diseases. Planting annuals near vegetables and fruit will encourage many beneficial and pollinating insects like hoverflies and bees.

In the descriptions on the following pages, the expected dimensions are given for every plant. Plants grow at different rates. Those shrubs described as short-lived make rapid growth in their first five years, but are past their best before ten years have passed. In contrast, many conifers sold as dwarf are, in fact, extremely slow growing, and over many decades will become tall trees. The dimensions can only be an approximate guide, however, as so much depends on local conditions. A plant's development is governed by a number of factors, including the site preparation and maintenance, and regional and local variables such as climate, soil and aspect. To a great extent these factors are interlinked. Climate is more than just a matter of latitude and elevation; changing weather patterns from year to year can have a profound effect on the garden. A series of dry springs and hot summers will take their toll among shallow-rooting evergreens and conifers, while many herbs and succulents flourish. Likewise, a plant's chances of survival during winter depends as much on drainage, exposure and snow cover as on the actual degrees of frost.

So, what's the answer? Successful planting comes down to research – matching plants to garden conditions. A plant growing in optimum conditions will always outdo another of the same species struggling in an unsuitable position.

1 Vegetables and herbs need not be hidden away from view. Bold chicory, linear Welsh onions and fine cotton lavender make a handsome, and edible, foliage display.
2 Ghostly-white stems of *Perovskia* 'Blue Spire' are clothed with filigree silver leaves and spikes of purplish blue flowers, contrasting pleasantly with the rounded *Allium sphaerocephalon* flowers; both plants suit drier climates.

3 Plums, here coated in delicate bloom, will perform best in sheltered spots, where frost is kept off early blossoms and warmth allows the succulent flavour to develop fully.

4 Foxgloves (*Digitalis purpurea*) are equally at home naturalized in woodland settings or scattered in herbaceous borders, where they are excellent hosts to bees.

4

5 Highly architectural and quite delicious, artichokes look stunning in the vegetable garden as well as elsewhere, as feature plants in shrub or herbaceous borders.

5

Trees and shrubs

Amelanchier lamarckii

Arbutus unedo

Betula utilis var. jacquemontii

Buddleja 'Lochinch'

Aralia elata

KEY TO SYMBOLS

◯ Prefers full sun

◑ Prefers partial shade

● Tolerates full shade

❋ ❋ ❋ Hardy below –8°C (18°F)

❋ ❋ Hardy to –7°C (20°F)

❋ Protect below 4°C (39°F)

These are woody plants which may have a single stem or trunk, in the case of a tree, or develop several stems from ground level to give a shrubby habit. As most trees and shrubs are long-lived and become increasingly difficult to move successfully once established, it is important to select a plant to suit your conditions. Prepare the soil well prior to planting and stake larger specimen trees until their roots are properly established. Mulch, and water generously in dry periods during the early years. Once settled, they demand relatively little attention.

Acer
MAPLE
◯ ❋ ❋ ❋

A versatile genus full of beautiful trees of great garden value. The slow-growing maples *A. palmatum* and *A. palmatum* 'Sango-kaku' (syn. *A. palmatum* 'Senkaki') are among the finest, with handsomely cut palmate leaves turning to fiery autumn colour. 'Sango-kaku' is quite upright, with pale green leaves and bright red winter stems, whereas the species often develops a more open, spreading habit. The paperbark maple, *A. griseum*, also makes a small tree, with wonderfully glossy mahogany-coloured flaking bark. Its deeply lobed leaves turn reddish purple in autumn.
● Prefers neutral to acid soils.
Height x spread:
A. palmatum
10yrs 3.5 x 3.5m (11½ x 11½ft)
20yrs 5 x 5m (16 x 16ft)
A. griseum
10yrs 4 x 2m (13 x 6½ft)
20yrs 6 x 3m (20 x 10ft)

Cercis siliquastrum

Amelanchier lamarckii
JUNEBERRY, SERVICEBERRY
◯ ❋ ❋ ❋

In spring, apricot-orange buds open to produce a huge white cloud of flowers, which envelop this small tree or shrub before the leaves emerge. In late summer purple-black berries attract the birds and in autumn the garden is treated to a spectacular display of fiery orange and red colour.
● Tolerant of acid, alkaline and wet soils.
Height x spread:
10yrs 5 x 5m (16 x 16ft)
20yrs 6 x 6m (20 x 20ft)

Aralia elata
JAPANESE ANGELICA TREE
◯ ❋ ❋ ❋

An architectural tree with particularly fine foliage. Dramatic palm-like leaves appear at the apex of spiky stems, but the plant looks very bare and knobbly in winter due to the absence of side branches. The look may be too stark for some tastes, in which case it is better placed in the background, behind medium-sized shrubs, rather than given centre stage. Flowers resembling decorative white plumes appear in summer.
● Prefers an acid soil.
Height x spread:
10yrs 3 x 2.5m (10 x 8ft)
20yrs 3.5 x 3m (11½ x 10ft)

Arbutus
STRAWBERRY TREE
◯ ❋ ❋ ❋

Slow-growing, beautifully shaped evergreen trees or large shrubs bear clusters of white, bell-shaped flowers from late summer onwards. These are quickly followed by red strawberry-like fruits, and some flowers and fruits can be seen at the same time. *A. unedo* is usually grown as a small shrub. *A. x andrachnoides* rarely fruits, but has particularly rich cinnamon-coloured bark which should be kept exposed by pruning out low-growing branches.
● Tolerant of alkaline conditions. Mulch with organic matter.
Height x spread:
10yrs 3 x 2.5m (10 x 8ft)
20yrs 5 x 5m (16 x 16ft)

Betula utilis var. jacquemontii
HIMALAYAN BIRCH
◯ ◑ ❋ ❋ ❋

This birch is noted for its eye-catching white bark, which peels in paper-thin scrolls. It makes an excellent feature tree or multi-stemmed specimen, especially when it is set against a dark background.

● Thrives on acid soils. Avoid siting it on waterlogged ground. Small plants establish quicker.
Height x spread:
10yrs 9 x 4m (30 x 13ft)
20yrs 12 x 6m (40 x 20ft)

Brachyglottis 'Sunshine'
SYN. *SENECIO* 'SUNSHINE'
◯ ❋ ❋ ❋

A low, hummocky evergreen shrub, noted for its silver leaves with white undersides. In summer, yellow daisy flowers are produced. It is a useful and reliable feature plant for small sunny gardens, or as part of a larger mass of shrubs.
● Grow in a well-drained, sunny place.
Height x spread:
10yrs 90 x 90cm (3 x 3ft)
20yrs 90cm x 1.5m (3 x 5ft)

Buddleja
BUTTERFLY BUSH
◯ ❋ ❋ ❋

Reliable, summer-flowering shrubs, sweetly scented and much loved by butterflies. The medium-sized *B.* 'Lochinch' has grey, woolly leaves and fragrant violet-blue flowers. *B. davidii* 'White Profusion' produces large, dense heads of pure white flowers, each with a yellow centre. *B. davidii* 'Black Knight' has long flowerheads of rich purple-black. Ideal for the back of herbaceous or shrub borders.
● Prune hard in late winter.
Height x spread:
10+20yrs 3 x 3m (10 x 10ft)

Buxus sempervirens
COMMON BOX
◯ ◑ ● ❋ ❋ ❋

A versatile, slow-growing evergreen shrub or small tree with small, glossy mid-green leaves. It is particularly suitable for hedges and for clipping into topiary shapes. It also makes good evergreen underplanting in woodland areas or in the background of a border.
● Although tolerant of most soils, the more fertile they are the stronger the growth will be. Grows best in shade.
Height x spread:
10yrs 1.5 x 1.5m (5 x 5ft)
20yrs 2.5 x 2.5m (8 x 8ft)

Carpinus betulus
COMMON HORNBEAM
◯ ❋ ❋ ❋

This is a beech-like tree but with duller green leaves, toothed at the margin. It is fast-growing and used to be coppiced for firewood, but today it is a popular hedging plant for boundaries, and for informal and wildlife gardens. This is partly because during winter it retains its dead reddish brown leaves, which tend to rattle in the wind.
● Tolerant of hard pruning and a wide range of soil types. Hedges should be clipped in late summer.
Height x spread:
10yrs 6 x 6m (26 x 20ft)
20yrs 12 x 9m (40 x 30ft)

Caryopteris x clandonensis
◯ ❋ ❋ ❋

A small shrub with grey aromatic leaves and clear blue flowers in late summer and into autumn. *C. x clandonensis* 'Heavenly Blue' is fairly erect in habit, with pale blue flowers. *C. x clandonensis* 'Kew Blue' has flowers in a deeper shade of blue. Plant it among perennials or shrubs, either singly or in masses.
● Cut back hard the current season's growth towards the end of winter to retain a compact shrub shape. Thrives in sun, in light loamy soil.
Height x spread:
10+20yrs 75 x 75cm (2½ x 2½ft)

Catalpa bignonioides
INDIAN BEAN TREE
◯ ❋ ❋ ❋

A handsome tree with spreading habit, ideal for providing summer shade in courtyards. It is grown for its large, pale green leaves, which open late, and masses of white summer flowers. These are followed by long, pendulous beans, which are retained throughout winter. Smaller growing is *C. bignonioides* 'Aurea', which has bright golden foliage.
● Although it will stand poor soil conditions, it prefers a moist loamy soil. Allow it plenty of root space.
Height x spread:
10yrs 8 x 9m (26 x 30ft)
20yrs 10 x 12m (33 x 40ft)

Catalpa bignonioides

Convolvulus cneorum

KEY TO PLANT SHAPES

The following symbols indicate the mature plant shape, but this may be affected by pruning, training or situation.

- Rounded or pyramidal tree
- Broad spreading tree
- Columnar or light-canopied tree
- Palm or tree fern
- Multi-stemmed shrub
- Low, hummocky shrub
- Clump-forming shrub
- Dome-like shrub
- Narrow or densely foliaged shrub
- Arching shrub

Ceanothus
CALIFORNIA LILAC

Most ceanothus are beautiful blue-flowered shrubs, very suitable for growing against warm, sunny walls. Among the hardiest are the evergreen early-summer flowering *C. thyrsiflorus*, with dark blue flowers, and the deciduous *C. x delileanus* 'Gloire de Versailles'. The latter produces large heads of soft blue flowers from late summer onwards, shortly followed by shiny mahogany-coloured seeds.
● Grow in well-drained soil.
Height x spread:
C. thyrsiflorus
10yrs 3 x 3m (10 x 10ft)
20yrs 4 x 4m (13 x 13ft)
C. x delileanus 'Gloire de Versailles'
10yrs 2.5 x 3m (8 x 10ft)
20yrs 5 x 4m (16 x 13ft)

Cercis siliquastrum
JUDAS TREE

A remarkable slow-growing deciduous tree with small clusters of purple pea-like flowers in spring. These appear before the circular leaves, not only on the terminal shoots but also along the main trunk. Foliage turns yellow in autumn.
● Prefers alkaline soils.
Height x spread:
10yrs 3 x 3m (10 x 10ft)
20yrs 6 x 6m (20 x 20ft)

Chaenomeles
FLOWERING QUINCE

Charming spring or early-summer flowering shrub, carrying virtually stalkless orange-red flowers on the previous year's wood. Cultivars are available in a variety of colours, from white to apricot and pink through to various shades of red and orange. Those that are fertile will bear yellowish quinces in late summer. It can be grown as a free-standing bush, although it tends to have an untidy habit, and looks much better trained against a wall. Take care with the sharp thorns.
● Grows in all fertile soils.
Height x spread:
10+20yrs 3 x 3m (10 x 10ft)

Chimonanthus praecox
WINTERSWEET

It is a real joy to have some shrubs that flower in winter, despite cold, frost and snow, and this is one of the most delightful and strongly scented. Caught in the first rays of sunshine, the waxy, bell-like, sulphur-yellow flowers appear translucent and emit a fragrance which is wafted far and wide. The shrub will grow taller than stated below if it is planted against a sheltered sunny wall.
● Grows in all well-drained soils, but is especially suited to chalky areas. Trim wall plants back after flowering. Free-standing shrubs need no pruning.
Height x spread:
10yrs 1.8 x 1.5m (6 x 5ft)
20yrs 2.5 x 2.5m (8 x 8ft)

Choisya ternata
MEXICAN ORANGE BLOSSOM

A medium-sized evergreen shrub, with attractive glossy green leaves that sparkle in the sunlight and are strongly aromatic when crushed. The white, sweetly scented flowers appear in small clusters during spring and early summer, and again, in lesser numbers, in autumn. It is a useful shrub with a good, rounded outline that can be used either as a feature or as background planting.
● Thrives on alkaline soils. Flourishes in sun or shade.
Height x spread:
10+20yrs 1.8 x 1.8m (6 x 6ft)

Convolvulus cneorum
SILVER BUSH

The silvery leaves have a silky sheen and combine beautifully with the large funnel-like flowers of white tinged with pale pink, which open all summer long. Unlike its bindweed relative, it is not invasive and its small size makes it suitable for associating with perennials in a rock garden, or, in larger quantities, with shrubs.
● Plant this short-lived shrublet in a sunny, well-drained position.
Height x spread:
10yrs 45 x 75cm (1½ x 2½ft)

Cornus
CORNEL, DOGWOOD

A genus which includes small trees as well as shrubs: some grown for their flowers, others for their colourful bark, and most for their autumn tints. The new stems of *C. alba* 'Kesselringii' are purple-black, while those of *C. stolonifera* 'Flaviramea' are olive-green to yellow, making both eye-catching features in winter. The latter prefers moister conditions, and is often grown on lakesides, so the stems are reflected in the water. *C. alba* 'Aurea' has golden foliage. *C. kousa* var. *chinensis* is a small tree of shapely habit, covered for many weeks in early summer with white petal-like bracts, which flush to pink as time goes by.
● Cut back dogwoods grown for stem colour to two buds in late winter, and mulch well with organic matter. This will encourage strong new colourful shoots.
Height x spread:
C. alba
10yrs 2.5 x 4m (8 x 13ft)
20yrs 3 x 4m (10 x 13ft)
C. stolonifera
10yrs 2.5 x 3m (8 x 10ft)
20yrs 2.5 x 4m (8 x 13ft)
C. kousa
10yrs 2.5 x 1.8m (8 x 6ft)
20yrs 4 x 4m (13 x 13ft)

Corylopsis pauciflora

A slow-growing shrub producing delightful short bunches of fresh, pale yellow, scented flowers in late winter, just before the leaves emerge. The young foliage is tinted pink. Plant among other deciduous shrubs.
● Requires an acid to neutral soil and cool conditions.
Height x spread:
10yrs 1.5 x 2m (5 x 6½ft)
20yrs 2 x 2m (6½ x 6½ft)

Corylus maxima 'Purpurea'
PURPLE-LEAF FILBERT

Intense purple foliage makes this a very desirable colour provider among other shrubs, or at the rear of large-scale herbaceous planting schemes. Filberts grow tall and upright, producing new shoots from an ever-widening base. Dark red catkins dangle decoratively in spring. In early autumn, when the husks turn yellow, gather the nuts before the squirrels take them.
● Old stems can be cut at the base and used for staking perennials.
Height x spread:
10yrs 4 x 3.5m (13 x 11½ft)
20yrs 4 x 6m (13 x 20ft)

Cotinus coggygria 'Royal Purple'
SMOKE BUSH, VENETIAN SUMACH

This shrub is grown for its smooth matt oval leaves of dark purple. It is suitable for planting among perennials, where it can be used as a powerful foil to other plants. Alternatively, it makes an excellent colour contrast with other shrubs. Plume-like flowerheads appear in summer and will remain on the bush into the autumn, at which time they resemble grey smoke.
● Pruning during winter is optional, but will help to keep the shrub shapely and medium-sized.
Height x spread:
10yrs 2 x 2m (6½ x 6½ft)
20yrs 4 x 4m (13 x 13ft)

Cratægus monogyna
COMMON HAWTHORN, MAY, QUICKTHORN

A beautiful small tree with spreading crown, also familiar as a hedging plant. In late spring it is covered with small, white, scented flowers, which are replaced in late summer and autumn by bright red berries, known as haws, and accompanied by coppery orange autumn leaves. Beware of the vicious thorns which make this a good choice for an intruder-proof boundary hedge. This excellent source of food and cover will encourage wildlife into the garden.
● Tolerant of a wide range of conditions, from wet to dry soils. Slow to establish. Trim hedges in summer and autumn to keep them dense.
Height x spread:
10yrs 6 x 4m (20 x 13ft)
20yrs 8 x 6m (26 x 20ft)

Cornus stolonifera 'Flaviramea'

Corylus maxima 'Purpurea'

Elaeagnus 'Quicksilver'

Genista aetnensis

Dicksonia antarctica

KEY TO SYMBOLS

◔ Prefers full sun

◑ Prefers partial shade

● Tolerates full shade

✳ ✳ ✳ Hardy below −8°C (18°F)

✳ ✳ Hardy to −7°C (20°F)

✳ Protect below 4°C (39°F)

Davidia involucrata
DOVE TREE, HANDKERCHIEF TREE
◔ ◑ ✳ ✳ ✳

An imposing specimen tree remarkable for its flowers.
In late spring the tree is covered in marble-sized flowers, each enclosed by two unequal-sized white bracts, resembling a handkerchief, or the wings of a dove. The inflorescences, suspended on long slender stalks, are best enjoyed from underneath the tree, so it is a good idea to plant it somewhere that will be accessible.
● It can take up to 15 years to flower, but planting in deep, fertile soil will encourage fast development.
Height x spread:
10yrs 6 x 4m (20 x 13ft)
20yrs 12 x 5m (40 x 16ft)

Dicksonia antarctica
SOFT TREE FERN
◔ ◑ ✳ ✳

Solid, dark brown hairy trunks, like elephant's legs, are topped with a superb whorl of large, fresh green fern fronds. The contrast between the chunky trunk and the delicacy of the foliage adds to the magic of this tree fern. Imposing in profile, the whorl of leaves should be viewed from

above to enjoy fully its stunning symmetry. The rusty brown unfurling fronds are also very spectacular.
● Fertile soil and warm, moist conditions will encourage good leaf development. Plant in a sheltered position and remember to protect from frost.
Height x spread:
10yrs 1.8 x 1.5m (6 x 5ft)
20yrs 3.5 x 2m (11½ x 6½ft)

Elaeagnus 'Quicksilver'
SYN. *E. ANGUSTIFOLIA* CASPICA GROUP
◔ ✳ ✳ ✳

A fast-growing oleaster of pyramidal habit. The glaucous leaves are silvery and deciduous, and in summer scented white flowers appear. Its high tolerance of salt-laden winds makes this shrub suitable for coastal plantings in particular.
● Avoid waterlogged soils. It suckers freely when growing conditions suit.
Height x spread:
10yrs 1.8 x 1.8m (6 x 6ft)
20yrs 3 x 3m (10 x 10ft)

Fagus sylvatica
COMMON BEECH
◔ ◑ ✳ ✳ ✳

One of the most imposing tall trees, beech makes a handsome feature plant, as well as a beautiful woodland tree with a smooth, silvery grey bark. Free-standing beeches develop monumental proportions. The spring foliage is a delicate pale green, turning darker as summer progresses and finally assuming an unsurpassed coppery red colour in autumn. Beech makes a stunning avenue tree, but is also suitable as a hedging plant, retaining its brown and rustling leaves through winter. Purple beeches, *F. sylvatica* Atropurpurea Group, are similar in habit and posture, but with purple-coloured leaves. Plant green-leaved and purple beeches together to make a tapestry hedge.
● Slow to establish, especially if planted with bare roots. Feeding and watering in the early years will encourage new growth. Hedges should be clipped in late summer.
Height x spread:
10yrs 7 x 5m (23 x 16ft)
20yrs 10 x 6m (33 x 20ft)

Genista aetnensis
MOUNT ETNA BROOM
◔ ✳ ✳ ✳

An elegant shrub or small tree of weeping habit with long, slender leafless shoots. During the summer months it is covered in scented, butter yellow flowers.
● Strongly dislikes pruning. Plant where it has space to develop fully.
Height x spread:
10yrs 4 x 4m (13 x 13ft)
20yrs 4.5 x 4.5m (15 x 15ft)

Ginkgo biloba
MAIDENHAIR TREE
◔ ✳ ✳ ✳

An atypical deciduous conifer, with curious fan-shaped leaves. It is slow growing, with a narrow crown that broadens with age. In the autumn the foliage turns a glowing yellow. Male and female flowers are borne on separate trees but, as the fruits exude an unpleasant odour in autumn, it is better to plant male trees.
● Very adaptable to all soil types and environmental conditions.
Height x spread:
10yrs 5 x 2.5m (16 x 8ft)
20yrs 10 x 4m (33 x 13ft)

Gleditsia triacanthos 'Sunburst'
◔ ✳ ✳ ✳

This thornless honey locust tree is topped with a mop of feathery foliage, which is particularly yellow in spring and evens out to a yellowish green during summer. The delicacy of the foliage lets a generous amount of light filter through to ground level, allowing underplanting to succeed. Its tolerance of air pollution makes it suitable for an urban garden.
● Grows on acid to slightly alkaline soil.
Height x spread:
10yrs 6 x 4m (20 x 13ft)
20yrs 8 x 6m (26 x 20ft)

Halesia monticola
◔ ◑ ✳ ✳ ✳

A particularly beautiful snowdrop tree, small in stature and grown for its delightful clusters of pendulous flowers, which appear in late spring. They are white and

bell-shaped, followed later in summer by large, green decorative winged fruits. The foliage colours well in autumn.
● Slow to establish.
Height x spread:
10yrs 3 x 4m (10 x 13ft)
20yrs 6 x 6m (20 x 20ft)

Hamamelis mollis
CHINESE WITCH HAZEL
◔ ◑ ✳ ✳ ✳

One of the most magical of all winter-flowering shrubs, producing stalkless clusters of warm yellow flowers, each consisting of four unfurling narrow petals. Most witch hazels are strongly scented, perfuming the entire garden on sunny winter days. Although slow growing, they flower at an early age. They tend to form wide branching plants of great charm. They also display beautiful autumn colour.
● Witch hazels grow better if the root zone is kept clear of other vegetation. Grow on an acid to neutral soil.
Height x spread:
10yrs 3 x 4m (10 x 13ft)
20yrs 5 x 6m (16 x 20ft)

Hydrangea
◔ ◑ ✳ ✳ ✳

Hydrangeas are invaluable for their late-summer flowers.
H. aspera Villosa Group form spreading shrubs with large tapering leaves, downy beneath, and large flat lilac-blue flowerheads. *H. arborescens* 'Grandiflora' produces huge rounded heads heavy with small white flowers, which dry on the shrub during winter.
● Plant in moisture-retentive soil.
Height x spread:
H. aspera
10yrs 2.5 x 2.5m (8 x 8ft)
20yrs 4 x 4m (13 x 13ft)
H. arborescens
10yrs 1.5 x 1.5m (5 x 5ft)
20yrs 2.5 x 2.5m (8 x 8ft)

Ilex aquifolium
COMMON HOLLY, ENGLISH HOLLY
◔ ◑ ● ✳ ✳ ✳

A tough, versatile evergreen which can be grown as a large shrub or small tree, or clipped as a hedge or to form large topiary. Mixed in with other hedgerow plants, the shiny

Hamamelis mollis

Hydrangea aspera **Villosa Group**

Lavandula angustifolia

Magnolia grandiflora

Malus **'John Downie'**

prickly holly leaves reflect the light and create an interesting contrast. Holly is suitable for underplanting large trees and can also be used for screening. If a male plant is nearby for pollination purposes, female trees produce an abundance of bright red (or yellow) berries, which show off well against the dark green foliage during the winter months. If a holly becomes too large, it can be cut back to the main stem in spring and will regenerate well as long as the plant is well mulched with rotted manure, and watered in dry periods.
● Easy to grow, but does best when planted on rich, moist soils.
Height x spread:
10yrs 5.5 x 2.5m (18 x 8ft)
20yrs 7 x 4m (23 x 13ft)

Lavandula
LAVENDER
Common lavender, *L. angustifolia*, is a robust species, producing large bushes with young grey growth, turning green as time progresses. The flower spikes, which appear in summer, are coloured lavender-blue. *L. angustifolia* 'Hidcote' is more compact in form, with dense spikes of dark lilac flowers and grey foliage. French lavender, *L. stoechas*, is slightly more tender, but equally well scented. It forms a neat bush clothed with narrow leaves. The broad purple flower spikes are topped with reddish purple sterile bracts, which look like little wings.
● Grow in well-drained sunny sites. Clip in mid-spring or after flowering, to stop the shrubs from becoming woody and shapeless. Lavenders are short lived and may not regenerate from old wood.
Height x spread:
L. angustifolia
10yrs 80 x 80cm (2½ x 2½ft)
L. stoechas
10yrs 50 x 90cm (1½ x 3ft)

Lavatera 'Rosea'
SYN. *L. OLBIA* 'ROSEA'
A fast-growing and rounded tree mallow that is covered in a never-ending display of pink flowers for most of the summer and into the autumn. The leaves are soft and downy

grey. Plant this shrub in a sunny spot sheltered from strong winds in order for it to thrive.
● Prune back the stems of this short-lived plant by two-thirds in late winter to reduce its size and improve its shape.
Height x spread:
10yrs 3 x 3m (10 x 10ft)

Liquidambar styraciflua
SWEET GUM
Beautiful slow-growing tree with a narrow pyramidal shape. It is renowned for its splendid appearance in autumn, when the deeply lobed shiny leaves turn from dark green to crimson, dark red and purple. The slim habit and slow growth rate make it a suitable feature tree for many gardens.
● Tolerant of most soils, including highly alkaline. Slow to establish.
Height x spread:
10yrs 6 x 4m (20 x 13ft)
20yrs 10 x 6m (33 x 20ft)

Magnolia
Magnolias count among the most impressive of flowering trees and shrubs. The evergreen bull bay (*M. grandiflora*) makes an imposing large shrub or tree, with huge glossy leaves. During summer it produces a succession of magnificent scented lemony cream flowers. It is often grown as a wall shrub. *M. x soulangeana* 'Alba Superba' opens its large white scented flowers in spring before the leaves emerge. It is tolerant of pollution and clay soils, but prefers those with an acid to neutral pH. For earlier spring show the star magnolia (*M. stellata*) offers an abundant display of scented narrow-petalled white flowers.
● To protect early flowers from frost, plant magnolias in a sheltered place.
Height x spread:
M. grandiflora
10yrs 4 x 1.8m (13 x 6ft)
20yrs 8 x 4m (26 x 13ft)
M. x soulangeana
10yrs 3 x 2.5m (10 x 8ft)
20yrs 6 x 5m (20 x 16ft)
M. stellata
10yrs 1.5 x 1.8m (5 x 6ft)
20yrs 2.5 x 4m (8 x 13ft)

Mahonia japonica
Bealei Group
Erect evergreen shrubs with large pinnate leaves that are glossy, dark green and spiny. The upright unbranched stems are topped with sprays of yellow scented flowers, which appear throughout winter and are followed by bunches of blue-black fruits. It is a useful evergreen height provider, suitable for small spaces. Similar, but more architectural in profile, is *M. x media* 'Charity', bearing enormous upright sprays of winter flowers.
● Prefers well-drained soils rich in organic matter, and should be sheltered from strong winds.
Height x spread:
M. japonica
10yrs 2 x 1.5m (6½ x 5ft)
20yrs 2.5 x 2.5m (8 x 8ft)
M. x media 'Charity'
10yrs 2.5 x 1.8m (8 x 6ft)
20yrs 3 x 2.5m (10 x 8ft)

Malus
CRAB APPLE
A crab apple tree is a great addition to any garden, producing a profusion of blossom in spring and colourful apples in late summer. *M.* 'John Downie' flowers white, and produces large, conical, orange-red fruits suitable for eating. *M. x moerlandsii* 'Profusion' has large red flowers followed by coppery new growth and, later on, sour red fruits.
● Avoid growing in waterlogged sites. If a good harvest of fruit is important, prune the tree to keep the centre open so light can penetrate and air can circulate freely.
Height x spread:
10yrs 6 x 3m (20 x 10ft)
20yrs 8 x 6m (26 x 20ft)

Morus nigra
BLACK MULBERRY
Many an old garden has its mulberry tree, which often looks older than its years due to the gnarled, burred appearance of its bark. In late summer the broad-crowned tree bears purple-red, raspberry-like fruits.

When fully ripe these are a delicious treat to steal straight off the tree, although beware of juice stains. Tolerant of urban and coastal environments.
● Take care when planting mulberries, as the fleshy roots are easily damaged.
Height x spread:
10yrs 5 x 2.5m (16 x 8ft)
20yrs 8 x 5m (26 x 16ft)

Parrotia persica
PERSIAN IRONWOOD
A slow-growing and wide-spreading shrub or small tree that flowers in late winter, producing dense brushes of red stamens. The autumn colours are brilliant gold, orange and bright red.
● Often associated with plants that love acid soil, parrotias also tolerate lime.
Height x spread:
10yrs 4 x 4m (13 x 13ft)
20yrs 8 x 10m (26 x 33ft)

Perovskia 'Blue Spire'
A wonderful silver-leaved shrub with elegant vertical growth. The leaves are deeply cut and aromatic, the stems virtually white, and the flowers, which appear later in summer, are blue.
● Will grow in relatively poor soils, but only if well drained. Best pruned close to ground level in spring. It is short lived.
Height x spread:
10yrs 1.2 x 1m (4 x 3ft)

Perovskia **'Blue Spire'**

Phyllostachys aurea

Rubus cockburnianus

KEY TO SYMBOLS

◖ Prefers full sun
◑ Prefers partial shade
● Tolerates full shade
❋❋❋ Hardy below −8°C (18°F)
❋❋ Hardy to −7°C (20°F)
❋ Protect below 4°C (39°F)

Philadelphus
MOCK ORANGE
◖ ◑ ❋ ❋ ❋

This is a shrub no garden should be without because of its sweetly scented flowers, produced in abundance in early summer. *P.* 'Belle Etoile' is compact and medium-sized, bearing single large white flowers with a maroon centre. Smaller and with double cream-coloured flowers is *P.* 'Manteau d'Hermine'. Even when they are planted in the background, the strong scent will permeate a wide area. Feature them individually in large perennial planting schemes or among shrubs.
● Tolerant of most soils.
Height x spread:
10yrs 2 x 1.5m (6½ x 5ft)
20yrs 2 x 2m (6½ x 6½ft)

Phyllostachys
◖ ❋ ❋ ❋

These bamboos make atmospheric features in gardens, adding a strong vertical element, movement of leaf and rustling sounds. The fishpole bamboo, *P. aurea*, produces pale green canes which fade to yellow as they mature. In contrast the canes of the black bamboo, *P. nigra*, are mottled brown at first before turning to black. The imposing size makes these species unsuitable for very small gardens.
● Moist, fertile soils rich in organic matter will increase the rate of development. Mulch when young.
Height x spread:
10yrs 3.5 x 1m (11½ x 3ft)
20yrs 3.5 x 2m (11½ x 6½ft)

Pieris formosa
◖ ◑ ❋ ❋ ❋

A slow-growing large shrub of the heather family, noted for its foliage and large clusters of bell-like flowers which appear simultaneously. The leaves open shiny bronze, turning dark green with age; they are an excellent foil to the creamy white blossom. Plant in a sheltered position, protecting the new foliage from late spring frosts with fleece.
● Requires acid soil.
Height x spread:
10yrs 1.8 x 1m (6 x 3ft)
20yrs 2 x 3m (6½ x 10ft)

Prunus laurocerasus

Pittosporum
◖ ❋ ❋

P. tenuifolium 'Purpureum' is a delicate form of the kohuhu, an evergreen shrub or small tree with pyramidal habit. Fine, wiry black stems carry soft, pale green leaves, which turn bronze-purple as they mature. A suitable feature plant in gravel gardens. *P. tobira* produces orange-scented white flowers in late spring and early summer. Its glossy leaves will tolerate salt spray. The sticky orange seedpods are a bonus.
● Provide well-drained soil, and shelter in cooler areas.
Height x spread:
10yrs 3 x 2m (10 x 6½ft)
20yrs 6 x 3m (20 x 10ft)

Prunus
CHERRY
◖ ◑ ● ❋ ❋ ❋

This genus contains a wide range of garden-worthy plants, from the tough evergreen cherry laurel, *P. laurocerasus*, to a whole range of deciduous flowering and fruiting trees. The cherry laurel is a reliable shrub, ideal for planting under trees, as a background or for a hedge. It has bold, glossy leaves which reflect sunlight, adding sparkle to a garden. In spring, spires of small white flowers open, followed later in the year by red fruits that turn black when ripe. Although it can grow into a large shrub, it copes with an occasional vigorous pruning to keep it under control. The Yoshino cherry, *P. x yedoensis*, is an elegant early-flowering deciduous tree with arching branches. The white flowers flushed with pink have a delicious almond scent. The autumn cherry, *P. x subhirtella* 'Autumnalis', produces a modest but continuous display of small, semi-double white flowers from autumn to spring. Both these cherries suit small gardens.
● Tolerant of most soils, but suffers in extremes of dryness and alkalinity.
Height x spread:
P. laurocerasus
10yrs 4 x 4m (13 x 13ft)
20yrs 5 x 5m (16 x 16ft)
Flowering cherries
10yrs 4 x 3m (13 x 10ft)
20yrs 7 x 4m (23 x 13ft)

Quercus ilex
HOLM OAK
◖ ◑ ● ❋ ❋ ❋

A majestic, slow-growing evergreen oak with a rounded crown. Initially the grey bark is smooth, becoming fissured as the tree grows older. The leaves are dark green above and silver-grey beneath, giving the tree a silvery appearance overall. It copes well with coastal conditions and can be clipped to make a good windbreak hedge for a seaside garden.
● A fertile, moist soil will accelerate establishment. This species does not thrive in cold situations.
Height x spread:
10yrs 5.5 x 3.5m (18 x 11½ft)
20yrs 8 x 5.5m (26 x 18ft)

Rhododendron luteum
◖ ◑ ❋ ❋ ❋

The common yellow deciduous azalea makes a vibrant display in early spring, ablaze with rich yellow flowers which spread their strong, sweet perfume across the garden. As the flowers fade, the pale green leaves open and develop magnificent autumn colours, ranging from orange to crimson and purple. There are numerous cultivars of deciduous azaleas, but the group of Ghent azaleas are among the finest. Most are deliciously scented and range in colour from pure white with a streak of yellow, as in *R.* 'Daviesii', to dark pink with a pale pink centre, as in the double-flowered *R.* 'Corneille', also noted for spectacular autumn colour. In the orange tones, the all-time favourite remains *R.* 'Coccineum Speciosum' with warm orange-red flowers in late spring.
● All members of the rhododendron genus require acid soil.
Height x spread:
10yrs 2 x 1.5m (6½ x 5ft)
20yrs 2.5 x 3m (8 x 10ft)

Robinia pseudoacacia
BLACK LOCUST, FALSE ACACIA
◖ ❋ ❋ ❋

A large suckering spiny tree with very light canopy and of somewhat oriental appearance. The acacia-like leaves are fresh green and feathery. The pendent clusters of white leguminous flowers appear in early summer. *R. pseudoacacia* 'Frisia' makes a small to medium-sized tree with red spines and a mop of golden leaves. It can be grown as a shrub. Both plants have brittle branches likely to break in very windswept conditions. They are tolerant of pollution.
● To establish quickly, plant a container-grown tree. Can also be cut back to the base in early spring and mulched well with organic matter to encourage strong new stems and a shrubby habit.
Height x spread:
10yrs 6 x 4m (20 x 13ft)
20yrs 6 x 6m (26 x 20ft)

Rosa
ROSE
◖ ❋ ❋ ❋

There is a vast range of roses available, as species and cultivars, both old and new. The shrub roses perform an invaluable role in the garden, offering not only flower colour and scents but, often, rose hips in late summer and autumn. *R. moyesii* grows into a tall shrub bearing single red flowers in early summer that hum with the sound of bees, then display bottle-shaped hips of vivid orange. *R. glauca* (syn. *R. rubrifolia*) is a smaller shrub, with new stems of reddish purple and distinctive glaucous leaves, red on the undersides. It produces clear pink single flowers, and small, round red hips. The sweet briar *R. rubiginosa* (syn. *R. eglanteria*) makes a small, dense, prickly bush with tiny dark green leaves and pink single flowers. Both foliage and flowers are apple scented. *R. x odorata* 'Mutabilis' (syn. *R. chinensis* 'Mutabilis') is a delightful China rose, with lax growth, few spines and dark purplish red slender stems. The large single flowers, produced throughout summer and autumn open buff and progress through rose to crimson. Another splendid shrub rose is *R.* 'Nevada', which in early summer is covered in creamy yellow flowers that open flat; a few repeat flowers appear during summer and these are often tinged pink, as they change colour in hot weather. The old hybrids have a special charm, even though their flowering season is short. The most delightful of all is *R.* 'Madame Hardy', a pure white Damask

Rosa glauca

Salix alba var. sericea

Sorbus hupehensis

rose with a lemony fragrance. It has perfect cup-shaped flowers filled with petals that surround a green eye.
● Plant in well-manured, loamy soil where no roses have grown before.
Height x spread:
R. moyesii
10yrs 4 x 3m (12 x 10ft)
R. glauca
10yrs 1.8 x 1.5m (6 x 5ft)
R. rubiginosa
10yrs 2.5 x 2.5m (8 x 8ft)
R. x odorata 'Mutabilis'
10yrs 2.5 x 1.8m (8 x 6ft)
R. 'Nevada'
10yrs 2.2 x 2.2m (7 x 7ft)
R. 'Madame Hardy'
10yrs 1.8 x 1.5m (6 x 5ft)

Rubus
△ ◑ ✳ ✳ ✳
Wild brambles have some sophisticated, but still prickly, relatives of great garden value.
R. cockburnianus makes a tall shrub with arching stems, but only suitable for large gardens where some wild areas are available. The young purple stems are covered in a ghostly white bloom, outstanding in winter. The ghost bramble itself, *R. thibetanus* (syn. *R. thibetanus* 'Silver Fern'), is of a more manageable size and could be planted in a more restricted site. The new growth also has a similarly chalky bloom to which the finely cut greyish leaves are a perfect addition.
● Cut back old shoots to the ground in late winter, and mulch to encourage formation of new growth.
Height x spread:
10yrs 2 x 2m (6½ x 6½ft)
20yrs 2 x 3m (6½ x 10ft)

Salix
WILLOW
△ ◑ ✳ ✳ ✳
Most willows thrive in damp sites, such as on river banks or in water meadows, but will grow in gardens providing sufficient moisture is available. If not, their roots will go in search of drains – beware! The silver willow, *S. alba* var. *sericea* (syn. *S. alba* f. *argentea*), is a small, round-headed tree with silvery white, narrow leaves. Another species with silky, silvery leaves,

especially when young, is the coyote willow, *S. exigua*. This produces long, thin grey-brown branches and forms a shrub or small tree. When coppiced, some willows produce unrivalled winter stem colour. One such is the golden willow, *S. alba* var. *vitellina*, with young shoots of brilliant orange-yellow.
● Tolerant of wet, waterlogged soils. Cut back willows grown for stem colour to two buds in late winter.
Height x spread:
S. alba
10yrs 8 x 3.5m (26 x 11½ft)
20yrs 9 x 5.5m (30 x 18ft)
S. exigua
10yrs 3 x 3m (10 x 10ft)
20yrs 4 x 4m (13 x 13ft)

Sambucus nigra
BLACK ELDER, COMMON ELDER, ELDERBERRY
△ ◑ ● ✳ ✳ ✳
Elders are a common sight in hedgerows, and two particularly appealing forms make interesting garden plants. The fern-leaved elder, *S. nigra* f. *laciniata*, is so called because of its finely cut leaves, giving it a very frilly, ferny appearance. *S. nigra* 'Guincho Purple' (syn. *S. nigra* 'Purpurea') has leaves that turn purple and flowerheads that are pink in bud and open white flushed pink. Both these elders are rapid-growing foliage shrubs suitable for mixed shrub borders or as single feature plants.
● Regular pruning is not essential, but it will regenerate new growth and keep foliage at eye level. Cut stems down to the base, or grow as a short-stemmed pollard for foliage at a higher level.
Height x spread:
10+20yrs 4 x 3.5m (13 x 11½ft)

Sorbus
MOUNTAIN ASH
△ ✳ ✳ ✳
The whitebeam, *S. aria* 'Lutescens', is an attractive small to medium-sized conical tree. Newly opened leaves are covered in dense white hairs, making the canopy look white early in the season, becoming gradually greener as summer wears on, and finally turning orange-yellow in autumn. This tree tolerates

polluted air and coastal conditions. Another good choice for a smaller space is *S. hupehensis*. This tree has a compact crown of glaucous tinted pinnate leaves which turn a magnificent red in autumn. At the same time it bears drooping trusses of white berries flushed pink, and these usually persist well into winter. Both species produce umbels of creamy white flowers during late spring and early summer.
● Whereas *S. aria* is commonly found in alkaline conditions, *S. hupehensis* prefers a neutral or slightly acid soil.
Height x spread:
S. aria
10yrs 6 x 4m (20 x 13ft)
20yrs 12 x 8m (40 x 26ft)
S. hupehensis
10yrs 5 x 2.5m (16 x 8ft)
20yrs 10 x 5m (33 x 16ft)

Taxus baccata
YEW
△ ◑ ● ✳ ✳ ✳
Few sights are more impressive than an ancient yew. Yew can be grown as a tree or shrub, clipped into hedges and topiary forms, or used as shrubby underplanting in woodland. The dull, dark evergreen foliage makes an ideal background for setting off the light and bright colours of other plants. In southern England and where summers are reliably warm, an old yew hedge can be rejuvenated by cutting it back to the main trunk in spring; the top and sunny side first, the shady side one or two years later. Before pruning, it is important to mulch, feed and water it well to encourage vigorous regrowth.
● Grows in all fertile soils, but will not tolerate waterlogging. Good ground preparation and mulching in early years will encourage quick establishment.
Height x spread:
10yrs 2 x 1.6m (6½ x 5ft)
20yrs 4.5 x 4.5m (15 x 15ft)

Trachycarpus fortunei
CHUSAN PALM, HEMP PALM
△ ✳ ✳
A fairly hardy palm which will survive in sheltered areas, growing from a shrub-like state to a small tree. It adds an exotic note to any planting scheme, and should be used

as a feature plant. The trunk, covered in a thick layer of rough fibres, is topped with a whorl of fan-shaped leaves reaching 2m (6½ft) across. Sprays of yellowish flowers may form in summer.
● Plant in a sheltered, well-drained site.
Height x spread:
10yrs 3 x 2m (10 x 6½ft)
20yrs 7 x 2m (23 x 6½ft)

Viburnum
△ ◑ ● ✳ ✳ ✳
Viburnums include many useful garden shrubs. Among them is evergreen *V. x burkwoodii*, with strongly scented flowers opening from pink-tinged buds during winter and spring, and fading to white as they mature. Another evergreen, but slightly more tender, is laurustinus, *V. tinus*, which makes a large mound of shiny dark green leaves and flowers from autumn through to spring. The clusters of pink buds open to display white flowerheads. This makes a good informal hedge tolerant of coastal conditions. Among the deciduous viburnums is the common guelder rose *V. opulus* and its cultivar *V. o.* 'Xanthocarpum', with maple-like leaves colouring vividly in autumn. In early summer, spheres of small white flowers tinged green appear resembling those of hydrangeas, followed by translucent yellow fruits. The most elegant of all viburnums is *V. plicatum* 'Mariesii'. It makes a medium-sized shrub of spreading growth. The horizontal branches are covered in white discs of flowers in late spring and early summer, standing on vertical stalks. Its autumn leaves are colourful.
● These viburnums can cope with most soil types, but only *V. opulus* will tolerate extremely wet and dry conditions.
Height x spread:
V. x burkwoodii
10yrs 1.5 x 1.5m (5 x 5ft)
20yrs 2 x 2m (6½ x 6½ft)
V. tinus
10yrs 2 x 2m (6½ x 6½ft)
20yrs 3.5 x 3.5m (11½ x 11½ft)
V. opulus
10yrs 3 x 3m (10 x 10ft)
20yrs 4.5 x 4.5m (15 x 15ft)
V. plicatum
10yrs 2 x 3m (6½ x 10ft)
20yrs 3 x 4m (10 x 13ft)

Trachycarpus fortunei

Perennials, bulbs and ferns

Allium hollandicum 'Purple Sensation'

Agave americana

Alchemilla mollis

All the following plants live for several years, and have the common characteristic that they do not possess a woody stem. Instead, they produce soft herbaceous growth that usually dies down each year. The root systems will live for many years, producing an annual cycle of stems, leaves, flowers and seeds, with the exception of ferns, which do not flower. Most perennials, bulbs and ferns have low labour demands and will establish quickly, giving effect within their first year. They are easy to lift and transplant, when most can be divided into smaller clumps or individual plantlets.

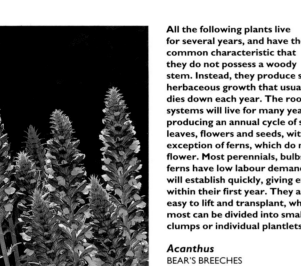

Acanthus spinosus

Acanthus
BEAR'S BREECHES
△ ✳ ✳ ✳
Extremely handsome plants of statuesque habit. In *A. spinosus* the glossy, dark green leaves are deeply cut and spiny. The foliage is topped in early summer by imposing spires of white flowers, each encapsulated in a purple bract. Plants of the *A. mollis* Latifolius Group have splendid, broad shiny leaves, strongly veined and lobed. Acanthus are ideal for mass planting.
● Grow in well-drained soil.
Height x spread:
1.2 x 0.6m (4 x 2ft)

Agapanthus
AFRICAN BLUE LILY
△ ◖ ✳ ✳ ✳
Rich blue tubular flowers form large round heads on upright stems, which rise out of soft, green strap-shaped leaves in late summer. Attractive border plants and handsome in containers, they also associate well with shrubs. Several are hardy in temperate regions, including the Headbourne Hybrids, which have large leaves and enormous spheres of flowers. More delicate is *A. campanulatus* 'Isis', with rich dark blue flowers, and the white-flowered *A. campanulatus* var. *albidus*.
● Mulch deeply in winter with leaves or straw to protect from frosts.
Height x spread:
0.6–1.2 x 0.6m (2–4 x 2ft)

Agave
CENTURY PLANT
△ ✳ ✳
Although most agaves are imposing succulents from tropical or subtropical regions, some are hardy in more temperate regions. *A. americana* has great grey-green fleshy leaves spiked at the tip. Each leaf carries the imprint of its neighbour, made before they unfurl to form a large rosette. The much

smaller *A. celsii* has broad green leaves in a solid clump. Due to their strong architectural presence agaves are best used singly as exotic punctuation points.
● Plant in full sun, in a well-drained position. Hardiness increases with age, so protect young plants during winter. Mulch deeply with straw and in severe weather enclose them in a tent of bubble plastic or horticultural fleece.
Height x spread:
0.75–2 x 0.75–3m (2½–6½ x 2½–10ft)

Ajuga reptans
BUGLE
△ ◗ ✳ ✳ ✳
This makes an excellent low-growing ground cover for semi-shaded spots among shrubs or other perennials. In late spring, elegant spires of blue flowers rise 15cm (6in) above the foliage. Although the species has dark green leaves, occasionally red tinged, several dark red- and purple-leaved variations are available, such as 'Atropurpurea'.
● Grow in moisture-retentive soils.
Height x spread:
15 x 30cm (6 x 12in)

Alchemilla mollis
LADY'S MANTLE
△ ◖ ◗ ✳ ✳ ✳
No garden should be without this versatile perennial, which flowers for weeks in early and midsummer. The pale greyish green, felty leaves are trimmed with pearl-like dewdrops on misty mornings, and make a good foil for thousands of tiny, starry lime-green flowers, appearing as one frothy mass. It is happy in most positions as long as sufficient moisture is available, and fits in well with perennials and shrubs alike. Planted in large masses or small clumps it will never fail to please.
● Cut back to the ground towards the end of the flowering period for a second flush of foliage and some repeat flowers in late summer.
Height x spread:
80 x 45cm (2½ x 1½ft)

Allium
△ ✳ ✳ ✳
Ornamental onions are equally invaluable in the garden as they are in the kitchen. The star of Persia, *A. cristophii*, makes huge transparent spheres of starry purple flowers up to 30cm (1ft) across, supported on stalks 45cm (1½ft) tall. In contrast, the slightly taller *A. hollandicum* (syn. *A. aflatunense*) carries dense heads, 10cm (4in) in diameter, of small, mauve flowers. Smaller still and later to open are the compact heads of the round-headed leek, *A. sphaerocephalon*. Held aloft on wiry stems up to 80cm (32in)

tall, the flowerheads turn from green to a rich maroon-purple as flowering progresses. All three flower from late spring to summer, and look charming scattered among other perennials.
● Plant bulbs in early autumn in a sunny, well-drained position.
Height x spread:
30–90 x 30cm (1–3 x 1ft)

Anemone
WINDFLOWER
△ ◖ ✳ ✳ ✳
Anemones vary enormously, ranging from small rhizomatous plants to tall perennials, and flowering from early spring to autumn. The small wood anemone, *A. nemorosa*, is one of the daintiest early-spring flowers with white petals flushed red. At the opposite end of the scale is the Japanese anemone *A.* x *hybrida* 'Honorine Jobert', with tall lanky stems which carry pure white flowers high above the dark green foliage in autumn. Colonizers by nature, anemones are best planted in large drifts to make an impact.
● As they are slow to establish, leave them alone as much as possible.
Height x spread:
A. nemorosa
15 x 20cm (6 x 8in)
A. x *hybrida*
30cm–1.2m x 10–45cm (1–4ft x 4–18in)

Astelia chathamica
SYN. *A. CHATHAMICA* 'SILVER SPEAR'
△ ◖ ✳ ✳
An evergreen perennial of good architectural value when planted singly as a feature. Its broad, sword-like leaves are the prime attraction, making long linear sheaths and covered in fine, silky hairs. The insignificant greenish flowerheads appear on tall stems in late spring. It is a good source of silvery foliage for planting in a shady situation.
● Grow in fertile soil.
Height x spread:
2 x 2m (6½ x 6½ft)

Aster
△ ◖ ✳ ✳ ✳
Asters are among the most reliable late-summer and autumn colour providers. In early autumn *A. divaricatus* will give an attractive display of small white daisies

with brown centres, set sparingly along dark wiry stems. This species is suitable for mass planting under trees. The delicate sprays of tiny pure white daisies of *A. pringlei* 'Monte Cassino' appear in later autumn and are favourites for cutting. The plant dries beautifully in the border and will retain a graceful shape throughout winter.
● Provide asters with a well-drained soil.
Height x spread:
75–90 x 60cm (2½–3 x 2ft)

Astrantia
MASTERWORT
△ ◖ ◗ ✳ ✳ ✳
The virtually translucent paper-like flowers look much more fragile than they really are. The greater masterwort, *A. major*, and its cultivars are the most valuable for the garden. The species has greenish white flowers with a flush of pink. *A. major rosea* is clear pink, while *A. major* 'Hadspen Blood' is a deep red. Masterworts look superb in large drifts.
● They prefer cool conditions and a soil rich in organic matter.
Height x spread:
30–90 x 30cm (1–3 x 1ft)

Calamagrostis x acutiflora 'Karl Foerster'
FEATHER REED GRASS
△ ✳ ✳ ✳
A non-invasive grass with stiffly erect leaves which have a purplish brown or silvery sheen. Loose, smoky pink flowerheads appear in early summer, turning fawn-yellow after flowering. Their strong vertical forms persist right through the winter.
● Cut down once the stems have fallen over in late winter.
Height x spread:
2 x 1m (6½ x 3ft)

Caltha palustris
KINGCUP, MARSH MARIGOLD
△ ✳ ✳ ✳
A moisture lover growing at water margins and in wet meadows or boggy conditions. The warm yellow flowers resemble large buttercups, and appear in spring above shiny fresh green leaves.
● Grow in wet soils.
Height x spread:
15–60 x 45cm (6in–2ft x 1½ft)

Astrantia major

Calamagrostis × *acutiflora* 'Karl Foerster'

Epimedium × *versicolor* 'Sulphureum'

Dicentra spectabilis 'Alba'

Camassia
CAMAS, QUAMASH
○ ◑ ✳ ✳ ✳
Bulbous perennials ideal for naturalizing or planting in groups. *C. cusickii* is strong growing, with dense spikes of delicate pale blue, star-like flowers. *C. quamash* is similar, but smaller in stature.
● They enjoy a moist soil.
Height x spread:
60–90 x 30cm (2–3 x 1ft)

Carex
SEDGE
○ ✳ ✳ ✳
Clump-forming evergreens with grass-like leaves. *C. comans* Bronze Form develops a dense mophead of fine trailing leaves which are bronze to yellowish green. *C. testacea*, which also has trailing foliage, is much looser. Both have insignificant flowers. Their evergreen habit makes them suitable for interspersing among low plants in naturalistic schemes.
● They enjoy a moist soil.
Height x spread:
45 x 60cm (1½ x 2ft)

Cimicifuga simplex Atropurpurea Group
BUGBANE, SNAKE ROOT
◑ ◐ ✳ ✳ ✳
Tall, slender spires of cream-white flowers are borne on dark red stems high above purplish leaves. Plant in drifts in front of pale green foliaged shrubs to enjoy the full effect of the ferny foliage and wand-like flowerheads, opening from late summer into autumn.
● They thrive in rich moist soils.
Height x spread:
1.2 x 0.6m (4 x 2ft)

Colchicum autumnale
AUTUMN CROCUS
○ ◑ ✳ ✳ ✳
The absence of chlorophyll is responsible for the eerie appearance of the waxy white stalks which carry the lilac-pink, crocus-like flowers in autumn. In spring, long after the flowers have been forgotten, the bold green leaves start to emerge.
● *C. autumnale* prefers a moist soil.
Height x spread:
15–30 x 15cm (6–12 x 6in)

Corydalis
○ ◑ ◐ ✳ ✳ ✳
Some dainty and charming garden plants can be found among the corydalis. *C. lutea* makes low evergreen mounds of soft green, ferny foliage, topped with small bunches of yellow flowers from spring till autumn. It thrives in dry cracks and walls. The blue-flowered *C. flexuosa* 'Père David' is a delicate long-flowering plant, which thrives in moist, shady positions and looks well associated with ferns.
● Provide a well-drained site for *C. lutea*. In contrast, *C. flexuosa* prefers cool conditions and soils enriched with plenty of organic matter.
Height x spread:
20 x 20–40cm (8 x 8–16in)

Crinum × powellii
○ ✳ ✳ ✳
Loose heads of elegant lily-like flowers curve down from the end of tall stems. The white and pink scented trumpets open between late summer and autumn. These stately bulbous perennials look their best when grown in large clumps in moist areas, preferably protected by a wall. *C.* × *powellii* 'Album' has pure white flowers.
● Keep well fed and watered, but in a well-drained soil. Mulch during the winter months to protect the crown from excessive moisture. The sap may irritate the skin, so wearing gloves is generally advisable.
Height x spread:
1 x 0.6m (3 x 2ft)

Crocosmia
MONTBRETIA
○ ✳ ✳ ✳
Cormous perennials with sword-shaped leaves and flowers in fiery colours. *C.* 'Lucifer' is a robust hybrid with vivid tomato red flowers. *C.* 'Solfaterre' is apricot-yellow with bronze leaves. They both flower for a long time, from late summer well into autumn, and make eye-catching colour accents in borders when planted in groups.
● In cold areas, protect during winter with a generous mulch of chipped bark or similar material.
Height x spread:
1m x 25cm (3ft x 10in)

Crocus tommasinianus
○ ◑ ✳ ✳ ✳
Crocuses bring much joy to early spring with their colourful flowers, followed by tufts of grassy leaves. *C. tommasinianus* is purple, often silvery on the outside. Ideal for naturalizing, it multiplies freely.
● Plant corms in well-drained soil.
Height x spread:
10 x 8cm (4 x 3in)

Dicentra spectabilis 'Alba'
◑ ✳ ✳ ✳
Delicate pale green ferny foliage looks attractive in association with other woodland and shade-tolerant plants. The arching flower stems are trimmed with pure white, intricate heart-shaped flowers emerging in late spring.
● Plant in moist but well-drained soil enriched with organic matter.
Height x spread:
75 x 60cm (2½ x 2ft)

Dierama pulcherrimum
ANGEL'S FISHING ROD
○ ✳ ✳ ✳
Fine, gracefully arching stems carry drooping sprays of pink fairy-like flowers. Later these are transformed into silvery seeds. Dieramas look stunning when free-standing alongside water and paths, or grown singly among low vegetation.
● Deep, well-drained soil is needed to accommodate the long roots. Can be slow to establish.
Height x spread:
1.5 x 0.6m (5 x 2ft)

Digitalis
FOXGLOVE
◑ ✳ ✳ ✳
Foxgloves, with their tall flower spikes, look most impressive naturalized in woodland clearings, especially the tall, white-flowered *D. purpurea* f. *albiflora*. Although perennial, this is short lived and more often treated as a biennial. Smaller, but as striking, is the sun-loving *D. ferruginea*, with dense spikes of small rusty orange flowers towering above silver-edged leaves. Both will naturalize happily if given the right conditions.
● Thrive in soils rich in organic matter.
Height x spread:
90cm–1.5m x 45cm (3–5 x 1½ft)

Dryopteris filix-mas
MALE FERN
◑ ◐ ✳ ✳ ✳
This large fern unfurls into an elegant shuttlecock of mid-green fronds. Plant in groups in shady corners, preferably near a path so you can look down on the beautiful whorls of leaves.
● Most luxuriant in moist, rich soil.
Height x spread:
1.2m x 90cm (4 x 3ft)

Echinacea purpurea
PURPLE CONE FLOWER
○ ✳ ✳ ✳
No garden should be without this late-summer flower with its large rust-coloured centre surrounded by a cheerful array of slender pink petals. The domed centres stay attractive long after the petals have faded and make useful cut flowers. The white petals of *E. purpurea* 'White Swan' are tinged green.
● Does best in rich soils.
Height x spread:
1.2m x 45cm (4 x 1½ft)

Epimedium
BISHOP'S MITRE
◑ ◐ ✳ ✳ ✳
An excellent ground cover for sunshine or shade, with tough, mostly evergreen leaves that take on attractive bronze and purple tones in winter. *E.* × *perralchicum* has dark green leaves and pendulous yellow flowers. *E.* × *versicolor* 'Sulphureum' combines sulphur-yellow flowers with red-tinted leaves.
● Cut back in late winter before the flowers develop.
Height x spread:
30 x 30cm (1 x 1ft)

Eranthis hyemalis
WINTER ACONITE
◑ ◐ ✳ ✳ ✳
Spring is announced when these bulbs start flowering. Bright yellow buttercup-like flowers are surrounded by a ruff of fresh green bracts. They make a cheerful show naturalized in huge drifts under trees and shrubs.
● Transplant in full leaf, just after the flowers have faded, into moist soil rich in organic matter.
Height x spread:
10 x 5cm (4 x 2in)

Foeniculum vulgare 'Purpureum'

Ligularia 'The Rocket'

Festuca glauca

Eremurus
FOXTAIL LILY

E. robustus produces broad rosettes of pale green leaves from a huge bud at ground level, followed by an awesome flower spike reaching 2.5m (8ft). This is covered with hundreds of soft pink starry flowers followed by marble-sized seedpods. *E. x isabellinus* Ruiter Hybrids are available in a mixture of colours, including yellow, salmon, apricot and orange tones. Foxtail lilies look superb mixed with ornamental grasses or mingled among perennials that will hide the foliage as it dies down.
● Plant in a sandy, well-drained soil and surround each plant with a collar of sharp sand or wood ash to protect the fleshy roots from winter moisture.
Height x spread:
2–2.5 x 1m (6½–8 x 3ft)

Erigeron karvinskianus

Modest, cheerful and long flowering. This low-growing plant is covered in a profusion of small daisies in white and pink tones, carried on short wiry stems. It loves growing in pavement cracks or in walls, and once established will happily seed itself.
● Enjoys a moist but well-drained soil.
Height x spread:
15 x 30cm (6 x 12in)

Eryngium giganteum

KEY TO SYMBOLS

◠ Prefers full sun
◑ Prefers partial shade
● Tolerates full shade
✳✳✳ Hardy below –8°C (18°F)
✳✳ Hardy to –7°C (20°F)
✳ Protect below 4°C (39°F)

Eryngium
SEA HOLLY

These thistle-like flowers are very sculptural. *E. agavifolium* has, as its name indicates, narrow, spiny agave-like leaves. The flower stems can reach 2m (6½ft) and are adorned with greyish, virtually spherical flowerheads in summer. *E. giganteum*, better known as Miss Willmott's ghost, is an attractive biennial of silvery green. The oval flowerhead, studded with tiny silver-blue flowers, is surrounded by spiny silver bracts. After it has flowered, the plant dies, turning an attractive brown-black. It will self-sow freely if conditions are right.
● Prefers a well-drained alkaline soil.
Height x spread:
50cm–2m x 30–60cm (1½–6½ x 1–2ft)

Euphorbia characias subsp. *wulfenii*

Eupatorium purpureum subsp. maculatum 'Atropurpureum'
JOE PYE WEED

This giant looks magnificent in late summer and autumn, when its tall purple stems are topped with large curved umbels of rich reddish purple, very long-lasting flowers which dry on the plant. All the way up the stems the purple-tinted leaves break out in whorls. Despite its enormous size the stems are strong enough not to need staking, and will stand well throughout winter. Its high architectural value means the plant can be used at the back of a border, or as a free-standing specimen in informal woodland areas.
● Rich, moist soil will guarantee huge, stately plants.
Height x spread:
2.5 x 1m (8 x 3ft)

Euphorbia
SPURGE, MILKWEED

Euphorbias are a very versatile group and include many garden-worthy plants of architectural value, adaptable to a variety of colour schemes. *E. characias* is extremely handsome and makes a large evergreen clump with upright branches and narrow grey-green leaves. In early spring yellowish green bracts start to form; these carry the flowers and later the fruit. These flowerheads stay beautiful until early summer, by which time the new shoots for the coming season will have formed. *E. dulcis* 'Chameleon' is also clump-forming and sun-loving, with dark red leaves which turn green in shade. *E. amygdaloides* var. *robbiae* produces glossy, dark green foliage rosettes against which the pale green flowerhead stands out well. *E. griffithii* 'Dixter' excels in moist soil and produces orange-tinged foliage and orange flowerheads. The latter two spread by creeping root systems and may need keeping within bounds.
● Euphorbias thrive in most soils and most prefer full sun. However, *E. amygdaloides* and *E. griffithii* prefer partial shade. Beware of the milky sap which can irritate the skin.
Height x spread:
0.5–1.5 x 0.5–1.2m (1½–5 x 1½–4ft)

Festuca glauca
BLUE FESCUE

The spiky mounds of glaucous foliage become bluer the higher the light intensity. It makes good punctuation marks among perennials or low-growing woody plants. It is not invasive.
● Grow in light soil. Remove dead leaves by hand or cut back plants in spring once new growth is apparent.
Height x spread:
30 x 30cm (1 x 1ft)

Foeniculum vulgare 'Purpureum'
BRONZE FENNEL

Although better known as a herb, bronze fennel is a valued infiller among perennials because of its delicate feathery bronze foliage, which enhances many flower colours. In summer the plant is topped with flat sprays of smoky yellow flowers. Leave flowerheads *in situ* to provide winter interest.
● Self-seeding can be a problem, but the winter stems are worth the effort.
Height x spread:
2m x 60cm (6½ x 2ft)

Galanthus nivalis
SNOWDROP

Unperturbed by frost or snow, these dainty bulbous plants open their nodding bells of sparkling white in the depth of winter. Best planted in huge drifts in woodland or under shrubs.
● Divide or transplant in full leaf, as soon as flowering has finished, into moist soil rich in organic matter.
Height x spread:
15 x 5cm (6 x 2in)

Galium odoratum
SWEET WOODRUFF

This fresh green ground cover with neatly arranged whorls of narrow leaves will form large carpets in shady places, spreading by means of creeping underground stems. In late spring the plants are covered with white flowers.
● Grow in well-drained rich soil.
Height x spread:
15 x 30cm (6 x 12in)

Geranium
CRANESBILL

The hardy geraniums and cranesbills are some of the most useful garden plants. They make excellent ground cover, have attractive foliage and flower for many months, from late spring to late summer. *G. macrorrhizum* 'Album' is a good ground cover, with large-lobed semi-evergreen leaves tinged red in late summer, and white flowers on sturdy stems. *G. phaeum* 'Samobor' has taller flower stems bearing dainty flowers of a rich plum-purple along their length. Matching purple spots mark the leaves. It is best grown in clumps, or intermingled with other woodland perennials. *G. psilostemon* has vivid magenta flowers with jet black centres carried at the end of very slender trailing stems. The flowering stems drape over adjacent plants, offering an easy means of enlivening non-flowering neighbours throughout summer. Geraniums can also be planted in free-draining wildflower meadows.
● All geraniums are top performers in soils enriched with organic material.
Height x spread:
50cm–1.2m x 30–60cm (1½–4 x 1–2ft)

Hakonechloa macra

A slow-spreading grass of great elegance. Flat, pale green leaves arch gracefully forward and are, therefore, most effectively planted near path edges. The yellow-variegated *H. macra* 'Aureola' is more widely available and makes a perfect companion to hostas, brightening up semi-shaded places.
● Incorporate plenty of leafmould into the soil before planting.
Height x spread:
30–45cm x 45cm (1–1½ x 1½ft)

Helleborus
HELLEBORE

Winter-flowering plants are welcome in any garden, especially such handsome evergreens as these, thriving as they do in shady positions where little else will grow. *H. foetidus* has deep-cut dark, shiny leaves which set off to perfection a multitude of cup-shaped, pale green

Galium odoratum

Helleborus foetidus

Geranium macrorrhizum 'Album'

Iris foetidissima

Miscanthus sacchariflorus

flowers, tinged maroon at the rim.
This long-flowering plant seeds freely,
but can be short-lived. The Lenten rose,
H. orientalis, flowers from early in winter
until spring and has ground-covering
foliage. The fascinating flowers vary in
their subtle colouring: from white and
pale pink to crimson and plum. spotted
inside with maroon and sometimes
flushed with green.
● Prune out dying flowerheads when
stems turn brown. These plants do
best in a fertile, moisture-retentive
but well-drained soil.
Height x spread:
60 x 60cm (2 x 2ft)

Hemerocallis
DAY LILY
○ ◖ ✳ ✳ ✳
The semi-evergreen leaves are long and
linear, and give a good vertical accent
to all planting schemes. The delicately
scented flowers appear from early to
midsummer, each one only lasting for a
day. *H. citrina* is adorned with fine open
trumpets of delicate yellow, whereas
H. 'Stafford' has larger broad-petalled
rust red flowers, velvety in texture. Day
lily petals also make a bright and tasty
addition to any salad.
● Provide well-manured soil. Day lilies
grow well in heavy clay.
Height x spread:
90cm–1.2m x 60cm (3–4 x 2ft)

Hosta
PLANTAIN LILY, FUNKIA
○ ◖ ◕ ✳ ✳ ✳
The strongly veined, decorative leaves
of hostas justify their popularity as
premier foliage plants. Drop-shaped
flowers in white or pale purple, borne
on sturdy stems, are an added bonus in
late summer. The elegant narrow leaves
of *H. lancifolia* are dark green and glossy,
whereas those of *H. sieboldiana* var.
elegans are enormous, heart-shaped,
matt and glaucous. Hostas look
magnificent planted singly, in a tub
(relatively safe from slugs) or in large
drifts. Their arching growth make them
perfect plants for the front of a border.
● A treat for slugs. Hostas flourish in
dappled shade and rich, moist soil.
Height x spread:
30cm–1.2m x 60–90cm (1–4 x 2–3ft)

Iris
○ ◖ ✳ ✳ ✳
Irises are much loved for their
extremely elegant flowers and their
vertical growth. The common bearded
iris produces large flowers of yellow,
blue or purple in spring and early
summer. The stinking iris, *I. foetidissima*,
thrives in shade. Modest yellow or
blue flowers in summer are followed
by an exciting show of orange berries
in autumn. Very impressive is the
tall yellow flag with variegated foliage,
I. pseudacorus 'Variegata', although the
stripes of cream and green fade to green
by the time the warm yellow flowers
open in early summer. It prefers half-
shaded, moist sites.
● In small gardens, lift and divide irises
regularly to curb their spread.
Height x spread:
90cm–2m x 60cm (3–6½ x 2ft)

Ligularia 'The Rocket'
○ ◖ ✳ ✳ ✳
Triangular, deeply frilled, dark green
leaves and black stems provide a
wonderful foil for tall spires of small
yellow flowers in late summer.
● Partial shade or plenty of moisture
are necessary to prevent the leaves
from drooping in the summer heat.
Height x spread:
1.8m x 90cm (6 x 3ft)

Lilium
LILY
○ ◖ ✳ ✳ ✳
Of all bulbous plants, lilies are without
doubt the finest. Each bulb produces a
single leafy stem topped by the flowers
in early summer. *L. martagon* produces
whorls of oval leaves up the stem,
above which dance elegant nodding
maroon flowers of a shape which give
the plant its common name of Turk's
cap lily. By contrast the regal lily,
L. regale, has a mass of narrow linear
leaves all the way up the stem. At the
top, heavily scented trumpets appear,
white on the inside and streaked
maroon outside.
● Provide well-drained soil and place
bulbs on a layer of coarse grit to protect
them from wet and slugs.
Height x spread:
1.2–2m x 30cm (4–6½ x 1ft)

Luzula sylvatica 'Marginata'
GREATER WOODRUSH
◖ ◕ ✳ ✳ ✳
A reliable tufted ground-covering grass
that can cope with dry, dense shade
found under trees, even beech trees.
The fairly coarse leaves are edged with
a white line made up of fine silky hairs.
Delicate frothy flowerheads appear in
late spring on wide-spreading stems.
● Although it tolerates dry shade, moist
shade is preferred.
Height x spread:
30–90 x 30–60cm (1–3 x 1–2ft)

Matteuccia struthiopteris
OSTRICH FERN, SHUTTLECOCK FERN
○ ◖ ◕ ✳ ✳ ✳
Pale lime-green fronds unfurl every
spring to form a large, trim shuttlecock.
The beautiful structure and colour
of the foliage makes these ferns good
companion plants for perennials and
shrubs, either in shady corners of
borders or in woodland, although
this fern also copes with exposure to
sun if kept moist. Plant in large drifts
if possible, or emerging from low-
growing ground cover.
● Mulch with plenty of organic material,
especially when grown in sunny sites.
Height x spread:
75 x 60cm (2½ x 2ft)

Miscanthus
○ ✳ ✳ ✳
Some of boldest clump-forming grasses,
and enjoyable all year round. In late
summer the flowers appear and dance
in the wind. The Amur silver grass, *M.
sacchariflorus*, spreads by underground
stems and can reach 2.5m (8ft), its
broad leaves 1m (3ft) long. The feathery
cream flowers are silky and do not
appear until late summer or early
autumn. Clump-forming Eulalia grass, *M.
sinensis* 'Gracillimus', is also favoured for
its foliage – much shorter and finer than

that of *M. sacchariflorus*. It makes dense
bushy clumps of tapering silvery leaves.
M. sinensis 'Silberfeder' has long-lasting
silvery feathery plumes. Both species
should be appreciated as individuals,
although several clumps of the Eulalia
grass together look very impressive.
● Do not cut back until new growth
emerges in spring, as the old stems give
protection over winter.
Height x spread:
1.2–2.5 x 0.9–1.5m (4–8 x 3–5ft)

Molinia caerulea
PURPLE MOOR-GRASS
○ ✳ ✳ ✳
Late-summer flowering, *M. caerulea*
subsp *arundinacea* 'Transparent' is a tall
grass with flowerheads so fine that they
are virtually transparent. *M. caerulea*
subsp. *arundinacea* 'Windspiel' is more
upright. *M. caerulea* subsp. *caerulea*
'Heidebraut' has stiffly erect and much
shorter yellower flower spikes. The
leaves are also shorter and more erect.
The plant turns rich yellow in autumn.
● Likes moist acid soils but is adaptable
to most garden conditions.
Height x spread:
1.5–2.5 x 0.9–1.2m (5–8 x 3–4ft)

Monarda
BEE BALM, BERGAMOT, HORSEMINT
○ ◖ ✳ ✳ ✳
Plant it close enough to touch and
enjoy the scented foliage. In summer
the leaves are often tinged purple and
the cheerful whorls of flowers appear,
each one resembling a little shrimp.
M. 'Cambridge Scarlet' has wine-red
flowers and *M.* 'Adam' has coral-red
ones, whereas in *M.* 'Beauty of Cobham'
they are soft pink.
● If badly affected by mildew (which has
a white, powdery appearance) move to
a moister area or to partial shade.
Height x spread:
1.2m x 40cm (4ft x 16in)

Monarda 'Adam'

Salvia × superba

Nerine bowdenii

Nymphaea alba

Persicaria amplexicaulis 'Alba'

Papaver orientale 'Beauty of Livermere'

Narcissus
DAFFODIL
◗ ◖ ◗ ✳ ✳ ✳
Although there are a host of different daffodils to choose from, the following are particularly beautiful and reliable to bring spring cheer. *N.* 'Tête-à-tête' is small and dainty with curled-back petals, and two or three rich yellow flowers to a stem. *N. jonquilla* produces stems of six highly fragrant and dainty flowers with short, dark yellow trumpets. *N.* 'Hawera' has nodding flowers with a gracious outer ring of widely reflexed petals, and a paler yellow, cup-shaped trumpet. Although most impressive in large drifts, these charming bulbs can be grown indoors in a pot.
● Do not remove the foliage until it has turned brown – usually five or six weeks after the flowers fade. This will allow the bulb to build up food reserves for next year's flowers.
Height x spread:
15–30 x 10cm (6–12 x 4in)

Nepeta 'Six Hills Giant'
CATMINT
◗ ✳ ✳ ✳
Provides indispensable foliage and colour all summer long. Plant this vigorous catmint either singly near the front of the border or as a low hedge. The grey velvety scented leaves make attractive mounds of foliage, extended by soft spikes of small blue flowers during the summer months.
● Cut back in mid- to late summer for a fresh mound of foliage and some more flowers for the end of the season.
Height x spread:
45 x 90cm (1½ x 3ft)

Nerine bowdenii
◗ ✳ ✳ ✳
Vibrant pink autumn-flowering bulb whose stems are topped by lily-like flowers with narrow wavy petals which curl backwards gracefully. Provides excellent late-season colour and a refreshing contrast to autumnal tints.
● Grow in a warm, sunny position, at the base of a wall.
Height x spread:
45–60 x 12–15cm (1½–2ft x 5–6in)

Nymphaea
WATER-LILY
◗ ✳ ✳ ✳
The most beautiful of water plants and bearing sumptuous and perfect flowers. Suitable only for a large pond is *N. alba*, the white water-lily, with scented brilliant white, semi-double flowers. The oval leathery leaves are red when young. For smaller ponds *N.* 'Caroliniana Nivea' produces large, scented white flowers and pale green leaves. *N.* 'Pink Opal' has delicate pink fragrant flowers and bronze foliage.
● Plant in still water, in an aquatic basket filled with loam and well-rotted manure, or directly into the pond bed.
Planting depth x spread:
N. alba
30cm–1.8m x 3m (1–6 x 10ft)
The rest
20–40 x 90cm (8–16 x 36in)

Paeonia
PEONY
◗ ✳ ✳ ✳
A favoured garden plant over many centuries. The opulent flowers atop clumps of handsomely cut foliage give great pleasure from late spring to early summer. *P. mlokosewitschii* is one of the earliest to flower, with delicate pale yellow single flowers and pale dusty green rounded leaves. Among the common garden peonies, *P. lactiflora* 'White Wings' has beautiful pure white single flowers with yellow stamens, and *P. officinalis* 'Rubra Plena' produces huge, very baroque double flowers of deep red. Use as front-of-border features.
● Plant just below the surface in rich, heavy but well-drained soil.
Height x spread:
75–90 x 60cm (2½–3 x 2ft)

Panicum virgatum 'Rehbraun'
SWITCH GRASS
◗ ✳ ✳ ✳
A tall grass with an open habit which brings a softness to planting schemes. The broad, flat leaves are streaked purple-brown. The flowerheads start as very tight plumes, opening out into fine sprays. Both leaves and flowers turn a warm orange-red in autumn, and will stand during winter if sheltered from battering winds. Plant them individually among other perennials, where the autumn sunlight can set them aglow.
● Although it is drought-tolerant, this grass will grow in moist areas too.
Height x spread:
1.8m x 60cm (6 x 2ft)

Papaver orientale
ORIENTAL POPPY
◗ ✳ ✳ ✳
The giants of early summer, the huge saucer-like flowers with the delicate texture of shimmering silk hover high above a base of hairy leaves which die down during summer. Most imposing is 'Beauty of Livermere' with large blood-red petals and dramatic purple-black stamens. Similar markings are found on the pure white petals of 'Black and White', and orange-red fringed petals of 'Curlilocks'. The smaller, more delicate 'Karine' has clear pink flowers marked with deep burgundy red. Plant singly in borders next to late-summer-flowering perennials so these can cover the empty space the poppies leave behind.
● Cut back foliage immediately after flowering. Lift and divide or take root cuttings during summer dormancy.
Height x spread:
45–90cm x 60cm–1.2m (1½–3 x 2–4ft)

Pennisetum villosum
FEATHERTOP
◗ ✳ ✳
Feathertop, a slightly tender grass, produces loose tufts of fine leaves. In late summer it is covered in long feathery flowerheads of soft pink. It is appealing on its own or in large masses.
● Sun is essential for the proper development of the flowers. Tolerant of dry conditions.
Height x spread:
60 x 60cm (2 x 2ft)

Persicaria
SYN. *POLYGONUM*
KNOTWEED
◗ ◖ ◗ ✳ ✳ ✳
These vigorous perennials are ideal for naturalistic plantings and informal border schemes. Excellent vertical accent is provided by the fine white spires of *P. amplexicaulis* 'Alba' and *P. amplexicaulis* 'Rosea' in pink. Both flower from late summer to late autumn. Strong-growing, non-spreading but less well known is *P. polymorpha*. It reaches 1.5m (5ft) and from late spring until early autumn bears white feathery plumes, which fade to peachy pink.
● Thrives in moist soils with abundant organic material.
Height x spread:
60cm–1.5m x 60cm–1.2m (2–5 x 2–4ft)

Phormium tenax
NEW ZEALAND FLAX
◗ ✳ ✳ ✳
Very large architectural evergreen which adds drama to any planting. Tall purple-red swords of foliage stand very erect, and in summer dark red flowers appear on purplish stems; much clearer in colour and form than the variegated varieties. Use boldly as a focal plant in a prominent place.
● Plant in moist soil. Mulch to give protection over winter.
Height x spread:
2–2.5m x 90cm (6½–8 x 3ft)

Pulmonaria officinalis 'Sissinghurst White'
◗ ◖ ✳ ✳ ✳
Shade-loving ground cover with distinctively mottled hairy leaves. The true lungwort, *P. officinalis*, has delicate blue flowers, but this cultivar is crisp white, which complements the white leaf markings well. It flowers in early spring, before the shrubs and trees under which it is planted come into leaf. An excellent plant to add lightness and relief in shady areas.
● Will suffer from mildew if planted in a dry position – look out for white powdery coating to the leaves. Cut back after flowering to produce a fresh longer-lasting foliage display.
Height x spread:
20 x 45cm (8 x 18in)

Sedum **'Herbstfreude'**

Stipa gigantea

Tellima grandiflora

Verbena bonariensis

Viola riviniana

Rheum palmatum 'Atrosanguineum'
CHINESE RHUBARB

One of the most architectural of all garden plants, with large, deeply cut rhubarb leaves, which are a rich dark red in spring. Tall, prominent red flower spikes also appear in spring and carry the pink, flushed white flowers. Plant in association with moisture-loving plants, as a single focal point or, if space permits, in bold groups.
● Thrives in deeply dug, well-manured, moisture-retentive soil.
Height x spread:
1.2 x 1.5m (4 x 5ft)

Sagittaria sagittifolia
JAPANESE ARROWHEAD, OLD WORLD ARROWHEAD

Handsome aquatic with two sorts of foliage. Spear-shaped fresh green leaves are borne on stalks standing 45cm (1½ft) clear of the water, while linear leaves are submerged. Sparkling white triangular flowers appear on stiff stalks in summer.
● Plant in water no deeper than 25cm (10in), in a planting basket filled with loam and well-rotted manure. They spread fast, so plant directly into the pond bed with caution.
Height x spread:
45–90cm x 2m (1½–3 x 6½ft)

Salvia x superba

Flowering from late spring till late summer, this ornamental sage is decorated with rich deep purple flowers held in vertical spikes. Use as a strong vertical accent in the foreground of perennial planting schemes.
● If flowering is finished by midsummer, cut back to encourage a second flush.
Height x spread:
60–90 x 45cm (2–3 x 1½ft)

Sedum 'Herbstfreude'
SYN. S. 'AUTUMN JOY'

This must be the best autumn-flowering perennial. Large, flat heads of small reddish pink flowers gradually develop on stems carrying pale green fleshy leaves. As the flowers mature, their colour turns deeper red and eventually they dry to a rich chocolate brown. In this state they stand beautifully throughout the winter, especially when covered with frost or snow. Dot through the front of any planting, formal or naturalistic, where they will provide a source of nectar for butterflies.
● Thrives in dry, sunny positions. Do not cut down until new foliage has started to grow in spring.
Height x spread:
45 x 60cm (1½ x 2ft)

Stipa
FEATHER GRASS, NEEDLE GRASS

Among the most decorative of all grasses, stipas form semi-evergreen tussocks. *S. gigantea* is most striking, with flowering stems reaching 2m (6½ft) or more, topped by loose tassels of glistening bronze from late spring onwards. If not too windswept they will dry and bleach blond until battered by winter. The pheasant's tail grass, *S. arundinacea*, has orange-green leaves throughout the year. The purplish flowers appear on a multitude of extremely fine arching stems, just above the upright foliage, at 60cm (2ft). *S. brachytricha* reaches 90cm (3ft) and is inexhaustible in the garden, producing fuzzy silver flowerheads from early summer until late autumn, ideal for cutting and drying. The elegantly waving plumes of *S. barbata* resemble foxtails as they ripen – grow them near a path to enjoy their tactile quality. All needle grasses are best displayed as single specimens, where they can catch the evening sunlight and the breeze.
● Divide and transplant in spring to keep clumps small. Once established they will tolerate drought.
Height x spread:
50cm–2m x 60–90cm (1½–6½ x 2–3ft)

Tellima grandiflora
FRINGECUPS

A reliable, low-growing, semi-evergreen ground cover. Long slender sprays of scented, green-tinted creamy flowers appear during late spring and early summer. Its modest character makes it ideal for naturalizing in woodlands and underplanting naturalistic shrubberies. The Rubra Group (syn. *T. grandiflora* 'Purpurea') are evergreen with copper-coloured winter foliage.
● Tolerates fairly dry positions.
Height x spread:
60 x 30cm (2 x 1ft)

Tiarella cordifolia
FOAM FLOWER

Short spires of frothy, creamy white flowers hover above fresh green hairy foliage in spring. A good ground cover for woodland planting in fertile soils.
● Prefers a moist soil, enriched with plenty of organic matter.
Height x spread:
30 x 30cm (1 x 1ft)

Verbena bonariensis
PURPLE TOP

Summer-flowering upright perennial that can be grown as an annual. Tall, thin, widely branching square stems carry sprays of small purple flowers for months during summer and autumn. Scatter throughout any planting; with their light, loose habit and slender stems they are virtually transparent.
● Thrives in hot, sunny situations.
Height x spread:
90cm–1.2m x 60cm (3–4 x 2ft)

Veronica gentianoides

An exquisite plant with an ever-expanding, evergreen carpet of glossy, dark green leaves. In early summer dainty spires of very delicate blue flowers with dark blue stamens rise above the foliage. Although its flowering life is short, a few small spaces should be found for it at the front of the border.
● Grow in a moisture-retentive soil.
Height x spread:
5–45 x 30cm (2–18 x 12in)

Vinca major
GREATER PERIWINKLE

An evergreen ground cover with glossy green foliage and starry blue flowers during spring. It produces long trailing shoots which insinuate their way into neighbouring plants. Shady sites encourage ground covering, whereas sunny sites produce a good show of flowers.
● Once established, tolerates dry soils.
Height x spread:
30 x 45–90cm (1 x 1½–3ft)

Viola
VIOLET

Perennial violets are modest but rewarding ground-cover plants. *V. riviniana* Purpurea Group (syn. *V. labradorica*) are tiny with small purple-red rounded leaves and miniature mauve flowers. They will happily sow themselves in semi-shade. The sweet violet *V. odorata*, has highly scented lilac or white pansy flowers and heart-shaped leaves. It makes an ideal front-of-the-border gap filler. Although it flowers naturally in spring, successive sowings will result in late-summer flowering. *V. tricolor* 'Bowles' Black' is a dramatically black-flowered form of the heart's-ease. Usually grown as an annual, but it self-seeds and stays true to type.
● A soil rich in organic matter will promote strong growth.
Height x spread:
5–30 x 10–30cm (2–12 x 4–12in)

Zantedeschia aethiopica
ARUM LILY, CALLA LILY

Rhizomatous perennial, producing elegant funnel-shaped white flowers and shiny arrowhead leaves. *Z. aethiopica* 'Crowborough' has snowy white flowers. It is a lush foliage provider and a powerful foil to other perennials.
● Performs best in boggy ground or standing in shallow water at the margin of a pond.
Height x spread:
90 x 45cm (3 x 1½ft)

Zantedeschia aethiopica **'Crowborough'**

Annuals and biennials

Nigella damascena 'Miss Jekyll'

Centaurea cyanus

Cosmos bipinnatus

Nicotiana sylvestris

Salvia sclarea var. turkestanica

KEY TO SYMBOLS

◠ Prefers full sun

◖ Prefers partial shade

● Tolerates full shade

✳ ✳ ✳ Hardy below –8°C (18°F)

✳ ✳ Hardy to –7°C (20°F)

✳ Protect below 4°C (39°F)

Annuals and biennials tend to flower over a long period, but have a short life span. Annuals flower, set seed and die within a single year, while biennials germinate and produce foliage one year, then complete their life the following year. Although the sowing and growing on of these plants can be very labour intensive, they make gardening flexible, as displays can be changed annually. Fertile, moist soils will produce the best results.

Centaurea cyanus
CORNFLOWER
◠ ✳ ✳ ✳
Hardy annuals with very slender stems, a few linear grey leaves and beautiful rich blue flowerheads. They are most striking when sown in large drifts, and will self-seed when conditions suit.
● Early and late-spring sowings will ensure a summer-long display.
Height x spread:
45–90 x 30cm (1½–3 x 1ft)

Cosmos
◠ ✳ ✳
Cosmos bipinnatus is a half-hardy annual, making erect stems with fresh green, finely cut foliage. Throughout the summer a constant supply of flowers is produced, mainly in vivid pink, purple and white. Rather different, and usually treated as an annual, is the tender perennial *C. atrosanguineus*, which has velvety brown, chocolate-scented flowers and coarse-cut foliage.
● Raise *C. bipinnatus* from seed sown under cover or *in situ*. *C. atrosanguineus* is usually propagated from softwood cuttings in spring.
Height x spread:
50cm–1.2m x 30cm (1½–4 x 1ft)

Erysimum cheiri
SYN. *CHEIRANTHUS CHEIRI*
WALLFLOWER
◠ ✳ ✳ ✳
Shrubby perennials, wallflowers are usually treated as biennials. The sweetly scented flowers produce a long, bright display, cheering up the garden in early spring. Although most wallflowers come in tones of warm yellows and oranges, the tall 'Rose Queen' is adorned with

Helianthus annuus
'Russian Giant'

rose and pink flowers, whereas 'Vulcan' is velvety crimson.
● Easy to grow, but plant where the spring sun will catch them and release their perfume. Sow in spring or autumn, or take softwood cuttings in summer.
Height x spread:
30 x 20cm (12 x 8in)

Eschscholzia californica
CALIFORNIAN POPPY
◠ ✳ ✳ ✳
Brightly coloured poppy-like flowers rest above a mass of greyish feathery foliage and close in late afternoon. Their usual colours are warm, rich yellow and orange, but some with white-, cream- or purple-flushed flowers are available under the names 'Alba', 'Ivory Castle' and 'Purple Gleam'. Plant in meadow-like masses or between perennials.
● Sow in sunny, dry sites.
Height x spread:
30–60 x 30–45cm (1–2 x 1–1½ft)

Helianthus annuus 'Russian Giant'
◠ ✳ ✳ ✳
This radiant giant, tallest of all annuals, reaches 3.5m (11½ft). The huge, bright yellow sunflowers will give height and cheer to any planting scheme, but should be planted towards the back so other plants mask their bare stems. Place them where their flowers, which face the sun, can be enjoyed properly. Great fun for children and adults alike.
● Sow directly in their growing position, in a well-prepared spot. Lavish care, feeding and watering will be rewarded with a gigantic display.
Height x spread:
3.5m x 60cm (11½ x 2ft)

Lunaria annua
HONESTY
◠ ◖ ✳ ✳ ✳
This large, hardy biennial is valued for its early-spring display of purple flowers. In summer the parchment-like seedheads develop, which dry to a beautiful silver. White flowers are also available in *L. annua* var. *albiflora*. Honesty is most attractive when scattered in between other spring flowers, where it self-seeds freely if conditions suit.

● Weed out systematically all the purple-flowered plants if you want to keep the white-flowered form, otherwise it will revert to purple.
Height x spread:
90 x 60cm (3 x 2ft)

Nicotiana
TOBACCO PLANT
◠ ◖ ✳ ✳ ✳
The biennial or short-lived perennial *N. sylvestris* is without doubt the most imposing tobacco plant, particularly when planted in big drifts. Large lime-green leaves are topped by a 1.8m (6ft) flower stem, with an elegant mop-head of pendulous tubular white flowers. The annual *N. langsdorffii* reaches half this height, has wiry stems covered in lime-green tubular flowers and looks best interplanted among other annuals. Of more conventional tobacco-plant appearance but no less valuable are *N.* Sensation Mixed, whose flowers come in a variety of mixed colours and are all scented in the evening.
● Tobacco plants cope well in partial shade and perform best in fertile soils.
Height x spread:
75cm–1.8m x 30–60cm (2½–6 x 1–2ft)

Nigella damascena 'Miss Jekyll'
LOVE-IN-THE-MIST
◠ ✳ ✳ ✳
A mist of fine feathery pale green foliage provides a background haze to the true-blue flowers of this hardy annual. After flowering the rounded green seedheads inflate. Although delightful when planted in a mass on their own, they also mingle well among other taller flowers. It self-seeds very freely.
● Sow in warm, well-prepared soil.
Height x spread:
60 x 30cm (2 x 1ft)

Omphalodes linifolia
VENUS'S NAVELWORT
◠ ✳ ✳ ✳
Narrow grey leaves become lost under a cloud of small, pure white forget-me-not-like flowers. A modest but delightful hardy annual, it looks its best among perennials, where it will self-seed.
● Sow in warm, well-prepared soil.
Height x spread:
30 x 30cm (1 x 1ft)

Papaver
POPPY
◠ ✳ ✳ ✳
These bright, uncomplicated flowers are a delight in early summer. Iceland poppies, *P. nudicaule*, are perennial but often grown as biennials. Their delicate silky petals in a range of pastel shades open wide to form virtually flat flowers. The annual opium poppy, *P. somniferum*, produces stiffly erect stems and glaucous leaves. The cup-shaped single or double flowers, some with frilly petals, come in all shades of pink, red and purple. *P. rhoeas* 'Mother of Pearl' produces single flowers in soft dusky and greyish pinks.
● Grow in well-drained soil. Sow freshly gathered seed, especially of *P. nudicaule*.
Height x spread:
30cm–1.2m x 45–60cm (1–4 x 1½–2ft)

Salvia sclarea var. turkestanica
◠ ✳ ✳ ✳
A handsome biennial clary with a basal rosette of large, rough-textured scented leaves from which the flower spikes develop. The flowers themselves are bluish white, but the surrounding bracts have subtle streaks of green, white and pink. Bracts and flowers merge to form a beautiful purple to pink haze, blending superbly with the greyish hairy foliage. A large plant which flowers for many months in summer and will self-sow.
● In the first season grow plants in pots or a nursery bed and plant out the following autumn or spring.
Height x spread:
1.2 x 1m (4 x 3ft)

Tropaeolum majus
INDIAN CRESS, NASTURTIUM
◠ ✳
A good trailing or climbing annual with bold, rounded leaves. Trailing Mixed comes in colours ranging from cream yellow and orange to red. *T.* 'Empress of India' has dark glaucous leaves and deep red flowers. Nasturtiums make an attractive, fast-growing ground cover and the spurred flowers add a delicious and decorative element to salads.
● Performs best in moist soil. In rich soils leafy growth swamps the flowers.
Height x spread:
30cm x 1.5m (1 x 5ft)

Climbers and wall shrubs

Hedera helix 'Buttercup'

Humulus lupulus 'Aureus'

Lonicera japonica 'Halliana'

Hydrangea anomala subsp. *petiolaris*

Vitis coignetiae

Although most climbers are woody their stems are not strong enough to support them alone; they therefore need the support of a neighbouring wall, fence, pergola, trellis, post or tree.

Akebia quinata
CHOCOLATE VINE

A semi-evergreen twiner with ornately lobed leaves. In spring, drooping clusters of reddish purple, vanilla-scented flowers open. In a hot summer, purple sausage-like seedpods ripen.
● Plant against a warm sheltered wall for flowers; it grows only foliage in shade.
Height:
9–12m (30–40ft)

Campsis radicans
TRUMPET HONEYSUCKLE

This self-clinging climber looks rather exotic, with its clusters of large, scarlet trumpet-shaped flowers in summer. Let it work itself along a sunny stone wall or over a shed roof which needs hiding.
● Full exposure to sun is needed in order to ripen the wood and ensure a good display of flowers.
Height:
10m (33ft)

Clematis
OLD MAN'S BEARD, TRAVELLER'S JOY

Spring has several fine examples to offer, starting with the vigorous evergreen *C. armandii* with white vanilla-scented flowers. More modest in size are *C. alpina* 'Frances Rivis', with elegant pale blue lanterns, and *C. macropetala* 'Markham's Pink', semi-double and dusty pink. Summer-flowering *C. viticella* hybrids are invaluable for their displays of rich shades of red, blue and purple.
● Plant deeply, burying at least 5cm (2in) of stem, to keep the roots cool and so, should clematis wilt attack, the plant can resprout from below ground. Cut out wilted shoots, which will not recover.
Height:
C. armandii
4.5–6m (15–20ft)
Others
Up to 2.5m (8ft)

Hedera
IVY

Ivy will find its own way up walls and trees and across beds and undergrowth. The Persian ivy, *H. colchica*, has large dark green reflective leaves. *H. helix* 'Buttercup' has yellow leaves, bright in full sun, but is less vigorous and more tender than *H. helix* itself.
● Grows almost anywhere, but humus-rich alkaline soils and partial shade promote the best growth.
Height:
10–15m (33–50ft)

Humulus lupulus 'Aureus'
GOLDEN HOP

Herbaceous twiner of yellow palmate leaves. In late summer the flowers appear, which enlarge to form papery fruits. Brightens a dark corner.
● Grows vigorously in moist, fertile soil.
Height:
3–8m (10–26ft)

Hydrangea anomala subsp. petiolaris

A deciduous, slow-growing climber, festooned with large, delicately scented lace-caps of pure white in early summer. It covers any structure without training or tying and is a useful ground cover.
● Initial growth rate is slow.
Height:
18–25m (60–80ft)

Lonicera
HONEYSUCKLE, WOODBINE

Many honeysuckles twine unaided up trees and fences. Two fragrant Japanese honeysuckles are *L. japonica* 'Halliana', opening white before turning yellow, and *L. japonica* var. *repens*, whose shoots and flowers are purple. Less rampant is *L. periclymenum* 'Graham Thomas'. The scented flowers open white and turn yellow. All flower for a long period during summer and their smell is strongest at dawn and dusk.
● They revel in cool conditions, moist soils and plenty of leafmould.
Height:
4–9m (13–30ft)

Parthenocissus quinquefolia
VIRGINIA CREEPER

Looks stunning scrambling through pine trees where its crimson autumn colour will provide a splendid contrast to the dark needles. It clings unaided.
● Give initial support until established and producing its own tendrils.
Height:
15–25m (50–80ft)

Passiflora caerulea
PASSION FLOWER

Passion flower will survive most winters to produce a vigorous tangle of growth that twines and clings by tendrils. Throughout summer and autumn flowers show their intricate structure in shades of blue, white and purple. Oval fruits ripen orange-red.
● Plant against a warm sheltered wall.
Height:
7–10m (23–33ft)

Rosa
ROSE

The deliciously scented flowers of *R.* 'Madame Alfred Carrière' are almost white with just a hint of buff. *R.* 'Mermaid' is vigorous once established, with delicately scented single blooms of a pale sulphurous yellow and dark glossy foliage. *R.* 'New Dawn' is pink budded, opening to delicate pale pink. *R.* 'Wedding Day' and *R.* 'Bobbie James' are both vigorous ramblers. They bloom only once, producing huge sprays of creamy flowers in summer.
● Provide well-manured, preferably loamy soils and an open position. Do not replant a rose where one grew before, to avoid rose sickness. Start pruning the third year after planting, removing the side shoots which flowered the previous year.
Height:
6–10m (20–33ft)

Solanum

The white-flowered potato vine, *S. jasminoides* 'Album', is a tender semi-evergreen but fast-growing shrub. It flowers in loose clusters through summer and autumn. *S. crispum* 'Glasnevin' is hardier, less vigorous, with purple-blue flowers.
● Performs best on a sunny wall in alkaline soils. Tie shoots in regularly. Prune after flowering.
Height:
4.5–9m (15–30ft)

Vitis
VINE

The leaves of the crimson glory vine, *V. coignetiae*, can measure up to 30cm (1ft) across and in autumn turn brilliant orange to crimson. The teinturier grape, *V. vinifera* 'Purpurea', is a purple form of the common grape vine. Its leaves open felty grey, turning purple.
● Poor soil will enhance autumn colour.
Height:
10–15m (33–50ft)

Wisteria

Most elegant of climbers, *W. floribunda* 'Alba' produces long, pendulous clusters of white flowers, reaching 60cm (2ft). *W. floribunda* 'Macrobotrys' has even longer trails of blue-violet. The fragrant Chinese wisteria, *W. sinensis*, has violet-blue flowers 30cm (1ft) long.
● Prune leafy shoots of the current season's growth to six buds in late summer. In winter, reduce the side shoots to two buds.
Height:
4–10m (13–33ft)

Wisteria floribunda 'Alba'

Vegetables, herbs and fruit

Courgette 'Gold Rush'

Asparagus 'Connover's Colossal'

French bean 'Purple Podded Climbing'

Lettuce 'Royal Oak Leaf'

Onion 'Red Torpedo'

Aubergine 'Easter Egg'

These vegetables, herbs and fruit are renowned for their culinary value. There is no need to confine them to the kitchen garden, as most are decorative and will more than hold their own in the ornamental borders of the garden.

VEGETABLES

Raise annual vegetables in small batches sown at monthly intervals during the growing season to provide the kitchen with a succession of fresh young produce. If you grow vegetables regularly, it is good gardening practice to rotate them so they only occupy the same bed every three years (or four years, if you grow potatoes). The crops are divided into four groups and rotated in the following order: legumes (such as beans and peas), potatoes, other rootcrops, and brassicas and other leafy crops. In this way, many pest and disease problems are avoided.

Artichoke, cardoon
⬒ ❋ ❋ ❋
These related, delicious perennials produce massive, deeply cut leaves of silvery grey and tall stems, topped with purple thistle-like flowers. Eat the blanched leaf stalks of cardoons, and the flower buds of the globe artichoke. 'Green Globe' is recommended. Plant both in flower borders for their foliage.
● Provide a sheltered, well-drained, fertile site. Blanch cardoon leaves by wrapping them in cardboard.
Height x spread:
1–2 x 1m (3–6½ x 3ft)

Asparagus 'Connover's Colossal'
⬒ ❋ ❋ ❋
Asparagus spears are cut shortly after emerging from the soil for eight weeks only, as the foliage must then be allowed to grow so the plants can replenish their reserves for the following year's crop. When fully grown, the stems produce a cloud of extremely fine, feathery foliage. These are long-term perennials best planted in a bed of their own.
● If your soil is well drained and grows good potatoes, it will grow asparagus.
Height x spread:
1.5m x 30–45cm (5 x 1–1½ft)

Ruby chard

Aubergine
EGGPLANT
⬒ ❋
In 'Long Purple' the well-flavoured fruits are elongated. More unusual is 'Easter Egg', whose white fruits should be picked when the size of a goose egg.
● Best grown in pots or beds in a greenhouse, minimum temperature 16°C (61°F), unless a sheltered, warm site can be guaranteed. Prepare the soil to a good depth. Allow only four fruits to develop per plant.
Height x spread:
60 x 45cm (2 x 1½ft)

Beans
⬒ ❋ ❋
The best known and most widely grown are broad beans, French beans and runner or string beans. The broad bean 'Red Epicure' has red flowers and red beans in the pod. Bush or dwarf French beans need not be green. Plant a yellow-podded cultivar like 'Mont d'Or', or deep purple 'Royal Burgundy'. Among the climbing French beans 'Purple Podded Climbing' has dark purple beans and stems. For a flavoursome runner bean select scarlet-flowered 'Painted Lady'.
● Broad beans are frost resistant and can be started in late winter in pots or sown direct in spring. French beans and, more especially, runner beans need warmth, shelter, plenty of moisture and a deeply dug bed enriched with organic material. Raise them under cover in pots in spring, or sow direct once the danger of frost is past. Runner beans and climbing French beans need firm support for their twining stems.
Height x spread:
30cm–2m x 30–45cm (1–6½ x 1–1½ft)

Beetroot
⬒ ❋ ❋ ❋
An annual root vegetable with attractive foliage. 'Barbietola di Chioggia' is an old Italian cultivar with alternate concentric rings of white and red, while 'Burpee's Golden' has yellow flesh. 'Bull's Blood' has a red root and superb red foliage.
● Grow in rich, light soil, manured the previous season.
Height x spread:
15–30 x 15cm (6–12 x 6in)

Brassicas
⬒ ❋ ❋ ❋
Brassicas include cabbages, Brussels sprouts, kale, calabrese, broccoli and cauliflowers. Cabbage comes in many varieties, and 'Ruby Ball' has very ornate purple foliage covered in a white bloom. Curly kale has wonderful, dark green, frizzy foliage. Less decorative but providing excellent flavour is calabrese 'Green Sprouting'.
● Leafy brassicas demand a rich soil. Raise them either in a seedbed or in pots, before transplanting firmly to their growing position. Brassicas are susceptible to several pests and diseases but will suffer less if planted in a slightly alkaline soil and among ornamentals.
Height x spread:
60–90 x 60–90cm (2–3 x 2–3ft)

Carrot
⬒ ❋ ❋ ❋
The plants have finely cut fresh green foliage and, when left to bolt, also produce dainty umbels of white flowers. 'Fly Away' is a sweet-flavoured cultivar, showing resistance to carrot fly. 'White Fodder' is interesting and tasty, with tender, white flesh. The spherical 'Balin' has excellent flavour. 'Ideal Red' is more traditional, with dark orange flesh.
● Carrots enjoy light soils with good drainage, well-manured the previous season. Plant them next to onions, leeks or garlic to keep carrot root fly at bay.
Height x spread:
20–45 x 10–15cm (8–18 x 4–6in)

Celery, celeriac
⬒ ❋ ❋
'Golden Self Blanching' is an early dwarf celery needing little or no earthing up. 'Giant Red', with red-tinged stems, makes an unusual foliage plant for the flower border. Celeriac is hardier and develops a tuberous root. 'Marble Ball' is large and flavoursome, and the leaves can be used to flavour soups.
● Germination can be erratic so sow indoors in pots in early spring, kept at an even temperature of 10°C (50°F) or just above. Celery requires a fertile soil and plenty of moisture during summer. Mulching celery is beneficial.
Height x spread:
60–75 x 25cm (2–2½ft x 10in)

Chard
⬒ ◗ ❋ ❋ ❋
Undemanding and handsome ruby chard grows taller than true spinach, and produces a constant supply of glossy, dark green leaves on wine red stems. In mild areas you can crop it through winter. Use this decorative plant in small patches among flowers.
● Sow in situ in early spring. Lift old plants as they start to bolt.
Height x spread:
60 x 45cm (2 x 1½ft)

Corn salad
⬒ ❋ ❋ ❋
A hardy winter salad plant also known as lamb's lettuce. It makes small rosettes of nutty flavoured leaves, which, if kept clear of snow, can be harvested throughout the winter months.
● Sow thinly in situ in late summer. An undemanding vegetable.
Height x spread:
5 x 10cm (2 x 4in)

Courgette, squash, cucumber
⬒ ❋
All of these are useful fast-growing summer vegetables. Courgettes are grown for their edible yellow flowers as well as their fruit. 'All Green Bush' is dark green and 'Gold Rush' a rich bright yellow. Closely related, but with a huge range of curiously shaped and colourful fruits, are the squashes. 'Early Butternut' is bush-forming, pale creamy yellow and delicious in flavour. The larger golden 'Vegetable Spaghetti', which makes spaghetti-like strands when cooked, is a trailing variety. Try growing it over an arch or another strong support: pinch out the growing point after six leaves have formed and train the resulting side shoots as required. 'Rebecca' is small, round and orange, and perfect for Hallowe'en. Cucumber is another relative; choose one for outdoors, such as 'Burpless Tasty Green', or the unusual round 'Crystal Apple'.
● All these plants are most productive on a well-manured, well-watered sunny site. Raise them in pots under cover or sow in situ once the soil has warmed up and frost is past, and mulch generously.
Height x spread:
60 x 75cm–1.5m (2 x 2½–5ft)

Potato 'Pink Fir Apple'

Rocket

Tomato 'Gardener's Delight'

Sweet basil

Bay

Lettuce
○ ✻

Of the many lettuces available, several – particularly the loose-leaved non-hearting types – make good foliage plants for shrub and flower borders. The red and pale green forms of lobed-leaved 'Royal Oak Leaf', and 'Lollo Rosso', a tight mass of frilly dark red foliage, look decorative scattered through borders or grown in masses. They extend into elegant spires when allowed to bolt.

● Sow in trays under glass from early spring onwards and transplant once the soil has warmed up in mid- to late spring. Later they can be sown outdoors in moist, light soil. More likely to bolt in dry, poor conditions. Look out for slugs.

Height x spread:
15–30 x 20cm (6–12 x 8in)

Onion, shallot, leek
○ ✻ ✻ ✻

Many different types, shapes and flavours of onion are available. Try sweet, red and elongated 'Red Torpedo', or violet-red and spherical 'Rossa di Bassano'. For everyday use and heavy cropping 'Bedfordshire Champion' is unbeatable. Shallots are more delicately flavoured than onions, and 'Sante' is about the finest. As for leeks, 'Musselburgh' is reliable and easy to grow. Planted at the back of a border leeks can be allowed to bolt and display dense, silvery pink, round flowerheads.

● Onions can be raised from seed sown early in spring, in pots or directly into the soil, or from sets – small bulbs planted in early spring so the tips show above the soil. Shallots are usually raised from sets planted in winter. Grow onions and shallots in soil well manured the previous season. Leeks do better in soil more recently manured. Raise them from seed in spring, sown *in situ* or for transplanting in pots.

Height x spread:
50 x 20cm (20 x 8in)

Parsnip
○ ✻ ✻ ✻

'Hollow Crown' is a reliable heavy cropper with a delicious flavour. 'White Gem' is resistant to canker, and its short, fat roots make it suitable for shallow stony or clay soils. If you can

resist eating these winter vegetables, they will produce handsome umbels of yellow flowers on tall stems during the following summer.

● Sow in mid-spring in soil that has been warmed by fleece or a cloche in order to improve germination and prevent canker. Parsnips will grow well in most well-drained soils.

Height x spread:
30–45 x 15–20cm (12–18 x 6–8in)

Pepper, chilli pepper
○ ✻

'Mavras' is sweet, dark aubergine in colour turning red when mature. 'Gypsy' is more elongated, pale green, ripening to red and very prolific. If you like something with pep, try 'Hot Gold Spike', a small, pale yellow chilli pepper.

● Peppers need to germinate in heat, 20°C (70°F), and are best grown in pots or beds in a greenhouse at 16°C (61°F) unless a warm sheltered site can be guaranteed, in which case mulch plants to prevent drying out.

Height x spread:
60 x 45cm (2 x 1½ft)

Potato
○ ✻

Many different potatoes are available, with early, mid-early and maincrop cultivars maturing at different times. The skins can be white, yellow, red or blue-black. The flesh also varies in colour and, after cooking, in texture – from floury to firm and waxy. 'Duke of York' is a delicious early potato, producing a heavy crop. 'Pink Fir Apple' is red-skinned, knobbly and very flavoursome, with a waxy texture that is ideal for salads.

● Raise from seed potatoes (small virus-free tubers) and sprout these in the light before planting them out at twice their depth in moisture-retaining fertile soil. Draw soil up round the stem to prevent the tubers becoming green and inedible. Early potatoes can be dug up from flowering time onwards, as use demands. Lift maincrop potatoes as soon as possible in autumn to avoid slug damage. Potato plants are best confined to the vegetable garden.

Height x spread:
60 x 45cm (2 x 1½ft)

Radicchio, red chicory
○ ✻ ✻ ✻

'Rosso di Verona' is a delicious Italian salad crop, producing dense small heads of intense red foliage. Do not banish it to the vegetable patch, for its dark green and red leaves laced with white veins are most appealing in a border.

● Sow in early spring for a summer crop, or in late summer for a winter crop. In cold areas winter crops may rot unless given cloche protection.

Height x spread:
20 x 30cm (8 x 12in)

Radish
○ ✻ ✻ ✻

Fast and easy to grow, tasty to nibble. There are the traditional pink-skinned radishes such as 'French Breakfast', but you could also try the long white ones like 'Tsukushi Spring Cross'.

● Sow in small batches in light fertile soil. Start as soon as the soil has warmed, or earlier under cloches.

Height x spread:
8 x 5cm (3 x 2in)

Rocket
○ ✻ ✻ ✻

A salad plant with a distinctive spicy smell and flavour, which can be eaten raw or cooked like spinach. Use the cream flowers for edible decoration.

● Sow several times during the season in order to ensure a constant supply of young, tender leaves.

Height x spread:
15 x 15cm (6 x 6in)

Tomato
○ ✻

A home-grown tomato in a salad makes it a special dish. For a love apple with a difference, try tall-growing sunny yellow 'Golden Sunrise', or 'Yellow Cocktail' with small pear-shaped fruits. For flavour, the small-fruited tomato 'Gardener's Delight' is hard to beat.

● Start under glass, in pots, as tomatoes are very frost sensitive and germinate ideally in a temperature of 16°C (61°F). Grow in well-manured, fertile soils in sheltered sunny sites. Support, and remove side shoots from tall varieties.

Height x spread:
30cm–1.5m x 30–60cm (1–5 x 1–2ft)

HERBS

Culinary herbs can be fitted into the smallest of gardens. Grow them in containers, mix them with flowers or vegetables, or fashion a separate herb garden. Some, like rosemary, can be clipped to form a low fragrant hedge, while thyme and chamomile form aromatic mats in sunny crevices.

Basil
○ ✻ ✻ ✻

Basil is one of the finest of culinary herbs. Sweet basil is highly flavoured with large, pale green leaves, while 'Napoletano' has crinkled leaves. Bush basil is neat, rounded and bushy and produces tiny leaves.

● Full sun enhances the flavour. Keep the shape neat and compact by regularly pinching out the shoot tips. Grow as an annual.

Height x spread:
30–45 x 30cm (1–1½ x 1ft)

Bay
○ ✻ ✻

Bay is evergreen and can form a tall tree in a sheltered position. In small gardens or cold areas, it is better grown in a tub and clipped to a shape; keep the prunings for flavouring dishes.

● Give winter protection in cold areas.

Height x spread:
3–9 x 2–3m (10–30 x 7–10ft)

Chamomile 'Treneague'
○ ✻ ✻ ✻

Non-flowering 'Treneague' is low growing and spreading and can make mats of aromatic, finely divided foliage, which releases scented oils when crushed. Although perennial, plants tend to be short lived, so keep a few in reserve for patching up gaps.

● Space plants of 'Treneague' 10cm (4in) apart to establish a dense carpet.

Height x spread:
10 x 15cm (4 x 6in)

Chervil
○ ◑ ✻ ✻ ✻

A delicate herb in appearance and in flavour, with fine feathery foliage and dainty umbels of white flowers. These attributes suit this hardy annual to a flower garden as well as among herbs.

Chives

Chervil

Parsley 'Moss Curled'

Rosemary 'Sissinghurst Blue'

Thyme 'Silver Posie'

French tarragon

Apricot 'Moor Park'

Currant 'White Grape'

KEY TO SYMBOLS

◌ Prefers full sun
◑ Prefers partial shade
● Tolerates full shade
❋ ❋ ❋ Hardy below –8°C (18°F)
❋ ❋ Hardy to –7°C (20°F)
❋ Protect below 4°C (39°F)

Purple sage

● In spring, sow seeds outdoors in their growing position. Chervil enjoys a light but moist soil, if possible in partial shade.
Height x spread:
15–45 x 20cm (6–18 x 8in)

Chives
◌◑ ❋ ❋ ❋
A mild onion-flavoured perennial herb that dies down in winter. The clumps of bright green, grass-like leaves make an attractive edging to formal beds. In summer it produces pink balls of flowers, which are a colourful addition to the salad bowl. Chinese or garlic chives are a flat-leaved relative, with a subtle garlic flavour and white flowers.
● Cut plants back after flowering to bring on a new crop of leaves, which will look fresh till autumn.
Height x spread:
25 x 15cm (10 x 6in)

Dill
◌ ❋ ❋ ❋
A decorative annual herb with extremely finely cut, blue-green leaves and umbels of smoky yellow flowers. It has great appeal planted in hazy drifts among flowers and will self-seed freely. The aniseed flavour, delicate in the leaves, is more intense in the seeds.
● Make successive sowings to ensure a constant supply of leaves and seeds. Keep separate from fennel as, in their early stages, they are indistinguishable.
Height x spread:
20cm–1.2m x 20cm (8in–4ft x 8in)

Garlic
◌ ❋ ❋ ❋
A strong-flavoured relative of the onion, indispensable in the kitchen and an excellent companion to aphid-susceptible plants. Garlic bulbs produce

grass-like, greyish foliage, and small globular heads of white flowers in summer. Unlike leeks and onions, which are weakened by flower development, when garlic develops flowers the quality of the underground bulb is unaffected.
● Tradition has it that the best-flavoured garlic is planted on the shortest day and harvested on the longest. Plant cloves to twice their depth, in well-drained soil.
Height x spread:
25 x 8cm (10 x 3in)

Marjoram
◌ ❋ ❋ ❋
A decorative perennial with strongly flavoured, small, rounded leaves, green or splashed with gold. Both common and golden marjoram carry clusters of small pink flowers from summer to autumn, unless these are sheared off to encourage a flush of fresh foliage.
● Grow in sunny, well-drained positions.
Height x spread:
30 x 30cm (1 x 1ft)

Mint
◌ ❋ ❋ ❋
These perennial herbs vary in their flavour and vigour: from less-invasive and delicately scented apple mint to rampant spearmint, and the more unusual black mint – the strongest of them all. In summer mints carry spikes of flowers, usually lilac or pinkish.
● Plant in a bottomless bucket sunk in the ground to stop the underground rhizomes from spreading.
Height x spread:
30–60 x 90cm (1–2 x 3ft)

Parsley
◌ ❋ ❋ ❋
Tightly curled dark green leaves make 'Moss Curled' desirable among flowers or herbs, planted in groups, singly or as bed edging. 'Flat-leaved Parsley' is preferred by some cooks for its stronger flavour, but it makes a slightly larger, less attractive plant. 'Hamburg' produces similar flat leaves, but with the addition of a parsnip-like, edible root.
● This biennial is slow to germinate and dislikes transplanting. Sow in well-prepared, warmed soil.
Height x spread:
20 x 30cm (8 x 12in)

Rosemary
◌ ❋ ❋ ❋
Rosemary is a densely twigged, evergreen shrub with aromatic, grey-green, needle-like foliage. Whorls of small blue flowers, tightly set, develop along the new growth; in 'Sissinghurst Blue' they are an intense blue.
● Grow in a sunny, well-drained place. Prune hard to keep the plants in shape.
Height x spread:
90cm–1.5m x 90cm–1.5m (3–5 x 3–5ft)

Sage
◌ ❋ ❋ ❋
Shrubby grey-leaved sage provides a splendid year-round foil to other plants in a herb garden. Besides the felty aromatic leaves, it produces spikes of purple-blue flowers in summer. Purple-leaved sages are even more decorative.
● A trim in spring and after flowering prevents plants from becoming leggy.
Height x spread:
60 x 45cm (2 x 1½ft)

Tarragon
◌ ❋ ❋ ❋
French tarragon is harder to obtain than Russian tarragon, but is infinitely more tasty and much less of a garden rogue. This perennial has untidy-looking stems bearing narrow, pale green, aromatic leaves. In midsummer, greenish white flowers are produced.
● Lift and divide occasionally.
Height x spread:
60 x 30cm (2 x 1ft)

Thyme
◌ ❋ ❋ ❋
Thymes are either carpet-forming or small shrubby bushes that are usually grown for culinary purposes. The following deserve a front-row position in the border, near to the kitchen door. Golden thyme has cheerful yellow lemon-scented leaves and lavender flowers, whereas the grey leaves of 'Silver Posie' are gracefully edged with a very fine white line, and the flowers are pale mauve. 'Porlock' has mounds of aromatic greyish leaves and mauve flowers that appear in spring.
● Grow in sunny, well-drained soil.
Height x spread:
10–25 x 10–30cm (4–10 x 4–12in)

FRUIT
Picking sun-warmed, perfectly ripe fruit is one of gardening's greatest pleasures. Strawberries and other soft fruit will fit into most gardens, but fruit trees need more thought. Because they do not come true from seeds they are grafted onto a rootstock that influences the tree's eventual size. On poor soils choose one more vigorous than you would for a deep fertile soil. A good nurseryman will help you select the right rootstock, offer advice on compatible cultivars – vital to ensure successful pollination and a plentiful harvest – and also supply ready-trained forms, with precise instructions for their future pruning and care.

Apple
◌ ❋ ❋ ❋
To ensure a good crop, plant at least two compatible trees. Cox-like 'Sunset' ripens early and is delicious, juicy and firm, but it does not store well. 'Kidd's Orange Red' will provide sweet fruit until midwinter. Two cookers unsurpassed for flavour, texture and keeping qualities are 'Bramley's Seedling' and 'Edward VII', which also becomes suitable for eating raw in late winter.
● For a large apple tree, select an MM.111 or M.2 rootstock. MM.106 is semi-dwarfing and suitable for an espalier, cordon or fan-trained apple. Bush trees are usually grafted on M.26, whereas the very dwarfing M.9 is used for dwarf bush trees.
Height x spread:
Controlled by rootstock

Apricot
◌ ❋ ❋ ❋
'Moor Park' is the most commonly planted late-summer fruiting apricot. As one of the first fruit trees to flower, it needs a sheltered place, such as against a south wall or under the overhang of a roof. When frost threatens, cover the branches with fleece or sheeting for added protection, as the pale pink blossoms are easily damaged.
● Plant in deep, well-drained, moisture-retentive soil, preferably loam. Apricots are usually grafted on 'St Julien A'.
Height x spread:
Controlled by rootstock

Gooseberry 'Whinham's Industry'

Fig 'Brown Turkey'

Kiwi 'Jenny'

Peach 'Peregrine'

Pear 'Williams' Bon Chrétien'

Raspberry 'Autumn Bliss'

Blueberry
◯ ✳ ✳ ✳
Blueberries are easy to grow and have good autumn colour. 'Bluecrop' is an early and heavy cropper, as is 'Herbert', which has a better flavour. Plant at least two different cultivars in your fruit garden in order to ensure cross-pollination and fruitfulness.
● Acid soil is essential.
Height x spread:
1.5 x 1.5m (5 x 5ft)

Currants
◯ ✳ ✳ ✳
Red- and whitecurrants are grown as a bush on a single stem, or can be bought ready-trained as cordons or standards. 'Jonkheer van Tets' is a tasty, heavy-cropping redcurrant. 'White Grape' is a mid-season cultivar of excellent flavour. For blackcurrants, it is advisable to buy stock certified as virus free to start off with strong healthy plants. Unlike red- and whitecurrants, blackcurrants crop on young stems as well as old. 'Blacksmith' bears huge quantities of large, fine-flavoured fruits in mid-season.
● Grow currants in open, sunny sites, well clear of frost pockets. Prune redcurrant bushes in winter by shortening the main branches by half and side shoots to one bud. Plant blackcurrants deeply to encourage new shoots from the base. After fruiting cut out a third of the old stems.
Height x spread:
90cm–1.2m x 1.2m (3–4 x 4ft)

Fig
◯ ✳ ✳
Figs perform best when fan-trained against a sheltered south-facing wall, where the warmth helps to ripen the fruit and it is easier to protect them from frost. Figs set fruit twice a year, in autumn and in spring. Remove the autumn fruits, as they rarely ripen before winter, to channel all energy into the rest of the plant. 'Brown Turkey' is the most reliable.
● Wear gloves when pruning figs, as the sap can cause an allergic reaction in some people. Figs grow well on most soils as long as they are well drained.
Height x spread:
2.5 x 3m (8 x 10ft), more if unpruned

Gooseberry
◯ ◑ ✳ ✳ ✳
Gooseberries are well suited to areas with cool summers. The fruits are red, green, yellow or white-skinned. 'Whinham's Industry' is red, crops heavily in mid-season, and has a good flavour. A white variety with excellent flavour is 'Langley Gage'. Gooseberries are, like redcurrants, traditionally grown on a single stem, but they can also be trained as elegant standards.
● Prune in winter, wearing heavy gloves to protect your hands, when main branches are shortened by half and side shoots are reduced to one bud.
Height x spread:
90cm–1.2m x 1.2m (3–4 x 4ft)

Grape
◯ ✳ ✳ ✳ / ✳ ✳
Not all grapes are suitable for outdoor cropping, but the delicious 'Chasselas' is an old, sweet, translucent yellow variety that stands the cold. 'Muscat of Alexandria' is suitable for warm climates, and 'Foster's Seedling' is a good choice for pots. 'Brant' is probably one of the most decorative for growing in a cool climate, with trusses of sweet, dark red grapes and stunning red and purple autumn colour in the foliage.
● Grow in deep, well-prepared soil and protect from late spring frosts. On outdoor grapes shorten new canes to six or seven buds, which will produce the following year's fruiting canes. After fruiting, all fruit-bearing canes are cut back completely and new shoots are shortened and tied in.
Height:
6m (20ft)

Kiwi
◯ ◑ ✳ ✳ ✳
The common kiwi is better known to some gardeners as the vigorous climber *Actinidia deliciosa* (syn. *A. chinensis*). Kiwis normally bear male and female flowers on separate plants, necessitating the presence of both. If you can ill afford the space for two, plant 'Jenny', which has flowers of both sexes on one plant.
● Grow in rich, loamy soil. Kiwis are best trained against a wall.
Height:
9m (30ft)

Peach
◯ ✳ ✳ ✳
Peaches perform well in sheltered sites and warm regions. To make optimum use of the warmth, grow them fan-shaped against a sheltered south wall. 'Duke of York' ripens in midsummer, 'Peregrine' a few weeks later. Both are fine flavoured and succulent.
● Peaches prefer an acid to neutral moisture-retentive soil and, to produce good fruit, warm springs and summers and dry autumns. The incidence of peach leaf curl can be reduced by covering the plants from midwinter to late spring with polythene or glass. Usually grafted on to 'St Julien A'.
Height x spread:
Controlled by rootstock

Pear
◯ ✳ ✳ ✳
'Williams' Bon Chrétien' is deliciously juicy, with a sweet musky flavour, and 'Concorde' is buttery sweet. Pears flower before apples and are consequently more endangered by frosts. Plant two or three different varieties to aid pollination.
● Pear trees cope with a range of soils and tolerate wet conditions, but they dislike drought. Quince rootstocks seem to encourage fruiting; 'Malling Quince A' and 'Malling Quince C' are suitable for most gardens.
Height x spread:
Controlled by rootstock

Plum
◯ ✳ ✳ ✳
Take care not to plant plums near frost pockets as the warmer and more sheltered the growing position, the better flavoured the fruit will be. The following self-fertile dessert plums do not need a pollinator, though 'Cambridge Gage', ready by midsummer, will produce a heavier crop if it has a pollinating companion. 'Golden Transparent' ripens in late summer and 'Victoria' is ready for eating at the end of summer and can also be used as a cooking plum.
● Plums tolerate most soils. They perform best in areas with a long, cold winter, short spring and hot summer. Prune leading shoots to 40–50cm (16–20in) and laterals to 15–25cm

(6–10in) in spring to reduce incidence of silver leaf disease. 'Pixy' is a dwarfing rootstock, 'St Julien A' is more vigorous.
Height x spread:
Controlled by rootstock

Raspberry
◯ ◑ ✳ ✳ ✳
Raspberries can be cropped over a long season. There are both summer and autumn-fruiting cultivars. For early summer 'Glen Moy' is heavy yielding, while 'Malling Joy' ripens a little later. 'Autumn Bliss' is the tastiest of the autumn croppers. An ever-increasing selection of raspberry relatives is available, including the loganberry, with elongated berries, slightly darker in colour and of sharper flavour.
● They perform best on slightly acid soils. Remove fruiting canes of summer raspberries after harvest, but cut down autumn-fruiting varieties in early spring.
Height:
1.2–1.3m (4–6ft)

Strawberry
◯ ✳ ✳ ✳
The smell of ripe strawberries is divine. 'Elsanta' is a high-yielding variety for midsummer. For late summer, treat yourself to the perpetual-fruiting 'Aromel'. The most delicate flavour of all belongs to the alpine strawberries. Just a handful will add a new dimension to fruit salads. Try the yellow-fleshed 'Alpine Yellow' – birds avoid them, thinking the berries are unripe.
● Plant in early autumn, when the soil is still warm, into soil enriched with rotted manure. Mulch plants with straw in spring to keep berries clean. Shear off foliage after fruiting.
Height x spread:
15 x 30cm (6 x 12in)

Plum 'Victoria'

Alpine strawberry

WALLS AND FLOORS

The following pages will show you a broad enough range of materials and styles of construction for paving, walls and fences to enable you to make an informed choice for the structural elements in your garden. These elements form the framework of the garden, created from materials that include bricks and mortar, concrete, stone and wood, together commonly known as the hard landscape. Hedges, although living, are widely used to mark boundaries and as informal screens within the garden. Plants may be trained or trimmed into arches and woven willow can form an arbour, fence or seat; lime or hornbeam can be pleached or stilted to make a screen or pergola. Use these 'living' structures in association with hard materials; although they need more regular maintenance, they will help keep costs down.

Walls or fences delineate the boundaries and enclose a garden. In the past this enclosure served a purely practical purpose, keeping animals in and intruders out. There may still be a need for this, but there are many other influences on the design and materials used to construct the boundary wall.

Security and privacy are important factors, especially in densely populated areas. You may want to screen an unsightly outlook, or simply define the boundary of the plot without obscuring the view. Once you have established your priorities, there are several other major considerations that should also influence your choice of materials. The boundary should be in keeping with the locality and the style of house, as well as being within your budget. The DIY enthusiast will look for ease of construction and availability of materials, while the durability and degree of maintenance will be important to everyone.

Gardeners often inherit walls and floors from a previous owner. Much can be done to break up large expanses of fence with trellis and planting; a concrete block wall can be rendered or painted for a decorative finish; and a bleak expanse of paving can be broken up by pockets of planting.

Your choice of paving materials also depends on how an area of the garden is to be used. High-use areas such as driveways, patios and front paths will need a smooth, hard-wearing surface and adequate foundations. Informal paths for strolling along may be laid more simply, as stepping stones, crunchy gravel or soft bark-wood chippings.

1 Pink colour wash on the rendered walls works well under blue skies, while the simple flow of cool water brings welcome relief to this arid landscape.
2 A circular opening within this old brick and flint wall frames a pastoral view over the immediate and more distant landscape.

3 A gravel path snakes through a lush lawn: here, two of the most effective and economical surfacing materials are used to create a strong visual impact.

4

4 Screens may be used as partitions to separate rooms within a garden as well as to frame views. Here the screens divide different areas of sculptural cacti and gravel and also frame a cactus beyond.

5

5 Pathways should reflect the character of their surroundings. This meandering path of loose slate links well with the rubble stone wall and is ideal for strolling through an informal garden.

Paving

■

■

RANDOM STONE

Random stone paving is bedded on a 5cm (2in) bed of stiff mortar over 10cm (4in) compacted hardcore. Avoid ugly straight joints, which spoil the random effect. Joints are filled with strong mortar and rubbed to a smooth finish. Some gaps may be left for planting with low plants like thyme.

GRANITE SETTS

For pedestrian use, granite setts should be bedded on 5cm (2in) mortar over a 10cm (4in) base of concrete. For driveways an extra sub-base of 10cm (4in) compacted hardcore should be introduced under the concrete, as shown here.

There is a great variety of paving materials available that can be used alone or in combinations with each other. Natural stone and gravel are traditional, while bricks or cobbles can provide interesting patterns and trim. These materials often have a timeless feel and, like timber, blend well with plants. Garden exhibitions are the fashion shows for landscape materials; although some people may throw up their hands in horror at rubber surfaces and steel mesh walkways, the innovative use of materials not normally associated with gardens should never be ignored.

SANDSTONE

In many ways this is the ideal paving stone. It is extremely durable and its mellow tones blend well with bricks and mortar, making it appropriate for both town and country gardens. Reclaimed secondhand flagstones are cheaper and have a more weathered appearance than new stone, but you should examine them before purchase as the surface may have been spoiled by oil stains. Buy secondhand stone by the square metre or square yard to ensure that the area

will be covered; slabs vary greatly in thickness and buying them by weight could lead to a shortfall. New stone is split from larger blocks into rectangular flagstones of random sizes with a riven (uneven or irregular) surface. Some 'dressing' or trimming of surface irregularities may be needed to avoid tripping. An alternative, very expensive material is diamond-sawn paving cut to specific thicknesses and widths and to measured lengths. This elegant paving can be further enhanced by the supplier 'distressing' the surface with heat treatment to improve the colour.

Laying Lay stone flags on a mortar bed approximately 5cm (2in) thick over a 10cm (4in) base of compacted hardcore, ensuring the depth is sufficient to bed slabs of uneven thickness. Falls, or a slope, of 1:40 or 1:50 should be built in to take surface water off the riven stone (see pages 72–3). Bed the slabs in stiff mortar (cement:sharp sand mix 1:6 or 1:7) so the heavy stone slabs do not settle. Wet-point slabs using a strong mortar (cement:sharp sand mix 1:3 or 1:4) and finish with a rubbed joint made with a length of dowelling.

Maintenance Natural stone tends to accumulate algae, which makes the surface slippery. Clean the stone with a high pressure jet once or twice a year.

LIMESTONE

As a paving stone limestone is much less durable than sandstone. It looks superb in its own locality used as a walling stone. When laid as paving it is prone to frost damage, causing the surface to become pitted and uneven.

Laying and maintenance This is the same as for sandstone (see above).

MARBLE

Marble comes in thin slabs which tend to suffer from the freeze-thaw action of frost and to crack if walked on frequently. The highly polished nature of marble makes it unsuitable for paving unless it is grit-blasted to produce a textured surface. Although it is used in Mediterranean climates, particularly in association with water, its high cost and general unsuitability mean marble is far more at home in an opulent hotel.

Laying and maintenance This is the same as for sandstone (see above).

SLATE

An extremely hard, dense, but fissile rock, which fits uneasily into garden settings other than in its natural locality, or those of a minimalist or modern style. Green and black slate come as thin sawn and polished flags which, although expensive, can look smart and crisp. One of the most attractive uses of

slate is to lay thin slices tightly on edge around an urn, a water feature or another such focal point.

Laying and maintenance This is the same as for sandstone (see above).

SETTS

Setts are small units of paving in natural stone or concrete. The best-known and most useful natural stone sett is cut from granite, an extremely hard rock. Granite setts are ideal for heavily used areas such as driveways and paths, but not for patios, where a more even surface is better. Setts provide an excellent non-slip surface and their small size is ideal for creating intricate patterns, like a fan or a fishtail layout. New setts are very expensive and come in colours from grey to pink, in cubes of 10cm (4in) or, less commonly, in random lengths. Granite setts are sometimes available secondhand, reclaimed from old roadways. These stones are cheaper and are pre-weathered.

■

BRICK PATH

Sandstone and limestone are used less frequently as stone setts. Their warmer colours are well suited to a garden setting, but they are not as durable as granite. Sandstone and limestone setts are available in random sizes as well as with a 'tumbled finish', achieved by turning them in a large concrete mixer to take off the edges and give a weathered appearance.

Concrete setts are cheaper than natural stone, and as they are of even thickness they are easier to lay. They also come in a wider range of colours, are readily available and have an acceptable appearance. Despite providing a more even surface than their natural stone counterparts, imitation setts are still better suited to driveways than patios.

Laying Bed setts on a 5cm (2in) layer of strong mortar (cement:sharp sand mix 1:3) over a base of 10cm (4in) lean-mix concrete (cement:aggregate mix 1:10 or 1:12) and a sub-base of

A temporary timber edge restraint has been used to retain this path laid in a basketweave pattern. Dry mortar is worked into the joints and watered in. Alternatively, a wet mortar mix may be trowelled into the joints, taking care not to stain the bricks.

■

4

1 **Cobbles and brick.**
2 **Marble paving.**
3 **Glass bricks.**
4 **Random stone paving.**
5 **Stone blocks with concrete surface.**
6 **Tiled floor.**

10cm (4in) compacted hardcore for a driveway; for pedestrian areas omit either the concrete or the hardcore layer. Granite setts are compacted to level by a vibrating plate. Brush dry mortar (cement:sharp sand mix 1:6) into the joints and lightly water to bind the setts. Use wet pointing for completely watertight joints around gulleys and along drainage channels. Falls for stone setts are 1:40 or 1:50, which will ensure run-off from an uneven surface (see pages 72–3).
Maintenance Setts need regular cleaning with a high-pressure jet to remove algae. Re-bed setts that become loose – a simple job of chipping out the old mortar with a bolster chisel and bedding the stone on a new strong mix.

BRICK BONDS

Stretcher

Soldier

Basketweave

Staggered basketweave

90-degree herringbone

45-degree herringbone

BRICK
As a paving material, brick often forms a good visual link between the house and other features in the garden. Ideally, the paving brick used should look the same as the house brick, but well-fired facing bricks, or engineering bricks, should be used instead as they are much more durable. Unlike house bricks they do not absorb water and consequently are not subject to frost damage and erosion. There are so many bricks made today that stock can always be found to tone with a house. Large builders' merchants often have brick libraries to help you select suitable bricks for your garden.

Extensive brick paving is expensive; however, bricks are visually more pleasing in smaller areas such as pathways. Bricks are useful for creating curved pathways or edging to other paving. Driveways are one area where bricks can be used over a wide area to good effect. Special clay paver bricks are used for this purpose. They are quick to lay and the cost is only fractionally higher than that of tarmac.

Concrete bricks lack any richness or warmth of colour and should be avoided. They look far more at home in pedestrianized streets and garage forecourts than in a garden.

Bricks can be laid in intricate bonding patterns. Some bricks even have built-in decoration, like the hard-wearing blue stable paver, which has either a diamond or a square pattern incised on its surface, giving an excellent grip.

Glass bricks over recessed lights make an unusual addition when laid as bands running through conventional brick or other paving materials.
Laying Brick paving for pathways is always laid between edge restraints to prevent sideways movement of the bricks. The edges may be of brick, mortared into place, or of timber, which can be removed once the path has been laid. Prepare a 10cm (4in) base of compacted hardcore overlaid with a level 5cm (2in) bed of dry mortar (cement:sand mix 1:4). Position the bricks and tap them down flush with the edge restraints, which act as a level guide. Brush dry mortar of the same strength between the joints and water in. An alternative method is to bed the bricks on wet mortar and point the joints with a wet mix. However, this is a slower process and care must be taken not to stain the brick face with the cement while pointing the joints.
Maintenance Brick paving may need cleaning once a year. Use a high-pressure jet, but ensure the pointing is strong enough to take the force or it may be washed out. A few bricks in a brick-paved driveway may settle, which

is easily repaired, although you may have to break a paver to give access to the surrounding bricks. Once this is done the settled pavers are lifted and the underlying sand relaid and compacted level prior to tamping the pavers back into position. Dry sand is then vibrated into the joints using a vibrating plate compactor.

TILES
Ceramic tiles can look wonderful in the garden, but they are expensive. You also need to be certain that the tiles you choose are exterior grade: in general, the darker coloured tiles – black, blue-black and dark brown – are more durable than those in shades of buff, and they will often have a frost-proof glaze. One way of achieving a hard-wearing and long-lasting tiled surface is to select one of the superb concrete imitations that provide a similar effect but which are much more durable.

Terrazzo tiles are also expensive but look outstanding in the right setting, for instance as a surround, highlighting fountains and other water features in a formal courtyard. These tiles are formed from a base of fine concrete inset with broken marble, and are available in various sizes.
Laying This is a job best tackled by specialist contractors as great accuracy is needed in producing a level concrete screed on which the tiles are bedded. Care must also be taken in laying the thin tiles on a very strong mortar (cement:sharp sand mix 1:4), which can easily mark the surface. An even stronger pointing mix (cement:sand mix 1:3), or grout, containing a waterproof additive, is needed for the joints. Ceramic tiles also need a thin mastic (waterproof filler) expansion joint for areas larger than 10m² (107 sq ft).
Maintenance Tiles need regular cleaning with a high-pressure jet.

5

GRAVEL AND SHINGLE
These two materials are practically synonymous. Always use local gravel to maintain continuity with other building materials, as the colours of different aggregates depend on the base rock. Avoid bright colours, which can look brash, and also white chippings, which appear artificial. Honey-coloured stone tends to look warm and it provides a good foil to foliage plants.

Gravel is cheap to buy, as long as local stone is selected, and cheap to install, so large areas can be covered at a reasonable cost. It forms a good surface for driveways, and is appropriate in both town and country. As gravel crunches underfoot it acts as a deterrent to would-be burglars.

Take care in selecting the size of aggregate: 1cm (½in) stones are about right, as anything smaller tends to scatter everywhere, and anything larger becomes awkward to walk on. The depth of a gravel surface should be no greater than 2.5cm (1in), otherwise walking will be like trying to wade through a pebble beach. Although gravel surfaces are to a degree self-draining, falls of about 1:40 should be built in to avoid puddling and deterioration of the surface (see pages 72–3). Gravel is best restricted to decorative areas of the garden rather than heavily used paths, where the stones tend to move more.

Self-binding gravel is an excellent material. Because it is made up of different grades of aggregate, including fine dust, it locks together after rolling to form a firm surface. It is ideal for paths as it does not move or deteriorate like loose gravel.

6

2

1 Slatted timber tiles.
2 Cobbles.
3 Bark chippings.
4 Concrete bridge.
5 Steel mesh walkway.
6 Curved timber
edging.
7 Brick edging.

Resin-bonded aggregates are more expensive and have a very crisp, smart finish. Follow the instructions for laying this material with care as different climatic conditions will affect the resin. One disadvantage is the smooth surface coat of resin which can be slippery, making it particularly unsuitable for use on sloping paths.
Laying Loose gravel is easy to lay between edge restraints of treated timber, bricks or granite setts. A base of compacted hardcore or, ideally, hoggin (binder clay) should be laid to a depth of 8cm (3in) for a pathway and overlaid with a 2.5cm (1in) layer of gravel, which is rolled into the hoggin. A greater depth of hardcore, 15cm (6in), is needed when gravel is used as a surface for driveways and parking areas. Free-draining geotextile membranes can be laid underneath to help prevent weeds germinating.
Maintenance Gravel paths and drives require regular surface raking and occasional weedkilling to keep them looking neat. After a while the surface may need to be topped up and re-rolled. Self-binding gravels need periodic watering, raking and rolling to maintain the surface.

COBBLES AND PEBBLES

The terms cobbles and pebbles tend to be used interchangeably. Rounded beach pebbles may be bedded flat into mortar to create an interesting, albeit slippery, path. They may also be bedded on end to project just above the mortar or set flush with the surface. This scheme is particularly suitable for surrounding a water feature or urn. Pebbles of different sizes and colours can be arranged to form simple patterns or intricate mosaics; loose pebbles can also be laid as a beach edging a natural pool. Like other aggregates, cobbles are available in bulk, in 1m³ (1.3 cu yd) sacks, or in smaller, more manageable bags for use in restricted areas.
Laying Pebble paths need edge restraints to retain the surface. Prepare a 10cm (4in) base of rammed hardcore and position the edge restraints. Then bed the stones into a 5cm (2in) dry mortar (cement : sand mix 1:4), which is also brushed across the pebbles and then lightly watered in.
Maintenance If necessary, clean with a high-pressure jet to remove algae, which make cobbled surfaces slippery.

TIMBER

Timber is an excellent surface material and blends extremely well with plants. Log slices and bark chippings are relatively cheap materials for a simple path in a woodland garden.

Decks of sawn timber make ideal patios in sunny positions and are especially useful for sloping gardens as there is no need for deep foundations and expensive retaining walls. To make the decking more interesting use timber slats in varying widths or lay them diagonally. The wood for decking should either be hardwood or treated softwood, and can be left with a natural finish or stained. Natural wood stains provide a finish which always blends with plants, while brighter colours such as light green or blue can work well in some schemes.

Reclaimed timber or railway sleepers are appropriate for decks set into the ground as they are highly durable. They are best for informal woodland areas as the surface may not be as level as that of planed timber. Take care when using old wood, as it may splinter, and bear in mind that tar can sweat out of timber sleepers on hot days.
Laying Log slices are laid over 5–10cm (2–4in) of hardcore, although on compacted soil, logs can be laid on a 2.5–5cm (1–2in) bed of sharp sand with an infill of gravel.

For decking, a specialist company can be employed to carry out the whole process, from initial design to final

1

construction. Low-level decks are laid with deck slats fixed to joists over brick footings. More commonly decks are raised on posts, 10 x 10cm (4 x 4in) in section, concreted into the ground or fixed into metal shoes. Bearers bolted to the posts support the joists onto which the slats are fixed. Both bearers and joists are commonly 15 x 5cm (6 x 2in) in section. Fix the slats in place with either galvanized nails or stainless-

3

steel screws. For a smart and splinter-resistant finish, use pencil-edged slats that have had the tops of their edges rounded by machine.
Maintenance Timber surfaces must be kept free of algae, which makes them slippery, so they should be cleaned at least once a year, especially if situated under trees. Use a high-pressure jet

and scrub them with a wire brush if necessary. As an extra precaution, decking slats are available with a ribbed surface to give extra grip, and some modern stains contain abrasive sands to give a non-slip surface. Cover log slices with chicken wire in order to give them enough grip.

BARK CHIPPINGS

Bark chippings make excellent, and relatively cheap, informal pathways through woodland areas, where they are far more in keeping than shingle or paved surfaces. To be successful, however, the chippings should be laid over compacted hardcore to avoid the possibility of the path turning to mud. Restraining edges will prevent the sides of the path from crumbling as well as keeping the chippings in place.

Bark is available in different grades – from fine shredded to chips or nuggets. Shredded bark tends to disintegrate quickly whereas nuggets keep their original form for longer and also look more attractive. Bark chips are available in 1m³ (1.3 cu yd) bulk bags or in smaller, more manageable sacks.
Laying Mark out the line of the path and remove the soft topsoil. Treated timber path edgings, 10 x 2.5cm (4 x 1in), are secured in position with driven timber pegs before compacting hardcore with a hand rammer or vibrating plate compactor to give a firm base 5–10cm (2–4in) thick. Finally, rake out the bark chips to a depth of approximately 5cm (2in).
Maintenance Little maintenance is necessary other than occasionally topping up and raking out the bark.

COBBLE INSERT

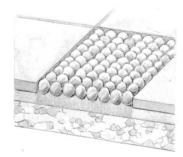

An interesting surface detail, cobbles may be used to break up a large expanse of paving. They should be packed tightly together and bedded into a 5cm (2in) bed of dry mortar; more mortar should then be brushed over the cobbles and watered in to hold them firm.

EXPOSED AGGREGATE CONCRETE

This is an excellent surface treatment for concrete, which can otherwise look drab. Just before the concrete has set hard, work at the surface with a stiff brush, applying water at the same time. This exposes the aggregate in the concrete and provides an attractive textured surface.

4

CONCRETE

Concrete slabs come in a range of colours and surface finishes, including non-slip, and form an economical alternative to natural stone paving. It is best to avoid garishly coloured slabs; buff tones tend to sit more comfortably with plants. Slab sizes also vary. Square slabs can create sharp geometric patterns, while small squares and larger rectangular slabs may be laid together in a softer, random pattern. Steer clear of slabs that pretend to be bricks or setts as they look contrived.

Imitation stone slabs vary from the good to the bad and the ugly. The good imitations are very good, showing saw marks and variations in the riven pattern. Their colouring can also be superb, with the only drawback being that, unlike natural stone, they never look weathered. The bad imitations have repetitive surface patterns that look completely unnatural. The ugly slabs are too bright, too glossy and look totally artificial. As you would expect, the good slabs tend to be more expensive than the others.

Concrete laid on site can look very good when the surface layer is brushed off just before it sets to expose the aggregate. This gives a textured surface that can vary in colour depending on the aggregate chosen. Great care is needed to ensure a satisfactory finished surface and for this reason it may be advisable to employ a specialist contractor to do the work.

Laying Lay concrete slabs on a full bed of mortar (cement:sharp sand mix 1:6) over an 8cm (3in) compacted layer of hardcore. Build in falls between 1:70 and 1:50 for the riven slabs to remove surface water (see pages 72–3). Laying slabs touching each other (known as butt jointing) works well for crisp-edged slabs, whereas slabs with uneven edges need an open joint, which must be filled or pointed. Use a strong mortar (cement:sharp sand mix 1:3 or 1:4) for pointing, and finish with a rubbed joint made with a length of dowelling.

Maintenance Concrete surfaces need occasional cleaning with a high-pressure jet. Re-bed loose slabs and repoint joints as necessary.

RUBBER

The growth of children's playgrounds over the last two decades and the concern for safety has brought about a revolution in the development of play surfaces. Rubber safety surfaces, which absorb shock, have been introduced to replace existing unforgiving tarmac.

Rubber surfaces are obviously suitable for children's play areas within the garden and, in the right setting, for

other surfaces that are more usually paved, like pathways or patios. Rubber is soft to walk on, durable, non-slip and virtually maintenance-free. Colours tend to be bright, though more muted tones and black are also available. It is not cheap, as manufacturers are geared up only for large playground sites, but this could change with time.

Laying This operation is carried out by a specialist contractor. The rubber is poured *in situ* over an existing sound base, or over a new base of concrete or compacted hardcore approximately 15cm (6in) deep. A timber or brick edging restraint is required.

Maintenance Apart from sweeping and the occasional washing down, a rubber surface needs no maintenance.

5

STEEL MESH

High-tech house design can be extended into the garden with walkways in steel mesh. The mesh must be painted unless galvanized, stainless or plastic-coated steel is used. Like rubber, it is not a cheap option, but it can be confined to a small area. Low-level walkways spanning water are particularly effective, as the water can be seen through the mesh.

Laying This is always carried out by a specialist contractor arranged by the manufacturer.

Maintenance Periodic cleaning, and possibly touching up the paint, may be necessary. Stainless and plastic-coated steel simply needs wiping clean.

EDGING AND TRIM

When linked to paving, both terms refer to a similar function of providing a crisp detail line to a surface material. The practical role of edging or, more precisely, edge restraint, is to confine a loose or flexible material like shingle or tarmac within an area, and at the same time to retain a lawn or planting bed.

Trim, however, has a slightly more aesthetic role in defining the edge of a paved area, or forming a neat link between two different surface materials. The practical use of trim is more as a maintenance strip than as a retainer – mowing edges are an obvious example. A brick edge allows the mower to run along the lawn edge, saving laborious trimming. A broader trim in the form of paving slabs laid next to a building allows access for cleaning windows. A shingle trim in such a position would provide a drainage channel.

Edging and trim should be functional and form a necessary part of the overall design. The materials should also fit their purpose: timber edging needs treating, while bricks and tiles must be well fired and frost-proof. They should also complement the property: concrete edging in the garden of a period home would look as wrong as Victorian tiles in a modern setting.

The small unit size of bricks makes them a versatile edging or trim. The many tones available mean suitable bricks can be found for most gardens. They are usually laid either on edge

7

6

or flat, set on a concrete footing and 'haunched' (supported up the sides) with concrete. Lay bricks flush with lawns for easy mowing but slightly proud to confine adjacent soil or gravel. Curved lines are usually achieved by laying bricks on end, and as such they form a neat finish to cut paving slabs or exposed aggregate concrete.

The granite sett is one of the most expensive, but probably the ideal edging stone. It is a small unit and can be laid to curves on a concrete footing with mortar-pointed joints.

Pressure-treated timber is cheaper than brick for edging a path of gravel or bark chippings. The long lengths of timber are simply nailed to timber pegs driven 45cm (18in) into the ground. Timber suits the edge of a woodland path, but it usually needs replacing after about ten years and is only practical for straight lines or shallow curves. Timber path edging is usually 10 x 2.5cm (4 x 1in), but may be used in larger sections such as 15 x 8cm (6 x 3in) to trim flexible material such as resin-bonded aggregate. Timber trim can be stained to match wooden decks or pergolas elsewhere in the garden.

TIMBER EDGING

Timber edging may be used as a temporary edge restraint to a brick path, or as a permanent edging to a flexible surface such as gravel or bark chippings. Pressure-treated timber should be used for permanent edging.

Lawns and meadows

1 Prairie-style
meadow planting.
2 Turf maze.
3 Striped lawn.
4 Grass path with
granite stepping stones.
5 Wildflower meadow.

LAWNS

As a living surface, grass is unsurpassed and, although lawns and meadows need regular care to look their best, if raised from seed either is a much cheaper option than hard paving. The texture of a lawn and its ability to withstand wear depends on its mixture of grasses. A fine-quality lawn provides a soft, smooth surface best appreciated in full view of the house; however, if you need a hard-wearing lawn where children can play and dogs can run about, it is better situated at a distance, where the coarser texture is less apparent.

Meadows tend to work best when they are given plenty of space. These informal mixtures of flowers and grasses encourage wildlife and in rural areas they suit the periphery of the garden, where they make a transition between the cultivated area close to the house and the more natural landscape beyond.

Lawns can be any shape, but those with straight edges look smart in formal settings, whereas gentle curves blend in with informal gardens. Avoid excessively wavy edges as these make mowing awkward. In any situation a trim facilitates mowing and prevents adjacent loose materials, such as gravel, from flicking onto the grass (see page 225). Although they need different treatments, a lawn can merge into a meadow along a gentle meandering curve.

Lawns are established from seed or from turf. Although it is possible to choose turf to suit your site and demands, a wider choice is available from seed. Seed is cheap and easy to sow, but you will need to weed the new sward and it will be some months before you can fully enjoy your lawn. Turf, on the other hand, is instant.

Lawns from seed The most widely available grass mixes are for a high-quality lawn (predominantly fescues and fine-leaved bents) or a hard-wearing lawn (mostly perennial rye grass). Other

mixtures are available for special purposes, including those able to cope with salt spray normally encountered in coastal regions, or alongside main roads; low-maintenance mixtures of shorter-growing grasses for steep banks and other areas where access is difficult; and shade-tolerant mixes for lawns overshadowed by trees or tall buildings. In subtropical or tropical climates the grasses suited to the cooler summers of Europe and North America will not perform well, so instead opt either for Bermuda grass or zoysia.

Lawns from turf Although suppliers can grow turf to a specification, most companies only offer a fine turf or a

MEADOWS

Meadows are established either by planting wildflowers into an existing sward, or by sowing an appropriate grass and flower mixture. A range of seed mixtures to suit many soil types is available from seed suppliers and garden centres. Alternatively, you can order from a specialist wildflower seed supplier who will offer the standard range and also some special mixtures, such as for wet soils, pond edges and woodland. It is important to match the mixture accurately to your conditions.

Maintenance Lawns and meadows need regular care, and how best to give this is described on page 254.

hard-wearing one. A turf usually covers one square metre or yard, but for an extensive lawn ask whether turf-laying equipment is available to lay long rolls, measuring approximately 13m (42ft). Depending on the area to be covered, the equipment is either pushed by hand or tractor-mounted. The large rolls work out marginally more expensive than the equivalent area of small sods, but laying is much quicker.

Buy turf from a reputable supplier to ensure it is weed-free, of good quality and of even thickness. Prepare the ground before delivery as turves should be laid as soon as possible, and certainly within two days, to prevent the roots from drying out and the grass yellowing.

Hedges

1 Terraced hedges.
2 Hedge with a view.
3 Wavy hedge.

Well-chosen and carefully maintained hedges give privacy and security, buffer sound and create favourable micro-climates by filtering wind. Although they take time to establish and require more attention, hedges are a cheaper alternative to walls and provide a sympathetic background for flowering plants. Fed and trimmed regularly, hedges will also last for a very long time. In addition, they have a flexibility that would be difficult and expensive to achieve with harder materials. Plant them in serpentine fashion; trim the top in the undulating form of a Chinese dragon or, more formally, into crisp crenellations. Such devices make little difference to the overall cost, but will bring movement into the garden.

Although evergreens may seem the obvious choice for a windbreak and for providing a dense screen all year round, a deciduous hedge gives greater seasonal variety, with the possibility of flowers (forsythia, berberis) and fruit (hawthorn, blackthorn). Some conifers, such as Leyland cypress, grow extremely fast and will quickly make

a thick hedge. However, this species is best avoided if at all possible, as once the desired height is achieved they need clipping several times a year to be kept under control. With the exception of yew, conifers do not lend themselves to hard, rejuvenating pruning if they become too large. They show little seasonal variation, making them less interesting than evergreens such as escallonia or pyracantha. Beech and hornbeam hedges retain their dead copper-coloured leaves during winter, giving extra protection and privacy.

Hedges for a formal garden must be solid-looking and immaculate. The desirable smooth, even surface is best achieved by using small-leaved evergreen plants. Box and yew are particularly suitable as they can be clipped to a precise shape and into decorative finials, should such exclamation marks be required. *Lonicera nitida* is a fast-growing alternative to box, but it needs more frequent trimming to retain a sharp outline. Low hedges edging beds and borders are often of dwarf box, with lavender and *Santolina chamaecyparissus* as grey-leaved alternatives.

Stilted hedges make formal elements out of trees such as lime or hornbeam. The canopies are clipped into large rectangular blocks or cubes while the trunks, kept bare, allow a clear view through to the area beyond.

Although beech and hornbeam can also be trimmed straight, they have a rustic appearance better suited to informal situations. The same is true for holly; its spiny leaves may be a drawback in some situations but they deter intruders. More informal still and also with glossy foliage is *Prunus laurocerasus*, the cherry laurel, which associates particularly well with woodland.

HEDGE PROFILES

Lawson cypress   Yew or privet   Beech

A tapestry hedge is made up of plants such as green and copper beech, holly, box and yew. During summer the difference between the plants is barely noticeable, but in spring and autumn the tapestry of greens and bronzes formed by the new foliage is beautiful.

Mixed hedges offer dense cover and food to wildlife. The choice of plants should reflect your local flora, but field

maple, hazel, hawthorn, blackthorn, privet, wild roses, elderberry and *Viburnum opulus*, the guelder rose, are all suitable. If space allows an occasional tree to grow up, so much the better.
Establishing a hedge As so many plants are needed, it is cheaper to buy young, bare-rooted stock rather than larger, container-grown plants. These should only be used if instant effect is required, or if planting has to take place in the height of the growing season. Prepare a broad, deep trench and incorporate plenty of organic matter. Space plants 15–30cm (6–12in) apart for low hedges; 30–45cm (1–1½ft) for medium internal hedges; 45–60cm (1½–2ft) for tall boundary hedges. After planting, water well and mulch with organic matter. Encourage bushy growth by pruning back the leading shoot of deciduous plants by one-third, or trimming off the top of evergreens. If this is not done, the hedge may attain the desired height more quickly, but will remain thin or bare at the base.
Maintenance Water well in dry periods until established and keep clear of weeds at all times. Trim regularly to maintain height and shape as follows.

Keep the height of low internal hedges at 30–60cm (1–2ft). Clip dwarf box (*B. sempervirens* 'Suffruticosa'), lavender (*Lavandula*) and *Santolina chamaecyparissus* in spring and in late summer or after flowering.

Keep medium internal hedges at breast height. Trim *Lonicera nitida* at least three times a year; box (*Buxus sempervirens*) and yew (*Taxus baccata*) in summer and autumn; and escallonias, berberis and roses after flowering.

For tall boundary hedges, clip holly, beech (*Fagus sylvatica*) and hornbeam (*Carpinus betulus*) in late summer; yew and hawthorn (*Crataegus monogyna*) in summer and autumn; privet (*Ligustrum*) and Leyland cypress (× *Cupressocyparis leylandii*) three times in the growing season; Lawson cypress (*Chamaecyparis lawsoniana*) and *Thuja plicata* 'Fastigiata' in spring to early summer; forsythia, hazel (*Corylus avellana*), blackthorn (*Prunus spinosa*) and *Cornus mas* after flowering.

3

Walls

BRICK BONDS

Free-standing garden walls should, ideally, be a full brick wide and in a bonding pattern to match the house walls. English and Flemish bond, along with their 'garden wall' variations, are commonly used.

English

English garden wall

Flemish

Flemish garden wall

BRICK RETAINING WALL

Retaining walls are load-bearing, having to withhold the pressure of wet earth. Brick retaining walls should be a minimum of one full brick wide, often built in English bond. Provision must be made to ease water pressure from behind the wall by back-filling with free-draining stone, and setting weep holes through the wall for drainage purposes.

Free-standing walls are used to form the external boundary of a garden and also to enclose smaller areas within the garden itself. Retaining walls, on the other hand, are load bearing, holding back earth at changes of level where a bank would be too steep. Water pressure may build up behind retaining walls, but by backfilling with free-draining aggregate and introducing weepholes, excess water can drain through the wall to a gully drain. Where the land is steeply sloping, a series of terraces, each supported by a low retaining wall, is a more effective method of soil retention than a single high wall. One type of retaining wall used to define a boundary is the ha-ha. This combines an open ditch with a wall to create a physical barrier while allowing an uninterrupted view.

Various materials are used in wall construction, some of which are specific to retaining walls. Select materials that are appropriate to the job in hand, within your budget and which harmonize with your garden style.

Curved or serpentine walls, and any wall higher than about 90cm (3ft), should be built by a professional. It is imperative that walls have adequate foundations, the depth of which will vary according to the height of the wall and the soil type. They must also be truly upright and level, with corners square and curves smooth and even.

BRICK

Brick is the most usual walling material. It is widely available, relatively cheap and often provides a good visual link with other areas of brick in the garden, including house walls. Choose well-fired facing bricks for your wall to avoid the

need for fussy coping stones and damp-proof membranes, both essential if you use interior quality, porous bricks. House bricks, which are often of this inferior quality, can be used for matching

garden walls but need the protection of coping stones. Glass bricks or blocks may be incorporated into a free-standing wall to add an interesting pattern and change of texture, as well as allowing light to filter through.

Ideally, garden walls should be at least one full brick in width; half-brick wide walls are weak and will need support from brick piers or pillars at regular intervals. The bonding pattern for garden walls is often chosen to match that of the house. This is usually stretcher bond laid in two skins to make the full width: two separate half-brick walls built up and linked together by brick ties. English bond and Flemish bond are also used, and both these patterns have a garden-wall variation for a traditional and unusual alternative.

Construction Laying bricks is a fairly straightforward operation, although great care has to be taken to ensure the brick courses run level and the face of the wall is kept upright and free of mortar. Bricks are bedded on mortar (cement:sand mix 1:6) over a concrete

foundation. The bottom of the wall needs protection from moisture and this is usually given by two courses of engineering bricks, as flexible damp-proof membranes do not adhere well to mortar, resulting in an unstable wall.

Start by building up the two ends so a string can be secured between them to act as a guideline. The line is to ensure that the bricks run level along the length of the wall; it is moved up after each course is laid. A line of bricks laid on edge will form a neat finish to the top of the wall. These may be laid over two courses of hard tiles known as creasing tiles for a neat detail as well as to give the wall extra protection. At the end of each session of brick laying, the mortar joints between the bricks must be finished with a rubbed joint made with a short section of pipe or a bucket handle.

Maintenance Well-constructed brick walls require little maintenance. If a coping brick is dislodged, re-bed it on strong mortar (cement:sand mix 1:3). If pointing becomes damaged either by climbing plants or frost, rake out the old mortar and repoint the joints with a new mix (E6).

CONCRETE

Infinitely adaptable, concrete can be coloured and structured into virtually any shade or shape required. Concrete blocks are a useful but under-used walling material. They are cheap, quick to lay and very strong. Although they are heavy to manoeuvre – each one measures 45 x 23 x 23cm (18 x 9 x 9in) – one block is equivalent in size to 12 bricks so a concrete wall is far quicker to build than one of bricks. Finished walls are often rendered and painted

Construction Mortared stone walls need a concrete footing 30–45cm (1–1½ft) thick depending on the soil, but dry-stone walls can be laid on a base of rammed earth if they are less than, say, 1.5m (5ft) high. The base of a stone wall is wider than the top, with the sides tapering into a 'batter' to give strength. To achieve this profile timber boards are set up at each end of the wall, linked by taut strings which act as guidelines for laying the stones. The widest stones are laid at the foot of the wall, including the 'tie stones', which span the width of the wall and are placed at intervals along its length. The finished wall is topped with coping stones set vertically and bedded into mortar.

Maintenance Any coping stones that are knocked loose should be re-bedded on a strong mortar (cement:sand mix 1:3) to keep the centre of the wall dry.

5

TIMBER

Timber is often used in the construction of retaining walls. Railway sleepers and telegraph poles are especially suitable for this purpose as both are extremely durable and well preserved. However, some care is needed when planting near them as the preservative may cause damage to soft foliaged perennials. Timber cribwalling also makes a neat retaining wall. This system is installed by a specialist contractor and is made up of interlocking timber units backfilled with free-draining aggregate to create an extremely strong wall. Pockets in the face of the wall can be filled with plants.

Construction Timbers for a low wall are usually laid on a concrete footing, although well-preserved railway sleepers may be laid directly on the ground. Lay sleepers – which are very heavy – and telegraph pole sections horizontally, overlapping each other in courses like brick bonding. To give the wall extra strength steel rods are bedded into the concrete footing and pass up through pre-drilled holes in the timber.

Maintenance Railway sleepers and telegraph poles are almost maintenance-free. All other timber should be pre-treated and may need occasional treatment to enhance the colour.

4

1 Serpentine concrete wall.
2 Painted brick wall.
3 Rendered concrete wall.
4 Stone retaining wall.
5 Mosaic wall.
6 Glass bricks and concrete.

with a masonry paint, and capped with a neat brick-on-edge coping. This type of wall suits contemporary gardens and can be enlivened by setting in stained-glass panels or coloured glass bricks.

Concrete is also ideal for retaining walls, either using concrete blocks reinforced with steel rods set into a concrete footing, or by setting concrete *in situ* behind temporary wooden boards known as shuttering. The wall can then be faced with a brick or stone veneer.

Construction Concrete blocks are laid and bonded in the same manner as bricks (see above), using a stiff mortar

STONE WALL

Dry-stone walls may be laid on a base of rammed earth, while mortared stone walls need a concrete footing to prevent movement and thus cracking of the joints. The walls are tapered to a batter to give them strength, with the angle of the batter constantly checked with a batter board and spirit level.

(cement:sand mix 1:5) to support the greater weight of the block. The joints are either rubbed or can be left flush if the wall is to be rendered.

Maintenance Rendered and painted walls need repainting about every two years; otherwise little work is needed.

STONE

Stone walls will soon weather and have a timeless quality, but they are fairly expensive to construct both in terms of material and labour. Sandstone and limestone are most often used for walling. Walls of random rubble or undressed stone look best in their own locality and generally suit rural rather than urban gardens. Dry-stone walls look wonderful in country gardens and may be laid truly dry or, for added strength, with mortar joints which are raked back to simulate dry-laid stone. Dressed stone, which is stone that has been cleaned and shaped into blocks, is equally at home in town or country. It makes a smart wall when laid in courses with mortar joints.

Stone may be laid in courses, at random or in patterns. There are regional variations, such as Cornish 'zig-zag', where thin stones are laid at an angle to the left and right in alternate bands or courses. Stone is also used as a veneer to a concrete or brick retaining wall in order to cut down on the high cost of a solid stone wall. Another interesting use of stone is in the construction of retaining walls using gabions. These are cages of galvanized steel, approximately 1m (3ft) square by 1m (3ft) high, backfilled with excavated rocks and pebbles. Gabions are appropriate in woodland settings to retain banks of streams or slopes.

6

Fences and trellis

Close-board

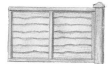

Timber panel

Hurdles

Hit-and-miss

Picket

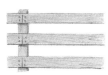

Post-and-rail

Chain-link

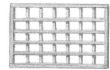

Trellis

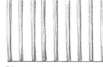

Rivetment

1

Like walls, fences are used for boundary enclosures and as divisions within the garden, but they are, in general, a much cheaper option. Choose a fence appropriate to your garden, taking into account its cost and ease of construction. A consideration for a boundary fence is the need for privacy, as this will determine whether your fence is solid or open. Privacy is less important for internal screens, where open trelliswork is often used. Fences are usually timber; steel is also an option.

CLOSE-BOARD FENCE

This style of fence is very strong and gives privacy if it is built to its usual height of 1.8m (6ft). Its most basic construction consists of a framework of posts and horizontal rails, known as arris rails, clad with overlapping vertical feather-edged boards. Variation is achieved by setting boards diagonally or using slats of different widths. By supporting the slats at the base by a horizontal board – a gravel board – they are lifted clear of the soil and prevented from rotting.
Construction The first fence post is set in a concrete footing, and a string line is stretched between this post and a temporary post at the end of the fence run. The framework of arris rails and posts is then constructed along the length of the fence, concreting in all the posts, which are spaced between 1.8m and 2.7m (6–9ft) apart. Allow at least two days for the concrete to set before nailing in place the gravel board and then the cladding boards. A capping rail will protect the tops of the boards; this is nailed to a counter rail (thinner in section than an arris rail) set between the posts. Pressure-treated timber should always be used and may be stained with a colour, if required.

Maintenance Treated timber needs staining with a suitable preservative every couple of years. Gravel boards may rot and need to be replaced from time to time if they are in contact with the ground. If gravel boards are not used set the panels approximately 5cm (2in) clear of the ground. Rotten fence posts need replacing. This awkward job is made a little easier by using concrete spurs – short concrete posts bolted to the original wooden post and concreted into the ground. The old concrete must first be removed prior to cutting back the rotten wood from the base of the post. The spur is then placed in the hole, bolted to the post and set in concrete.

TIMBER PANEL FENCE

This cheaper version of close-board fencing uses ready-made panels of overlapping or interwoven slats set between posts. The slats often have a wavy edge. They are also very thin and when interwoven can break quite easily. Purchase pre-treated panels and posts, and a lead cap on the top of each post will protect against the weather.

A more substantial variation on this style of fencing is one where timber panels are set over concrete gravel boards and between concrete posts. Although this type of fence is strong and long-lasting, it looks stark and does not blend in well to a garden setting.
Construction The first post is set in a concrete footing and a string line is stretched to a temporary post at the

end of the fence run. Consecutive posts are concreted in a panel-width, about 1.8m (6ft), apart, each secured with a temporary strut until the concrete has set. Fix the panels in position – the last panel in the run may need to be cut to fit the remaining space. Timber gravel boards fixed along the bottom of the fence are not essential but they will protect the panels from rot.
Maintenance This is the same as for a close-board fence (see above).

HURDLES

Woven hazel and willow hurdles form a solid, albeit expensive, fence. They look best as a backdrop to shrubs in country gardens where they will provide a

2

temporary screen until the planting has established. You will be lucky if they last five years before deteriorating.
Construction Hurdles are simply fixed to timber posts or angle-iron stakes with strands of plastic-coated wire. It is almost impossible to set the panels to a true level, so just follow the general contour of the ground. Hurdles usually measure 1.8 x 1.8m (6 x 6ft).
Maintenance As hurdles are by nature temporary, it is not worth trying to maintain or repair them. Hazel hurdles tend to last longer than willow ones.

3

CONSTRUCTING A TIMBER FENCE

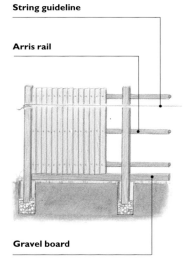

String guideline

Arris rail

Gravel board

CLOSE-BOARD FENCE

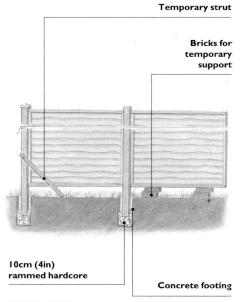

Temporary strut

Bricks for temporary support

10cm (4in) rammed hardcore

Concrete footing

PANEL FENCE

Excavate a hole for the first upright, 60cm (2ft) deep for a fence 1.8m (6ft) high. Ram in hardcore and wedge the post in position, checking it is vertical, giving support with a temporary strut. Run a guide along the length of the fence: Erect the second post and attach the arris rails. Continue in this way until the framework is complete. Check posts are vertical and pour in concrete. When the concrete has set, first nail in place the gravel boards, then the cladding boards. Uprights for a panel fence are erected in a similar manner. Nail the panels in place once the concrete has hardened.

4

5

HIT-AND-MISS FENCE
This fence is supported by timber posts, square in section, with horizontal boards fixed on alternate sides. The fence gives privacy when built to its usual height of 1.8m (6ft), but the horizontal boards are easy to climb and offer no security. It is an excellent choice for windy situations.
Construction The first post is concreted into position and the lowest board nailed on to indicate the position for the next post, about 1.8m (6ft) along the line. This process is continued on down the fence line, concreting in each post and holding it firm with a temporary strut until the concrete has set. After about two days, when the concrete has set hard, the upper boards are nailed alternately on either side of the fence posts. The boards are usually 15 x 2.5cm (6 x 1in) in section.
Maintenance Rotten posts need to be replaced, as they would for a close-board fence (see above). Treated timber needs staining with a preservative every couple of years. Avoid coloured stains and paints, as it is almost impossible to ensure complete coverage

PICKET FENCE
A low fence of vertical pales clads a framework of posts and horizontal rails. Timber may be sawn and treated or, more expensively, prepared and painted. The height is normally no more than 90cm (3ft) and, although the fence offers some protection, its main function is to delineate the boundary of a cottage-style garden. The tops of the pales are pointed or rounded and finish level with the post tops. Ready-made panels of rails and palings are a cheaper option than a bespoke fence.
Construction Posts are concreted in at 1.8m (6ft) intervals. The rails are then secured to the posts using either mortise joints or nails. The pales are then nailed to the rails to finish level with the post tops and approximately 5cm (2in) off the ground. Space the pales at gaps equal to the width of the pale or less. Ready-made panels are simply fixed to posts with brackets.

6

Maintenance Broken pales can easily be replaced. The fence should regularly be stained or painted. Rotten posts are repaired using concrete spurs, as for a close-board fence (see above).

POST-AND-RAIL FENCE
This is the traditional stock fence of rural areas, offering no privacy or security. It is a strong fence using relatively large-section timbers, which are necessary as cheaper, undersized posts and rails will not last long.
Construction The first post is concreted in and a string line is run to the temporary post at the end of the fence line. A rail is used to mark the position of all holes prior to concreting in all the posts. All rails are nailed into position when the posts have set firm.
Maintenance Damaged rails need to be replaced as necessary. Rotten posts are repaired with concrete spurs, as for a close-board fence (see above).

CHAIN-LINK FENCE
Plastic-coated wire mesh is fixed to strained wires set between angle-iron stakes. It makes an extremely secure fence as, at 1.8m (6ft), it is almost impossible to climb, but it offers no privacy at all. It comes in black or dark green and is not beautiful, but set among plants it can become almost invisible.
Construction Angle-iron straining units are concreted in at either end of the fence run, with intermediate stakes

driven in at 3m (10ft) intervals along this line. Straining wires are run along the top and bottom of the fence, through the intermediate stakes, and pulled taut. A metal bar is inserted in one end of the netting roll and bolted to one of the end units. Then the roll is pulled out tight against the straining wires and secured at the far end. Small clips hold the netting onto the wires. For extra security set the bottom of the mesh 15cm (6in) below ground level and bury it. This precaution will also help to keep out rabbits.
Maintenance Little aftercare is required other than making sure that the mesh of the netting does not unwind in places.

7

TRELLIS
Trellis now plays a significant role in many gardens as a semi-permeable screen, a garden division and, often, a *trompe l'oeil*. The market accommodates a wide range of companies, including those who produce trellis from the cheapest of softwood panels and others who install made-to-measure hardwood trellis of the finest quality.
Trellis panels are normally in 15cm (6in) square grids, but squares can be smaller for greater privacy, or much larger, acting as windows into the garden. Trellis with a natural finish, or stained blue or light green, looks superb with planting.

Construction Trellis screens are constructed in the same way as a timber panel fence, with the posts concreted into the ground (see above).
Maintenance The trellis battens may break on the cheaper softwood panels but they are easily replaced. Treat trellis periodically with a stain or wood preservative to maintain a smart look.

RIVETMENT FENCE
Round, pointed chestnut stakes are driven into the ground at regular intervals, usually between 8 and 10cm (3–4in). The open nature of the fence gives little privacy. Some security can be achieved by placing the poles closer together. It is useful for internal barriers; there are no strained wires or rails, so curved screens and divisions can be created more easily than by using rigid panels.
Construction Timber poles, approximately 8cm (3in) in diameter, are peeled of bark and may be dipped into preservative to prolong their life. Ram them into the ground at set spacings to give a fence height of between 90cm and 1.2m (3–4ft). For a straight fence drive in the poles against a string line, but for a curved or serpentine screen draw out the line of the fence on the ground with a spray marker paint. If the ground is hard, use a crowbar to make the initial opening, then drive home the pole with a sledgehammer or a two-handled post rammer, called a drivall. Check the poles for vertical alignment with a spirit level, or by eye if the poles do not have a smooth edge. A more interesting fence can be achieved by varying the height of the poles and opening up the spaces between them along different sections.
Maintenance Replace rotten poles as necessary. Preservatives and stain may be applied to extend the life of the timber and to add colour.

1 Slatted timber fence.
2 Rough picket fence.
3 Woven bamboo hoops.
4 Screen of curved metal slats.
5 Corrugated steel fence.
6 Log store as garden divider.
7 Lattice-work bamboo screen.

Steps

1 Metal steps.
2 Shallow gravel steps.
3 Stone risers, grass treads.
4 Steps with glazed tiles.
5 Tiled steps.

1

2

The style of garden steps should be influenced by their surroundings and by their intended use. For quick access, construct a straight flight with several steps of short treads. Wider treads and landings encourage a slower pace for meandering up a slope, often preferable to a shorter, steeper ascent. Where there is space, a gentle ramp may be more practical than steps, as it will allow barrows and garden machinery to be wheeled easily. Ramps should not have a gradient exceeding 1:10. If there is not enough space for a ramp, then ramped steps with low risers may be the answer.

Steps are costly to build, but there is no place for short cuts in their construction, as safety is vital. Provide handrails where there is any danger of falling and also to assist with the ascent, but check them regularly, as fixings may need tightening. Landings make a welcome break on a steep flight of steps and one should be introduced at intervals of at least every thirteen steps.

Planting either side of steps in a grass bank allows the grass to be maintained easily by machine. Planting is also useful for softening wide flights of steps, which can be achieved by growing plants in pockets built into the step treads.

STEPS

The style of steps must be in keeping with their location and proposed use. Brick steps are smart and crisp, suiting a more formal setting close to a house. Their concrete foundations ensure no movement and cracking of mortar joints. Steps made of logs or log slices are better in an informal woodland setting, needing no such elaborate foundations.

NATURAL STONE

Rectangular stone flags are normally used as treads with risers in either brick or walling stone. It is important that each tread has a fall of 1:50 towards the front edge to allow water to run off, as stone can be very slippery.
Laying On a sloping site bear in mind that you may have to excavate soil before laying steps. Careful planning is necessary to ensure that all the steps up a bank are of equal height, as steps with uneven risers are potentially lethal. A comfortable tread to riser ratio is 45cm (18in) to 15cm (6in). Concrete footings must first be laid for step risers. In order to ensure stability, concrete foundations should be used in all but the smallest and simplest steps.
Maintenance Regular and careful maintenance is necessary to ensure safety. Clean occasionally with a high-

3

pressure jet, and if tread slabs become dislodged they should be replaced immediately on a bed of fresh mortar.

ROCK

Rough hewn blocks of rock probably form the simplest steps, involving little construction as the strength comes from the mass of the rock set into the ground. The skill is in selecting appropriately shaped rocks with a flattish area for the tread. Rock steps are most appropriate when laid in rock gardens. They can be used as ramped steps with a gravel tread.
Laying Bed the rocks firmly in the soil.
Maintenance Firm them if they wobble at all.

TIMBER

Sawn timber steps visually link with areas of decking, whereas railway sleepers or preserved log poles are more at home in woodland. Log slices are also effective in such a setting. Slices of different diameters can be fitted together with the occasional planting pocket to give variation.
Laying log slices Compact the soil and cover with a 2.5cm (1in) layer of sand. Over this spread a 2.5–5cm (1–2in) layer of gravel into which the log slices are bedded.
Maintenance Log slices can become very slippery, so cover them with chicken wire to give grip. Also scrub them occasionally with a wire brush.
Laying log poles Compact the soil and position the log poles. Hold them firm with wooden pegs, 5cm (2in) in section, driven 15cm (6in) into the soil. Backfill the risers with compacted hardcore or ballast and top-dress with a 5cm (2in) layer of gravel or chipped bark.

5

Maintenance You will need to top up the gravel or chipped bark from time to time as necessary.

BRICK

Steps with brick risers and brick treads look very smart. The top of the riser is usually of bricks laid on edge; these also form the leading edge of the tread. The rest of the tread can be of bricks laid flat in a pattern to match adjacent paving.

4

Laying This is similar to the method described for natural stone (see above), with the difference that here a complete concrete foundation for both riser and tread will make construction easier and stronger.
Maintenance Replace any loose or dislodged bricks immediately.

STONE SETTS

As with brick steps, a row of stone setts forms the riser and leading edge of the tread. Smaller setts can be used to construct the remainder of the tread.
Laying and maintenance This is similar to bricks (see above).

CONCRETE PAVING SLABS

A concrete paving slab forms the tread, with the riser built in brick. The slab should overhang the brick riser by about 1cm (⅓in) to create a shadow line and mask the bedding mortar joint. Special concrete steps are also available composed of tread and riser in one neat unit. These are easy to install and a cheaper solution than using brick. They link in well, physically and visually, with paving and walling in the same material.
Laying and maintenance This is similar to natural stone (see above).

Log pole steps

Log slice steps

Brick steps

Doors and gates

2

Doors and gates are more than an entrance to a garden; they form an integral part of the overall design. The gate must be compatible with the style of the boundary fence or wall; for instance, a close-board or picket fence should have a gate to match. A gate set into a wall or hedge should be complementary. An imposing stone wall needs a sturdy timber or iron gate. A picket or railing gate would suit a hedge. As with fences, a choice must be made between a solid or an open-work gate. If total privacy is required then a solid wood or close-boarded gate is the answer. Open trellis-work or wrought-iron gates can be used to lead the eye to a view beyond. The cost of gates varies as much as the styles, ranging from very cheap hurdles to expensive, highly detailed and electrically operated wrought-iron gates.

Installing gates Boundary gates should ideally open into a property for safety and must be set 5–8cm (2–3in) above ground level to ensure that they open easily. If the ground slopes down from the garden towards the entrance, set the gates back into the property and let them open outwards.

Hanging posts or piers take a great deal of strain and should, therefore, be of sturdy construction, reinforced and set at least 75cm (2½ft) into the ground, in a concrete footing.

Metal gates and posts are hung as one unit supported by temporary struts until the concrete around the posts is set. The posts for a wooden gate, however, are set in position prior to hanging the gate. The two posts are set in concrete at a spacing to allow for the width of the gate and hinge fittings. Gates hung between posts only open to 90 degrees, whereas gates hung on the post face open to 180 degrees. The opening edge of the gate may be hung slightly higher than the true level as, in time, its weight will pull it down.

Maintenance Because of the continual strain put on the hanging posts, they may need to be pulled

3

upright and reconcreted from time to time. Renew hinges on sagging gates. Where a gate binds against the shutting post, plane back the timber until the gate swings freely. All timber needs regular treating or painting, particularly at ground level, where rot is most prevalent. Wrought iron gates will need regular painting.

PICKET GATE

This is a very simple form of gate constructed to match a picket fence, in either painted or stained timber. Made-to-measure versions look sturdier and will last a lot longer than those bought off the shelf.

POST-AND-RAIL GATE

The traditional five-bar gate is associated with post-and-rail and other types of stock fencing. In country gardens the gate looks equally at home set between stone walls and brick piers. Pedestrian gates and wider driveway gates are also available, with a combination of the two often being used across wide driveways.

1

SOLID WOOD GATE

These are often constructed from tongue-and-groove timber set into a frame and are more like doors than gates. They may be used for pedestrian access or across driveways. Hardwoods may be left in their natural state to weather, while softwoods look smarter when stained. These are heavy-duty gates that need the support of substantial posts or piers.

RAILING GATE

This type of gate, similar to a picket gate, needs to match the design of the fence in which it is set.

WROUGHT-IRON GATES

These can be bought off the shelf or purpose-made by a blacksmith. They combine strength and security, if required, with a light, open and decorative structure, but need regular painting or they will rust. Gates of great originality can be made of this material, from fancy filigree to starkly modern.

MOON GATE

This is not a gate at all but an oriental concept: a circular opening in a wall which frames a view and visually links two areas of the garden. To afford some security, wrought-iron gates may be hung within the opening.

4

1 **Reclaimed timber door.**
2 **Picket gate.**
3 **Rustic gate.**
4 **Laurel arch.**
5 **Metal wave gate.**
6 **Double gates.**

GATE HARDWARE

Automatic latch

Ring latch

Thumb latch

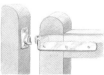

Loop over

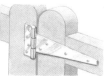

Strap hinge

5

6

Double strap hinge

FURNITURE AND FEATURES

Furniture and features should be chosen not for fussy details but rather for their simplicity, clean lines and practicality. At the same time they need to harmonize and be in scale with their surroundings. This applies throughout the garden to all items: from a large natural pool to a simple light fitting, from an ornamental gazebo to a humble bench. Before any extra item is added to the garden it should be judged both visually and practically appropriate.

Furniture and containers are not only functional; they add substance and character to their surroundings. A large urn or a piece of sculpture can make a fine focal point, but on too small a scale it would look inconsequential. Retreats such as pergolas and summer-houses should invite you to linger, away from the cares of the home, but will work only if they form an integral part of the garden plan. Remember, too, that these structures can be living. Woven willow arbours and stilted hedges can serve a similar purpose to a pergola. Such features need to blend with both the living and the architectural landscape, and this may well govern your choice of material.

As well as garden centres and flower shows, seek out other sources of furniture and containers. Potteries, country house sales and antique shops all hold promise. Church pews can make fine garden seats, solidly built, if very heavy. Weight is important if you like moving furniture and pots around. On roof gardens and balconies heavy containers are unacceptable because of the safety factor – moist compost is heavy enough, without adding a stone urn for the roof to bear. There are interesting and stylish alternatives to plastic, such as aluminium or woven cane. With the convenience of a plastic liner, items not usually intended for use as containers can add zest to a planting scheme.

Much of the success of a feature depends on it being well sited. Formal pools naturally associate with house, paving and hard materials. But to attract wildlife to a pond you must choose a relatively secluded spot with nearby shrubs and trees offering cover. Water flows downhill, so 'natural' pools will always look more convincing in a depression; but a blatantly artificial swimming pool can crown a ridge with panache. Lighting is installed in the garden for reasons of safety and security, and its positioning is crucial. It can also be used to create magical effects, which must not be spoilt by unsightly fixtures.

1 Clean lines and practicality – here a narrow window lowers to become a glass table. Its success lies both in the idea's ingenuity and in the effective link between streamlined and roughcast materials.
2 A study in simplicity and harmony. The warm colours of the stone walls and timber decking tone with the fabric of the butterfly chairs, positioned under the welcome shade of a simple canvas awning.

3 A lightweight metal gazebo over matching table and chairs forms the focal point at the end of an illuminated avenue of trees.

4 Water will always bring a garden to life, no matter how large or small the feature is. Here a simple fountain brings movement and light to a dark corner.

5 Unlike heavy timber furniture, which stays in a permanent position, the classic deckchair is lightweight and portable, looking good in almost every garden.

4

5

Seating and tables

1 **Metal seat encircling a tree trunk.**
2 **Metal, wood and wicker furniture.**
3 **Plastic Adirondack chairs.**
4 **Driftwood throne.**
5 **Concrete table.**

Choosing outdoor furniture is largely a matter of personal taste, compatibility with the surroundings and budget. Looks are important, but they are of little consequence if the furniture proves to be uncomfortable, so try out seats before you buy. Cushions will help, of course, and they can be chosen in colours to fit in with an overall theme. Cost is another major consideration, so hunt around, from chainstore or garden centre to country-house craft fair, to compare prices. Some timber furniture is extremely expensive, but there are some equally good and agreeable alternatives on the market at a fraction of the cost. Hammocks are blissfully comfortable, but do ensure that the ropes are securely attached and in good condition, and that the supporting trees are strong enough to take the strain. For absolute simplicity, don't forget rugs, with a waterproof backing, and cushions.

Portable furniture should be light enough to move around with relative ease; some of the most elegant and lightweight is made from rattan and wickerwork. On the other hand, permanent seating will, due to its weight, remain in a fixed position. This type of furniture may be built in, such as a tree seat or a bench recessed into a wall, and could well form a focal point.

WOOD
Wood looks good in any garden, in town or country and whether it is contemporary or period in style. There is some quite superb, top-of-the-range hardwood furniture, including tables, chairs and benches as well as terrific slatted loungers called steamers. A large canvas umbrella with a wooden pole complements this furniture beautifully, although it is heavy to move about. For conservation reasons, furniture made from tropical hardwoods should be avoided.

At the cheaper end of the price range, but just as comfortable, is the humble classic deckchair, which can conveniently be folded away. The canvas material can be chosen to combine with your colour scheme, and it is a fairly simple process to replace it.
Maintenance Lightweight wooden furniture can often be dismantled or folded away for storage during the winter months. Wood left in the open will be damaged by sunshine as well as by rain and frost, so ensure that all timber is well treated initially and thereafter maintained regularly with preservative. Check also that nuts and bolts on folding or self-assembly furniture are kept rust-free and in good order to avoid a painful disaster.

PLASTIC
Plastic furniture is fairly cheap and easy to move around. Suites of furniture are readily available, including sunloungers and matching umbrellas. The chairs are usually fairly comfortable, but cushions are available in a huge range of colours and designs to complement almost any scheme. However, plastic, or lacquered resin as it is more correctly described, never acquires the patina of age. For this reason it suits modern housing better than the garden of a period home, where it can look harsh and out of

place. In a modern minimalist setting the bright clear colours of plastic furniture can make a lively addition. Its light weight also makes plastic a sensible choice for a balcony or roof garden.
Maintenance Plastic furniture may stay out of doors all year and only requires a wipe over with a damp cloth to keep it clean. However, permanent exposure to weather can make the plastic turn brittle and eventually crack. So, if space permits, it is wise to store it under cover for the winter months.

1

METAL
Cast-iron seats and round tables look good on the small breakfast terrace of a country house, but they are heavy, often not very comfortable and a little cold without cushions. This type of furniture is not cheap, either. It comes in a limited choice of colours: green or black tend to blend better into most garden surroundings than the alternative white, which looks rather stark. In contemporary gardens, tubular steel frames with wire seats and backs work well, although their looks tend to be superior to their comfort.
Maintenance Metal furniture is often too heavy or too cumbersome to move and put in storage. Ensure that any painted metal is regularly maintained to prevent rusting. Plastic-coated metal will avoid this problem. Like tubular steel, it needs only a wipe over from time to time to keep it clean.

PERMANENT SEATS
Seats of stone or concrete slabs set into a recess in a wall offer a sheltered retreat and also form an interesting feature. A large, ornate stone bench acts as a grand focal point in a prime position, such as at the end of a formal pool or terminating a long path. But just as effective in its own way is a group of boulders or logs on which to perch. Seats around trees look attractive and inviting, and are available in kit form made of hardwood. Alternatively, they can be designed and built to suit the style and needs of your garden.
Maintenance Stone or concrete seats are maintenance-free apart from brushing off any plant debris. Wooden tree seats will need treating or painting initially and thereafter they should be regularly maintained with paint or preservative. Check regularly for signs of rot at the base of the legs.

4

5

3

Containers

1 Tin can pots.
2 Wooden half-barrel.
3 Terracotta pot.
4 Metal containers.

There is a place for pots and planters in every garden; in some cases they will provide the only medium for growing plants at all. If you are really pushed for space, there is nearly always room for a well-planted hanging basket or windowbox, and both can be the source of wonderful floral displays all year. Flats with balconies and mews houses with no gardens are brightened up no end by planted tubs and trailing baskets. Pots can be home to tender plants that are brought out in spring and returned to their shelter in autumn. Bright annuals often look better in pots and hanging baskets rather than dotted among shrubs in open borders. Favourite plants which would not survive in the local soil can be included in the planting scheme, with, say, acid-loving plants in pots in an area of alkaline soil. Here, azaleas and pieris will flourish in pots of ericaceous compost, where otherwise they would sit and suffer in a limy soil.

The positioning of containers is important, too, as haphazard displays look messy and uncomfortable. Pots may be used as a safety device – to define the edge of a patio or to indicate a flight of steps. They may also be used in pairs to frame a doorway, or singly to provide a focal point, such as a single large urn placed to end a vista.

If pots are to be planted up for balconies and roof gardens then a soilless compost is preferable to one based on soil as it is lighter and, therefore, safer, as well as enabling the pots to be moved more easily. Drainage holes in the base are essential, and should be covered

with broken terracotta or stones to prevent blockage by the compost. Often there is no need to plant up pots at all, as some of the large urns, for example, are so pleasing to the eye they need no further adornment.

A huge range of containers is available, varying in material, size, shape, colour and cost. Sometimes it is worth paying extra for a large pot in a natural material for a special position. Otherwise, look around as there are some good imitations of glazed clay in painted fibreglass and of terracotta pots in plastic at a fraction of the cost. Pots should be frostproof unless they are to be brought inside during the winter.

TERRACOTTA AND STONEWARE

Hand-made terracotta always looks good in the garden and even large pots can be inexpensive, but care should be taken to select frostproof pots to avoid them flaking to pieces. Frostproof pots tend to be hand thrown, using good-

quality, well-prepared clay, and fired at a high temperature. The pot's shape also has a bearing on its ability to withstand frost. One which flares outwards allows thawing compost to move upwards more easily than an Ali-baba type, which narrows toward the rim. This style of pot is better left unplanted if it is to pass the winter out of doors.

Stoneware is a clay that is also fired at a very high temperature and, although more expensive than ordinary terracotta, the wonderful colours produced make these pots desirable.
Maintenance Although containers do not need much maintenance they do need scrubbing out thoroughly between repottings or before new planting. Terracotta and stoneware containers,

particularly new ones, should be well soaked before planting up so they do not rob the compost and plants of water. New pots of stone, terracotta and unglazed stoneware can be 'aged' in several ways. Painting them with a weak solution of manure will encourage lichens to form. New terracotta can be bleached by rubbing lime on the surface and wetting it regularly.

STONE

Natural stone, lichen-covered urns are particularly appropriate for a classic-style country garden. They can be bought from dealers in antique garden ornaments, but are often very heavy and extremely expensive. Old stone sinks and troughs once so cheap and plentiful, are now scarce. They are especially suited to alpines or small shrubs and need to be raised above the ground for drainage purposes.

Reconstituted stone is a more economical alternative and one which is certainly more readily available.
Maintenance Apart from cleaning out between repottings or before new planting, stone containers need little maintenance. New containers can be 'aged' by painting them with a weak solution of manure to encourage lichens to form. Use of a plastic liner makes changing seasonal displays easier.

WOOD

Versailles planters are square box-like containers, normally made from hardwood slats with a plastic inner liner for the compost. Their cost varies depending on size and whether hardwood or treated softwood has been used. The wood can be treated or painted with a modern stain to match a colour scheme within the garden. These planters look very elegant holding a single foliage plant or topiary specimen.
Maintenance Wooden containers are normally lined, which protects the wood. However, they should be cleaned out occasionally. Softwoods need treating with a preservative harmless to plants. Hardwood containers often carry guarantees against rot for up to 30 years. If this is not the case, oil to keep them in good condition.

PLASTIC AND FIBREGLASS

Plastic is cheap and lightweight, which is useful, although it often comes in gaudy colours, making it difficult to place other than in modern settings. However, plastic pots and troughs are useful liners for large or heavy containers of wood or stone, for window boxes and also for protecting antique containers from the sometimes harmful effect of fertilizers and filling with compost. Apart from

their protective function, the liners enable plantings to be changed quickly, easily and without mess.

Fibreglass pots are also light to move, and come in a range of moulded shapes, some simple, others more fussy. Like plastic, fibreglass can be painted but with more pleasing and subtle results.
Maintenance Clean thoroughly after use. Plastic tends to become brittle and crack, so liners may need replacing every two or three years.

METAL

Commonly used for street planters, metal can also be used in its various forms for garden containers. There is a wide variety of metal containers, ranging in style and cost from old coal scuttles and tin baths to specially commissioned bronze or lead planters. Metal containers are heavy and need careful siting as they will form permanent fixtures. Lead, bronze and galvanized steel tend to be used for traditional designs and therefore suit period properties. Shining stainless steel containers look more at home in a contemporary garden.
Maintenance Little is necessary. Paint steel planters to avoid rust and polish stainless steel to keep it bright.

Garden structures

TYPES OF ARCH

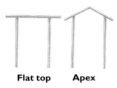

Flat top   **Apex**

Round top   **Gothic**

Pergolas and summer-houses, simple tree houses and ornate gazebos are among the wide range of permanent structures that can be built in the garden. Awnings, tents and parasols, although of a temporary nature, should also be carefully considered. Whichever you choose, it is vital that they are constructed of sturdy materials and, in order to ensure a long life, are maintained properly and regularly.

PERGOLAS, ARBOURS AND ARCHES

Historically, pergolas supported vines and provided lightly shaded corridors extending from the house. Pergolas continue to serve gardens well, although they are now just as likely to be festooned with fragrant and colourful climbers as they are with vines. The framework of overhead beams, draped with climbing plants, provides a neat link

ORIENTAL PERGOLA
This is the traditional timber pergola which is used to span walkways. Square, sawn timber, either a hardwood or treated softwood, is notched and bolted together to form the framework. The posts may be set directly into the ground and held firm with concrete, or may be supported with a variety of metal shoe fixings which keep the timber clear of the damp ground and thus avoid rot.

between the horizontal plane of a terrace and the vertical wall of the house, often framing views out into the garden and providing a cool canopy in summer. Pergolas constructed over paths invite you to walk on towards a view or focal point, or lead you from one area of the garden to another.

Arbours, although constructed in the same manner as pergolas, are smaller and tend to be focal points in their own right. They are often shady retreats within the garden, half hidden by climbers and other plants.

Archways form a simple link between two areas or frame a view beyond. Arches over gates are usually of brick or wrought iron, with timber commonly used for free-standing archways often constructed in the style of a small pergola. Archways focus on a view and, by doing so, create a sense of direction within the garden. The focus will be stronger if the archway is set in planting, rather than standing in isolation.

All structures need to be sturdy enough to support the weight of plants, but not so overpowering as to detract from the plants themselves. Before building begins plan the position with care and check posts are not directly in front of a window. Overhead beams at least 2.1m (7ft) high are necessary to give adequate head clearance, especially when they are covered in trailing plants.
Timber Although combinations of materials can be used in the construction of pergolas, all-timber frameworks are the most popular as they are fairly cheap, straightforward to build and suit most gardens. Treated softwood is commonly used and may be stained. Oak and other hardwoods are more expensive but need no treatment and turn silvery grey as they weather. Softwoods do require regular treatment to prolong their life. Flimsy lengths of wood will bow like boomerangs and should be avoided, but do not be unduly alarmed by wood cracking and twisting; this is quite normal and adds character. Square and sawn timber, ready notched and bolted, is standard for pergola construction, usually with rafters notched over crossbeams, which are in turn bolted to the posts. Rounded timber poles can also be used, but they work best away from the house, in a woodland or rural setting. In these instances, treated machine-rounded posts, 13cm (5in) in diameter, with 10cm (4in) crossbeams, are usually better than rustic poles with bark on, which tend to deteriorate quickly. Lean-to pergolas are fixed to a wall by means of joist hangers or a timber wall plate, which has been notched to support the overhead beams.

Brick and timber Brick and timber pergolas are constructed with well-built brick piers, no less than 35cm (14in) square, supporting sturdy beams in oak or treated softwood. Due to the imposing scale of the construction, brick and timber pergolas are better suited to large country gardens. The brick piers, set on concrete footings, have a central reinforcing rod. Once the bricks have set the cavity is backfilled with concrete. The beams are either recessed into the brickwork or held in metal brackets. The quantity of materials involved and the necessarily slow construction make this a relatively expensive structure.
Stone and timber Stone piers may be used instead of brick to form an equally substantial structure, again looking best in country gardens. Dressed stone, bedded in mortar with rubbed or raked joints, gives neat crisp edges to the pier. Where budget allows and the style is compatible, an impressive colonnade can be formed from reconstituted stone columns with overhead beams.
Tubular steel Tubular steel is strong and makes a light, open pergola at a reasonable cost. Galvanized metal, often coated in plastic, must be used. This is normally black, but other colours could

be used in the right contemporary setting. There are companies that supply kits for steel arbours, which, although not cheap, are quick to install and create a light and airy structure. The connection points are rather ugly but are soon camouflaged by plants. Tunnels made from lightweight tubular steel appear quite delicate. In fact, they are

Aluminium Aluminium pergolas are lightweight, airy constructions which come in kit form, fixed together with nuts and bolts in a similar fashion to an aluminium-frame greenhouse. This material is, however, fairly malleable and therefore only suitable for supporting delicate climbing plants, as heavy climbers may distort the structure.

Constructing a timber pergola
The most common form of construction uses 10 x 10cm (4 x 4in) timber posts, which are either set in concrete footings or fixed in metal shoes driven into the ground, thus avoiding potential rot. All joints should be constructed before setting posts upright and lifting beams up into position. Crossbeams – 15 x 5cm (6 x 2in) in section – are either set alongside the tops of the posts or notched into the posts, and in both cases bolted together, incorporating a toothed washer for added strength. The rafters, often the same dimensions as the crossbeams, are notched halfway into the beams, or a halving joint is made into both timbers so that when pushed together their tops finish flush. Galvanized nails are normally used for securing the rafters, although galvanized or brass screws can also be used. The rafters should extend beyond the beams by about 30cm (1ft), and the ends can either be shaped or left square. Plastic-coated wire can be secured by vine eyes to the posts to support climbing plants.

Maintenance Timber should be treated or stained periodically and all bolt fixings checked regularly.

SUMMER-HOUSES

A summer-house should be large enough to accommodate several people sitting comfortably, with doors opening out on to a verandah. They are, literally, garden rooms and, although expensive, they can look very handsome. However, all too often summer-houses are not big enough, so they are stuffed full of toys and garden furniture, and serve more as garden sheds with windowboxes.

Summer-houses are available as prefabricated sectional buildings, which are not cheap, but you could make your own, incorporating all your needs. Timber should be treated or stained to blend in with the surroundings.

Construction Sectional buildings that come with floor, side panels and roof can be put together by most keen amateurs, but a helper is essential. If you doubt your DIY capabilities, most suppliers offer an assembly service.

Before erection prepare a solid and level foundation of compacted hardcore, approximately 10cm (4in) thick. Over this foundation a 10cm (4in) concrete base is laid. A simpler and

4

cheaper alternative for lightweight buildings is to lay timber bearers – 8 x 8cm (3 x 3in) timber posts – level and at 90 degrees to the floor joist of the summer-house. Lay a strip of damp-proof membrane along the bearers before lowering the floor section into position. Bolt on the side panels and the roof, but leave the final tightening of the

bolts until minor adjustments have been made. Cover the roof with felt tiles or wooden shingles. Treat the building with paint or preservative, unless it is cedar wood, when no treatment is necessary.

Maintenance Check door hinges and all other fittings. Treat wood regularly with paint or preservative if necessary. Roof tiles may need replacing.

1 Metal arches.
2 Arbour.
3 Timber pergola.
4 Rustic gazebo.

very strong and look magnificent when completely covered with plants. Tubular steel is also used to support overhead wooden beams; the steel uprights are set into metal shoes and support purpose-made headframes to hold standard timber beams. The almost fragile appearance disguises the strength of this structure too.

RUSTIC PERGOLA

This construction will look best in a more informal setting away from the house. Round poles, often larch, are notched and nailed together to create a rustic framework for climbers. A smarter look will be gained by using treated machine-rounded poles. These will also last longer than true rustic poles, which keep their bark on and are untreated.

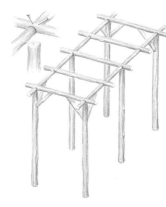

LEAN-TO PERGOLA

Lean-to pergolas are fixed against walls to provide an area of semi-shade close to the house. Their construction is similar to the oriental pergola, but with one end of the overhead beams secured to the wall. This fixing is normally by means of a joist hanger screwed into the wall, supporting the timber beam.

or half-wood, half-glass sides and measure 1.8 x 2.5m (6 x 8ft) or 2.5 x 3m (8 x 10ft). The space-age glass domes that were popular in the 1960s look dated now and would form a focal point for all the wrong reasons.
Construction Greenhouse suppliers offer an assembly service, or the structures can also be erected by amateurs but with at least one helper. Always employ a qualified electrician to run power lines from the mains for heating and lighting, and a plumber to install a water supply.

Before erection prepare a solid and level foundation of compacted hardcore, approximately 10cm (4in) thick, over which are laid concrete slabs (see page 225), or, more often, two courses of brick wall (see page 228) around the edge, on to which the frame is fixed.

Assemble the frame on the base and bolt it together loosely. Leave the final tightening of the bolts until minor adjustments have been made to the frame, but before fitting the glass.
Maintenance Keep the glass clean, and the door and ventilator fixings oiled and in good condition.

SHEDS
Sheds are the main storage buildings of the garden. They are available in many sizes, from tiny units to hold garden tools to large buildings capable of housing ride-on lawn mowers. Sheds need good access as they will be in regular use, and it is ideal to have an area of hard paving around the entrance to take the wear. Self-assembly buildings are available with pent (flat) or apex roofs. There is no need to hide or screen a shed if the design is good.

GAZEBOS
These are covered buildings, often hexagonal in shape, with open sides, positioned to command views, often forming a focal point in themselves. There are some extremely good but expensive gazebos on the market that are made of timber and also of ornate metalwork. Home-made versions are often rustic in style and are best suited to woodland gardens.
Construction Ready-made gazebos are built in much the same way as summer-houses; home-made gazebos are constructed similarly to timber pergolas (see above for both).
Maintenance Little maintenance is needed. Metal may need painting to prevent rust. Rustic timber is not treated and will rot quietly. Any loose spars can be banged into place.

GREENHOUSES
These common utility buildings require an open, sunny site. They are most conveniently placed in or near a fruit and vegetable garden. Greenhouses come with aluminium or cedar-wood frames, and in a wide range of shapes and sizes. The most usual have a span roof and either wall-to-floor glass sides

Construction Sheds come in a self-assembly kit with floor, side panels and roof, and they can be put together by most keen amateurs, but a helper is essential. If you doubt your DIY capabilities, shed suppliers normally offer a cheap assembly service.

Before erection prepare a solid and level foundation of compacted hardcore, approximately 10cm (4in) thick. This should be the size of the floor, plus an extra 10cm (4in) all round. Over this foundation can be laid a concrete base; 10cm (4in) thick is normally adequate, but for large structures that store garden machinery and for workshops a thickness of

15cm (6in) is advised. Alternatively, concrete paving slabs can be laid on a full mortar bed (see page 225) and wet pointed. The simplest and cheapest option is to lay timber bearers and to proceed as described for summer-houses (see above). Cover the roof with felt, which can come in rolls, strips or tiles. Treat the building with paint or preservative, unless it is cedar wood, when treatment is not necessary.
Maintenance The roof may need refelting from time to time, otherwise maintenance is the same as for summer-houses (see above).

TREE-HOUSES
Children – and adults – love to hide away in secret dens, so the tree-house must be the ultimate garden sanctuary. They should not be too high up in the tree, and obviously they must be strong and secure. Access can be controlled by a removable ladder. A tree-house should be exciting and could resemble a pirate ship or a castle, for example.
Construction Usually built to your design, it must fit the tree perfectly.
Maintenance This is much the same as for summer-houses (see above), but remember to check regularly that the structure is secure.

AWNINGS, TENTS AND PARASOLS
These lightweight structures are designed to reduce glare and provide welcome respite from the sun without the need for a heavy construction of overhead beams and the associated building costs. As they are not permanent fixtures, they have the added

4

1 Children's play-house.
2 Tree-house.
3 Garden tent.
4 Parasol.
5 Sail awning.
6 Shade from
overhead climbers.

5

advantage of being easy to move and maintain, and of folding away when not in use. Take care when choosing the colour for these furnishings; cream, off-white and green look good and will not foreshorten the distance when set away from the house. Bright colours are better close to the house, with yellow, in particular, giving a warm, sunny feeling on a grey and overcast day.

Awnings may be simple, canvas-covered frames which are wound out from the house wall above the windows, similar to those used above shop fronts

or restaurants. They provide comfortable shade and also protect interior furnishings from the bleaching effects of sunlight. Fabric is also used to cover permanent structures, such as pergolas, to create a more intimate outdoor room. The flaps of the awning are tied back to the posts to create openings and allow breezes through.

Garden tents are far more glamorous creations than those normally used by backpackers; in fact, they bear a closer resemblance to marquees. Small versions will easily accommodate a garden table and chairs, while larger tents are ideal for parties and barbecues. In the evening the interior can be lit by a string of lights. Choice of colour is important; gaudy, striped canopies will look too much like a hospitality marquee at a country show.

Brightly coloured sun brollies have been surpassed by the large and elegant free-standing parasols which associate so well with wooden furniture. Their large, sail-like canopies are adjusted by means of a rope tie and provide a wide area of welcome shade.

Construction Awnings may be a sheet of canvas, cut to fit, secured over an existing pergola and tied back to the

posts. Purpose-made awnings fixed to the house wall are normally installed by the manufacturer.

Garden tents are easy to assemble. The supporting frame is often of lightweight, anodized aluminium or zinc-plated tubular steel and the sections simply push-fit together. The covers are usually coated nylon or PVC and are, therefore, weatherproof. Large tents hired for special occasions are erected by the hire company.

Parasols normally have a hardwood pole with a rope and pulley system to open and close the canopy. The material for the canopy is a proofed cotton or sometimes marine acrylic, which is waterproof, resistant to ultra-violet light, does not get mildewed and does not shrink when washed. A sturdy metal base gives support on paving, or a metal spike can be used on a lawn.

Maintenance Canvas for awnings, tents and parasols should be wiped clean regularly and may also be removed for more thorough cleaning. Oil the timber poles of parasols in order to keep them in good condition. All structures should be stowed away, clean and dry, in neat, zip-up bags for storage over winter.

6

Water features

1

POOLS

Close to the house a formal pool of square, rectangular or circular outline works well. Such simple shapes can fit in with the ground pattern of paving, and the edging of a raised pool doubles as a sitting area. A pool in an open, sunny position is more likely to stay clean and provide a reflective surface than one in a shady place with overhanging trees.

In contrast, informal pools blend in with the softer lines of the natural landscape and are often linked with waterfalls and running streams. A bog garden is an appropriate adjunct to an informal pool, and may be formed by digging a depression, approximately 30cm (1ft) deep, and lining it with an extension of the pool liner. This extension is punched with holes so that the bog garden is not permanently waterlogged. Overlay the liner with coarse gravel 5cm (2in) deep to ensure the holes do not become blocked. A mound of soil separating the main pool from the bog garden prevents permanent flooding while letting the pool overflow during heavy rainfall.

Open water is both an attraction and a danger to toddlers and older children so, for peace of mind, a contained water feature, such as a millstone or a drilled bubble fountain, is a sensible choice. Outdoor electric sockets must be waterproof and an electric current circuit breaker is essential whenever any outdoor electrical equipment is installed, such as a submersible pump.

Constructing a formal pool Square or rectangular pools may be built quite inexpensively from small units, such as bricks or blocks, tied into vertical reinforcing rods for strength. A concrete foundation, 10cm (4in) thick, forms the base of the pool on to which the side walls are built. The base and the side walls are subsequently covered with two skins of waterproof render. The top of the side walls are finished with a neat brick-on-edge or paving-slab coping. Ideally this should overhang slightly to create a shadow line on the pool side to hide the joint of the coping, the water mark or any change in the water level. Do not introduce any fish for at least a month, as they will

most likely die due to the lime coming out of the mortar. The walls can be treated with a sealant to neutralize the lime. Choose one in a dark colour.

Constructing an informal pool
Informal pools tend to be free-flowing shapes fitting into the natural contours of the garden. They are best built with flexible materials that can, depending on scale, be fairly inexpensive. The traditional material used for lining pools was puddled clay, which does not guarantee a watertight seal, often cracking in dry weather. Concrete is a more elaborate and expensive construction technique, using a reinforcing mesh throughout, and it, too, can crack. Pre-formed fibreglass pools are relatively cheap and easy to install. The outline of the pool excavation is made by propping the form upright on the ground and marking around the edge; symmetrical forms can merely be inverted. Excavate the ground to the correct shape and firm the soil, removing any sharp stones, then spread a layer of sand over the base before setting in the pre-formed pool. Check that it is sitting absolutely level before backfilling around it with more sand. The drawbacks of this type of pool are that you are governed by the shapes manufactured and that it is almost impossible to disguise the wide, rigid lip around the top in a natural way. The development of flexible plastic and rubber pool liners has revolutionized the construction of informal pools. These are relatively light and easy to handle, simple to install and come in a range of dark colours, including black, which gives the best surface reflections.

Constructing an informal liner pool A simple, informal pool may be constructed using a flexible pool liner. Mark the proposed shape of the pool on the ground and fix pegs around the outside to indicate the finished level. Before you excavate, calculate the amount of liner required. The total length of liner equals twice the maximum depth of the pool plus its maximum length; the total width of liner equals twice the maximum depth of the pool plus its maximum width; the area of liner required equals the total width multiplied by the total length. If you think you might overdig you can order the liner once the hole is finished.

Excavate the pool to the desired depth, usually between 45cm and 75cm (1½–2½ft), with slightly sloping sides and marginal shelves, approximately 23cm (9in) below the surface and 25cm (10in) wide, for planting baskets. Throughout the excavation check that the perimeter is level. Remove any large stones or roots that protrude from the

2

surface before spreading a layer of geotextile membrane, or a 5cm (2in) layer of sand, over the excavated surface to protect the liner from sharp stones working through the soil. Pull the liner taut over the hole and secure temporarily round the edge with a few bricks. Then start filling the pool with water from a hosepipe directed to the centre of the liner. As the pool fills up move the bricks so the liner fits snugly in place. Once the pool is full of water, the liner is trimmed to leave an excess of about 15cm (6in) that can be masked by a suitable edging material.

Edging a pool The edging is crucial to the success of a pool, and a credible solution is simple to achieve when using a flexible liner, as it can be hidden in a number of ways. Access to the water for wildlife, as well as for maintenance purposes, may be created by extending the lawn to the water's edge or to a beach area of loose pebbles. Timber decking may be built out to form a pier or boardwalk overhanging the water. Rocks mortared into position are another option. Where the pool comes up against formal paving, brick or stone is set round the edge to overhang by about 5cm (2in) and form a shadow line.

POOL EDGINGS
The treatment of a pool edging is critical to ensure its successful overall appearance; flexible liners can be masked in a variety of ways. Beach pebbles or turf can cover the edge of a liner for a natural pool. The liner can also be tucked behind an overhanging timber jetty or under a brick coping for a more formal kind of pool.

Beach pebbles

Timber decking

Brick edging

POOL WITH FLEXIBLE LINER
Flexible liners of plastic or rubber may be used for formal pools, but they are better suited to the free-form lines of an informal pool. A layer of sand or geotextile membrane protects the liner from sharp stones, and the edge of the liner is then concealed by a suitable edging stone.

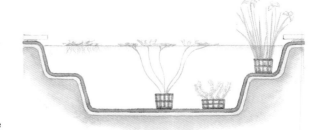

3

Maintenance Although regular work is involved in feeding and breeding fish, dividing plants and planting up new baskets, the pool water may only need changing every five years, or when it becomes choked with rotting vegetation. To help prevent this, skim off fallen leaves before they sink, or net the pool in autumn. The water level will need topping up from time to time, particularly in a hot summer and where a fountain is installed. If you have fish, a small area of the pond should be kept ice-free in winter, either by placing a plastic ball on the surface to take up the pressure of the expanding ice, or by introducing an electric pool heater. This will also prevent the sides of concrete pools from cracking.

FOUNTAINS

Although fountains are normally thought of as eye-catching focal points in formal pools, the term is also used to cover other types of running water – from a cheap and simple bubble jet set amid pebbles to much more costly waterfalls and rocky streams.

In formal pools, a fountain should be set centrally to avoid wind gusting the jet of water out and, in time, emptying

4

the pool. Bubbling millstones and drilled boulders are safe water features but have become fairly commonplace. Use your imagination to link sculpture or containers with moving water, employing the same principle of a hidden reservoir.

Wall-mounted fountains are also safe for children, and can be fitted into the tiniest courtyard. Those in kit form are simple to install. Some of the most familiar examples are where the water spouts through the mouth of a mask. Whatever the design, make sure the jet is aimed towards the centre of the bowl so that water is not lost from the system. Drain mask-type fountains in winter as such a small amount of water in an exposed position will freeze and damage the pipe and pump.

A series of formal pools may be connected by means of stone- or tile-clad canals known as rills. Informal pools may be linked by streams. In a wild setting, rocky streams contained within a flexible liner should vary in width to create differing rates of flow: fast straits broadening out into meandering curves. Mark slight changes of level by small waterfalls linked by level streams. It is important that natural waterfalls fit in with the surrounding contours and do not rise out of flat ground. The best waterfalls, in an informal or formal setting, need a clear fall of water. This can only be achieved with a pump powerful enough to lift the water and a horizontal lip of slate or perspex to ensure an unbroken sheet of water.

Constructing a drilled-boulder water feature This example of a safe water feature illustrates the basic construction method for other variations. A hole is dug either to house a fibreglass tank or to be lined with a flexible liner, which will act as a reservoir. Once the tank or liner is in place, a submersible pump is set at the bottom. A length of hose is attached to the pump and passes up to a pipe through the centre of the boulder. The boulder is supported on concrete blocks or bricks and surrounded by a

wire mesh strong enough to carry beach pebbles. There should be a hinged lid in the mesh to give access to the submersible pump for maintenance. The reservoir is filled with water and the pump is connected up, ready for use. Water flows up through the boulder and back down through the pebbles. **Maintenance** Clean the pump filter occasionally and top up the reservoir with water as necessary.

SWIMMING POOLS

Swimming pools range from relatively cheap, small, above-ground pools, adequate for a splash, through to large sunken pools for serious swimming. Whichever type of pool is selected, the installation should be carried out by experienced professionals to avoid costly mistakes.

Great care must be taken in siting a swimming pool, as it is such a dominant feature in a garden. This is particularly important when a pool is close to the house; despite the advantage of changing facilities in the house, the pool requires extra-careful detailing to fit in with its surroundings. Away from the house banks of planting will shield the pool from view, but the need for a changing room has to be considered. However, pools do not always need screening, and they can be eye-catching features when well designed. When a pool is set on high ground, overlooking the view below, the water-line can be brought up to an almost invisible metal strip at the far end, so the water and sky seem to merge in a breathtaking effect.

Pools are constructed from concrete blocks or steel frames or, at the top of the range, free-form pools are built using tile-clad gunite concrete (a mixture of cement, aggregate and

5

water sprayed on to a metal mould). When planning a swimming pool consider the siting of and cost of extras such as steps, a pool cover and diving boards, as well as their regular upkeep. Never forget comfort and safety; low planting around the perimeter will give welcome shelter from cool breezes, and a surrounding low fence with lockable gate will ensure peace of mind if there are toddlers about.

DRILLED-BOULDER WATER FEATURE

This is a simple, safe feature, with no open water surface. A hidden reservoir containing a submersible pump is covered with a steel mesh to support beach pebbles. Water is pumped up through the boulder, filtering back through the stones into the reservoir. The device is controlled by a switch in the house.

1 Still water.
2 Brick edge between formal pond and lake.
3 Swimming pool.
4 Waterfall.
5 Simple water spout.

Types of lighting

1

Lighting brings a garden to life, extending the period of enjoyment beyond the daylight hours and creating magical night-time pictures through all the seasons. Lighting may be functional or used for purely aesthetic reasons, or may be a combination of the two. A soft illuminating glow makes late-night summer suppers in the garden all the more enchanting. A light shining through branches creates a shadow play against a wall. Clever lighting near water can imply that a shallow pool has unfathomable depths, while a simple spotlight accents the elegant form of a favourite tree. In every case lighting provides some security by discouraging intruders.

It is sensible to seek professional help for electrical installation work, although there are now some cheap and simple low-voltage lighting systems on the market aimed at the DIY customer. There are also specialist lighting companies who design and arrange complete garden lighting systems. These companies offer a demonstration of their products at night-time to show the different effects that are possible. Specialist lighting companies will install both low, 12 volt, and mains, 240 volt, systems. The low-voltage circuits incorporate a transformer to step down the voltage. These systems benefit from

FUNCTIONAL LIGHT

Spread lighting

a smaller lamp size and, therefore, smaller fittings that are easily concealed. They are ideal for compact gardens as they require shorter cable runs and have a reduced light intensity. The lower voltage supply also means greater safety. The mains fittings, with their higher output, are ideal for lighting mature trees or large landscapes. Mains fittings are essential on long cable runs and where a long lamp life is required. Low-voltage fittings can be combined with mains fittings by using transformers.

Whether employing professionals or doing it yourself, carefully plan a simple and effective scheme, as too much lighting lacks subtlety and is a form of pollution, disturbing to wildlife and annoying for neighbours. Remember, too, that it is the effect of the light that is important rather than the light itself, so choose unfussy fittings that blend into the surrounding foliage. Safety must be a priority, so ensure all outside sockets and connections are in waterproof housings and circuit breakers are fitted to cut off the power if a cable is damaged. Ideally, wiring for garden lighting systems should be in PVC-sheathed armour cable (essential for mains voltage lights) and buried to a minimum depth of 45cm (18in).

FUNCTIONAL LIGHTING

You may decide that you need some functional lighting for utility areas, such as sheds and greenhouses, enabling you to potter or tend your plants late into the autumn evenings. Such lighting also serves leisure areas, such as tennis courts and swimming pools. Safety is also an important function, as lighting may be needed to illuminate steps and pathways which would otherwise be hazardous in darkness. The lighting units used for these purposes are often referred to as spread lights. They provide broad beams or pools of light that may, for example, be positioned close to the ground to indicate a change of level or the edge of a path.

Security is an important function of lighting. It need not be a harsh floodlight, as any garden lighting can act as a deterrent to intruders. Security lights activated by sensors need to be positioned with care, as they can all too easily be switched on by passing traffic or animals. This is a problem that applies particularly in small gardens.

ACCENT LIGHTING

This may be as simple a matter as running up a string of coloured lights through a tree at Christmas or used more dramatically in the form of a narrow beam to illuminate a specific feature in the garden. There are a number of interesting aesthetic effects that can be achieved in the garden by positioning or angling the light source in different ways, and some of the most effective of these are described here.

Use accent lighting sparingly – one dramatically silhouetted tree has far more impact than an assortment of illuminated focal points dotted about in the gloom. One other word of caution regarding lighting: choose white lights only, as these will enhance the natural colours of plants. Coloured lights will change the natural colours and create a fairy grotto effect – best reserved for special occasions only.

Uplighting In this case a light source positioned at ground level beams up to illuminate the branches of a mature tree against dark surroundings. The light

2

ACCENT LIGHTS

Uplighting

Moonlighting

Spotlighting

Silhouetting

Shadowing

Grazing

3

1 Fairy lights.
2 Spread lights.
3 Wall-mounted spread lights.
4 Bollard light.
5 Dichroic lighting.
6 Sculptural globe light.
7 Uplighting.

4

fitting should be aimed away from the direction of view to avoid glare. If lights are aimed from many directions, fit them with louvres to prevent glare.

Moonlighting A series of lights are set in a tree to direct a soft glow down through the branches to imitate the light of the moon. Moonlighting, or

6

downlighting, also provides general security as well as creating depth and, therefore, a sense of perspective.

Spotlighting This dramatic technique is used to highlight a piece of sculpture or other focal point.

Silhouetting A tree or architectural feature of an interesting shape is lit from behind to create a dramatic silhouette. The fixture should be hidden from view, so set lights flush with the ground, or recessed and surrounded by plants.

Border lighting This is the type of lighting provided by low-level spread lights to define the edge of a path, driveway, lawn or border. Some such spread lights may define an area within an arc of 180 degrees.

Mirror effect Here a formal pool will remain unlit while trees and other objects to one side are dramatically uplit in order to create a mirror effect on the surface of the water.

Shadowing As you would expect, a light shines directly at an object or plant with a sculptural branch structure, to cast shadows on a wall or fence behind. Different effects are achieved according to the intensity of the light and how close it is to the object.

Grazing Designed to highlight a strongly textured relief. The light is cast at an angle across the surface of a wall catching the high points and throwing depressions into deep shadow. Exciting abstract patterns can often be achieved with this technique.

Fibre-optic lighting A single source sends light through strands of glass fibre to create many individual twinkling pinpoints. The fibres, which are almost invisible, can be run through water safely and look particularly intriguing when sparkling through moving water.

Dichroic lamps These are another relatively modern development in garden lighting, although they were originally designed for shop interiors, where accurate representation of colour and texture are important. A series of mirrors directs the light from a recessed halogen lamp in a controlled manner, with an angle of beam ranging from 8 to 60 degrees. The lamps have a five-year life and colour filters are unnecessary.

MOUNTINGS

Adjustable spike This is one of the most common types of mounting. It is suitable for use in lawns or borders, carrying adjustable angled lights to illuminate trees and shrubs.

Wall- or post-mounted lights These fixed mountings are usually for downlighters, although some fittings may combine both an uplighter and a downlighter. The fixtures are widely used in conjunction with entrances, steps and pergola walkways.

Fixed tall spike This usually supports a fixed downlighter to provide a narrow light for highlighting a pathway. A tall spike may carry two adjustable lights for a more flexible scheme.

Recessed lights These useful and unobtrusive fixtures are normally set low down into a side wall to throw light over an adjacent surface. They can also be hooded to conceal the light source.

5

Recessed 'brick lights' are designed to be the same size as a standard brick and therefore fit neatly into the bonding pattern of a brick wall. This fitting is ideal for lighting steps and pathways, and may have louvred covers to angle the light down to where it is needed. Floor-mounted recessed lights in stainless steel or brass come complete with toughened glass for walkways and driveways. The angle of the light beam may also be adjusted.

Maintenance Ensure all connections are sound and that there are no exposed or damaged wires. The lights must be kept clean at all times.

7

Garden design is first about planning – the creative stage – and then about turning your finished plan into reality – the practical stage. The latter requires the mastery of certain technical skills and putting these into practice to make your vision happen can be just as enjoyable as the design stage. To garden successfully, you will need to employ such essential techniques as ground preparation, planting and propagation, caring for lawns and meadows, pruning and training, and dealing with problems of all kinds.

Your plants deserve the best start in life, and what they take out of the soil needs to be replenished with organic matter. In the wild, soil is invariably covered with a protective eiderdown of growth, rotting vegetation, sand, gravel or rocks. In the garden, the surface is often laid bare in the process of weeding and cultivation. By applying generous, regular mulches of organic matter, nature can be imitated.

Planting your garden is an exciting process, but should be the result of careful research. Whether you intend to buy them or raise them yourself, find out all about the plants you wish to grow, their needs, their speed of growth and their eventual size. Decide which plants will combine together practically as well as aesthetically – are their growth rates in balance, or will one dominate all too soon?

Although gardening inevitably involves manipulation, try always to work in harmony with nature. Welcome helpful animals into your garden with wildflowers, a small pool and some cover. Meanwhile, much can be done quite literally to nip problems in the bud if you take a regular stroll around your garden, watching out for pests, picking up fallen fruit and snipping off spent flowers as you go.

The basic structural elements of a garden need to be clothed with plants in order for it to come alive. You should learn how to provide your plants with the best conditions for them to flourish, and also how to maintain them correctly so that they continue to give long-lasting pleasure.

Ground preparation

To give your precious plants the best possible start, pay particular attention to preparing the ground before you plant them. Soil is composed of particles of sand, silt and clay in varying amounts. The soil also contains organic matter of plant and animal origin, various minerals and a huge number of living creatures. The balance between these components dictates the type of soil you have.

SOIL TYPES

You can feel the soil type by rubbing a sample between your fingers. Sandy soils feel gritty because they are composed of relatively large particles. They are quick draining, easy to dig and they warm up rapidly. On the negative side, they dry out fast during drought, and nutrients are quickly washed through. By adding organic matter, either as a mulch or by digging it in, the soil will become much more moisture retentive.

Clay soils feel greasy and can be rolled in a malleable ball when moist. They are heavy to work and slow to heat up, but are rich in nutrients and retain water. However, when they dry out they become brick-like and impossible to dig. With frequent applications of organic matter the texture will improve and they will become easier to work. Applications of gypsum (also known as sulphate of lime) help to improve drainage and aeration, but without increasing alkalinity.

Loamy soils combine the best points of sandy and clay soils. They are fertile, moisture retentive and well aerated, but to maintain these good qualities they too need applications of organic matter.

If you are gardening on a wet clay soil where waterlogging is a regular problem, drainage can be improved either by digging in plenty of coarse sand or gravel if the problem is minor, or by installing a drainage system. This can be simply an open drainage ditch, about 1.2m (4ft) deep, with slightly sloping sides, dug along the lowest part of the site. To disguise it, the trench can be turned into an unobtrusive French drain.

FRENCH DRAIN

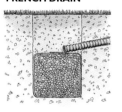

This is a drainage ditch lined with a geotextile membrane and filled in with gravel. Fold the geotextile over the gravel and cover with soil. To guide surface water into the drain install a herringbone pattern of corrugated plastic drainage pipes in gravel-filled trenches 60cm (2ft) below the ground. Space the pipes 5–8m (16–26ft) apart.

ACID OR ALKALINE?

Once you have established the soil type, the next step is to determine whether it is acidic or alkaline – low or high in calcium, commonly known as lime. Look at the plants growing in neighbouring gardens: where camellias, heathers and rhododendrons flourish the soil will be acidic, while clematis, weigelas and ceanothus prefer alkaline soils. Soil acidity or alkalinity is measured on a pH scale of 1 to 14: acid soils have a low pH, below 7, while alkaline soils have a pH of above 7. A pH of 7 is considered neutral and most plants grow well in such conditions.

With the help of a simple pH testing kit obtainable from garden centres, you can test your own soil. Take samples from different parts of the garden, as levels can fluctuate within quite small areas. It is also worth repeating the test every two years or so to check whether the pH has changed.

FEEDING PLANTS

Plant foods are divided into two groups: those needed in substantial amounts and those required in tiny quantities. In the first group are the three most important plant nutrients: nitrogen (N), which promotes leafy growth, phosphorus (P), which encourages root development, and potassium (K), which encourages flowering and fruiting. In addition, calcium (Ca), magnesium (Mg), and sulphur (S) are also necessary in fairly large amounts in order to ensure strong healthy growth. The minor nutrients, or trace elements, include iron, manganese, chlorine, zinc, copper, molybdenum and boron. Though these are required in only tiny amounts, a deficiency is detrimental to plant growth and is usually first apparent in the foliage that has begun to sicken, turning yellowish or brown in the process of dying.

All these nutrients are available in most soils, but in the competitive situation of the garden demand is great and regular supplements are needed in the form of regular applications of garden compost and rotted manure. These bulky organic materials contain nutrients in small amounts, and they also encourage soil organisms whose activities make more nutrients available to the plants. Nutrients can also be added in a concentrated form as fertilizers, described as organic or non-organic, or artificial. In general, organic fertilizers are derived from natural products. They are less soluble and, because of this, act more slowly over a longer period than many of the artificials. Bonemeal and fish, blood and bone are good organic sources of nitrogen and phosphate.

Among the non-organic fertilizers are both soluble and slow-release formulations. The soluble ones are immediately available and can be used to give a quick boost to growth. They need to be applied regularly at low doses and they tend to be leached out of sandy soils rapidly. It is vital to apply them as recommended, for at high concentrations soluble fertilizers can even burn plant tissue. Slow-release fertilizers, or nutrient 'prills', help make container gardening easier as they supply the nutrients over many months, usually necessitating only one application per growing season.

MAKING COMPOST

Nothing is more satisfying than using home-made compost and leafmould on the garden. They are both superb organic soil improvers and sources of humus.

Garden compost should never smell and has a light, crumbly texture. Ideally the heaps should consist of layers of different types of material. The material that activates the rotting process and decomposes quickly, such as grass clippings, should be mixed with fibrous material, such as straw or the stems of herbaceous perennials, that takes longer to break down but gives bulk. If you can add a layer of manure every 30cm (1ft), so much the better. The finer the material is cut or shredded, the quicker it will rot down. The more often the heap is turned, the faster the composting process will be. There must be sufficient ventilation and

1 Making compost is a useful means both of recycling kitchen and garden waste and of creating an excellent soil improver for plants.

1

moisture. Kitchen waste can include all vegetable trimmings, tea leaves, coffee grounds and crushed eggshells. Do not add scraps of meat or fish, dirty nappies or dog or cat litter. Most garden waste can be used, although perennial roots, diseased material and seeding flower-heads are best not added; unless the heap heats up considerably you could be storing up problems, particularly if the compost is used as a mulch.

There is a variety of compost bins available, and very small gardens may benefit from a rotating bin turned with a handle. These bins take only a limited amount of compost at a time, but the process is quick. Another option for small gardens are plastic bins. Aesthetically more pleasing and better ventilated are bins made of wooden slats; these stack on top of each other, facilitating access to the bottom of the pile.

LEAFMOULD

Autumn leaves are best composted separately in an open wire-mesh bin and allowed to rot for at least a year before use. To speed up the process leaves can be shredded by running over them with a rotary mower. This has the added advantage that most mowers spew out the leaves in rows, making collection easier.

MULCHING

A mulch of organic material spread at least 5cm (2in) and preferably 10cm (4in) deep performs several vital functions. It helps maintain soil fertility and acts as an insulating blanket. In winter, the frost will not penetrate so deeply and in summer the ground will be kept cool and moist, a tremendous advantage in areas susceptible to water shortages. Light cannot penetrate to the soil level, so weed seeds are less likely to germinate. However, before a mulch is applied the ground must be cleared of perennial weeds, or these will push through and delight in their improved situation. Different materials can be used for mulching, both organic and inorganic.

ORGANIC MULCHES

These can be home-made by composting garden waste or leaves, as described above, but you can also use commercial waste products, such as manure or bark. What you choose will depend greatly on availability. By the end of the growing season most organic mulches will have disappeared, broken down by soil organisms. Although this means they need to be reapplied on a regular basis, organic mulches will not only provide nutrients to help plant growth, reducing the need for fertilizers, but they will also greatly improve the soil structure.

Once rotted, manure is a superb mulch. It should be allowed to decompose for three to twelve months before being spread on the garden; used fresh it will burn your plants. If you cannot obtain fresh farmyard manure, it can be bought dried, powdered and ready bagged. This is easy and light to handle and makes a good fertilizer, but it is too concentrated and not bulky enough to act as a mulch.

Spent mushroom compost is a useful by-product of the commercial mushroom growing business, but make sure that it has been sterilized. The presence of added gypsum makes little difference to alkaline soils but it should not be used around acid-loving plants.

Cocoa shells are the lightweight waste product from the chocolate manufacturing industry. They are pleasant to handle and form a mat once wetted, preventing them from blowing about. They also act as an efficient cat deterrent.

Chipped bark is a by-product of the forestry industry. It can be bought in large quantities, or you can make it yourself with a shredder. Shredded material should be composted for a year; if used fresh it will rob the soil of nitrogen, a mineral used by micro-organisms in the process of decomposition.

For many years peat was a popular mulch, but it is no longer used for this purpose as it stems from a non-renewable resource. One substitute for peat is coir, a waste fibre from coconut shells. It is

expensive because of the high cost of transportation and is best used on a small scale as a potting compost.

GREEN MANURE

Although not strictly a mulch, sowing a crop of green manure is another way of covering the ground and adding organic matter and nutrients while improving the soil structure. Plants, particularly leguminous plants belonging to the pea and bean family, are excellent as they make nitrogen available in the soil. Green manures should be dug into the soil before the first flowers begin to open.

INORGANIC MULCHES

Gravel, stones or rocks will last a long time, but their suitability depends on your garden style and the type of plants you want to grow. In a cool humid climate, plants that naturally prefer a drier environment benefit from a gravel mulch. The gravel not only reduces mud splash, but also reflects the sunlight and retains heat. Gravel gardens can be low-labour if a sheet of porous membrane is laid over the soil before spreading the gravel. The membrane allows rain water through but prevents weed seeds from germinating, and planting holes can easily be cut into it.

Black plastic, ready-woven to allow water to penetrate, or sheeting, is an excellent weed suppressor. Cover it with chipped bark to improve its appearance.

LEAFMOULD BIN

Stack autumn leaves into a bin made from four posts 10 x 10cm (4 x 4in) in section, and wire mesh, which can be unhooked on one side. The bin should be at least 90 x 90cm (3 x 3ft). As well as a mulch, leafmould is also a useful base for home-mixed peat-free potting compost. In a small garden, add layers of leaves to the compost heap.

COMPOST BINS
Wooden bins should be at least 90 x 90cm (3 x 3ft) and fitted with a lid. (The leafmould bin, lined with straw or old carpet and kept covered, would be a cheaper option.) A garden should have a minimum of two, but ideally three, bins: one being built, one rotting down and one in use. Soft material, shredded or cut, should be ready for use in a few months.

Planting and propagation

PLANTING A BARE-ROOTED TREE OR SHRUB

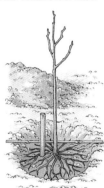

1

2

3

4

HEELING IN
If your bare-rooted plants arrive too early, or you are unable to plant because the soil is too wet or frozen, heel them in by the following method. Dig a shallow trench in a sheltered part of the garden. Lay the plant at an angle in the trench. Cover the roots with soil, then mulch with a layer of straw or old carpet.

Dig a generous hole and fork in plenty of rotted manure or compost (1). With a helper to hold the plant, spread out the roots and bang in a short stake (see page 257) 10–15cm (4–6in) from the stem on the windward side. Check that the soil mark on the stem is level with a cane laid across the hole (2). Backfill, working the soil between the roots with your hands and firming with your heel (3). Fix stem to stake with a tree tie (4). Water and mulch the root area, leaving the base clear. Plants in containers or balled are treated in a similar way.

One of the most thrilling parts of making a garden is choosing plants. Browsing through mail order catalogues as you compile your shopping list and visiting specialist nurseries, flower shows, garden centres and other people's gardens for ideas can be extremely pleasurable gardening pastimes.

For an instant effect you must buy some fairly mature plants, and the more money you have to spend, the larger the specimens you can afford. If time is no object, you can also raise your own plants. Propagating plants is satisfying, creative and also saves a lot of money.

BUYING PLANTS

The search for specialist nurseries is enjoyable but takes up a lot of time. Garden centres are more accessible, but usually only stock a standard range of plants and may not have everything on your shopping list. If you are looking for

many plants it is worth sending off for catalogues from nurseries that operate a mail-order service. By ordering early you will be more likely to get your first choice of bulbs, seeds and plants. Good nurseries will also be happy to advise you on the best time to plant and on aftercare, and may well help with your planting ideas, often over the telephone.

The first plants to buy are trees and shrubs, the foundation plants. These can be bought bare rooted or container grown. Bare-rooted specimens can only be planted during the dormant season, whereas container plants can go in at any time of the year, providing they are watered during dry spells. Bare-rooted plants need to be handled with care and kept constantly covered as their roots will dry out quickly unless well protected. Prepare the planting site in advance of delivery and soak the roots in a bucket of water before planting as soon as possible

after they arrive. Although bare-rooted plants undergo quite an upheaval, in the long run they will often perform better than those grown in containers. Bare-rooted plants have had the advantage of growing in soil, as opposed to compost, and will adapt more quickly to their new environment. Plants from open ground may also be stockier than container-grown plants, which tend to have lusher growth encouraged by feeding.

Most nurseries grow their container stock in soilless compost, which is very different from garden soil. The roots may remain within the soilless environment and never penetrate the surrounding soil, particularly if it is heavy clay. To help overcome this, tease out some of the roots and gently, with your fingers, work compost into the planting hole as you plant.

Although people are attracted to large plants, they are not necessarily the most cost-effective. Larger bulbs will flower

SOWING UNDER COVER
Fill a pot or seedtray with compost and firm the surface with a presser (1). Sow seeds thinly (2). Cover with sieved compost (3). Stand pot or tray in a bowl of water until the compost surface is thoroughly moist (4). Stand pots in a propagator, preferably a heated one, until seedlings emerge (5).

1

2

3

4

5

Before sowing annuals or vegetables outside, prepare a seed bed by firming the soil and raking it finely. Draw out a shallow drill with the corner of a hoe or rake against a string line (1). If the soil is dry, water the bottom of the drill. Sow seeds thinly and label each row with the plant name and the date (2). Cover seeds to about twice their depth (3). Firm the soil with the back of the rake (4).

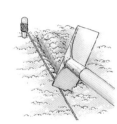   

1   2   3   4

DIVISION

Fibrous roots

Fleshy roots

Split up clumps of herbaceous perennials every three or four years. Prise fibrous-rooted perennials apart using two forks. Congested clumps of fleshy-rooted plants, such as hostas, are better cut into pieces.

better than undersized specimens, but most herbaceous perennials grow so fast that a plant bought in a small pot will reach the same size within one growing season as a more mature plant in a larger container. This also applies to faster-growing trees and shrubs, including plants for hedges such as some of the willows, poplars, privet and hawthorn. However, slow-growing trees and shrubs will give more immediate impact if they are bought as larger specimens.

Large trees should only be bought from reputable nurseries where they transplant or cut the rootballs regularly to ensure trees have a compact root system, and prune the crown accordingly. If this has been done semi-mature trees will resume growing without much delay, but without this preparation they take a long time to establish and you are better off buying a younger – as well as cheaper – specimen which will grow faster.

For large-scale woodland planting and for establishing a hedge or a meadow it is more economical to plant trees, shrubs and perennials that have been raised in small individual modules, known as cells or plugs. Because these plants are sold in the small containers they were raised in and are still very young, they are cheap and will establish very quickly given the necessary care.

PROPAGATION

If you are bitten by the propagation bug or if you have a limited budget, then raising your own plants is the answer. With the help of a warm, bright but not sunny window-sill and, if possible, a cold frame and a small heated propagator, it is possible to propagate quite an extensive range of plants. A greenhouse and mist bench makes the task easier, but are by no means essential.

Plants can be raised from seed or can alternatively be propagated by division, cuttings, layering or grafting. The first four methods are straightforward, but grafting is a specialized technique used by nurserymen to control vigour or to overcome disease problems. Most roses, fruit trees and flowering cherries are the products of grafting.

GROWING FROM SEED

This is an excellent way of producing large quantities of annuals, biennials and most perennials as they will offer quick results. If you buy seeds, the packets will tell you how and when to sow, but you can also collect your own seed. Although most species will come true from seed, some cultivars will not and should be propagated by other means. Seeds of trees and shrubs can take up to two or even three years before they germinate, and then take several more years before reaching a plantable size. Bulbs grown from seed will take several years before they reach flowering size.

DIVISION

Many perennials, including aquatics and grasses, are divided during the dormant season. The easiest way of doing this is by driving two forks, back to back, through the middle of a clump and pushing them away from each other. The roots are teased apart and the many small plants can be separated. Congested clumps may also be cut into pieces with an old kitchen knife. Whenever you move perennials it is advisable to divide the old clump and replant the young outer plantlets, discarding the old central portion. This process rejuvenates the plants, which will re-establish much more quickly and can be left unattended for a longer period.

ROOT CUTTINGS

Some perennials with fleshy roots are propagated from root cuttings taken in the dormant season. Oriental poppies, for example, go dormant during the summer

DIVIDING BORDER IRIS

1

2

Lift rhizomes in mid- to late summer. Select plump sections bearing a shoot and roots and discard the central wrinkled portion (1). Trim the leaves and replant them, leaving just the top of the rhizome exposed (2).

Prick seedlings out as soon as they are large enough to handle, usually when they have developed four true leaves. Ease seedlings out with a widger or pencil, holding them by a leaf, never the stem (1). Transfer to individual modules and water them in (2).

1   2

ROOT CUTTINGS

1

Select small lateral roots for cuttings. When cutting the roots, trim each section straight across the top and slanting at the base, in order to distinguish the top

2

from the bottom (1). Insert the cuttings in the compost the correct way up, so that the top is level with the surface. Cover the compost with a 1cm (⅛in) layer of gravel (2).

SEMI-RIPE CUTTINGS

1

Trim the stem immediately below a leaf joint (here choisya) and remove the lower leaves from the cutting (1). Dip the base of the cutting in rooting hormone powder and

2

remember to tap off any excess. Insert the cutting through the layer of sharp sand so that the base of the stem sits just below the surface of the soil or compost (2).

SOFTWOOD CUTTINGS

1

Gather softwood cuttings early in the morning and have everything ready in advance so you can insert them without delay. Trim the stem

2

just below a leaf joint (here pelargonium) and remove the lower leaves from the cutting (1). Insert the cuttings in sandy compost and water them well (2).

HEEL CUTTINGS

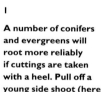

1

A number of conifers and evergreens will root more reliably if cuttings are taken with a heel. Pull off a young side shoot (here rosemary) in such a way that a strip of the

2

previous year's wood is attached (1). Trim off the ragged tail of the heel, dip in rooting hormone powder, remembering to tap off any excess, and insert in gritty compost (2).

with the compost and covered with 1cm (½in) of gravel. Keep the cuttings fairly dry to prevent them from rotting. Root cuttings can also be taken from woody plants which have a tendency to sucker from the roots, such as aralias, catalpas and chaenomeles.

SOFTWOOD CUTTINGS

Spring is the time of year to take softwood cuttings of shrubs and perennials. Choose young, vigorous growth that is still soft and green and will root without too much difficulty. Although it is quite possible to take softwood cuttings well into the late summer, the success rate will decrease as the season progresses. Because softwood cuttings wilt very quickly, put them in a plastic bag and keep them in a cool place if you are unable to set them in compost straight away. If you have never taken cuttings before, start with something easy like fuchsia or dianthus. If you need a lot of cutting material, for example from dahlias, overwinter plants in a frost-free environment, and in late winter cut them back hard and water to bring them into growth. The new shoots produced within the next few weeks make perfect material as soon as you can cut a shoot with three to six leaf joints. This strong new growth with a healthy leaf bud at the end (not a fat flower bud) will root very quickly. With a sharp knife cut just below a leaf

HARDWOOD CUTTINGS

Insert hardwood cuttings in a V-shaped trench in open ground. Backfill with soil and firm in. The layer of sharp sand or grit at the base ensures good drainage so the cutting does not rot.

months. Lift the plant and, after cutting off a few strong healthy roots, replant the mother plant. Use the small lateral roots. Cut across the top at a right angle and trim the bottom at a slanting angle to give a larger surface from which the new roots can develop. This will also help you to distinguish top from bottom. Cuttings to be raised in the open should measure at least 10cm (4in), those destined for a cold frame 5cm (2in) and for a heated propagator 2.5cm (1in). Before inserting them into a gritty compost, it is advisable to dust the cut surfaces with a fungicide. The top of the cuttings should be level

INTERNODAL CUTTINGS

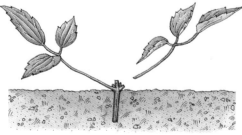

This technique is used for climbing plants (here clematis) with a lengthy stem between the leaf joints, or internodes. Trim

above a leaf joint and insert about 2–3cm (1in) of stem in gritty compost. Remove some of the leaves to cut down water loss.

LAYERING

This is a reliable method of propagating shrubs with low-growing branches, such as rhododendrons (shown here), pieris and magnolias. Climbers can be increased by pulling down a long shoot, wounding the stem and pegging it down.

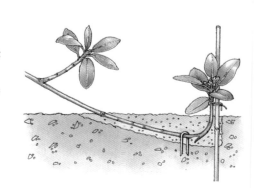

joint, or node, and remove the lower leaves. You can dip the base in a rooting hormone powder, although cuttings often root as well without. A fungicidal dip is a useful precaution, or remove wilting or rotting material as soon as it becomes obvious. Insert the cuttings round the edge of a pot of freely draining compost, such as one part coir to one or two parts sharp sand. Cover with a polythene bag or, for faster, more reliable rooting, put them into a heated propagating case at a constant temperature of 24°C (75°F). A small case fits on a wide window-sill and is plugged into the mains.

SEMI-RIPE CUTTINGS

Shrubs, trees and climbers, including evergreens, are more often propagated from semi-ripe cuttings in late summer or from hardwood cuttings during the winter months. Take semi-ripe cuttings when the new season's growth starts to harden. Cut terminal growths 10–15cm (4–6in) long. Remove leaves from the lower half of the stem, dip the base in rooting hormone powder and insert into soil or gritty compost, topped with a 2.5cm (1in) layer of sharp sand, in a shaded cold frame. To save space cut large leaves like mahonia or cherry laurel (*Prunus laurocerasus*) in half. Take cuttings of conifers in a similar way, but with a heel. This means pulling side shoots from the main stem so they come off with a small strip of old wood, known as a heel.

HARDWOOD CUTTINGS

Easy subjects for your first hardwood cutting experiments are willows and *Cornus sanguinea* cultivars. In winter, just after leaf-fall, cut lengths of hardened woody stem bearing at least three buds. Trim the bottom end at an angle and the top end level, just above a bud. Insert the cuttings into a V-shaped trench in open ground, leaving the top buds showing, and firm them in. In heavy clay, mix some sharp sand into the soil and also place some at the base of the trench to ensure good drainage.

TRANSPLANTING A LARGE SHRUB

1   2

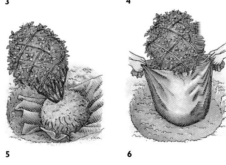

In the first year expose and trim back back the outer roots (1). Refill the trench with compost (2). The following autumn tie up the branches so that they are not broken during the move, and re-open the trench (3). Excavate the rootball (4). Ease the plant onto a large plastic sheet (5). Lift it out of the hole (6). Secure the rootball and move to its new site (7). Replant, water in and mulch generously (8).

3   4

5   6

7   8

LAYERING

Many shrubs and climbers are propagated by layering. In late winter or early spring select a strong new stem that will reach down to ground level and prepare the soil at this point by forking in garden compost and grit. Pull down the stem and make a slanting cut halfway through to encourage root formation. Peg the cut branch down into the prepared soil with the end tied vertically to a stake. Water in dry weather and transplant when the roots have established, which should be towards late summer or autumn.

MOVING TREES AND SHRUBS

Even the best gardeners make mistakes and occasionally need to move a plant to a more suitable position. The best time is late autumn, as the plants will have ample opportunity to re-establish their root system before summer and dry weather set in. Although dormancy can continue into late spring, plants moved late will be slower to establish due to the drier conditions, and will need more aftercare. A day or two before moving small shrubs, soak them well. Prepare a generous planting hole, fork in a quantity of organic matter, and water.

Moving trees and larger shrubs needs some more forethought and preparation. A year ahead of time, dig a 60cm (2ft) trench around the plant to the size of the rootball and fill with garden compost. This encourages the production of new feeding roots. When the time comes to transplant, prepare a generous planting hole, fork in plenty of organic matter and water well. Have ready some hessian, sacking or strong polythene sheeting in which to wrap the rootball. Then dig around the rootball and, with some assistance, slide the sheeting underneath so that the plant can be lifted out of the hole. If the original root system has been drastically reduced, it is advisable to cut back the crown to compensate for the loss of roots. When replanting is complete, stabilize the plant with guy ropes and keep it watered during the first season.

Lawns and meadows

SOWING GRASS SEED

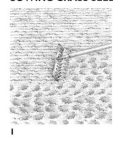
1

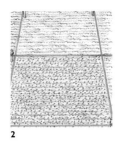
2

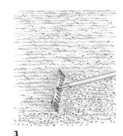
3

Soft turf is like no other surface, cool under foot and soothing to the eye. But behind a perfect lawn there is more than just mowing – you must add time spent trimming edges, fertilizing, weeding, raking and aerating. If an immaculate lawn does not suit your garden you may prefer a meadow studded with wildflowers. Meadows do not require weekly attention but the first cut is laborious. This aside, they are one of the most attractive solutions to an impoverished soil.

ESTABLISHING A LAWN

Whether you opt for seed or turf, a well-prepared and absolutely level surface is vital, as it is difficult to rectify mistakes once the lawn is established. The site should have topsoil at least 15cm (6in) deep. Dig over the area, incorporating some organic matter and removing stones, roots and perennial weeds. Badly compacted soil needs double digging and heavy clay can be improved by adding quantities of sharp sand or installing a drainage system (see page 248). Once it has been dug, the soil must be meticulously levelled. Prepare a 'stale seedbed' by leaving the ground for ten days or so. This gives weed seeds time to germinate and they can then be hoed off.

Sow lawn seed in a spell of warm, moist weather during either the autumn or the spring. Autumn-sown grass will have

become established by late spring, and spring-sown lawn will be ready for use by the following autumn. When the grass is 5cm (2in) long, roll it to even out any humps and to encourage tillering and rooting. A few days later, give it its first cut with the mower blades set high at 4–5cm (1¾–2in).

Turf is best put down in autumn or late winter, so that the grass has time to establish before dry weather sets in.

LAWN CARE

Regular care will keep your lawn growing well and looking smart. Cut the grass at least once a week in the growing season, but not too short. During early spring, autumn and dry weather set the mower blades to 2.5cm (1in), but leave heavily used grass slightly longer. Leaving the clippings protects the grass during dry spells, although this is not good general practice as it can lead to a build-up of moss and dead matted grass.

Feed lawns regularly, from spring till late summer, with a high nitrogen fertilizer, or apply a slow-release fertilizer in spring. In autumn a feed high in potash and phosphate will encourage good root development. In late spring apply a mosskiller if necessary. Weed treatment is most effective when weeds are in full growth, shortly after feeding. To control creeping weeds scarify them (rake vigorously) prior to mowing; remove rosette weeds by hand. In early autumn scarify and spike the lawn and clear fallen leaves.

MEADOWS

Cut once or twice a year, wildflower meadows are your own private piece of countryside. Unlike lawns, they thrive on poor, unfertilized soil where competition from grass species is less aggressive. Be careful to choose a meadow mix that suits the soil and conditions in your garden, otherwise you risk a failure rather than a flowery success. Before sowing, clear the soil of unwanted weeds by preparing a stale seedbed and hoeing off any weeds that germinate.

An alternative to sowing is to establish weed-free turf of fine grass before planting wildflowers and bulbs. Strip small patches of turf or spot treat with a herbicide so that flowers can establish without competition. Do not collect plants or seeds from the wild. If an existing lawn is converted to meadow, reduce soil fertility first by mowing regularly, not fertilizing and collecting the grass cuttings.

Spring-flowering meadows are usually left to grow until early summer and are ready for cutting when they start to seed. Summer meadows are cut regularly until mid-spring, then allowed to grow and flower, and cut again in late summer or

Before sowing tread the soil firm and rake level (1). For even sowing divide the area into rectangles of known area. Measure out the correct quantity of seed for each division and scatter by hand or use a seed applicator. Go over the site twice, at right angles to one another, to ensure even coverage (2). Lightly rake in the seeds (3).

LAYING TURF

1

2

3

early autumn. It is important to wait until seeds are shed and bulbs have died down before cutting meadows with a scythe, strimmer or heavy-duty rotary mower. Once cut, rake up the hay. You will be left with pallid rough grass, but it will green up in a few weeks. For the rest of the year leave the meadow rough; a cut every three to four weeks is sufficient.

MOWERS

Cylinder mowers give an immaculate cut and smart stripes, ideal for fine turf, but they choke on long, rough grass. Rotary mowers cope with rough, wet grass and meadows. Hover mowers float on an air cushion, which makes them easy to use on steep banks. All are available as either electric or petrol-driven machines. Electric ones are cheaper, quieter and lighter but less powerful. Most models come with a grass collecting box.

Unroll the turves and butt them closely together (1). After laying, firm the turves gently using the back of a rake or a light roller (2). Top-dress with sharp sand and compost or soil mixed in equal parts, brushing the dressing into any gaps and crevices (3). Water thoroughly and irrigate in dry spells until the lawn is properly established.

AUTUMN LAWN CARE

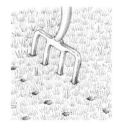

Scarification

Aeration

Scarify the lawn to remove dead matted grass, known as thatch. Then spike with a fork or hollow tiner, to a depth of at least 10cm (4in) every 15cm (6in)

or so to relieve compaction and to improve aeration and drainage. Top-dress with a mix of sharp sand, loam and rotted organic matter.

Pruning and training

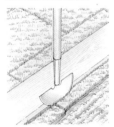

Straight edge

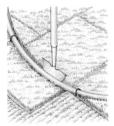

Curved edge

Slice down vertically with a half-moon edger to give a crisp outline. Cut against a plank for a straight edge. For a curve, pin down a hose pipe and use this as a guide. Trim lawn edges regularly with edging shears; strimmers or petrol-driven edge trimmers are quick but do not give such an immaculate finish.

In nature plants do not depend on pruning for their survival but in the artificial setting of the garden things are rather different. Plants often need a little help to keep them shapely and growing and flowering well. Sometimes trees or shrubs are manipulated into decorative forms like topiary, hedges, standards, fans or espaliers, which need precise and regular attention to keep in shape. Occasionally plants get out of hand and their growth needs to be curtailed.

The methods of pruning fall into three categories. These are formative pruning, regenerative pruning to revitalize the plant, and the removal of dead, diseased or weak growth, which is applicable to all plants and is an essential part of good garden management.

FORMATIVE PRUNING

Many gardeners are very understandably wary of pruning a healthy shrub. But formative pruning in the early years can be a way of avoiding problems later in life and ensuring a pleasing, well-balanced form. This, and a regular trim to keep the proportions right, will prove in the long term far less traumatic for pruner and plant alike than having to confront an oversized, misshapen mature shrub.

Newly purchased shrubs and trees may need some light pruning to establish an open framework of branches. If a young tree has two leading shoots, one should be removed. This will ensure a strong central trunk and an elegant

shape and avoid the possibility of a cleft trunk in the future. When planting a large bare-rooted tree or shrub it is advisable to compensate for the loss in roots by reducing the crown size.

Some trees and shrubs, particularly fruit trees, can be purchased ready-trained as fans, espaliers or standards. The formative pruning has already been taken care of by specialists, making life much easier and instructions on future pruning requirements are often supplied along with the plant.

Small woody shrubs, like lavenders, santolinas and rosemary, can become unappealingly leggy at a very early age unless they are trimmed regularly after flowering and in spring. If this is not done, a vigorous trim to where buds break from the stem may revive the plant, but in view of their short lifespan it may be easier to replace them.

REGENERATIVE PRUNING

Some plants such as willows, dogwoods, rubus, eucalyptus and paulownias, benefit greatly from heavy annual pruning. This will encourage the production of healthy, colourful new stems and large, strong leaves. Old stems soon lose their vibrant colour, so bushy new growth must be encouraged by pollarding or by coppicing the shrubs.

Other shrubs, particularly roses and fruit, will retain their vigour and produce more and better flowers if they are pruned annually. Thinning out old wood,

Always cut just above a bud. Where buds are alternately arranged (left) slant the cut as shown; where the buds are opposite (right), cut straight across.

FORMATIVE PRUNING

After planting cut out basal shoots to encourage vertical growth (1). The following year remove weak growth at the base and any shoots competing with the main leader (2). In the third year remove lower branches to establish a clear trunk and any badly placed or crossing branches (3).

1   2   3

RENOVATING A SHRUB

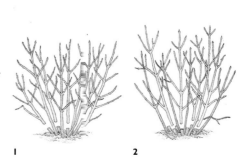

1   2

Renovate an overgrown shrub over two years. Start by cutting out about half the stems including any that are dead, damaged or diseased. Trim back the remaining shoots if necessary (1). The following year will bring new growth from the base, when the remaining old stems can be removed (2).

PRUNING TOOLS

Bow saw

Pruning saw

Long-arm pruner

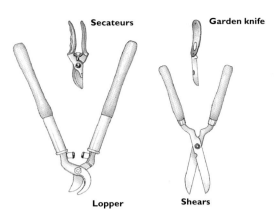

Secateurs

Garden knife

Lopper

Shears

COPPICING

This way of restricting the size of a plant also encourages plenty of new growth. Cut back all stems to the base, but not into the swollen woody crown that will develop over the years. Do this every year for a show of colourful stems.

POLLARDING

Similar to coppicing except that a head of shoots sprouts from a single stem. In the first year, cut the plant down to a strong bud at ground level. In the following years, in late winter or early spring, cut back all stems to two buds from which will sprout new growth.

especially from the centre of the plant, and cutting back stems that have finished flowering or fruiting will ensure new strong, healthy growth. If a plant is well fed, the harder it is pruned the more vigorous the new growth will be. This makes it all the more important, both visually and to avoid disease problems, that the centre of the plant is kept open to let in plenty of light and allow air to circulate. A plant pruned on a regular basis will suffer less than one pruned sporadically; pruning also becomes simpler and less time-consuming because it is easier to distinguish between old and new wood.

Clematis also rewards regular pruning with an abundant display of flowers and no unsightly tangle of bare stems. Prune summer-flowering clematis hybrids right back to a strong pair of buds near ground level during the winter months. Spring-flowering clematis produce their buds on the previous season's growth and are usually only lightly pruned back to two or three buds from the main framework stems after they have finished flowering, in early summer.

After a heavy bout of pruning, always compensate your plants with a dose of slow-release fertilizer and a generous mulch at the start of the growing season. Such attention will reap rich rewards in the form of strong and healthy growth.

ATTACHING CLIMBERS TO A WALL

Trellis

Train climbers and wall shrubs along strong wires that have been run through vine eyes fixed firmly in the wall or fence. Trellis can also be used, but it

Vine eyes

must be mounted on battens, otherwise thickening stems will force it apart. Train in shoots regularly using soft twine and a figure of eight tie.

REMOVING DEAD WOOD

An essential part of good garden management is to check all trees, shrubs and climbers every winter. Any diseased, damaged or dead wood should be cut out and, if possible, burnt to prevent disease from spreading. Weak, twiggy stems will never produce strong growth and need removing. Cut out any crossing branches; if they are allowed to rub together an open wound will form and provide an entry point for disease.

THE RIGHT TIME TO PRUNE

Plants grow most rapidly in spring; once dry summer weather arrives, the growth rate slows. Consequently, if you want to encourage vigorous new growth, prune hard in early spring. If, on the other hand, you want to clip your conifer or evergreen hedge just once a year, trim in mid- to late summer so that there will only be modest regrowth before the onset of winter and you will be able to enjoy the crisp outline when there is relatively little happening in the garden. During mid- to late summer is also the best time to remove any dead or damaged shoots from free-form evergreens and conifers, which otherwise need little pruning.

If in doubt about the right time to prune a plant, have a close look at its flowers. If the flowers form on new growth produced in the current season, like *Buddleja davidii* and large-flowered clematis hybrids, then the plant can be pruned at any time during late autumn, winter or spring. If you prune too early in autumn, the plant will produce new shoots which will not have time to harden off before the frosts set in. However, plants that show sensitivity to frost, such as fuchsias, are best left unpruned until the spring. The slightly warmer micro-climate created by the network of branches will fend off a certain amount of frost and prevent it from penetrating into the centre of the plant too easily.

If the flowers are borne on woody growth formed the previous year, as is the case in many of the winter and spring-

SHAPING A HEDGE

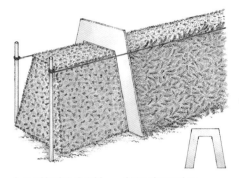

A good hedge should be dense and well covered down to the ground. It will keep its shape better if the profile is tapered, so the top is narrower than the bottom. To achieve a really sharp outline cut a template

from plywood to the shape required. Stretch a line between two posts, either side of the hedge, to indicate the height. First trim along the top then clip the sides, moving the template along as you work.

flowering plants like philadelphus and deutzias, allow the plant to flower first, then prune soon after the flowering period is over. This way the plant will have time to produce new growth, which will carry next year's flowers.

PRUNING TOOLS

Before you start to prune, spend some time selecting a few good tools. Handle them before you buy to make sure they will be comfortable to use. Look out for

CRISS-CROSS ROSES

Climbing roses can be trained along wires in order to cover a wall or make a fence. As they grow, pull down the branches and cross them over one another, weaving in

the side shoots so that the area is evenly covered. In this way the whole plant will eventually become smothered with flowers and make a solid barrier.

manufacturers who offer a repair and maintenance service, as this will extend the life of your equipment dramatically. A good sharp pair of secateurs will take care of much of the regular pruning work. If you have a great deal of pruning it is worth investing in secateurs with a rotating handle as these lie better in the hand and prevent blisters.

Never attempt to hack through a branch with a tool inappropriate for the job. For thick twigs and medium-sized branches, loppers, long-handled secateurs or a small fold-away pruning saw are advisable, whereas large branches should always be sawn through. A slim-bladed pruning saw is easily manoeuvred between the branches without causing unnecessary damage. A sharp pair of shears is essential for topiary work and neat hedge trimming, but for clipping seemingly endless hedges powered hedge-trimmers are the answer. Although they have the disadvantage of a cable, electric trimmers are much lighter to handle than petrol-driven models.

Keep all blades well sharpened so they cut cleanly and easily, with no snags or tears where diseases can find an easy entry point. Always clean blades after use and keep them well oiled. Such regular care makes good hygienic practice, prolongs the life of expensive tools and ensures they do a good job.

TRAINING

Climbers and scramblers trained along walls or trellis, over arches or pergolas, can link house to garden and hide unsightly structures. Some climbers support themselves by means of aerial roots or suckers, such as ivy, Virginia creeper and climbing hydrangea, and need no help to work their way over a wall or fence. Morning glories and runner beans twine themselves around anything they are given. Roses and blackberries scramble through shrubs and trees, hanging on by their thorns; in a garden they need regular tying if you want to keep them under control. Slightly tender shrubs can be trained against walls, where they will benefit from the extra protection These include ceanothus and fremontodendrons, but hardier plants like forsythias or pyracanthas can also be used in this way to create a fine display.

Even self-supporting climbers benefit from a little training, otherwise you will find your clematis flowers over the wall in your neighbour's garden. Lateral shoots off a main stem will produce ample flower buds as long as the main stems are trained horizontally and the side shoots can grow upwards. It may be tempting to fan-train a climbing rose, but this will result in flowers only at the extremities. However, if you pull the branches down and criss-cross them to produce a loosely woven network, the side shoots will be encouraged and the entire plant will be covered in flowers.

Train climbers and wall shrubs along wires run through vine eyes or over some trellis, which should be mounted on battens unless free-standing. Use soft twine, raffia or other natural materials for tying back. If overlooked, these will break or disintegrate when the branches increase in diameter, whereas plastic and metal ties can cut into the bark and strangle stems by inhibiting the flow of sap. In any case, you should check all plant ties regularly and loosen those that are beginning to get tight.

STAKING TREES

Newly planted trees need anchoring for two or three years while they establish their roots. Recent research has proved that trees supported with short stakes, reaching to approximately one-third of the trunk height, develop a much better root system more rapidly than those with tall stakes. Because the canopies of trees are free to move with the wind, the roots anchor themselves quicker and more securely than if the tree is held virtually immobile. This does not apply to larger trees which, if moved, need strong tall stakes or a system of guy ropes; mature trees are invariably moved by a specialist contractor with the benefit of specialist equipment. Always check the tree ties regularly and loosen them before they cut into the bark.

Very young trees that lack any side branches, or whips, can be planted in plastic tubes which will act as a temporary greenhouse, giving shelter during the initial years of establishment. These tubes are fixed in the ground with a stake and act as support for the plant, also protecting it from rabbits and deer.

SUPPORTING PERENNIALS

Once upon a time staking herbaceous perennials was routine and gardens were all too often awash with canes. Many perennials that traditionally needed staking are now available in more compact or sturdy self-supporting varieties. However, some plants still need support. Double-flowered peonies are top-heavy but by growing them through wire mesh their sumptuous blooms will be held aloft. The tallest delphiniums benefit from individual treatment, tying the stem of each magnificent flower spike up high to a bamboo cane.

Good staking should be invisible within three weeks, hidden by vegetation. The most inconspicuous stakes are fan-shaped hazel branches. Push them in the earth around clump-forming perennials and bend over the tops to make a web of small twigs through which the plants can grow. Bamboo canes are widely used and, unlike hazel twigs, they are reusable and come in different lengths. Place three or four around a clump and hold plants in position by means of garden twine.

A number of galvanized or plastic-coated metal supports are available. They include L-shaped stakes hooked into each other, around or across plants, and circles filled with wide wire mesh through which plants can grow. Large metal hoops simply hold back masses of vegetation that are on the verge of flopping across the border. All of these types of support are effective in their own way but are not necessarily cheap.

Avoiding trouble

To many gardeners, avoiding trouble means controlling pests, diseases and weeds but it should also include avoiding accidents. With a little forethought, your garden need not be a hazardous place.

AVOIDING PESTS AND DISEASES
Keep plants healthy and in vigorous growth; they will be far less susceptible to pest and disease attack than sickly plants. Clear up fallen leaves, fruits and other plant debris that could harbour diseases and prune out weak, damaged or dead stems. Crop rotation is usual in the vegetable garden but it can be applied elsewhere. New fruit trees and roses, in particular, require a fresh site. Choose plants to suit your garden and look out for disease-resistant varieties.

Try to catch problems as soon as they arise. Better still, deal with the cause rather than just treating the symptoms. For instance, powdery mildew is a sign of dry, exposed conditions, so by moving vulnerable plants to a moist spot, their health will improve. Encourage beneficial wildlife. A patch of stinging nettles or a few logs will offer a winter home for ladybirds who, in summer, will feast on your greenfly. Hoverflies – even more efficient predators of aphids – lay their eggs near infestations, on plants such as calendulas and fennel. Some long grass and a pool will attract slug-eating frogs and toads. Other garden friends besides bats, bees, birds and hedgehogs include earthworms, centipedes, ground beetles and lacewings.

CONTROL MEASURES
If your preventative measures fail, there are biological, physical and chemical controls to turn to. Biological control consists of introducing organisms that parasitize the pest and cause its death. They are available to control slugs, vine weevils, whitefly in the greenhouse, red spider mites and caterpillars.

Barriers and traps are physical control methods. A broad collar of grit placed around vulnerable plants, like hostas, deters slugs. Yoghurt cartons of beer sunk into the ground to show 2.5cm (1in) of the rim are good slug traps. A grease band round the trunk of a fruit tree will prevent harmful insects from crawling up. Codling moth and cockroach traps are baited with pheromones (female sex hormones) to lure unsuspecting males onto a sticky sheet, leaving the females unfertilized and the population reduced.

Chemical controls are either contact or systemic. The former must hit the target to succeed, whereas systemic sprays are absorbed by the plant and circulate in the sap stream; they will kill an insect feeding on the plant or a fungal disease trying to infiltrate.

WEEDS
Weeds are plants growing in the wrong place and some perennials are very persistent. They will compete with more choice plants and invade planting schemes. They will resprout from a tiny portion of root, so attempts to dig out, say, bindweed only increases the numbers. Other nightmares include ground elder, couch grass and horsetails. Most annual weeds are easily pulled by hand and perennials can be spot-treated with weedkiller. A chemical-free way of dealing with weeds on paths and drives when conditions are dry is to use a flame gun. To clear large weed infestations, cover the area with old carpet or black polythene sheets for a growing season. This will starve the weeds of light and water, killing them off in a harmless way.

If you can't wait, you may have to resort to herbicides. One application may not kill everything but reoffenders can be spot treated. Most herbicides are residual: they remain active in the soil for a specified time during which planting cannot take place. Others, glyphosate for example, become inactive soon after they have made contact with the soil. As glyphosate also travels through the plant systemically to the root system, it is especially suitable for treating persistent perennial weeds.

CHEMICAL SAFETY
Use the right product for the job, and dispose of it exactly according to the instructions. Never store a chemical in a container other than the one it is sold in. Keep all chemicals under lock and key in a dark, cool place, away from children. Spray in still weather when there is no danger of drift, preferably in the evening when bees have gone to rest. Always cover up and wear rubber gloves and goggles. Try to use the product which will cause least harm to the environment.

AVOIDING ACCIDENTS
Wear sensible clothes; goggles, trousers and sturdy footwear (steel-capped boots are best) are essential when strimming, mowing and laying paving slabs. Before mounting a step ladder, open it fully and ensure it is absolutely firm. Check safety guards are intact on lawn mowers and power tools. Clean tools and equipment after use, and hang them up tidily. Store dangerous tools in a locked shed.

Electricity can be quite lethal. Outdoor electric sockets must be special waterproof units. Always fit residual current circuit breakers, as these will cut off power immediately a cable is damaged. Never leave electrical equipment plugged in and unattended and always unplug equipment before you maintain or repair it. Keep cables well away from water.

Water can kill, and small children are most at risk. Fit water butts with a secure lid and install a pond only when children are old enough to understand danger. Always supervise children playing in a paddling pool and empty it after use. Similarly, never leave barbecues and bonfires unattended and site bonfires well away from buildings and trees.

Attend immediately to any loose or uneven paving slabs or steps. Site play equipment over a soft surface of grass or bark chippings; swings must be well clear of paths, walls and greenhouses. Fit cane protectors on all stakes. Keep boundary fences, walls and gates secure at all times so pets and children do not stray.

Plant maintenance calendar

Gardening is very much governed by the weather, which, of course, does not follow a set pattern every year. There are also wide regional climatic differences that need to be taken into account. Within the broad regions there are local variations based on whether your garden is on a chilly hilltop or in a sheltered valley. Work with the prevailing weather conditions; for instance, it is far better to wait until the soil warms up than to waste seeds by sowing them on half-frozen ground.

SPRING

Routine jobs
- Prepare soil for planting when it is not too wet.
- Apply slow-release fertilizers to borders, fruit and perennial vegetables.
- Mulch beds and borders when the soil is moist and weed-free.
- Any plants that have been heavily pruned over winter need feeding and a generous mulch.

Annuals
- Sow seeds of hardy annuals *in situ* when the soil has warmed.

Bulbs and perennials
- Lift and divide clumps of snowdrops and winter aconites when still in leaf.
- Plant dahlia tubers and summer-flowering bulbs.
- Remove spent flowerheads of narcissus and tulips.
- Lift and divide ornamental grasses and other perennials.
- Stake tall perennials.

Trees, shrubs and climbers
- Complete winter plantings early in the season.
- Remove winter protection.
- Prune slightly frost-sensitive shrubs such as lavateras and many of the silver-foliaged plants in early spring.
- Prune after flowering shrubs such as forsythia, ribes and early-flowering clematis.
- Check and adjust ties.
- Guide climbers along their supports regularly.
- Layer shrubs and climbers.
- Take softwood cuttings in mid- to late spring.

Fruit and vegetables
- Sow vegetables in moist soil which has had the chance to warm up. To speed up this process, cover the soil with plastic film, fleece or cloches.
- Sow small quantities of vegetables in succession for a continuous supply of succulent young produce.
- Protect early fruit blossom.

Lawns and meadows
- Make a new lawn by laying turf or sowing seed when conditions are favourable.
- Mow established lawns as soon as the grass starts growing.
- Weed and feed in late spring and, if necessary, apply a mosskiller.
- Do not cut summer-flowering meadows after mid-spring.

Pools
- In late spring clean out dirty or overgrown pools and ponds.
- Plant aquatic plants.
- Lift and divide all aquatic plants as necessary.
- Remove pool heater and reinstate pump after its winter service.

Indoors/under glass
- Sow half-hardy annuals, perennials and vegetables, hardening them off towards the end of spring.
- Take softwood cuttings of tender perennials for container display.
- In early to mid-spring pot up dahlia tubers to bring them into growth before they are planted out.
- Plant containers for summer display.

SUMMER

Routine jobs
- In early summer plant up containers for summer display, or move those prepared in the greenhouse outside.
- Feed container plantings regularly unless using a slow-release fertilizer.
- During prolonged periods of dry weather water plants showing signs of stress or that are not yet fully established, including trees and shrubs planted during the past two to three years.
- Deadhead plants to encourage new flower buds.

Annuals
- In early summer sow a second batch of annuals in plugs to replace early sowings once they are past their best.

Bulbs and perennials
- Leave bulb foliage to die down naturally. Remove spring bulbs from containers to die down and dry off in a vacant corner of the garden.
- Order bulbs for spring display.
- Lift and divide bearded irises as soon as they have finished flowering.
- Collect seeds.
- Take softwood cuttings of those plants you are worried about losing during the winter, such as diascias and penstemons.

Trees, shrubs and climbers
- Prune late spring- and early summer-flowering shrubs and climbers, such as deutzias, lilac and philadelphus, after flowering is over.
- Check climbers regularly, and tie back any wispy growths.
- Trim evergreen and coniferous hedges and topiary.
- Remove any dead or damaged shoots from free-form evergreens and conifers.
- Towards the end of summer take semi-ripe heel cuttings of shrubs, trees and evergreens.
- In late summer order trees and shrubs for winter planting.

Fruit and vegetables
- Continue to sow vegetables in small batches.
- Pick soft fruit and vegetables regularly.
- Feed vegetables regularly unless a slow-release fertilizer was applied in the spring.
- Towards the end of summer, harvest and store vegetables and fruit for winter consumption.

Lawns and meadows
- Make the first cut of a spring-flowering meadow.
- Feed lawns regularly as long as grass is growing.
- In dry weather raise mower blades and remove grass box so clippings act as a mulch.

Pools
- There is still time to clean out your pool in early summer, and to plant or to lift and divide water-lilies and other aquatic plants.
- Top up water level in hot weather.
- Thin out foliage of water-lilies if leaves become overcrowded.

Indoors/under glass
- Shade and ventilate plants growing under glass.
- Clean, tidy and paint the greenhouse ready for autumn.

AUTUMN

Routine jobs
- Clear containers of summer bedding and plant up winter displays.
- Collect fallen leaves and pile them into bins for leafmould.
- On heavy clay soils dig beds to allow winter frost to break up the soil.
- Turn compost heaps and spread rotted compost over beds and borders for winter protection.

Annuals
- Clear away annuals and biennials when they have finished flowering, but remember that some have attractive seedheads which can be dried or left *in situ*.

Bulbs and perennials
- Plant spring-flowering bulbs, in the garden or in pots, as soon as your order arrives.
- Lift dahlias and other tender bulbous plants after the first frost has knocked them back and store them in a cool, dry, frost-free environment.
- In late autumn mulch bulbs of borderline hardiness over winter.
- Lift, divide and replant perennials.
- Tidy up herbaceous borders by cutting back perennials when they become unsightly and putting the shredded or chopped-up material on the compost heap.
- In late autumn apply a thick mulch of organic material to protect perennials of borderline hardiness over winter.

Trees, shrubs and climbers
- Take hardwood cuttings just after leaf fall, before the soil is cold.
- Plant trees and shrubs as the dormant season commences.
- Protect slightly tender woody plants by screening them with bracken, conifer branches or matting over winter.

Fruit and vegetables
- Continue to harvest fruits and vegetables.
- Prune soft fruit bushes and summer-fruiting raspberries.
- Pick and store apples, pears and nuts for winter.
- Plant fruit trees, bushes and strawberries.

Lawns and meadows
- Cut spring- and summer-flowering meadows.
- Early in the season apply autumn feed if lawns have suffered from drought or hard use during the summer.
- Scarify, spike and top-dress lawns
- In mild spells a new lawn can be established from seed or turf.

Pools
- Skim off fallen leaves.
- Remove dying foliage.
- Take out pump towards the end of autumn, and service and store until spring.

Indoors/under glass
- Bring tender plants inside before the first frosts arrive.

WINTER

Routine jobs
- Now is the time to plan any changes to your garden, based on your observations throughout the year.
- Continue to collect fallen leaves and tidy up beds and borders, cutting plants back and clearing away plant debris.
- Dig beds for next season when weather permits, incorporating plenty of manure or other organic matter.
- Protect vulnerable plants over winter.
- Maintain fences, trellis, paths and garden structures while plants are dormant.
- Tidy up shed and clean tools.
- Clean and prepare propagators, seed trays and pots ready for spring sowing.
- Check plant labels and replace any that are fading or brittle.
- Order fertilizers, stakes, twine and any other garden sundries for the year ahead.
- Take root cuttings of fleshy-rooted perennials.

Trees, shrubs and climbers
- Prune trees, shrubs, roses and climbers, even if the weather is slightly frosty.
- Check all woody plants for dead and diseased wood, removing and destroying any infected stems or branches.
- In late winter layer shrubs and climbers.

Fruit and vegetables
- Prune fruit trees.
- Plan next year's crop rotation for the vegetable garden.
- Order seeds of vegetables and herbs.

Lawns and meadows
- Rake up leaves.
- Make sure mower is serviced and blades are sharpened in readiness for the new season.

Pools
- Keep an area ice-free by installing a pool heater or floating a plastic ball on the water. This is essential if you have fish.

Indoors/under glass
- If you have not already done so, bring under cover any tender plants in containers.

Useful addresses

ADVICE

**Arboricultural Advisory
and Information Service**
Alice Holt Lodge
Wrecclesham
Farnham
Surrey GU10 4LH
Wide-ranging advice on trees

British Agrochemicals Association
4 Lincoln Court
Lincoln Road
Peterborough
Cambridgeshire PE1 2RP
*Trade association which publishes guide to
products for amateur gardeners*

Common Ground
Seven Dials Warehouse
44 Earlham Street
London WC2H 9LA
*Promotes links between the environment
and social culture*

Composting Association
National Centre for Organic Gardening
Ryton-on-Dunsmore
Coventry
Warwickshire CV8 3LG
*Promotes composting as sustainable organic
waste management practice*

**Henry Doubleday Research Association
(HDRA)**
National Centre for Organic Gardening
Ryton-on-Dunsmore
Coventry
Warwickshire CV8 3LG
Promotes organic gardening methods

**Dry Stone Walling Association of
Great Britain**
YFC Centre
National Agricultural Centre
Stoneleigh
Kenilworth
Warwickshire CV8 2LG

Gardening for the Disabled Trust
Hayes Farm House
Hayes Lane
Peasmarsh
East Sussex TN31 6XR
Provides advice, grants and information

Good Gardeners Association
Pinetum Lodge
Churcham
Gloucestershire GL2 8AD
Promotes practice of companion planting

Health and Safety Executive
Information Centre
Broad Lane
Sheffield
South Yorkshire S3 7HQ
Concerned with gardening health and safety

Horticultural Therapy
Goulds Ground
Vallis Way
Frome
Somerset BA11 3DW
Provides advice and information

The London Ecology Unit
Bedford House
125 Camden High Street
London NW1 7JR
*Publishes guide to using plants on roofs,
walls and pavements*

**National Inspection Council for
Electrical Installation Contracting
(NICEIC)**
Vintage House
37 Albert Embankment
London SE1 7UJ
*Produces a list of approved electrical
installation contractors*

Northern Horticultural Society
Harlow Carr Botanical Gardens
Crag Lane
Harrogate
North Yorkshire HG3 1QB
*Advice, publications, events, membership
benefits*

Permaculture Association
8 Hynter's Moon
Totnes
Devon TQ9 6TJ
*Encourages the practice of permaculture,
the use of ecological, organic and bio-
dynamic principles for sustainable cultivation*

Royal Caledonian Horticultural Society
28 Silverknowes Southway
Edinburgh EH4 5PX
*Advice, publications, events, membership
benefits*

Royal Horticultural Society
80 Vincent Square
London SW1P 2PE
*Advice, publications, events, membership
benefits*

Royal Horticultural Society of Ireland
Swanbrook House
Bloomfield Avenue
Donnybrook
Dublin 4
Republic of Ireland
Publications, events, membership benefits

Soil Association
80 Colston Street
Bristol
Avon BS1 5BB
*Promotes sustainable relationship between
plants, soil, animals, people and the
biosphere to protect and enhance the
environment*

GARDEN DESIGN COURSES

English Gardening School
Chelsea Physic Garden
66 Royal Hospital Road
London SW3 4HS

Harlow Carr Botanical Gardens
Crag Lane
Harrogate
North Yorkshire HG3 1QB

Open College of the Arts
Houndhill
Worsborough
Barnsley
South Yorkshire S70 6TU

Royal Horticultural Society
Education Department
RHS Garden
Wisley
Woking
Surrey GU23 6QB

*Many horticultural/agricultural colleges,
universities and adult education centres
also offer garden design courses*

GARDEN DESIGNERS

*There are a number of ways to find a
professional garden designer to provide
design advice or design your garden:*
● *Personal recommendation is possibly the
best option.*
● *Many garden centres have an in-house
designer, or can recommend a local
designer (most designers work on a regional
basis, and it is generally more practical
to employ a relatively local one).*
● *Many garden landscaping contractors
have an in-house designer, or work in
association with one or more garden
designers.*
● *Garden design areas at shows like Chelsea,
Hampton Court and BBC Gardeners'
World Live.*
● *Classified section of gardening magazines.*
● *Yellow Pages listings under 'Garden
Designers' or 'Landscape Architects'.*

The Society of Garden Designers (SGD)
6 Borough Road
Kingston upon Thames
Surrey KT2 6BD
*List of Full Members, whose work has passed
an assessment. Full Members number
around 60 but account for less than 10 per
cent of the Society's total membership*

**The Garden & Landscape Designers
Association (GLDA)**
73 Deerpark Road
Mount Merrion
Co Dublin
Republic of Ireland
List of Full Members

GARDEN CONTRACTORS

*As with designers, there are a number of
ways to find a good garden landscaping
contractor:*
● *Personal recommendation is possibly the
best option.*
● *Most garden designers can recommend a
number of contractors to their clients.*
● *Many garden centres have an in-house
construction service, or can recommend a
local contractor.*

**British Association of Landscape
Industries (BALI)**
Landscape House
9 Henry Street
Keighley
West Yorkshire BD21 3DR
List of approved members

**Association of Professional Landscapers
(APL)**
Creighton Lodge
Hollington Lane
Stramshall
Uttoxeter
Staffordshire ST 4 5ES
List of approved members

Arboricultural Association
Ampfield House
Ampfield
Romsey
Hampshire SO51 9PA
*Directories of Approved Arboricultural
Contractors and of Registered Consultants*

GARDEN STRUCTURES

Agriframes
Charlwoods Road
East Grinstead
West Sussex RH19 2HG
*Steel pergolas, arches, arbours, bowers,
obelisks*

Alitex
Station Road
Alton
Hampshire GU34 2PZ
Aluminium glasshouses

Amdega
Faverdale
Darlington
Co Durham DL3 0PW
Softwood conservatories and summer-houses

Appeal Blinds
6 Vale Lane
Bedminster
Bristol
Avon BS3 5SD
Conservatory blinds

Continental Awnings
Unit 14
Torbay Trading Estate
New Road
Brixham
Devon TQ5 8NF
Sun protection for glazed roof buildings, terrace awnings

Deckor Timber
Matrix House
55 East Parade
Harrogate
North Yorkshire HG1 5LQ
Softwood retaining structures, gazebos, pavilions, pergolas, decking, trellis, planters, seating

Anthony de Grey Trellises
Broadhinton Road
77A North Street
London SW4 0HQ
Trellis, pavilions, gazebos, pergolas, arbours, decking, planters

English Hurdle
Curload
Stoke St Gregory
Taunton
Somerset TA3 6JD
Willow hurdles, summer-houses, arches, arbours, bowers, seats, benches, chairs, tables, plant climbers

Garden Heritage
The Studio
Braxton Courtyard
Lymore Lane
Milford on Sea
Hampshire SO41 0TX
Bamboo poles and screens

Good Directions
15 Talisman Business Centre
Duncan Road
Park Gate
Southampton
Hampshire SO31 7GA
Cupolas, clocks, weathervanes

HLD
The Old Shipyard
Gainsborough
Lincolnshire DN21 1NG
Hardwood and softwood retaining structures, bridges, gazebos, pergolas, decking, trellis, fencing, planters, seating

Haddonstone
The Forge House
East Haddon
Northampton
Northamptonshire NN6 8DB
Reconstructed stone architectural components for balustrading, pergolas, pavilions, steps, etc

H S Jackson & Son
75 Stowting Common
Ashford
Kent TN25 6BN
Specialist supplier and installer of timber and metal fencing and gates

Jungle Giants
Plough Farm
Wigmore
Herefordshire HR6 9UW
Bamboo poles, screens, fencing, gates

Lloyd Christie
1 New Kings Road
London SW6 4SB
Hardwood and softwood conservatories, summer-houses, gazebos, pavilions, decking, pergolas, trellis, planters, seating

M&M Timber Co
Hunt House Sawmills
Clows Top
Nr Kidderminster
Worcestershire DY14 9HY
Softwood retaining structures, bridges gazebos, pavilions, pergolas, decking, trellis, fencing, gates, planters, seating

Marston & Langinger
192 Ebury Street
London SW1W 8UP
Conservatories

Portland Conservatories
Portland House
Ouse Street
Salford
Manchester M5 2EW
Hardwood conservatories

Raffles Thatched Garden Buildings
Laundry Cottage
Prestwold Hall
Prestwold
Loughborough
Leicestershire LE12 5SQ

Redwood Decking
Bridge Inn Nurseries
Moss Side
Formby
Liverpool L37 0AF
Hardwood and softwood retaining structures, bridges, gazebos, pavilions, pergolas, decking, trellis, planters, seating

The Secret Garden Company of Ware
Ware
Hertfordshire SG12 0YJ
Iroko and cedar gazebos, summer-houses

The David Sharp Studio
201A Nottingham Road
Somercotes
Derbyshire DE55 4JG
Reconstructed stone components for balustrading, pavilions, steps, etc

Stuart Garden Architecture
Burrow Hill Farm
Wiveliscombe
Somerset TA4 2RN
Hardwood gazebos, pavilions, pergolas, bridges, decking, trellis, gates, planters, seating

Thatching Advisory Services
Faircross Offices
Stratfield Saye
Reading
Berkshire RG7 2BT
Thatched sunshades, prefabricated thatch tiles, split cane screening, peeled reed screening, heather screening, reed panels, willow and wattle hurdles, bamboo fencing

PAVING, WALLING & STONE

Atlas Stone Products
Westington Quarry
Chipping Campden
Gloucestershire GL55 6EG
Paving slabs and walling

Baggeridge Brick
Fir Street
Sedgley
Dudley
West Midlands DY3 4AA
Clay pavers and accessories, facing and engineering bricks, plus specials

Bardon Natural Stone
Thorney Mill Road
West Drayton
Middlesex UB7 7EZ
Granite and sandstone cubes, setts and paving, plus rockery and walling stone, boulders, feature stones, cobbles, and decorative aggregates

Blanc de Bierges
Eastrea Road
Whittlesey
Peterborough
Cambridgeshire PE7 2AG
Modular creamy buff concrete paving slabs and setts, plus seats and planters

Blockleys Brick
Sommerfield Road
Trench Lock
Telford
Shropshire TF1 4RY
Clay pavers and accessories, and facing bricks, plus specials

Border Hardcore
Middletown Quarry
Nr Welshpool
Powys SY21 8DJ
Natural stone boulders, cobbles/pebbles, large rocks, rockery stone, obelisks and decorative aggregates

Butterley
Stewartby
Bedford
Bedfordshire MK43 9LZ
Hand-made and machined clay pavers and accessories, facing and engineering bricks, plus specials

CAMAS
Holland Ward
Ashbourne
Derbyshire DE6 3ET
Slabs, walling, concrete block pavers, and setts and accessories

Civil Engineering Developments (CED)
728 London Road
West Thurrock
Grays
Essex RM20 3LU
Natural stone paving, setts, boulders, cobbles/pebbles, mosaic cubes, large rocks, rockery stone, aggregates

Freshfield Lane Brickworks
Dane Hill
Haywards Heath
Sussex RH17 7HH
Clay pavers and facing bricks, plus specials

Ibstock Building Products
Leicester Road
Ibstock
Leicestershire LE67 6HS
Hand-made and machined clay pavers and accessories, facing and engineering bricks, plus specials and ceramic tiles

Marshalls
Southowram
Halifax
West Yorkshire HX3 9SY
Concrete paving, block and sett paving and accessories plus clay pavers and accessories, facing and engineering bricks, and specials

Michelmersh Brick
Hillview Road
Michelmersh
Romsey
Hampshire SO51 0NN
Hand-made and machined clay pavers and facing bricks, plus specials

Silverlands Stone
Holloway Hill
Chertsey
Surrey KT16 0AE
Natural stone paving, walling, rockery stone, imported stone, decorative aggregates, plus reclaimed materials and man-made paving and walling

Stone Heritage
Portaway Mine
off Dudwood Lane
Elton
Derbyshire DE4 2BD
*New and reclaimed natural stone paving,
setts, boulders, walling, rockery stone*

Stonemarket
Old Gravel Quarry
Oxford Road
Ryton-on-Dunsmore
Warwickshire CV8 3EJ
Reconstituted stone paving, edging, walling

Town and Country Paving
Unit 10
Shrublands Nurseries
Roundstone Lane
Angmering
Littlehampton
West Sussex BN16 4AT
Paving slabs and terracotta tiles and bricks

The York Handmade Brick Co
Forest Lane
Alne
North Yorkshire YO6 2LU
*Hand-made clay pavers and accessories,
facing brick, specials and terracotta tiles*

LIGHTING AND IRRIGATION

City Irrigation
Bencewell Granary
Oakley Road
Bromley Common
Kent BR2 8HG
Irrigation system design and installation

Garden and Security Lighting
23 Jacob Street
London SE16 4UH
*Initial design consultations, lighting
proposals and demonstrations, product
supply, and installation*

H₂O Irrigation
Formula House
West Haddon
Northamptonshire NN6 7AU
Automatic watering systems

Hartland Irrigation
Unit 4, Manor Farm Business Centre
Kingston Lisle
Wantage
Oxfordshire OX12 9QL
Irrigation system design and installation

Leaky Pipe Garden Systems
Frith Farm
Dean Street
East Farleigh
Maidstone
Kent ME15 0PR
*Supply and installation of sub-surface
or sub-mulch porous hose system*

Outdoor Lighting Supplies
3 Kingston Business Centre
Fullers Way South
Chessington
Surrey KT9 1DQ
*Design consultations, specification, supply
and installation*

Porous Pipe
PO Box 2
Colne
Lancashire BB8 7BY
Porous hose made from recycled car tyres

FURNITURE AND ORNAMENT

Barbary Pots
45 Femshaw Road
London SW10 0TN
Hand-thrown Moroccan terracotta pots

Humphrey Bowden
6 Park Terrace
Tillington
Petworth
West Sussex GU28 9AE
Sculptures and copper fountains

The Bulbeck Foundry
Reach Road
Burwell
Cambridgeshire CB5 0AH
Lead statuary, fountains, pots, urns, planters

Capital Garden Products
Gibbs Reed Barn
Pashley Road
Ticehurst
East Sussex TN5 7HE
Fountains, urns, pots, planters, lead cisterns

Julian Chichester Designs
121 Sydney Street
London SW10 0TN
Teak seats, benches, tables

Chilstone
Victoria Park
Fordcombe Road
Langton Green
Tunbridge Wells
Kent TN3 0RE
*Hand-made reconstituted stone statuary,
pots, urns, planters, seating, fountains,
obelisks, columns, balustrading*

Connoisseur Sundials
Lane's End
Strefford
Craven Arms
Shropshire SY7 8DW
Brass and bronze sundials

The Conran Shop
Michelin House
81 Fulham Road
London SW3 6RD
Tables, chairs, shades, pots and planters

Andrew Crace
49 Bourne Lane
Much Hadham
Hertfordshire SG10 6ER
*Bronze sculptures, bronze pots and urns,
gazebos, seats, benches, tables, umbrellas*

Serena de la Hey
The Willows
Curload
Stoke St Gregory
Taunton
Somerset TA3 6JD
Willow sculptor

Fairweather Sculpture
Hillside House
Starston
Norfolk IP20 9NN
Hand-made ceramic sculpture

Frolics of Winchester
82 Canon Street
Winchester
Hampshire SO23 9JQ
*Ornamental trellis, trompe d'oeil, silhouettes,
seats, benches, chairs, tables, planters*

Forsham Cottage Arks
Goreside Farm
Great Chart
Ashford
Kent TN26 1UJ
*Dovecotes, poultry and waterfowl housing,
aviaries*

Garden Heritage
The Studio
Braxton Courtyard
Lymore Lane
Milford on Sea
Hampshire SO41 0TX
*Carved granite, marble and sandstone
statuary, water basins, Japanese lanterns,
bamboo poles, screens and water features*

Gaze Burvill
Plain Farm Old Dairy
East Tisted
Alton
Hampshire GU34 3RT
English oak seats, benches, chairs, tables

Haddonstone
The Forge House
East Haddon
Northampton
Northamptonshire NN6 8DB
*Reconstructed stone statuary, seating, urns,
planters, paving, tiles*

David Harber Sundials
The Sundial Workshop
Valley Farm
Bix
Henley on Thames
Oxfordshire RG9 6BW
Sundial maker and restorer

The Heveningham Collection
Weston Down
Weston Colley
Micheldever
Winchester
Hampshire SO21 3AQ
Hand-crafted wrought-iron furniture

Indian Ocean Trading Co
28 Ravenswood Road
London SW12 9P
Teak furniture, umbrellas

Ironart of Bath
61 Walcot Street
Bath
Avon BA1 5BN
Wrought-iron and steel seats, benches, tables

Vanessa Marston
Gorwell House
Goodleight Road
Barnstaple
Devon EX32 7JP
Bronze and bronze-resin sculpture

Minsterstone
Station Road
Ilminster
Somerset TA19 9AS
*Stone seating, planters, staddle stones,
balustrading, paving, tiles*

Oak Barrel Co
Yew Tree House
Nuneaton Road
Over Whitacre
Coleshill
Warwickshire B46 2NE
Cast iron pumps, oak barrels, water features

Pearson/Lloyd
39–41 Folgate Street
London E1 6BX
Furniture and industrial design

Pots and Pithoi
The Barns
East Street
Turners Hill
West Sussex RH10 4QQ
Cretan pots, antique Mediterranean pots

Christine-Ann Richards
Chapel House
The Street
Wanstrow
Shepton Mallet
Somerset BA4 4TB
Ceramic vases, planters, water features

Rusco Marketing
Little Faringdor Mill
Lechlade
Gloucestershire
GL7 3QQ
*Wrought-iron, teak and iroko furniture,
umbrellas, hammocks*

Sandridge House Sculpture
Sandridge Hill
Melksham
Wiltshire SN12 7QU
Hand-carved natural stone ornaments

The David Sharp Studio
201A Nottingham Road
Somercotes
Derbyshire DE55 4JG
*Reconstructed stone urns, planters, statuary,
benches*

Sundialman
Cae Gwyn
Capel Gurig
Betws-y-Coed
Gwynedd LL24 0DH
Brass and slate sundials

Rupert Till
Harristown Estate
Brannocks Town
Nuas
Co Kildare
Republic of Ireland
Lifesize wire sculptures

Whichford Pottery
Whichford
Shipston-on-Stour
Warwickshire CV36 5PG
Hand-made terracotta pots and urns

SPECIALIST NURSERIES

Apple Court
Hordle Lane
Hordle
Lymington
Hampshire SO41 0HU
Ferns, grasses, hostas, South American plants

Anthony Archer-Wills
Broadford Bridge Road
West Chiltington
West Sussex RH20 2LF
*Aquatics. Also specializes in water garden
design, construction and maintenance*

Architectural Plants
Cooks Farm
Nuthurst
Horsham
West Sussex RH13 6LH
Foliage plants, hardy exotics

Ausfern Nurseries
Tytherleigh House
Hubert Road
Brentwood
Essex CM14 4RF
*Australian and New Zealand plants, ferns,
palms*

David Austin Roses
Bowling Green Lane
Albrighton
Wolverhampton
Shropshire WV7 3HB
*Over 900 varieties of antique, climbing,
rare and unusual roses*

Peter Beales Roses
London Road
Attleborough
Norfolk NR17 1AY
*Over 1,000 varieties, especially
old-fashioned and climbing roses*

Blooms of Bressingham
Bressingham
Diss
Norfolk IP22 2AB
Herbaceous perennials, alpines, conifers

British Wild Flower Plants
23 Yarmouth Road
Ormesby St Margaret
Great Yarmouth
Norfolk NR29 3QE

Celyn Vale Nurseries
Allt-y-Celyn
Carrog
Corwen
Clwyd LL21 9LD
Eucalyptus and acacias

John Chambers Wild Flower Seeds
15 Westleigh Road
Barton Seagrave
Kettering
Northamptonshire NN15 5AJ

The Beth Chatto Garden
Elmstead Market
Colchester
Essex CO7 7DB
Unusual perennial plants

The Citrus Centre
Marehill Nursery
West Mare Lane
Pulborough
West Sussex RH20 2EA

Coblands Nursery
Trench Road
Tonbridge
Kent TN10 3HQ
Bamboos, grasses, ferns

Countryside Wildflowers
Chatteris Road
Somersham
Cambridgeshire PE17 3DN

Deacon's Nursery
Moor View
Godshill
Isle of Wight PO38 3HW
Soft fruit and fruit trees

Drysdale Garden Exotics
Bowerwood Road
Fordingbridge
Hampshire SP6 1BN
*Bamboos, foliage plants, Mediterranean
plants*

Emorsgate Seeds
The Pea Mill
Market Lane
Terrington St Clement
King's Lynn
Norfolk PE34 4HR
Native wildflowers and grasses

Fibrex Nurseries
Honeybourne Road
Pebworth
Stratford-on-Avon
Warwickshire CV37 8XT
Ferns, ivies, hellebores

Global Orange Groves
Edgarton Road
Canford Heath
Poole
Dorset BH17 9AY
*Over 30 varieties of citrus, including lemons,
mandarins and kumquats*

Hoecroft Plants
Severals Grange
Wood Norton
Dereham
Norfolk NR20 5BL
Grasses, foliage plants

Iden Croft Herbs
Frittenden Road
Staplehurst
Kent TN12 0DH
Herbs, wildflowers

Jekka's Herb Farm
Rose Cottage
Shellards Lane
Alveston
Bristol
Avon BS12 2SY
*Medicinal, culinary and aromatic herbs,
wildflowers*

Jungle Giants
Plough Farm
Wigmore
Herefordshire HR6 9UW
*Bamboos, plus bamboo poles, screens,
fencing, gates*

Langley Boxwood Nursery
Langley Court
Rake
Liss
Hampshire GU33 7JL
Over 50 varieties of box, topiary

Mattocks Roses
The Rose Nurseries
Nuneham Courtenay
Oxford
Oxfordshire OX44 9PY
*Over 350 varieties, especially new and old
ground-cover and shrub varieties*

Ken Muir
Honeypot Farm
Factory Road
Weeley Heath
Clacton on Sea
Essex CO16 9BJ
Soft fruit and fruit trees

The Palm Centre
533 Upper Richmond Road West
London SW14 7ED
*Palms for interior and exterior use, bamboos
and cycads*

PW Plants
Sunnyside
Heath Road
Kenninghall
Norfolk NR16 2DS
Bamboos, grasses

Reads Nursery
Hales Hall
Loddon
Norfolk NR14 6QW
*Citrus, fig and other fruit trees, vines, yew,
box hedging, topiary*

The Romantic Garden Nursery
The Street
Swannington
Norwich
Norfolk NR9 5NW
Topiary including holly, box and yew

Trevor Scott
Thorpe Park Cottage
Thorpe-le-Soken
Essex CO16 0HN
Grasses

Simply Plants
17 Dunhoe Brook
Eaton Socon
Cambridgeshire PE19 3DW
Grasses, bamboos

Stapeley Water Gardens
Stapeley
Nantwich
Cheshire CW5 7LH
*Aquatics, fish, filters, fountain jets, pool
liners, preformed pools*

Wevale Nurseries
Bagshot Road
Chobham
Surrey GU24 8BD
Bamboos

Index

Page numbers in italic refer to illustrations

Acknowledgments

The publisher thanks the following photographers and organizations for their kind permission to reproduce the photographs in this book:

1 Antoine Bootz (Architects: Studio Morsa);
2-3 Holt Studios International;
5 Vogue Living/Simon Kenny;
6-7 Clockwise from top left: Sculptor: Peter Randall-Page ('Granite Song', 1991); Arcaid/Richard Bryant (Architect: Philip Johnson); The Image Bank/ Carlos Navajas; Richard Felber; Roger Foley (Designers: Oehme, van Sweden);
8-9 Marianne Majerus/Conran Octopus;
10 Maison & Jardin/Nicolas Bruant (Designer: Thierry W. Despont);
12-13 **1** Christian Sarramon; **2** The Garden Picture Library/Rex Butcher; **3** The National Trust Photographic Library/John Bethell; **4** Claire de Virieu (Private garden);
14-15 **1** Jerry Harpur (Crowninshield, Hagley, Delaware); **2** Curtice Taylor; **3** Osamu Nobuhara (Designer: Tokuzo Kubo); **4** Michael Latz (Designer: Peter Latz & Partner); **5** Designer, Sculptor, Photographer: Janis Hall;
16-17 **1** World of Interiors/Jacques Dirand; **2** Gary Rogers; **3** Antoine Bootz (Architects: Studio Morsa); **4** Marianne Majerus (Designer: Reuben Godden); **5** Karen Bussolini; **6** Derek Fell;
18-19 **1** Dan Pearson (Sculptor: Daniel Harvey); **2** Architectur & Wohnen/Stefan Maria Rother; **3** Andrew Lawson (The Gnome Reserve, West Putford); **4** Ianthe Ruthven; **5** Marianne Majerus; **6** Belle/Justine Kerigan; **7** Allan Mandell (Tom Chakas garden, Berkeley, CA);
20-21 **1** Bilderberg/Eberhard Grames; **2** Schöner Wohnen/Camera Press; **3** Dan Pearson (Saiho-ji Temple, Moss Garden, Kyoto); **4** Marijke Heuff (Garden: Ton ter Linden, Holland); **5** Allan Mandell (Redgate Farm, Lopez Island, Washington);
22-23 **1** Bilderberg/Milan Horacek; **2** The Interior Archive/ Fritz von der Schulenburg; **3** Image du Sud; **4** Kate Gadsby; **5** Marion Nickig; **6-7** Kate Gadsby; **8** Vogue Living/Geoff Lung; **9** Richard Felber;
24-25 **1** Wallpaper/Chris Chapman; **2** Photonica/ Y. Akimoto; **3** Arcaid/Lucinda Lambton; **4** Delaney, Cochran & Castillo (Pemberton; **5** David Gamble; **6** Architectur & Wohnen/ Ivan Terestchenko; **7** Gary Rogers; **8** Daniel Harvey (Artists: Heather Ackroyd & Daniel Harvey);
26 Ken Druse (Designers: Steve Martino & Cliff Douglas, Arizona);
28-29 **1** Derek Fell; **2** Colorific Photo Library Ltd./ Michael Yamashita; **3** Ken Druse (Tower Hill Botanic Gardens, Boylston, Massachusetts);
30-31 **1** Marijke Heuff (Designer: Gilles Clément, France); **2** The Interior Archive/Cecilia Innes; **3** Steven Wooster (Designer: Christopher Lloyd); **4** Marianne Majerus (Designer: David Hicks);
32-33 **1** Alberto Giacometti 'Femme' 1928, bronze, cast number 3/6, 19 x 15½ in. (48.2 x 39.4 cm) Private Collection/Courtesy Yoshii Gallery/ © ADAGP, Paris & DACS, London 1998; **2** Ianthe Ruthven (Designer: Charles Jencks); **3** World of Interiors/Fritz von der Schulenburg; **4** James Pierce; **5** Bilderberg/Eberhard Grames;
34-35 **1** Jerry Harpur (Designer: Edwina von Gal, NY); **2** Arcaid/Richard Bryant (Architects: Sergio Puente & Ada Dewes); **3** Richard Felber; **4** Earl Carter (Designers: Rae & Anthony Ganim)/Conran Octopus; **5** Ken Druse (Stoddard Garden,

Massachusetts, designed by Fletcher Steele);
36-37 **1** Jerry Harpur (Designer: Tim du Val, NY); **2** Roger Foley (Designers: Oehme, van Sweden); **4** Gary Rogers (Designer: Erika Jahnke); **5** Derek Fell;
38-39 **1** The National Trust Photographic Library/ Eric Crichton; **2** Brigitte Perdereau; **3** Jerry Harpur (Wesley & Susan Dixon, Lake Forest, IL); **4** Mick Hales;
40-41 **1** Georges Lévêque; **2** Jacqui Hurst; **3** Ken Druse; **4** Mark Fiennes;
42-43 **1** Colorific Photo Library Ltd./Michael Yamashita; **2** Jerry Harpur (Namaqualand, SA); **4** Jerry Harpur (Designers: Oehme, van Sweden, Washington DC);
44-45 **1** Ross Honeysett (Architects: Engelen Moore); **2** Shodo Suzuki; **3** Richard Felber (Designers: Robert Jakob & David White); **4** Jerry Harpur (Designer: Isobelle C. Greene, Santa Barbara, CA);
46-47 **1** The Garden Picture Library/Gil Hanly; **2** Georges Lévêque (Designer: Erwan Tymen); **3** Marijke Heuff (Designer: Jean Mus, France);
48-49 **1** Todd Eberle (Designer: Steve Martino, CA); **3** Beatrice Pichon-Clarisse (Designer: Sylvie Devinat);
50-51 **1** Curtice Taylor (Designer: Edwina von Gal, NY); **2** Claire de Virieu (Private garden);
52-55 Andrew Lawson/Conran Octopus, courtesy of Terence Conran;
56-57 **1** Georgia Glynn-Smith; **2** Shodo Suzuki; **3** Roger Foley (Designer: Oehme, van Sweden); **4** S. & O. Mathews; **5** Lanny Provo (Landscape Architect: Raymond Jungle; Architect: Carlos Zapota, Golden Beach, Florida);
58-59 **1** Delaney, Cochran & Castillo (Randall-Denny); **2** Delaney, Cochran & Castillo (Stamper); **3** Roger Foley (Designers: Oehme, van Sweden); **4** Claire de Virieu (Designer: Mark Rudkin); **5** Michèle Lamontagne (Festival de Jardins, Chaumont sur Loire);
60-61 **1** Image du Sud/Le Studio/Résidence; **2** Inside/ C. Sarramon; **3** Beatrice Pichon-Clarisse; **4** Leigh Clapp; **5** Schöner Wohnen/Camera Press;
62-63 **1** Landscape Design (Owner/Designer: Ivy Rosequist); **2** Mark Darley/ Esto (Owner/Designer: Ivy Rosequist); **3** Nicola Browne (Designer: Dan Pearson; Pebble Work: Blot Kerr-Wilson); **4** William P. Steele; **5** Elizabeth Whiting & Associates/Jerry Harpur;
64-65 **1** Eric Morin; **2** The Garden Picture Library/ Ron Sutherland; **3** Arcaid/Richard Bryant (Architects: Silvestrin & Pawson); **4** Roger Foley (Designers: Oehme, van Sweden);
66-67 **1** Sofia Brignone (Designer: Arabella Lennox-Boyd); **2** Marianne Majerus; **3** Ken Druse;
68-69 **1** Chris Parsons; **2** John Glover; **3** The Garden Picture Library/Steven Wooster (Gibbs Garden, New Zealand); **4** Andrew Lawson (Designer: Arne Maynard);
70-71 **1** Belle/Simon Kenny (Designer: Vladimir Sitta, Terragram Pty. Ltd., Australia); **2** Tom Sitta (Designer: Vladimir Sitta, Terragram Pty. Ltd., Australia); **3** Conran Octopus/Jerry Harpur; **5** Osamu Nobuhara (Designer: Shodo Suzuki);
72-73 **1** The Garden Picture Library/Juliette Wade; **2** Country Living/Graham Kirk; **3** Michèle Lamontagne (Designer: Erwan Tymen);
74 Richard Felber;
76 Conran Octopus/Hannah Lewis;
78-79 **1** Gary Rogers; **2** Arcaid/Richard Bryant (By kind permission of the Mount Vernon Ladies' Association of the Union); **3** Elizabeth Whiting & Associates/

Jean-Paul Bonhommet; **4** Andrew Lawson (Courtesy John Miller, Cornwall); **5** Steve Speller (Designer: Thomas Heatherwick); **6** Arcaid/Dennis Gilbert (Architect: Bill Dunster); **7** Arcaid/Richard Bryant (Architect: Sergio Puente & Ada Dewes); **8** Arcaid/Natalie Tepper (Architect: Eric Owen Moss);
80-81 **1** Richard Felber; **2** Arcaid/Richard Bryant (Architect: Kevin O'Neill); **3** Thomas Heatherwick (Designer: Thomas Heatherwick/Collection: Terence Conran); **4** Roger Foley (Designers: Oehme, van Sweden); **5** Ken Druse (Mohonk Mountain House, New Paltz, New York); **6** Derek Fell; **7** Arcaid/Richard Bryant (Architect: Philip Johnson); **8** Ken Druse (Artist: Patrick Dougherty, Chapel Hill, North Carolina, USA);
82-83 **1** Marijke Heuff (La Casella, Côte d'Azur, France); **2** Marianne Majerus (Bourton House); **3** Mise au Point/Frédéric Didillon; **4** Gary Rogers; **5** J.C. Mayer & G. Le Scanff (Designer: Hiroshi Teshigahara, Festival de Jardins, Chaumont sur Loire); **6** Earl Carter (Designers: Robert Grant & Murray Collins)/ Conran Octopus; **7** Mark Fiennes;
84-85 **1** Roger Foley (Designers: Oehme, van Sweden); **2** Leigh Clapp (Designer: Diana Pringle); **3** Roger Foley (Designers: Oehme, van Sweden); **4** Gary Rogers; **5** Michèle Lamontagne; **6** J.C. Mayer & G. Le Scanff (Designer: Alain Prevost, Ville de Paris, Parc André Citroën);
86-87 **1** Beatrice Pichon-Clarisse; **2** Shodo Suzuki; **3** Martha Schwartz (Designers: Schwartz, Smith, Meyer Inc./Dickenson Residence, Santa Fe, NM 1992); **5** Stirling Macoboy/Camera Press; **6** Andrew Lawson (Private garden, Quebec);
88-89 **1** Howard Sooley (Derek Jarman); **2** Jerry Harpur (Sculptor: Peter Randall-Page at Manor House, Bledlow); **3** Vivian Russell (Sir Frederick Gibbard); **4** Peter Baistow; **5** Peter Baistow (Sculptor: Ben Nicholson, Sutton Place); **5** The Garden Picture Library/Sunniva Harte (Sculptor: Peter Gough); **7** 'Two Together' (Sculptor: David Nash, Goodwood Sculpture Park/Annely Juda Fine Art, London);
90-91 **1** Steve Speller (Designer: Thomas Heatherwick, Hat Hill Sculpture Foundation); **2** Andrew Lawson (Private garden, Maine, USA); **3** Andrew Lawson (The Lost Gardens of Helgan, Cornwall); **4** Clive Nichols (Sculptor: Herta Keller/The Hannah Peschar Gallery, Surrey); **5** Timothy Hursley (Sculptor: Gary Slater); **6** Colorific Photo Library Ltd./Michael Yamashita; **7** John Gollings (Sculptor: Jim Sinatra); **8** Georgia Glynn-Smith;
92-93 **1** Dean Cardasis; **2** Delaney, Cochran & Castillo (Che); **3** Shodo Suzuki; **4** The Garden Picture Library/Ron Sutherland; **5** Richard Waite (Designers: David Connor); **6** Bilderberg/Ellerbrock & Schafft;
94 Hannah Lewis/Conran Octopus;
96-97 **1** John Glover; **2** Juliette Wade; **3** Susan Roth; **4** Marianne Majerus; **5** Elizabeth Whiting & Associates/Rodney Hyett. **7** William P. Steele;
98-99 **1** Jerry Harpur (Designer: Mai Arbergast, San Francisco, CA); **2** Juliette Wade; **3** Elizabeth Whiting & Associates/Spike Powell; **4** Georges Lévêque (Designer: Camille Muller); **5** Ianthe Ruthven; **7** Jacqui Hurst; **8** Jerry Pavia; **9** Andrew Lawson;
100-101 **1** Hugh Palmer (Antony House); **2** Claire de Virieu (Private garden); **3** Marianne Majerus; **4** J.C. Mayer & G. Le Scanff; **5** The Interior Archive/Fritz von der Schulenberg; **6** Jacqui Hurst (Heale Gardens and Nursery); **7** Andrew Lawson;
102-103 **1** The Interior Archive/Christopher Simon-Sykes (McCabe); **2** Juliette Wade; **3** Image du Sud/

Bea Heyligers; **4** Andrew Lawson (Shan Egerton, Hay-on-Wye, Powys); **5** Maggie Oster (Cedar Falls); **6** Jerry Harpur (Helmingham Hall, Suffolk); **7** J.C. Mayer & G. Le Scanff (Marc Meneau, Vezelay, France) from 'The Art of French Vegetable Gardening'/Artisan; **8** Susan Roth (Duff Garden);

104-105 1 Richard Felber; **2** Marianne Majerus (Designer: Christina Stapley); **3** Elizabeth Whiting & Associates/ Jerry Harpur; **4** Susan Roth; **5** Erica Lennard (Designer: Nicole de Vesian); **6** Grant Heilman Photography Inc./Jane Grushow; **7** Beatrice Pichon-Clarisse (Wy-dit-Joli-Village); **8** Georges Lévêque (Designer: Jean-Louis Bajolet);

106 Hannah Lewis/Conran Octopus;

108-109 1 Simon McBride; **2** Steve Speller (Designer: Thomas Heatherwick/Hat Hill Sculpture Foundation); **3** Gary Rogers; **4** Richard Felber; **5** J.B. Visual Press/Horst Neumann; **6** Nicola Browne (Designer: Dan Pearson) **7** Claire de Virieu (Kenzo); **8** Arcaid/Alberto Piovano (Designer: C. Rutherford); **9** Jerry Harpur/Conran Octopus;

110-111 1 Elizabeth Whiting & Associates/Neil Lorimer; **2** Maggie Oster; **3** Maggie Oster (Humes Japanese Stroll Garden); **4** Elizabeth Whiting & Associates/ A. Kolesnikow; **5** Arcaid/Richard Bryant (Designer: Gabriel Poole); **6** Verne Fotografie (Designer: Anne Tack); **7** Elizabeth Whiting & Associates/ Karl Dietrich-Bühler;

112-113 1 Images Colour Library; **2** J.B. Visual Press/ Horst Neumann; **4** Vogue Living/Tom Eckerle; **6** Gary Rogers; **7** Mark Darley (Architects: Jim Jennings & Bill Stout)/Esto; **8** Vogue Living/Simon Kenny/The Blind and Drape Store (Designers: Stephen Bonnitcha & Leon Czeto);

114-115 1 Hugh Palmer (Trebah Garden, Cornwall); **2** Jerry Harpur (Montecito, CA); **3** 'Garden Doctors' by Dan Pearson & Steve Bradley, published by Boxtree; **4** Gary Rogers (Designer: Henk Weijers); **5** Earl Carter (Designers: Rae & Antony Ganim)/ Conran Octopus; **6** Gil Hanly; **7** Derek Fell;

116-117 1 William P. Steele (Designer: Luis Ortega); **2** Roger Foley (Designers: Oehme, Van Sweden); **3** Simon McBride & Richard Waite (Designer: David Connor); **5** Earl Carter (Architect: Leonard Hamersfield)/Conran Octopus; **6** Arcaid/Richard Bryant (Architects: Silvestrin & Pawson); **7** Pascal Chevallier (Michèle Gayraud-Belaiche)/Agence Top;

118 Hannah Lewis/Conran Octopus;

120-121 1 The Garden Picture Library/Ron Sutherland; **2** Ken Druse (Designer: Susanne Jett, Santa Monica, CA); **3** Marianne Majerus; **4** Roger Foley (Colonial Williamsburg); **5** Ken Druse (Designers: Steve Martino, Cliff Douglas, Arizona); **6** Belle/Simon Kenny (Designer: Vladimir Sitta, Terragram Pty. Ltd., Australia);

122-123 1 Gary Rogers; **2** Reiner Blunck; **3** Reiner Blunck; **4** Arcaid/Annet Held; **5** Peter Baistow; **6** Schöner Wohnen/Camera Press; **7** The Garden Picture Library/Michael Howes;

124-125 1 Belle/Simon Kenny; **2** Peter Aprahamian (Designer: Anthony Noel); **3** Derek St Romaine (Designer: Johnny Woodford); **4** Deidi von Schaewen (Owner: Françoise Dorget, Morocco); **5-6** Earl Carter (Designers: Jergen Plecko & William Simson)/Conran Octopus; **7** The Garden Picture Library/Henk Dijkman (Designer: Henk Weijers); **8** Nicola Browne (Designers: Avant Gardener);

126-127 1 Camille Muller; **2** Inside/Claire de Virieu; **3** Jerry Harpur (Designer: Delaney, Cochran & Castillo, San Francisco, CA); **4** Jerry Harpur (Designer: Isobelle

C. Greene, Santa Barbara, CA); **5** Scott Frances/Esto; **6** Richard Felber; **7** Colorific Photo Library Ltd./ Michael Yamashita;

128-129 Nicola Browne/Conran Octopus;

130-131 1 Jean-Pierre Godeaut (Designer: Gilles Clément); **2** Marijke Heuff (Westpark, Munich); **3** John Neubauer (Selby Gardens, Sarasota, FL); **4** Claire de Virieu (Private garden); **5** Juliette Wade;

132-133 1 Marijke Heuff (Painter: Joseph Bayol, France); **3** Jerry Harpur (Designer: Heide Baldwin, Santa Barbara, CA);

134-135 1 Clive Nichols; **2** John Hall; **3** Charles Mann (Designer: Ruth Bancroft); **4** John Neubauer;

136-137 1 Bilderberg/Klaus D. Francke; **2** Tony Stone Images/James Randklev; **3** The Garden Picture Library/John Ferro Sims (Savernake Forest, Wiltshire); **4** Nicola Browne (Church Norton);

138-139 1 Claire de Virieu (Private garden); **2** Jerry Harpur (Wesley & Susan Dixon, Lake Forest, IL); **3** Sunniva Harte (Goldcrest Nursery); **4** Dan Pearson; **5** Roger Foley (Designers: Oehme, van Sweden);

140-141 1 Colorific Photo Library Ltd./Michael Yamashita; **3** Maggie Oster (Chantilleer); **4** Ianthe Ruthven;

142-143 1 Marijke Heuff (Mrs L. Goossenaerts, Holland); **3** Jerry Harpur (Designer: Mark Rios, Los Angeles, CA); **4** Sunniva Harte (Spinners); **5** Richard Felber;

145 1 Piet Oudolf, Holland; **2** Clive Nichols (The Old Rectory, Burghfield, Berkshire);

146-7 1 Andrea Jones; **2** Richard Felber; **3** Gary Rogers; **4-5** Nicola Browne/Conran Octopus;

148-149 1 Marijke Heuff (Walenburg); **2-3** Nicola Browne/ Conran Octopus; **4** Dan Pearson; **5** Ken Druse;

150-151 1 Marijke Heuff (Garden: Ton ter Linden); **2** Allen Rokach; **3** John Glover; **4-5** Nicola Browne;

152-153 1 Roger Foley (Designers: Oehme, van Sweden); **2** Roger Foley (Designers: Oehme, van Sweden); **3** Roger Foley (Designer: Sheela Lampietti); **4** Georges Lévêque;

154-155 1 Pamela Harper; **2** Bilderberg/Stephan Elleringmann; **3** Nicola Browne/Conran Octopus; **4** Gary Rogers; **5** Bilderberg/Stephan Elleringmann; **6** Gary Rogers;

156-157 1 Nicola Browne/Conran Octopus; **2** Georges Lévêque (Designer: Jacques Wirtz); **3** Michel Arnaud; **4** Colorific Photo Library Ltd./Michael Yamashita (Saiho-ji Temple Garden, Kyoto); **5** Roger Foley;

158-159 1 Stephen Robson (Tresco); **2** Richard Felber; **3** Lanny Provo;

160-161 1 Jerry Harpur (Ryoan-ji Temple, Kyoto); **2** Jane Gifford; **4** Andrew Lawson (Designer: Dan Pearson); **5** Richard Felber; **6** Andrew Lawson;

162-163 1 Jerry Harpur (Powis Castle, Powys, Wales); **2** Ken Druse;

164-165 1 Tim Street-Porter (Taft-Ojai);

166-167 1 Jacqui Hurst; **2** Delaney, Cochran & Castillo (Pemberton); **3** Marion Nickig; **4** World of Interiors/ Polly Farquharson; **5** Marijke Heuff (Designer: Gilles Clément, France);

168 1 Andrew Lawson (Designer: Dan Pearson);

168-171 2-8 Nicola Browne/Conran Octopus (Designer: Dan Pearson);

172-173 1 Andrew Lawson (Designer: Arne Maynard); **2** Vivian Russell (Logan); **3** Solvi Dos Santos; **4** Ken Druse; **5** Roger Foley (Designers: Oehme, van Sweden);

174-175 1 Ianthe Ruthven; **2** Dency Kane (Ellen & Gordon Penick Garden, Ruther Glen, VA); **3** Ken Druse (Designer: Steve Martino); **4** Andrew Lawson; **5** The Interior Archive/Fritz von der Schulenburg;

176-177 1 Jerry Harpur (Designer: Neil Diboll, Michigan); **2** Gill C. Kenny; **4** Marijke Heuff (Garden: Ton ter

Linden, Halland); **5** Richard Felber;

178-179 1 Allen Rokach; **2** Bilderberg/Wolfgang Kunz; **3** Roger Foley; **4-5** Roger Foley (Designers: Oehme, van Sweden); **6** Jerry Harpur (Designers: Oehme, van Sweden);

180-181 1 Arcaid/Richard Bryant (Architect: Philip Johnson); **2** Gary Rogers; **3** J.C. Mayer & G. Le Scanff (Jardin de Talos, France); **4** Image du Sud/A. Moya; **5** Jacqui Hurst (The Old Stores, Suffolk);

182-183 1 Andrew Lawson (Designer: Caroline Burgess, Canada); **2** The Garden Picture Library/Ron Sutherland (Beth Chatto Garden); **3** Jane Gifford; **4** The Garden Picture Library/Marijke Heuff (Ter Kiule Garden, Holland); **5** The Garden Picture Library/Howard Rice;

184-185 1 Charles Mann (Designer: Ruth Bancroft); **2** Michel Arnaud; **3** The Garden Picture Library/ Didier Willery; **4** Jerry Harpur (Designers: Stanton & Jean, Armour, IL); **5** Jerry Harpur (Huntington Arboretum, Los Angeles, CA);

186-187 2 Wulf Brackock (Designer: Jacques Wirtz); **3** Andrew Lawson (Lower Slaughter, Glos.); **4** Michèle Lamontagne (Mt Koya); **5** Jerry Harpur (Château Gourdon, Alpes-Maritimes, France); **6** Deidi von Schaewen; **7** Marijke Heuff (Huis Bingerden, Holland);

188-189 1 Mark Fiennes; **2** Bilderberg/Milan Horacek; **3** Neil Campbell-Sharp (Lakemont, Co. Cork); **4** John Neubauer (Nymans, West Sussex); **5** The Garden Picture Library/John Glover; **6** Jerry Harpur; **7** Marijke Heuff;

190-191 1 J.C. Mayer & G. Le Scanff (Jardin de Talos, France); **2** Colorific Photo Library Ltd./Michael Yamashita (Ritsurin Garden, Takamatsu, Japan); **3** Claire de Virieu (Private garden); **4** Maggie Oster (Stan Hywet); **5** Gary Rogers;

192-193 1 The Garden Picture Library/Zara McCalmont; **2** Richard Felber; **3** John Hall; **4** John Glover; **5** Jerry Harpur (Keith Kirsten, Johannesburg, SA); **6** Bilderberg/Frieder Blickle;

194-195 1 Hugh Palmer (Jenkyn Place); **2** Andrew Lawson (Designer: Dan Pearson); **4** Juliette Wade; **5** Häuser/Camera Press; **6** Nicola Browne (Designer: Dan Pearson);

196-197 1-3 Andrew Lawson (Designer: Dan Pearson); **4-5** Nicola Browne (Designer: Dan Pearson);

198 Todd Eberle;

200-201 1 Jacqui Hurst; **2** Richard Felber; **3** Marion Nickig; **4** S. & O. Mathews **5** Marion Nickig;

202-203 Clockwise from top left: Derek Fell; John Fielding; S. & O. Mathews; The Garden Picture Library/ Brigitte Perdereau; Andrew Lawson; John Fielding; Andrew Lawson; Clive Nichols; Andrew Lawson; Andrew Lawson;

204-205 Clockwise from top left: John Fielding; The Garden Picture Library/John Glover; Andrew Lawson; Andrew Lawson; PhotoNats/Robert E. Lyons; Andrew Lawson; John Fielding; The Garden Picture Library/Michèle Lamontagne; The Garden Picture Library/Morley Read;

206-207 Clockwise from top left: Derek Fell; Clive Nichols; Andrew Lawson; Andrew Lawson; S. & O. Mathews; The Garden Picture Library/Vaughan Fleming; Andrew Lawson;

208-209 Clockwise from top left: S. & O. Mathews; Andrew Lawson; The Garden Picture Library/Ron Evans; The Garden Picture Library/J.C. Mayer & G. le Scanff; Andrew Lawson; Marion Nickig; Derek Fell; Marion Nickig;

210-211 Clockwise from top left: John Fielding; The Garden

Picture Library/John Glover; J.C. Mayer & G. Le Scanff (Jardins de Bellevue, France); The Garden Picture Library/John Glover; Jo Whitworth; Andrew Lawson; The Garden Picture Library/John Glover; Marion Nickig; Derek Fell; Derek Fell; The Garden Picture Library/J.S. Sirra;

212-213 Clockwise from top left: Andrew Lawson; Clive Nichols; Marion Nickig; Andrew Lawson; The Garden Picture Library/Sunniva Harte; Andrew Lawson; Marion Nickig; John Fielding; Clive Nichols; The Garden Picture Library/John Glover; Andrew Lawson;

214-215 Clockwise from top left: Andrew Lawson; Allan Mandell; John Fielding; Andrew Lawson; S. & O. Mathews; Andrew Lawson; The Garden Picture Library/Clive Nichols; Andrew Lawson; S. & O. Mathews; Clive Nichols; Ken Druse; Derek Fell;

216-217 Clockwise from top left: Marion Nickig; Derek Fell; Marion Nickig; John Fielding; John Fielding; John Fielding; Andrew Lawson/Conran Octopus; Andrew Lawson; John Fielding; John Fielding; Marion Nickig; Marion Nickig; Roger Foley; Marion Nickig;

218-219 Clockwise from top left: John Fielding; Andrew Lawson; Marion Nickig; Andrew Lawson; Marion Nickig; Marion Nickig; The Garden Picture Library/David Askham; Holt Studios International; Derek Fell; The Garden Picture Library/J.S. Sirra; The Garden Picture Library/Neil Holmes; Marion Nickig; S. & O. Mathews; Richard Felber; Jo Whitworth;

220-221 1 Todd Eberle (Designer: Steve Martino); 2 S. & O. Mathews (Polesden Lacey); 3 Arcaid/Richard Bryant; 4 J.C. Mayer & G. Le Scanff (Festival de Jardins, Chaumont Sur Loire); 5 Andrew Lawson/Conran Octopus (Designer: Dan Pearson);

222-223 1 Derek Fell; 2 Lanny Provo; 3 Arcaid/Richard Bryant (Architects: Sergio Puente & Ada Dewes); 4 J.B. Visual Press/Horst Neumann; 5 Maggie Oster; 6 Mark Fiennes;

224-225 1 Michèle Lamontagne; 2 Robert Harding Syndication/Geray Sweeney/Homes & Gardens; 3 Allan Mandell (McMenamin's Edgefield garden, Troutdale, OR); 4 Belle/Justine Kerrigan; 5 Earl Carter (Designers: Rae & Anthony Ganim)/Conran Octopus; 6 Chris Mead; 7 Andrew Lawson (Designer: Lynda Miller, NY);

226 1 David Muench; 2 The Garden Picture Library/Marianne Majerus; 3 Dency Kane (Designer: Charles F. Gillette, Bemiss Garden, Richmond, VA,); 4 Brigitte Perdereau; 5 Andrew Lawson;

227 1 The Interior Archive/James Mortimer; 2 Claire de Virieu (Private garden); 3 Jacques Merles;

228-229 1 Belle/Garry Sarre; 2 Richard Felber; 3 Verne Fotografie (Carlo Scminck); 4 Roger Foley (Designers: Oehme, van Sweden); 5 Lanny Provo (Coral Gables); 6 Lanny Provo;

230-231 1 Chris Meads; 2 Ken Druse; 3 Andrew Lawson; 4 Vogue Living/Jack Sarafian; 5 Michèle Lamontagne; 6 Elizabeth Whiting & Associates/Rodney Hyett; 7 Colorific Photo Library Ltd./Michael Yamashita;

232 1 Verne Fotografie (Arhnen); 2 J.C. Mayer & G. Le Scanff (Chez 'Agapanthe', France); 3 Karen Bussolini; 4 J.C. Mayer & G. Le Scanff (Jardin Majorelle); 5 The Interior Archive/Cecilia Innes;

233 1 Mark Darley/Esto (Owner/Designer: Ivy Rosequist); 2 Andrew Lawson; 3 Ken Druse; 4 Andrew Lawson; 5 Charles Jencks; 6 Mark Darley/Esto (Architect: Ned Forrest);

234-235 1 Marie Claire Maison/Gilles de Chabaneix (Stylist: Catherine Ardouin); 2 Arcaid/Earl Carter/Belle;

3 Hort-Couture Landscape Lighting; 4 Roger Foley; 5 Elizabeth Whiting & Associates/Di Lewis;

236 1 Richard Felber; 2 Richard Felber; 3 Schöner Wohnen/Camera Press; 4 Juliette Wade; 5 Marie Claire Maison/Gilles de Chabaneix (Stylist: Marie Kalt);

237 1 Debbie Patterson/'The Decorated Garden Room' by Tessa Eveleigh (Lorenz Books, £14.95); 2 The Garden Picture Library/Brigitte Perdereau; 3 The Garden Picture Library/Friedrich Strauss; 4 Australian House & Garden/Russell Brooks;

238-239 1 Andrew Lawson (Designer: Caroline Burgess, Canada); 2 Andrew Lawson (The Priory, Charlbury, Oxon.); 3 Maggie Oster (Orton Plantation); 4 Marianne Majerus;

240-241 1 Marijke Heuff; 2 Ken Druse; 3 Gary Rogers (Owner: Barbara Hammerstien); 4 Gary Rogers; 5 Vogue Living/Simon Kenny; 6 Guillaume de Laubier (Maxime de la Falaise);

242-243 1 Roger Foley (Designers: Oehme, van Sweden); 2 Earl Carter (Designers: Robert Grant & Murray Collins)/Conran Octopus; 3 Marie Claire Maison/Gilles de Chabaneix (Stylist: Catherine Ardouin); 4 Roger Foley (Osamu Shimizu); 5 Richard Felber;

244-245 1 Gary Rogers; 2 Schöner Wohnen/Camera Press; 3 Martha Schwartz (Designers: Schwartz, Smith, Meyer Inc./Dickenson Residence, Santa Fe, NM 1992); 4 Schöner Wohnen/Camera Press; 5 Gardens Illustrated/Jonathan Lovekin; 6 Shodo Suzuki; 7 Gary Rogers (Designer: Henk Weijers);

246 The Interior Archive/C. Simon-Sykes (McCabe);

249 Hugh Palmer (Cringletie House);

Pages **45, 5**; **48-49, 2**; **87, 4**; **132, 2**; **140, 2**; **163, 3** from 'The Gardens of California' by Nancy Goslee Power, photographs copyright © 1995 by Mick Hales. Reprinted by permission of Clarkson Potter, a division of Crown Publishers Inc. All gardens designed by Nancy Goslee Power.

Every effort has been made to trace the copyright holders, architects and designers. We apologize in advance for any unintentional omission and would be pleased to insert the appropriate acknowledgment in any subsequent edition.

ILLUSTRATIONS
The publisher thanks the following illustrators whose work appears throughout the book as follows:

Paul Bryant: **222-3**; **224-5**; **228-9**; **239**; **232-3**; **238-9**; **242-3**, **244**
Terence Conran: **53**
Lesley Craig: **133**; **134**; **142**; **144-5**; **161**; **165**; **186**; **195**
Vanessa Luff: **227**; **248-1**; **250-1**; **252-3**; **254-5**; **256**
Agneta Neroth: **76-7**; **94-5**; **106-7**; **118-19**
Dan Pearson: **168**
Angus Shepherd (Garden design by Andrew Miller): **37**; **39**; **43**; **47**; **51**; **67**; **71**; **73**
Angus Shepherd: **97**; **99**; **112-13**

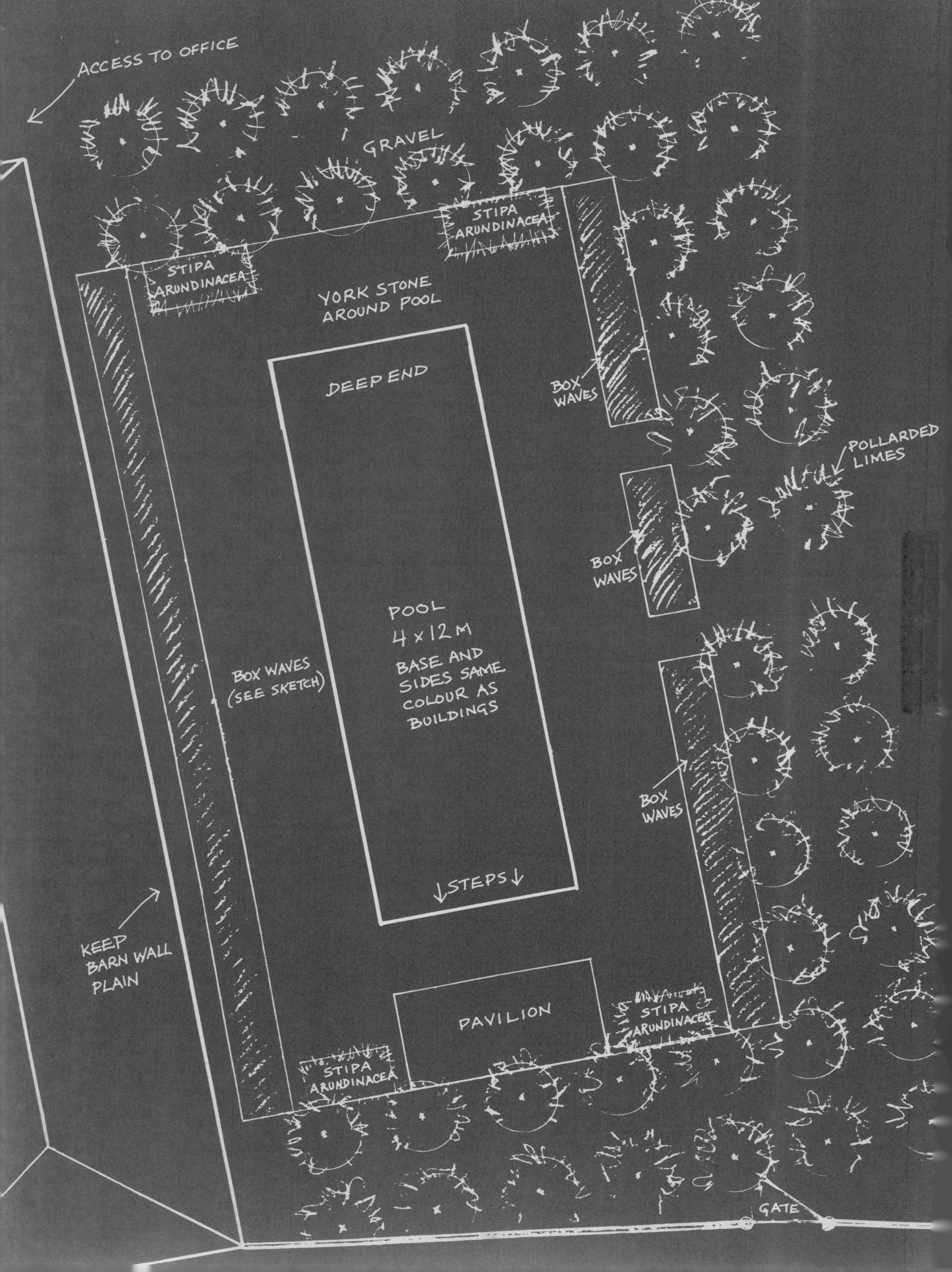

ACCESS TO OFFICE

GRAVEL

STIPA
ARUNDINACEA

STIPA
ARUNDINACEA

YORK STONE
AROUND POOL

BOX
WAVES

DEEP END

POLLARDED
LIMES

BOX
WAVES

BOX WAVES
(SEE SKETCH)

POOL
4 x 12 M
BASE AND
SIDES SAME
COLOUR AS
BUILDINGS

KEEP
BARN WALL
PLAIN

BOX
WAVES

↓STEPS↓

PAVILION

STIPA
ARUNDINACEA

STIPA
ARUNDINACEA

GATE